Harsh Mander is one of India's most trusted and courageous social justice and human rights activists. He works with survivors of mass violence and hunger, as well as homeless persons and street children. He is the director of the Centre for Equity Studies, a research organization based in New Delhi, and has also served as a special monitor for the National Human Rights Commission to the detention centres for 'declared foreigners' in Assam.

Mander is also the author of several acclaimed books on contemporary India, among them, *Looking Away: Inequality, Prejudice and Indifference in New India*; *Ash in the Belly: India's Unfinished Battle Against Hunger*; *Fatal Accidents of Birth: Stories of Suffering, Oppression and Resistance*; and *Locking Down the Poor: The Pandemic and India's Moral Centre.*

Navsharan Singh is a Delhi-based researcher and human rights activist. She has worked and published extensively on informal-sector workers, especially women workers and the precarity of their work and lives. She has also been working on the vulnerability of internally displaced people and those affected by mass sectarian violence. She was previously the Senior Program Specialist for the Women's Rights and Citizenship Program at the International Development Research Centre's Asia office, New Delhi.

Her publications include *Landscapes of Fear: Understanding Impunity in India*; *Blood, Censored: When Kashmiris Become the 'Enemy'*; and *Gender Justice, Citizenship and Development.*

This Land Is Mine, I Am Not of This Land

CAA-NRC and the Manufacture of Statelessness

Edited by Harsh Mander
and Navsharan Singh
(with Varna Balakrishnan and
Mihika Chanchani)

SPEAKING
TIGER

SPEAKING TIGER BOOKS LLP
4381/4, Ansari Road, Daryaganj
New Delhi 110002

Published by Speaking Tiger Books in paperback 2021

ISBN: 978-93-90477-18-0
eISBN: 978-93-90477-26-5

10 9 8 7 6 5 4 3 2 1

Typeset in Sabon Roman by SÜRYA, New Delhi
Printed at Chaman Enterprises, New Delhi

CONTENTS

Human Cost

Gendered Exclusions

PART THREE: THE CITIZENSHIP AMENDMENT ACT, 2019 AND A PAN-INDIA NRC

PART FOUR: CONTESTATIONS AROUND THE CAA-NRC-NPR

INTRODUCTION

'THIS LAND IS MINE, I AM NOT OF THIS LAND'

Harsh Mander

Almost a hundred years have passed since a battle was launched for the soul of this ancient, diverse land. At stake was the country we would build together after the British left our shores.

This was in the years just after Mahatma Gandhi had returned from South Africa, in 1915, to join India's freedom struggle.[1] Gandhi's immense popularity was proof that the majority of Indians—Hindu, Muslim and those of other faiths—shared his vision of a country which would be inclusive and humane, which would welcome people of every belief and ethnicity to be equal citizens. This ideal later formed the very foundation of the Constitution of the Indian Republic crafted with great care and foresight by Babasaheb Ambedkar.[2]

However, the Hindu Mahasabha[3] and the Rashtriya Swayamsevak Sangh (RSS)[4] have bitterly contested these ideas of inclusiveness and equality all these hundred years. Their vision for India is of a nation belonging to India's Hindu majority—specifically, to Hindus who subscribe to their narrow, political and militant interpretation of Hinduism—in which Muslims and Christians would possibly be 'allowed' inclusion but only as second-class citizens. Though less explicitly enunciated, in this dispensation, people of the most disadvantaged castes and tribal ethnicities would also be lesser citizens. The Mahasabha-RSS ideas were mirrored in many ways by the Muslim League which argued that India was not one but two nations—a Hindu India and a Muslim Pakistan—and that Muslims would not be able to achieve equality, security and justice in a Hindu-majority country. They fought for and accomplished the calamitous Partition of the country into India and Pakistan, Pakistan being carved out of Muslim-majority regions in both the eastern and western flanks of the country.

The turbulent struggle between these opposing ideologies took a toll of over a million lives, including Gandhiji's, and caused the largest cataclysmic distress displacement of human populations on the planet in history[5] (barring the movement of enslaved populations from Africa to the Americas).

Today, the people of India find themselves at a decisive phase of this very same battle. The RSS is probably the largest civil society organization in the world, with unparalleled penetration into villages and urban settlements and branches all across the country. India is led today by men who have spent all their adult lives as staunch members of this Hindu supremacist formation. They are convinced that their time has come, to remould India into the muscular, unequal and resentful nation of their imaginings.

~

I was born eight years after India won her freedom. I recall a childhood in which the idealism of the freedom struggle, although rapidly fading, still endured. We were raised without bigotry, taught to be thrifty and kind. Friendships across religions were common (though much less, I realize now, across caste). Our cinema, our poetry, our music and theatre, all celebrated our plural identities. It was an unequal India, but comfortable in its diversity, imbued with the hope of building a better future for *all* our people, of every faith, caste and class.

Today, my little grandson is being raised in a worryingly altered India. From the time he makes sense of his world, he will routinely hear conversations of bigotry and exclusion, in living rooms, in classrooms, on his phone and laptop, on his television screen, from the most prominent political leaders of the country. He will also join a section of the world that is complacent in its comfort and vulgar overconsumption, indifferent to the stark penury and want outside its doors.

It would be a mistake to believe that India suddenly changed in recent years. The slide started much earlier. When I entered college in the 1970s, idealistic students of earlier batches had disappeared into the countryside to fight rural oppression. We rallied against the corruption and authoritarianism of the Congress government and against the Emergency[6] imposed by the then prime minister, Indira Gandhi. The 1980s saw vast fractures in India's plurality: calamitous communal massacres, regressive mobilization against the rights of Muslim women, a violent campaign to destroy a medieval mosque in Ayodhya,[7] campaigns to demonize the Muslims and construct a sense of permanent grievance in the Hindu people. In all of these, the Congress leadership abjectly bent before the most regressive elements of the Hindu, Muslim and Sikh faiths, and cynically allowed the core of India's secular republic to be steadily eroded.

Since 2014, however, India hurtled far more rapidly and treacherously downwards to become a country increasingly dangerous and unwelcoming to its minorities, especially its vast Muslim populace of nearly 200 million people. Fear and hate became inseparable from public life, for both minorities and for those who stood with them. Elected leaders, especially of the ruling party, indulged in vitriolic and runaway hate speech[8] with impunity, legitimizing and valorizing bigotry and hatred, and these became the dominant markers of social life. Crowds gathered to lynch Muslims and Dalits in the name of cow protection, and proudly posted videos of the lynchings on social media.[9] Relationships between Muslim men and Hindu women were stigmatized as 'love jihad'.[10] Christian priests, nuns and shrines were attacked. Dissenters were pilloried as anti-national. A new slur was adopted and bandied about even by the Prime Minister, of 'Urban-Naxals'[11] or Urban-Maoists, a contradiction in terms, applied pejoratively (and menacingly) to left and liberal dissenters (including, incidentally, this writer).

In the midsummer elections of 2019, the Bharatiya

Janata Party (BJP) government won an expanded mandate, despite economic collapse, mounting farm distress and rising unemployment that peaked to a 45-year high. It is significant that of the 37.6 per cent votes won by the BJP, 36 per cent were votes by Hindus. Even one in three Dalits voted for the BJP. This was interpreted by the BJP leadership as a mandate to decisively further their vision for India of a land owned, dominated and controlled by Hindus; and they moved to actualize it in statute and law with resolve and swiftness, hubris and recklessness. Diminishing the only Muslim-majority state in the Indian Union, Jammu and Kashmir, to a Union territory[12] and engineering the judicial ruling for a Ram temple[13] at the site of a demolished mosque were pivotal steps towards fulfilling the long-prized agenda of the RSS of converting India into a Hindu nation.

The next, even more critical step for this raging Hindu supremacist juggernaut was to create by law, for the first time, a hierarchy of citizenship rights based on religion. The Citizenship Amendment Act (CAA), passed by Parliament in December 2019, threatened to strip India's Muslims of all rights. It promised citizenship to migrants of the 'Hindu, Sikh, Buddhist, Jain, Parsi or Christian community from Afghanistan, Bangladesh or Pakistan'. It mentioned only these three countries and it did not mention Muslims. This Act—as we shall see—if followed by the National Register of Indian Citizens (NRIC) based on the National Population Register (NPR), would thrust India's Muslims into the same vortex of permanent fear and desperate insecurity that had been the fate for decades of the Bengali-origin people of Assam.

The edifice of India's Constitution has continued to endure, although under constant siege and subversion ever since it was written, and despite the numerous onslaughts on it during the Modi regime since May 2014, and especially May 2019. However, when Parliament, overwhelmingly dominated by the BJP and its allies, passed the CAA, it was an assault under which India's constitutional structure threatened to finally cave in. Make no mistake. The Constitution would not need to be rewritten. But through the CAA coupled with the NRIC and NPR the soul of the Constitution would be annihilated. A new nation would emerge from the rubble—wrathful, muscular, majoritarian and inhospitable and unjust to its minorities.

This law brings the tangled contestations of belonging and rights that had haunted the enslaved nation as it struggled for freedom into stark relief. Who would belong to India, and on what terms? And indeed, who would India belong to? A young Bengali-origin Assamese poet, Kazi Neel, laments, 'This land is mine, I am not of this land'; he loves India, but India refuses to own him.

~

Citizenship ultimately is the right to have rights. Who in this country should have rights, and from whom should these be withheld?

The answer to these fraught questions seemed settled within the humanist and inclusive framework of the Indian Constitution. Its iridescent central premise was that religious faith had no bearing on eligibility for Indian citizenship. India belongs equally to its Muslim, Christian and Parsi residents, as much as to its Hindu, Sikh, Buddhist and Jain citizens.

It was the idea of religion as the defining principle of politics and national identity that tore India apart. The Muslim League regarded religion as key to citizenship, which was why they believed that India was not one but two nations—Hindu India and Muslim Pakistan. V.D. Savarkar, one of the founders of the Hindutva ideology and president of the Hindu Mahasabha, concurred. But even after Partition and the creation of Pakistan on the basis of Muslim identity, India's Constituent Assembly steadfastly rejected the idea that India belonged only or even primarily to its Hindu majority. Jawaharlal Nehru, among the tallest leaders of the freedom movement and India's first prime minister, declared, 'We accept as Indian anyone who calls himself a citizen of India.'

But by introducing the Citizenship Amendment Act, the BJP-led government deliberately reopened old wounds, reviving and cynically further stoking the old fears, anxieties and hatreds of Partition. This law, in effect, endorses the two-nation theory by creating a hierarchy of citizenship based on religious faith that lowers Muslims in the hierarchy. This is why this 1,000-word law threatens to destroy the Constitution of India: there will be no need to actually formally rescind or annul the Constitution; the CAA will annihilate its very soul—the pledge of equal citizenship for all.

The moral fig leaf offered by the Union government for this law was that it intends to provide humanitarian refuge to people suffering religious persecution in neighbouring countries. If religious persecution were truly the yardstick for eligibility for Indian citizenship, then few neighbours are more deserving than the Ahmadiyyas in Pakistan who face death for even worshipping in a mosque, the Rohingyas battling genocide in Myanmar and the Uighurs held in internment camps in China. Why is refuge assured to persecuted people of Hindu, Buddhist and Sikh identity, but not to Muslims who suffer the same and sometimes even worse persecution? Why is it presumed that minority communities in Hindu-majority Nepal or Buddhist-majority Sri Lanka face no persecution?

Until 1987, to be eligible for Indian citizenship it was sufficient that a person be born in India. Then, spurred on by populist violent movements of the preceding decade, especially in Assam, alleging massive illegal migrations from Bangladesh, citizenship laws were first amended to lay down that birth in India would no longer be enough; to be eligible for citizenship the additional requirement would be that at least one parent must be Indian. Then, through the Citizenship (Amendment) Act, 2003—brought in by another BJP-led government, headed by Atal Bihari Vajpayee, and given Presidential assent in January 2004—the law was amended further. This law prescribed that it was not enough that just one parent be Indian; in addition, the other should not be an 'illegal immigrant'. This means that you would be eligible for citizenship if one parent is indisputably Indian and the other from any part of the planet, *except someone whom the Indian State brands as an illegal immigrant*. Read this now with the CAA-NRIC-NPR package and it becomes apparent why it fostered such widespread unease and dread. The CAA 2019 creates pathways for the State to fast-track and grant citizenship to undocumented people of various religious identities *except* Muslim (and small groups like Jews and Bahais). Therefore, even if they are undocumented and therefore 'illegal immigrants' according to existing Indian laws, people of various religious identities barring, importantly, Muslims have nothing to worry about. CAA can enable them to acquire Indian citizenship, and it would also free their children from the barrier to citizenship created by the 2004 amendment. Except for Muslims. If Muslims are judged to be 'illegal immigrants', the 2004 amendment would bang firmly the doors not only on them from becoming Indian citizens, but also on their children born in India who have known no other country. Even people whose families have for generations lived in India would become 'doubtful citizens' if they fail to provide documents confirming that at least one of their parents is or was Indian and the other, if not 'legally' Indian, a 'legal' refugee.

The disappointment and dissatisfaction of the BJP-led governments of India and Assam with the outcomes of the updated National Register of Citizens (NRC) in Assam (released in August 2019) was that—by all accounts—a much larger number of Bengali-origin Hindus and people of 'indigenous' tribes and other ethnic groups were excluded from the register than Muslims. If these Hindus and indigenous people were judged to be illegal immigrants, not just they but their offspring would become so because of the 2004 amendment.[14] The CAA alone could rescue the BJP from this political conundrum. It could treat the undocumented Bengali Hindus as refugees eligible for citizenship, and only Bengali-origin Muslims and their later generations would become 'illegal immigrants', even if they were born in India or had lived here for decades.

Treating Bengali-origin Hindus excluded from the Assam NRC as persecuted refugees from Bangladesh, however, will require multiple extraordinary leaps of official faith. Not one of these persons would have claimed in any official forum—NRC offices, Foreigners' Tribunals (FTs) or police stations—that they were illegal Bangladeshi immigrants. They would have strenuously tried to establish exactly the opposite. But, after the CAA, to secure Indian citizenship, they would have to claim to be illegal foreigners! There would also be thorny questions of evidence. How would they prove that they were citizens of neighbouring countries and that they were persecuted? The truth is that most had not crossed any border but were unable to produce the documents that could officially prove that they were Indian citizens. The government would find ways out of this legal predicament: it could just seek a self-affidavit from non-Muslim undocumented persons, or go further to simply presume that they are persecuted refugees from neighbouring countries even without any claim or affidavit from the undocumented persons only on the strength of their religious identity.

The Union Home Minister had often spoken of chronology: we will first pass the CAA, he declared, and then introduce a nationwide NRC, or NRIC. By first passing the CAA, the government clearly signalled that if people of any identity except Muslim anywhere in the country were unable to produce the required documents, they could now lawfully be accepted as refugees and given citizenship. This meant that the burden to actually prove that they are Indian citizens, if and when the NRIC exercise is undertaken, falls on Indian Muslims, because *only they* risk statelessness. Most Indians—including me—would find it impossible to put together the documents required to prove citizenship, but only document-less Muslims would face the prospect of detention centres, expulsion or being stripped of citizenship rights.

And then, since this imagination of citizenship is all vested in documents, which documents would provide the proof of religion? At present, it is only one's own declaration during the decadal census which is official evidence of one's religious persuasion. I can be born to a religion and reject it when I become an adult. I can be born to parents who claim no religion. But if religion becomes the principal fulcrum of whether or not one is a citizen, then which document would the State rely upon to decide what my religion is, and, based on that, whether I am a persecuted refugee or whether I am an infiltrator who should be thrown into a detention centre?

Creating a numerically immense population, running into many millions, of potentially stateless persons exclusively based on their religious identity would mark the demise of the secular republic built on guarantees of equality and non-discrimination on the basis of religion. The responsibility for this catastrophic collapse of the edifice of our Constitution would lie of course with leaders of the elected government who owe allegiance to a vision for India that contravenes fundamentally the guarantees of the Constitution; but the responsibility must also be shared by a timid political opposition bereft of the courage to defend the moral and political convictions and foundational principles of our democracy.

The CAA-NRIC-NPR poses the gravest threat to India's democratic Constitution since India became a republic, and it has to be fought by a nationwide civil disobedience movement. The contours of this struggle would be worked out by 'We, the People'. On the day that the CAA was being debated in the Rajya Sabha, the upper house of Parliament, I declared my own form of civil disobedience. If the CAA was passed, followed by a national NRIC, I would, in solidarity with those whose citizenship would be contested, declare myself Muslim in any government survey which sought a declaration of one's religion. And, when the NRIC would be organized, I would boycott it, refusing to produce any documents. I would then demand that I be given the same punishment my undocumented Muslim sisters and brothers were being subjected to, be it detention, the extinguishing of my citizenship rights or the threat of expulsion.

~

To comprehend even a fraction of the full dangers of the CAA-NRIC-NPR, one needs only to look back at the experience of the NRC project in Assam, and the mind-numbing injustices and immense human suffering it left in its wake. Assam even today continues to battle through the throes of the prolonged and uncertain tumult that the NRC provoked. Through a complex and tortuous process with no parallels in any other part of the country—and few, if any, in the world—millions of Assamese residents were called upon to produce documents that proved that they were Indian citizens.

It is not often remembered that it was not just Punjab and Bengal that were partitioned in 1947, but also Assam, when after a referendum Sylhet district was transferred to Pakistan. Migration from Sylhet and other parts of Bengal to Assam had continued until then for two centuries, fuelled by land-hunger and the attraction of creating farmlands in the vast virgin forest tracts and river islands of Assam, and encouraged by the colonial State. The cataclysms of Partition in 1947 and the Bangladesh Liberation War of 1971 spurred fresh migrations of Bengali people into Assam.

From the late 1970s, a massive and sporadically violent movement against 'foreigners' by people who saw themselves as 'original inhabitants' of Assam rocked the state. The updating of the NRC resulting in a national register that excluded from citizenship 19 lakh, or nearly two million, people was in fulfilment of the agreement reached by the agitators with the Union government in 1985, that persons who migrated to Assam from across the international border after 1971 would be identified and deported.

In 2007 the Supreme Court of India ruled that it was not the duty of State agencies to prove their claim when charging a person of being a foreigner. Instead, it was for those who claimed citizenship to prove that they were citizens. This was the most lethal blow to the vast populations of poorly lettered and impoverished residents of Assam, turning on its head the natural law that a person is innocent until proved guilty.

As a result, these disadvantaged people were required to garner official documents—such as documents of birth, landownership and voter identification—to establish their citizenship credentials. The majority of indigent rural people not just in Assam but in all of India would be unable to prove their citizenship for a whole host of reasons. Birth certificates are rare; many do not attend school; many have migrated for work or been married off as mere children; land records are poorly maintained and, in any case, many of these people are either landless or unrecorded tenants or encroachers on government land. To top it all, voters' lists are replete with omissions.

It is also important to reiterate that the flawed process of the NRC was monitored and indeed driven by the Supreme Court of India, in ways that did little to defend the constitutional rights of the residents of Assam. The burden of proof was shifted to the residents to prove that they were citizens, but even when they succeeded in producing the required documents, these were often rejected for small discrepancies such as in the English-language spelling of Bengali names, or in the ages reported, even though it is well known that most rural people do not know their dates of birth. And then, in the middle of the NRC process, an arbitrary category was introduced of 'indigenous' Assamese, who were treated much more leniently even when they could not produce the required documents.

The underlying chauvinism of the process was exposed also by official orders, again ratified by India's Supreme Court, which exempted 'persons who are originally inhabitants of the state of Assam' from any 'further proof or inquiry'. The 'original inhabitant', thus made eligible for automatic inclusion in the NRC, is nowhere defined, but in practice original inhabitants are taken to exclude people who speak Bengali, Nepali, Hindi or Santhali, even if they have lived in Assam for generations.

The tragedy of the Assamese people is that the labyrinthine NRC authority is not the only agency empowered to identify non-citizens in Assam. In fact, three parallel processes, mostly dependent on low-level bureaucratic and police discretion, run side by side, in what poet Manash Bhattacharjee aptly describes as the 'sniffer-dog' idea of the state, hunting down 'foreigners'. One of these 'sniffer-dog' processes began in 1997 when, on the pretext of extensive revision of electoral rolls, the Election Commission of India summarily and without any due process marked 3.7 lakh voters as doubtful, or 'D-voters'. This stripped them of their voting rights, and their cases were referred to a Foreigners' Tribunal. Election officials still continue to brand many residents as 'doubtful'. Yet another empowered agency is the Assam Police Border Organisation, which deputes police officials in many police stations to identify possible non-citizens and refer their cases to FTs.

People who do not speak Assamese, and are not from indigenous tribes, are in this way beleaguered from all sides. They do not know when challenges to their citizenship may come, from the NRC executives, election officials or the local policeperson.

In 2006, the Police Border Organisation referred Ajbahar Ali, a small farmer in Kheluwapara village in Bongaigaon district of western Assam, to an FT. With trepidation, he answered the summons from the Tribunal. He learned that the Tribunal in an *ex parte* judgment had already declared him a foreigner. Without any advance warning, he was whisked away from the Tribunal directly to a detention centre built inside a jail. In desperation, his wife Balijan Bibi sold their farmland, cattle and the only cell phone they owned to pay a lawyer to challenge the FT order and get her husband released from detention. Their older son Moinul Haque travelled to the Gauhati High Court to hear the judgment, while his mother waited anxiously at home for news. He returned the next morning only to inform his mother that the Court had rejected their plea. The Supreme Court, Moinul explained, was beyond their reach. Balijan Bibi did not speak much, just asked her son to rest. After a while he found her hanging from the ceiling.

Months later, our Karwan-e-Mohabbat team visited the family. The children were in the darkest despair. Their father was in a detention centre with no prospect of release, their mother was dead, and their land and all they owned had been sold. There are at least 28 cases of suicide committed by people who had lost hope of proving they were citizens of this country and found no reason to live.

This is the collective tragedy of literally millions of religious, linguistic and ethnic minorities in Assam, living daily under the shadow of a hostile state that is using multiple tangled and opaque ways of establishing that they don't belong. And their predicament continues to worsen, with no light visible even on the distant horizon, because the Union and state governments are completely silent about the fate of those who in the end are declared foreigners. Over a thousand such people have been housed indefinitely in hellish detention centres and jails, in flagrant violation of constitutional guarantees and international law. But if the numbers tomorrow run into possibly millions, where will they be detained?

~

In his historic address to the World's Parliament of Religions in Chicago in 1893, Swami Vivekanand[15] declared, 'I am proud to belong to a nation which has sheltered the persecuted and the refugees of all religions and all nations of the earth.' It is ironic then that a political party which conspicuously proclaims its allegiance to Swami Vivekanand has restricted by law, 126 years later, citizenship to people on grounds of both religion and nation.

The CAA 2019, passionately contested by people across the country, which introduces these filters of religion and nation, also reminds us urgently of the moral imperative of an expansive and humane refugee law. A law that conforms to what is finest in India's civilizational ethos, and to the morality of India's Constitution. This urgency is underlined further by the decision of the Indian executive in October 2018, backed by the Supreme Court, to send seven Rohingya men who had been detained in Assam since 2012 back to Myanmar.[16]

Looking back, it is pertinent to ask why Jawaharlal Nehru, an international statesperson and a leading moral voice in the community of nations, refused to sign the 1951 Convention Relating to the Status of Refugees. Scholars suggest that whereas he was committed to the principles enshrined in the Convention, he was unwilling to legally bind his country to its obligations. The Convention defines refugees as persons fleeing persecution on grounds of race, religion, nationality, social group or political opinion. Refugees get legal rights, most important of which are 'non-refoulement', which prevents states from sending them back to their home countries against their will. They also get secondary rights, such as to education, work and property. India has long argued that even without signing the Convention, in practice it is one of the leading refugee-receiving countries in the world. Refugees include Sri Lankan Tamils, Tibetans, Chin minorities from Burma, and Hindus from Bangladesh and Pakistan. It may then be legitimately asked why India needs a refugee law which conforms to the

Refugee Convention if in practice it has been hospitable to refugees.

The answer lies in the discrimination exercised in the recognition of refugees and the award of citizenship, embedded sometimes in laws and rules and, at other times, in official practice. These include the morally indefensible, indeed shameful, decision of the Indian government to send the Rohingyas back to conditions which the International Court of Justice had recently deemed genocidal. It also includes the changes made to the Passport Rules even prior to the passage of the CAA which in effect discriminate between people on the basis of their religion.

There are many problems with the Indian law relating to refugees. The first of these is that our law does not distinguish between 'foreigners' and 'refugees'. This means that refugees depend on the discretion of the State, indeed on its 'benevolence' rather than having inherent rights. The second is that the law assumes that the executive will act on principles of humanism and non-discrimination. This may have been true of an India led by Nehru. Governments which followed his have had mixed records in this regard. It is certainly not true of the government that we have today, driven as it is by the ideology of the RSS, which is openly hostile to Indian Muslims, and which believes that India should be (like Israel) the natural home of persecuted Hindus, not Muslims.

In the absence of explicit recognition by Indian law of the category of refugees, or of their legally binding rights, even the guarantees of Fundamental Rights to life, equality and non-discrimination and humanitarian obligations did not prevent India from violating the core principle of non-refoulement, of not sending back people to situations of persecution, such as those faced by the Rohingyas. Let us rewind to the litigation in the Indian Supreme Court, challenging the government's proposed deportation of seven Rohingyas in 2018. When the seven repatriated Rohingya men were only hours away from the border with Myanmar, human rights activists who had just found out about this, made a dramatic urgent intervention in the Supreme Court, pleading to immediately stop the Rohingyas from being thrown into a genocidal situation. The Supreme Court bench, which included Chief Justice Ranjan Gogoi, refused to stay their deportation, basing its ruling primarily on a brief Union government affidavit which claimed that Myanmar had accepted the refugees as 'citizens' and the men had orally agreed to be repatriated. The Court unconscionably refused to stop the deportation despite the transparent unreliability of these claims, since the men did not have access to legal counsel nor to the United Nations High Commissioner for Refugees (UNHCR) to determine whether their consent was freely expressed. Also, that they may have chosen the risks only because the option they were given to deportation was to remain indefinitely in detention. The media later reported that these men had been detained in Myanmar for 'illegal entry' and had been given the controversial National Verification Card (that does not recognize their religion or ethnicity), not citizenship. We do not know what has happened to them since.

The moral culpability of these decisions both of the Union government and the Supreme Court are further highlighted by the unanimous judgment of the International Court of Justice on 23 January 2020 that concluded that the Rohingya face genocidal intent.[17] The case against Myanmar was brought to the International Court by a small African Muslim nation, The Gambia. It rejected Aung San Suu Kyi's testimony on behalf of her government, where she described the allegations brought by The Gambia as 'an incomplete and misleading factual picture' of the prevailing conditions in Rakhine State. The International Court warned the Myanmar military against any conspiracy to commit genocide and directed the Myanmar authorities to take steps to protect its minority Rohingya population.

For the Indian government and the Supreme Court, this judgment should have been a moment of both introspection and atonement. But it was not, and it will not likely be. The government has never referred to the Rohingya as refugees. Instead, they have been branded illegal immigrants, security threats and potential terror threats. They cannot lawfully be considered eligible for citizenship under the 2019 amendment because the law excludes them due to both their religion and country of origin. So they are often the subject of communally charged political stigmatization by the ruling party, amidst calls for the expulsion of the desperately impoverished tiny population of around 40,000 that subsist by picking rags and carrying out the most menial tasks, living in dismal shanties unsupported by the Indian State.

The Supreme Court continues even until the time of writing to rule that the principle of non-refoulement—prohibiting States from forcefully returning undocumented persons to conditions where they would face discrimination on the basis of their religion, ethnicity, language, sexuality, political beliefs or any other grounds—does not apply to India because it has not signed the international convention for the protection of refugees. But even a first-year law student could educate the learned judges that the fundamental right to life under Article 21 of the Indian Constitution applies to every *person* and not just to every citizen. Therefore, returning Rohingya to the genocidal conditions that prevail in their home country is a violation of Article 21 of the Indian Constitution that guarantees the protection of life and liberty to all persons, both citizens and those who are not Indian citizens.

Our treatment of the Rohingyas, and the introduction of the discriminatory CAA must compel every Indian committed to ensuring India remains a humane and inclusive country to fight not just for the abrogation of the CAA-NRIC-NPR trinity, but also for India to bring in a refugee law that conforms to international conventions. This would firstly recognize eligible undocumented immigrants as refugees, based on evidence determined by due process of their persecution in their home countries. It would also assure them of a set of binding rights. The most important of these would be the guarantee that they would not be forced to return to the conditions of persecution that they escaped from. The second is that they be assured of lives of dignity within India, with education, health care and sustainable livelihoods. Only then would India become the country which Swami Vivekanand was so proud of, a haven to the persecuted of the world, untainted by discrimination based on religion or nation.

~

India today is as far as it can be from the nation envisioned by Vivekanand and Gandhi, more profoundly divided than it has ever been since it became a republic. Despite the unprecedented, but mostly peaceful, popular protests against the CAA-NRIC-NPR trinity that continued for over three months and the resolutions of eleven state Assemblies against the trinity, the government remained stubborn in its resolve to roll out the NPR countrywide from 1 April 2020.

At protest sites in many corners of the country, a poignant word I heard repeatedly was *bemulk*, literally, 'without a country'. With the announcement of the NPR, the threat of being made stateless seemed imminent. There were new questions that had been introduced in the NPR form—the place of birth of one's parents, for instance—which were of no relevance at all in a population register. What was the purpose of these questions? Naturally, then, people feared that the information that the State gathered from them in the NPR could be used to render them without a country, locked up in detention centres for life—because this was the only land where they belonged; where would they be deported to? The NPR was set to become the flashpoint for even more irreconcilable and dangerous social and political fractures, till the Covid-19 pandemic and lockdown came in the way of the government's plans. But the plans have certainly not been suspended.

As the citizenship protests gathered strength in the winter of 2019–20, Prime Minister Modi first announced that his government had not taken any decision to undertake an NRIC.[18] Then, in Parliament, Home Minister Shah declared that no documents would be sought during the NPR, that people would have the right to refuse certain questions, and that the government would not investigate and identify 'doubtful' citizens during the NPR. So, he said, 'nobody has to fear the process of NPR', that 'false propaganda' was 'being spread on CAA'.

Yet, millions in India remain convinced that the NPR would pave the path for their possible disenfranchisement. Let us examine the citizenship law. What does it say? The seeds of the crisis—the horror—of statelessness that the CAA-NRIC-NPR could result in were laid by the Vajpayee government.[19] As already noted, its amendments to the citizenship law prescribed that a person could not claim citizenship, even if born and raised in India, if even one of her or his parents was an 'illegal immigrant'. The Citizenship Rules, 2003 also state in clear, unambiguous terms that the National Population Register will become the basis for preparing a Local Register of Indian Citizens (LRIC) at the tehsil or taluka level and a National Register of Indian Citizens (NRIC). Thus, *NPR is integral to the 'initialization' of the NRIC.*

It may be argued that details of this law, perhaps any law, are not common knowledge, and when that is the case, why have the declarations of the two most powerful men in the country failed to allay the intense fears of a significant proportion of Indians?

This is, first, because the trust of the ordinary citizen in the words of her government has never been as low as it is today. It is disingenuous for the Home Minister to ask why so many Indian citizens fear the NPR and NRIC, because it is he who has been the most assiduous in fostering and feeding this fear, with references to immigrants as 'infiltrators' to be deported from every square inch of the country and 'termites'[20] (presumably to be exterminated); in declaring that a nationwide NRIC would be implemented for this purpose; and in ensuring that the CAA precedes the NRIC, thereby protecting the citizenship rights of every religious community except Muslims.

Second, the Union government has not assured people that it will never undertake an NRIC. Its assertion has always only been that it has not taken any decision to prepare an NRIC for the present. The NRIC therefore remains a weapon the government can opt to unleash on its people at any time of its choosing.

Third, the government has offered no convincing explanation why it remains determined to ram through the NPR despite the apprehensions of millions of citizens and the unprecedented opposition of several state governments. If the Union government does not intend to draw up an NRIC in the future based on information collected from the NPR, there is no convincing reason for it to ride roughshod over such massive democratic and federal opposition to the NPR.

Fourth, fears persist because of the experience of Assam. It is now several years since the people of Assam were thrust into a tumult born from the chronic fear of disenfranchisement if they were unable to muster vintage documents which many of us would find difficult to collect. People have sold their meagre belongings to pay lawyers and bribe government functionaries, to argue their claims before merciless officials and biased tribunals, not to speak of the stories of the horrors of detention centres. That this might become the fate of vast numbers across the country has hardened the resolve of people to oppose the NPR and NRIC at all costs.

And, most importantly, assurances never override the law. Unless the law and rules are amended to remove provisions for both the NRIC and the NPR, the danger of the government using the NPR to identify 'illegal immigrants' for the NRIC will always hang over our heads like the proverbial sword of Damocles.

Some state governments suggest that an NPR with just the 2010 questions will be benign. This is completely misleading. It is not as though 'doubtful' citizens will be identified by a scientific algorithm analysing their answers. The NPR with *any* set of questions unleashes a process which gives sweeping powers to the executive to ask any resident to prove her or his citizenship through decades-old documents. This unbridled power is highly susceptible to being misused for rent-seeking, and for communal, gender or caste targeting.

It is true, as Mr Shah says, that the NPR functionaries will not seek documents, nor will they designate people as doubtful citizens.[21] But this is no reassurance, because anyway the rules did not intend for them to do this. The rules provide that *after* the compilation of the NPR, the executive will identify 'doubtful' citizens. The powers to do so are vested with junior officials from the tahsildar upwards. There are no guidelines, so officials have complete discretion to classify 'doubtful' citizens as they please. They can also demand that any person of their choosing provide any information or documents. Even more dangerous for social harmony, the draft NRIC will be made public to invite objections or claims for inclusion or corrections—any person aggrieved by anyone's exclusion or inclusion order can appeal to the district registrar and the officials will examine these objections. So not only does the government give itself and its functionaries the power to strip anyone it chooses of citizenship rights, it also recruits the mob in the project.

If the government really wishes to win back the faith of the people, to convince them that it has no intention of threatening their citizenship, there is only one way to do so. It must abrogate the clauses brought in in 2003 prescribing the NRIC and rules for the NPR and identifying 'doubtful' citizens. But the hubris of our rulers and their commitment to their communal ideological project makes the likelihood of this happening most improbable. To meet their ends, they are prepared to put in unprecedented peril the Indian people and nation.

~

In early May 2021, results of elections in four states, including Bengal and Assam, were declared. Bengal saw the emphatic rejection of the openly and aggressively divisive agenda of the BJP, led from the front by the Prime Minister and his closest confidant, the country's Home Minister. But in Assam, the BJP and its allies returned to power with a convincing majority.

Bengali-origin Muslims of Assam have confided in me that they are terrified by the results. Although it had been close to two years since the NRC list was released in Assam, the BJP-led government in the state and the national government had not taken the next steps prescribed under law—they have not given 'speaking orders' to the nearly two million people who were excluded from the final NRC. These 'speaking orders' with detailed reasons for their exclusion are the last chance the excluded persons have to press their claims for citizenship in the Foreigners' Tribunals. The conundrum confronting the state and Central governments is apparent: until the CAA 2019 is operationalized to create pathways to citizenship for the excluded Hindus, taking the NRC forward would be political suicide for the BJP as it would exclude from citizenship twice as many Hindus as Muslims. BJP leaders in Assam had spoken widely before the elections of rejecting the NRC, and reopening the agonizing process of a new NRC either in all of Assam or, more likely, in eight border districts with high Muslim populations. The agenda is clear—to exclude millions of Bengali-origin Muslims, and not Bengali Hindus. This is all speculative at the time of writing. But that these widespread fears exist in the targeted community reflect how fragile their right to citizenship remains.

Not surprisingly, uncertainty, fear and disquiet continue

to grip nearly two million residents of Assam and their loved ones. And the unremitting tragedy of the Bengal-origin people of the state is that even those whose names appear on the updated NRC list have no assurance that they will not be deemed illegal immigrants sometime in the future. They are a people for whom there is still no closure, no prospect of the permanent security of citizenship.

Legitimate anxieties about land, culture and migration have created entrenched fissures in the social and political life of Assam for decades. Blood has flowed, many lives have been destroyed. People on all sides of these bitter divides had hoped that the conclusion of the six-year-long process of updating the 1951 citizen register in Assam would finally resolve this long-festering dispute. But despite the immeasurable toll of human suffering that the process has exacted from millions of very impoverished people, it is evident that it has resolved nothing.

The Bengali-origin Assamese have always maintained that the estimates of illegal immigration are grossly exaggerated, and that most Bengali-origin people in Assam, regardless of faith, are descendants of people who came in legally when this was one country, and that since the cutoff date of 1971, illegal immigration has taken place on a relatively small scale. The relatively low final tally, even after a highly flawed process which was entirely loaded against them, seems to vindicate their stand. But this is cold comfort and assures them no security when influential demands are being raised to once again reopen the process of the NRC with a fresh process of reverification.

For supporters of the Assam agitation, it has long been an article of faith that millions of immigrants from Bangladesh have continued to illegally penetrate the porous border that Assam shares with Bangladesh, and that these immigrants will take over their culture and language and edge them out of their lands and forests. Estimates of the numbers of these illegal immigrants that the leaders of the Assam Movement have tossed around range from five to 10 million. The final figure of less than two million in the new NRC has sorely disappointed and enraged them.

For the BJP establishment, clearing out Muslim 'infiltrators' has been as integral to its core agenda as abrogating Article 370 and building the Ram Temple at the exact site of the demolished Babri Mosque in Ayodhya. In Assam, specifically, it is only Bengali-origin Muslim immigrants who constitute a threat to Assam and the Indian nation, according to the BJP; Bengali Hindus are not 'infiltrators' but 'refugees' and India is their natural home. We do not yet have an official break-up of the 19 lakh people excluded from the NRC in Assam, but indications are, as we have noted, that more than half of them are Hindu or members of tribes regarded as 'indigenous'.[22] Assamese sub-nationalism has never been communal: its supporters are agnostic when it comes to Bengali Hindus or Muslims; for them, both are equally unwelcome. For the BJP, on the other hand, disenfranchising or deporting Bengali Hindus would be political suicide, sacrificing their core constituency. Therefore, BJP leaders in Assam and Delhi are today cunningly rejecting the very biased process that their own governments drove, describing it as 'biased' against *them*! The only way in which the NRC could work for them is if the openly discriminatory CAA is implemented or the NRC in Assam is selectively reopened to ensure that Muslims alone are excluded.

What does the future hold for the Bengali-origin people of Assam? Those excluded from the NRC, once they are given reasoned speaking orders, will have the option of appealing to FTs. This is a frightening prospect for them because the FTs have operated in ways that are openly hostile and arbitrary. The presiding officers of FTs are often lawyers with no judicial experience, appointed with no security of tenure by the state government, who follow no due process, and are reportedly driven by informal targets to maximize the numbers of persons they deem to be foreigners.

There is also the enormous workload that the appeals will engender. Today there are 100 FTs. There were statements to the effect that these would be doubled but that hasn't happened yet. In our observation, an average case in the FT takes one year or longer to dispose of. I did a back-of-the-envelope calculation that even if there were 1,000 FTs that decided one case per working day, it would take more than six years for them to decide 19 lakh cases. Given their actual rate of disposal, it could take three or four times that. And as we have seen, disappointed by the smaller numbers of Bengali Muslims in the final list of excluded names, the state government has already indicated that it will continue to verify even those whose names are included in the NRC, and if it believes that they could be foreigners, it will refer them too to the FTs.

The biggest question then is what the fate will be of those people who at the end of this process are declared illegal immigrants. There is no question of Bangladesh accepting them—the Indian government knows this too and is not even negotiating this with Bangladesh. The Assam agitation was clear in its demand of 'detection, deletion (from electoral rolls) and deportation'. Home Minister Amit Shah has declared that his government will deport 'illegal immigrants' from every square inch of Indian land. How will this be accomplished? Will these millions be pushed by force into Bangladesh at the risk of war? Will they be thrown into the sea? Or will they be locked in massive detention centres that would have to be built for millions of people—and if that, then for how long?

Since the Indian government is not even negotiating an extradition treaty for the return of these persons with the Bangladesh government, if they are to continue to live in India as non-citizens, are we not manufacturing a horrific Rohingya-like situation within our country? Because the only realistic probability is that, in the end, they will be allowed to live in India, but stripped of all citizenship rights, of voting, owning land and social security. They would be a marked people, powerless and without rights, susceptible always to social violence and intense State scrutiny and targeting. They will become people no country wants, with futures bleak and obscure, profoundly let down even by the highest courts of the land, and indeed liberal civil society. Assam is sitting on a volcano of further mass suffering and conflict.

Think then of the grand ideological project of Prime Minister Modi and Home Minister Amit Shah of extending the NRIC to all of India. Think of throwing 200 million Indian Muslim people into the perpetual hell of fear, uncertainty and absolute hopelessness. More than any other step that the government might take in resolute pursuit of its majoritarian agenda, this will mean the end of India as we know it, as a democracy, a civilization.

~

But the Indian people have risen. The peaceful mass uprising against the trinity of the CAA-NRIC-NPR in the winter of 2019–20 lasted for 100 days before it was silenced by the nationwide lockdown in the wake of the pandemic. But while it lasted, it was a movement without precedent in the journey of the Republic. Resolute both in their solidarity and their resistance, in cities and towns across the country people of various faiths and identities came out in the hundreds of thousands. With no single leader, at the vanguard of this rising were young people and working-class Muslim women. Its icons were Mahatma Gandhi and Babasaheb Ambedkar and its symbols the Tricolour and the Constitution. The national anthem, sung rousingly in every protest, became a protest chant. With fear and silence broken, voices of dissent rang out loud and clear. We were stirred by defiant poetry and slogans celebrating our unity and freedom, the country and the Constitution.

Like a sudden flash of brilliant light in a stormy night, the revolt broke through the darkness which had shrouded this land. By refusing to allow their nation to be divided by hate, young and working people challenged the government's hubris. The movement might or might not have been sustainable, particularly when confronted by an elected autarchy of the kind that rules India. But the fact that it happened at all was miraculous proof that vast numbers of us, including the young, have the moral fibre to fight for the kind of country that Gandhi imagined and fought for a hundred years earlier. These protests were, at their core, popular moral assertions founded on fraternity of a kind we have not seen for a long time, perhaps not since our freedom struggle.

The ruling establishment responded with its well-used playlist of attempts to communalize and discredit the protesters; to confuse people with falsehoods; and to deploy crushing State force. But this time none of it worked. The police brutalized students in the two national universities identified with India's Muslim heritage—Jamia Millia Islamia and Aligarh Muslim University. But the same night that news filtered in of injured Jamia students rounded up in police stations in Delhi, large crowds spontaneously gathered outside the police headquarters and refused to move until the early hours of the morning when the police was forced to release the students. Students and faculty from more than 50 universities around the country surged out in support. As more people were detained, sleep-deprived lawyers kept vigil every night outside police stations where the protesters were detained.

The Prime Minister taunted the protesters saying he could identify them by the clothes they wore,[23] an unmistakable reference to their Muslim identity. In response, people of every visible identity joined the protests. Choir singers in Kerala wore skullcaps and hijabs while singing Christmas carols. A young Hindu lawyer travelled from Jabalpur to the protest in Delhi, stripped in the freezing cold to his boxer shorts, and then asked the Prime Minister to recognize him by his clothes.

Solidarity and courage shone through at every protest site. Posters read: 'There are two words which break my heart: Except Muslim'; '*Woh todenge, hum jodenge. Yeh mulk hamara hai*' (They'll break it, we'll put it back together. This country belongs to us); 'You divide. We multiply'. Newlyweds circulated pictures holding posters that said: 'Say no to CAA-NRC-NPR'. Many wrote this in henna on their hands.

In recent years, for the first time in my life, I had found my optimism frayed, even ebbing. My personal politics have always been grounded in a dogged, even naïve optimism, a belief in the inevitability of human goodness and a conviction that hatred and tyranny will not prevail. But during the journeys of the Karwan-e-Mohabbat with my colleagues and friends to meet families whose men had been lynched, we found that several people, mostly young men, who had led the mobs targeting Muslims and Dalits with an inexplicable ferocity and cruelty, were completely without remorse, proudly circulating videos of the brutal slayings. No one had come forward in defence of the men who had been killed. In most cases the police had encouraged the mobs, protected the killers and criminalized those victims who had somehow survived. It appeared that the BJP and its ideological family had been able to demonize and completely marginalize the Muslims by uniting every other caste and religious group in a pact of hate against them. I began to dread that India was trapped in a long, dark night of hate. But the protests led by young Indians celebrating Hindu–Muslim unity and the equal rights of people of every identity reignited my hope. I'm sure crores of others across India felt infected by the same optimism.

The great import of the moment was that it was in its spirit the continuance of the battle which began 100 years ago. As I recalled in the opening pages of this book, Mahatma Gandhi had returned from South Africa to lead India's freedom struggle marked by a humane and inclusive nationalism, and the idea of a country which would welcome as equal citizens people of every faith and identity. In stark contrast was the imagination of the Hindu Mahasabha and RSS that dreamed of a Hindu nation in which religious minorities would be forced to live as second-class citizens; and of the Muslim League, which too was unashamedly communal, convinced that Muslims could only achieve equality and security in a separate Muslim-majority nation. Those holding power today seem determined to prove that Gandhiji was wrong and Savarkar and Jinnah were right. But young and working-class Indians, 70 years after Gandhi was killed for his beliefs—and after Ambedkar incorporated the idea of secularism and fraternity into our Constitution—have picked up the mantle to fight for a country which is equal, just and kind.

The protests have certainly led to great unease in the ruling establishment. The Uttar Pradesh administration declared war on its Muslim citizens and other protesters.[24] Delhi too burned in the communal carnage ignited by the brazen hate-mongering of the highest leaders of the BJP. The Prime Minister tried to defend his government with astounding barefaced falsehoods, claiming that his government never spoke of a national NRC,[25] whereas his Home Minister had announced it repeatedly in Parliament and outside, linking it with the CAA[26] and signalling unmistakably that Hindus would be protected, but not Muslims. The Prime Minister also claimed that India had no detention centres,[27] whereas I have personally seen and entered these hell-like centres in Assam. And the Home Minister has announced that states have been asked to build detention centres across the country;[28] indeed, construction of such centres is underway in some states.

The final assault on the protest movement was to charge both young people and older activists with sedition, accusing them of hatching a conspiracy of insurrection and terror. Many young people have been in jail for over a year already. In a few cases the courts, including the Supreme Court, have granted them bail; in many others, a brazenly partisan police has managed to subvert justice repeatedly, starting with a 1,000-page chargesheet with wild claims.[29]

As I see it, despite repression and criminalization, despite the temporary physical suspension due to the pandemic, the protests have already won. They have succeeded in halting—at least until the time of writing—a national NRIC. This is an enormous victory, because it was the combination of the CAA with the NRIC which threatened to thrust India's 200 million Muslims into the same vortex of dread and insecurity that the Bengali-origin Assamese people have been trapped in for the past several years. Even allies who cynically voted with the ruling party in support of the CAA have announced, influenced by popular revulsion, that they will not implement the NRIC. Eleven state governments have categorically ruled out the NRC, as noted above.

Those who worry about the success of the movement mistake the character of the resistance. It is a gross error to view this merely as a battle against the CAA-NRIC-NPR trinity. It was a rebellion against the audacity of a government asking its citizens to prove that they belong. It was a warning that the government must listen to its people. It was a spontaneous rising against fear, hate, discrimination and violence, and the dangerous project of militarist Hindutva nationalism.[30] It was an uprising against a government which crushes and demonizes students, dissenters and minorities, even as it fails to address the hopeless realities of everyday life, of joblessness, farm distress, violence against women and a broken economy.

Its paramount success was that it was the first national movement for Hindu–Muslim unity after Mahatma Gandhi was taken away from us by an assassin's bullet in 1948. Indeed, it was a movement for the unity of people of various religious and caste identities. When poor Sikh farmers camped out on cold nights in Shaheen Bagh to prepare *langar* for their protesting sisters, it represented the triumph of what is finest in our civilizational traditions. 'We have seen the suffering of

1947,' one elderly farmer said. 'We want to ensure that this never happens again.'

A second success of the movement has been the re-politicization of students in universities across India. For too long, most universities had become sterile sites deprived of both political and ethical reflection. In this movement, students were teaching their elders not to hate, showing the way to a more caring and equal country.

A third accomplishment was the reassurance to India's Muslim people. For Muslims, the past years have been harrowing and terrifying. They were rendered politically irrelevant and were treated as a political liability by every political party. Bigotry, hate speeches and lynchings became an acceptable part of life. I had the privilege to be invited to speak at protest sites and massive rallies in different parts of the country. In these protests led by Muslim women, I found the mood electrically festive. Less protests, these were more celebrations of the reassurance that India was still equally their country, that we all stand together.

A fourth achievement was the reclaiming of the idea of nationalism by those Indians who unite rather than divide. Those who truly love their country would not want it to be divided by hate, fear and violence. The resentful divisive nationalism of the Right has been countered by the patriotism of Rabindranath Tagore and Mahatma Gandhi, whereby you love your country by loving all its people and respecting every other country.

A fifth victory was in making the Constitution the soul of the people's movement. I got goose bumps each time, in mass as well as street-corner protests, crowds, usually led by young women, recited the preamble of the Constitution. What could be more apt than 'We, the people of India' coming together to defend the Constitution at a time when it was most threatened.

The final triumph of the movement was that it compelled the reluctant, morally ambiguous non-BJP parties to take a public stand at last to defend the Constitution, which they were willing to betray for petty electoral considerations. It also clearly rattled the Union government, leading to the lie that the NRIC had not been its agenda.

I am convinced that the movement will, possibly after the passing of the humanitarian crisis created by the pandemic and lockdowns, ride again on these brilliant successes to move into its next phase. While protests and rallies will continue as long as people have the stamina and conviction to persist with these, the main focus of the movement must now shift to non-cooperation, specifically with the NPR and NRIC. If the NPR is allowed, it will enable the government at any time of its choosing to identify 'doubtful citizens' for exclusion from an NRIC.

A flawless NPR-NRIC is an unimplementable project. Its real aim is to push all of India's Muslims, and with them all vulnerable and dissenting groups, into a permanent state of insecurity and dread—to make them forever fearful, force them into silence and invisibility. The movement must therefore compel state governments to refuse to implement the NPR and to decouple it from the Census, which must continue.

And it would be unconscionable for a movement that defends the Constitution to ride on the shoulders of India's Muslims who are already being brutally targeted by the present regime. So, the call for a citizens' boycott of the NPR must focus on non-Muslims, because for Muslims the cost of disobedience will be intense and grave.

Finally, we must heed Maulana Azad:

> Today if an angel were to descend from the Heaven and declare from the heights of the Qutab Minar that India will get Swaraj within 24 hours provided she relinquishes Hindu–Muslim unity, I will relinquish Swaraj rather than give up Hindu–Muslim unity. Delay in the attainment of Swaraj will be a loss to India but if our unity is lost it will be a loss to entire mankind.[31]

The movement must, always and in every way, deepen our unity and solidarity. It must address not just the State but each of us. In the end the kind of country we become will be determined not by laws or judgments, but by whether our hearts are ruled by love or colonized by hate. At the height of the protests when so many streets and squares all over India were alive with fellowship, this solidarity was clearly visible, brilliant and incandescent. It must return and grow ever stronger, brighter.

The Hindutva Right believes that Partition will be complete only with the transfer of every Muslim Indian to Pakistan and Bangladesh, and of every Hindu from these nations to India. It believes in the eternal supremacy of the bigoted Hindu. The freedom struggle, by contrast, was founded on the idea of equal rights for all, including Muslims. This vision was first imperilled by the tragic ruptures of Partition. It was the moral lodestar of Mahatma Gandhi in the final months of his life which steadied India and steered it back in the direction of the values of the freedom struggle, aided by leaders like Nehru, Ambedkar and Maulana Azad.

But, as the decades passed, with the rising clout and influence of Hindutva politics, and the parallel moral and political enfeeblement of secular political formations, it appeared that the legacy of the freedom struggle and inclusive nationalism was fading, even spent. In recent years, it appeared instead that militant, narrow and perpetually resentful Hindutva nationalism had triumphed, that most of India had coalesced against the common 'adversary' within, the Indian Muslim, and the enemy outside, Pakistan.

The 2019 election results and the months that followed seemed to signal the hegemony of this social and political consensus, of the prior and higher right of the Hindu majority to the nation. Political parties almost across the spectrum, and all public institutions including the higher judiciary, the civil services, the armed forces, universities and the media seemed to accept this new consensus. The letter of India's secular

Constitution was not altered, but its spirit and indeed its practice appeared to have reversed.

But this long night of darkness was suddenly interrupted for a hundred days by bursts of light in every corner of the land. Our young people were rebelling against the hate that older generations have raised them in. The popular movement led by India's young and its working-class Muslim women for secularism and solidarity, for a just and kind country, was indeed picking up the unfinished business of the freedom struggle.

Many people have spoken about the dangers of fascism, and the eerie echoes of Nazi Germany in India today. The similarities with Nazi Germany are indeed many. But Germany in the 1930s never saw the kind of pushback from non-Jews that India is witnessing today. And it never saw the federal resistance that many state governments have offered, by refusing to implement the NRIC.

The hundred days of protests against the amended citizenship regime have accomplished one thing above all: they have demonstrated conclusively that there is no hegemonic consensus in support of the idea of a Hindu Rashtra. That significant numbers of people of various religious identities, including Hindu, are opposed passionately to the divisive and majoritarian Hindutva agenda. That the idea of India—defined by hope and equality rather than fear and dominance—for which millions battled during the freedom struggle is still precious to a vast number of people in this land. They were on the streets to reclaim the values of our freedom movement and our Constitution. And they will return.

Mahatma Gandhi would surely have approved.

Notes

1. After 21 years in South Africa as a lawyer and civil rights activist fighting against the racist policies of the British, Gandhi returned to India on 9 January 1915. By this time, he was already well known in India for his activism. Over the next 30 years, Gandhi and his methods of peaceful civil disobedience became instrumental in the Indian freedom movement.
2. Upon India's independence on 15 August 1947, the new Congress-led government invited Ambedkar to serve as the nation's first law minister, which he accepted. On 29 August, he was appointed Chairman of the Constitution Drafting Committee, and was appointed by the Constituent Assembly to write India's new constitution. Granville Austin, a well-known historian of the Indian constitution, described the Constitution drafted by Ambedkar as 'first and foremost a social document': 'The majority of India's constitutional provisions are either directly arrived at furthering the aim of social revolution or attempt to foster this revolution by establishing conditions necessary for its achievement.' The text prepared by Ambedkar provided constitutional guarantees and protections for a wide range of civil liberties for individual citizens, including freedom of religion, the abolition of untouchability, and the outlawing of all forms of discrimination. Ambedkar argued for extensive economic and social rights for women, and won the Assembly's support for introducing a system of reservations of jobs in the civil services, schools and colleges for members of Scheduled Castes and Scheduled Tribes and Other Backward Classes, a system akin to affirmative action. India's lawmakers hoped to eradicate the socio-economic inequalities and lack of opportunities for India's depressed classes through these measures. The Constitution was adopted on 26 November 1949 by the Constituent Assembly.
3. The Akhil Bharatiya Hindu Mahasabha, formally named so in April 1921, was an umbrella organization for all the previous 'Hindu Sabhas' which had been taking place over the past decade. Initiated as an organization to foster 'Hindu unity', the core ideology of the Hindu Mahasabha was rooted in its identification of India as a Hindu Rashtra ('Hindu Nation') and belief in the primacy of Hindu culture, religion and heritage. It was founded around 1915. The Mahasabha advocates that Sikhs, Jains and Buddhists are identical to Hinduism in terms of teachings and cultural, national and political identity. It argues that Islam and

Christianity are foreign religions, and that Indian Muslims and Christians are simply descendants of Hindus who were converted by force, coercion and bribery. At various points in its history, the party called for the re-conversion of Muslims and Christians to Hinduism. The Mahasabha is widely seen as the ideological and political root of the RSS (see note 4 below), and the Bharatiya Janata Party, the party currently in power in India. See Christophe Jaffrelot, *Hindu Nationalism: A Reader*, Princeton, NJ: Princeton University Press, 2007.

4. K.B. Hedgewar founded the Rashtriya Swayamsevak Sangh (RSS; 'Association of National Volunteers') in 1925 in response to the threat posed to Hindus by Muslims and the British. The ideology of Hindutva was centred on the equating of Indian identity to Hindu identity. Religious minorities within the Indian state were to 'pledge allegiance to Hindu symbols of identity, assuming that these epitomize Indian national identity' (Jaffrelot, *Hindu Nationalism*, p. 97). Hindutva also assumed an upper-caste Brahmanical understanding of Hinduism that reaffirms the caste system. Hindutva organizations like the RSS advocated a model of citizenship based on ethno-nationalistic principles. There were, however, two different understandings within the RSS about the place of religious minorities. Savarkar argued that religious minorities should enjoy equal formal citizenship and rights, while Golwalkar (the second director of the RSS) believed the minorities did not respect Hindu religion and should therefore have a subordinate position in the State. For Golwalkar, religious minorities could stay in the country 'claiming nothing, deserving no privileges, far less any preferential treatment, not even citizen rights' (Golwalkar, 1939, quoted in Jayal, *Citizenship and Its Discontents*, p. 217). The idea clearly did not gain prominence, as the Constitution of India granted equal citizenship rights to all minorities. However, the ideology of Hindutva, propagated through the RSS, and subsequently other organizations within its fold, has grown steadily through the years. See Achin Vanaik, *The Rise of Hindu Authoritarianism: Secular Claims, Communal Realities*, London: Verso Books, 2017; N.G. Jayal, *Citizenship and Its Discontents: An Indian History*, Cambridge: Harvard University Press, 2013; and Jaffrelot, *Hindu Nationalism*.

5. The Partition of India of 1947 was the division of British India into two independent dominion States, the Union of India and the Dominion of Pakistan by an Act of the Parliament of the

United Kingdom. As described by historian Urvashi Butalia, 'the political partition of India caused one of the great human convulsions of history. Never before or since have so many people exchanged their homes and countries so quickly. In the space of a few months, about twelve million people moved between the new truncated India and the two wings, East and West, of the newly created Pakistan... Slaughter sometimes accompanied and sometimes prompted their movement; many others died from malnutrition and contagious diseases. Estimates of the dead vary from 200,000 (the contemporary British figure) to two million (a later Indian estimate) but that somewhere around a million people died is now widely accepted'. See U. Butalia, *The Other Side of Silence: Voices from the Partition of India*, Penguin, 2017.

6. In India, 'Emergency' refers to a 21-month period from 1975 to 1977 when Prime Minister Indira Gandhi had a state of emergency declared across the country. Officially issued by President Fakhruddin Ali Ahmed under Article 352 of the Constitution because of the prevailing 'internal disturbance', the Emergency was in effect from 26 June 1975 until its withdrawal in January 1977. The order bestowed upon the Prime Minister the authority to rule by decree, allowing elections to be suspended and civil liberties to be curbed. For much of the Emergency, most of Indira Gandhi's political opponents were imprisoned and the press was censored. Several other human rights violations were reported from the time, including a forced mass-sterilization campaign spearheaded by Sanjay Gandhi, the Prime Minister's son. See P.N. Dhar, *Indira Gandhi, the Emergency and Indian Democracy*, Oxford University Press, 2001.

7. On 6 December 1992, Hindu militants pulled down a Mughal mosque, the Babri Masjid, stone by stone as two hundred thousand people watched and cheered. They were clearing the ground for a massive temple to Rama on the site they believe to be his birthplace a site, therefore, where no mosque ever belonged. Riots occurred once again all over India after Muslims attacked symbols of the State which had not been able to protect the mosque. Hundreds were killed in retaliation, mostly by the police, in Bombay, Bhopal, Surat and other places. The *Ram Janmabhoomi* ('Rama's birthplace') dispute is a long and complicated one. Essentially, it was contended by various groups, including the Hindu Mahasabha, RSS and its cultural wing, the Vishwa Hindu Parishad ('World Hindu Council'), that the site

of a fifteenth-century Mughal mosque was actually the original birthplace of Lord Rama and that the mosque should be razed and a temple erected in its stead. The destruction of the mosque and the immense violence that followed is seen as a 'turning point' in the Hindu nationalist movement in India, described by a journalist who was present at the site as 'the most significant triumph for Hindu nationalism since Independence and the gravest setback to secularism'. The movement to build Rama's temple and the demolition of the Babri Masjid led to the BJP's meteoric rise in electoral politics—from two seats out of 541 in the Parliament in 1984 to forming a national government in 1998. The campaign for Rama's temple ushered in an era of majoritarian politics in defiance of the promise of secular nationalism that has held together this multi-religious country since 1947.

8. Refer to the 2017 Law Commission of India Report (No. 267) on Hate Speech (https://www.scribd.com/document/362912579/Law-Commission-Report-No-267-Hate-Speech#from_embed, last accessed 28 July 2021).
9. Ibid.
10. Love jihad, also known as Romeo jihad, is a conspiracy theory, developed by proponents of Hindutva, purporting that Muslim men target Hindu women for conversion to Islam by means such as seduction, feigning love, deception, kidnapping, and marriage. Although allegations of 'love jihad' have consistently been proven false, there have been numerous cases of violence perpetrated against men and women of the Muslim community for this. Furthermore, the theory was noted to have become a significant belief in the state of Uttar Pradesh by 2014 and contributed to the success of the Bharatiya Janata Party campaign in the state. For more information on love jihad, see https://economictimes.indiatimes.com/topic/love-jihad.
11. The term 'Urban-Naxal' gained popularity on social media, TV news and other mediums after the 2018 arrest of five prominent human rights activists—Sudha Bharadwaj, Gautam Navlakha, Varavara Rao, Arun Ferreira and Vernon Gonsalves—in connection with an incident of caste-based violence in Maharashtra termed as the 'Bhima Koregaon incident'. The phrase loosely means people of a Naxalite bent of mind who reside in urban areas and work as activists, supporters and protectors of the ideology. In recent years the term seems to be used to describe anyone who speaks out against the government. Prime Minister Narendra

Modi, Home Minister Amit Shah and several other senior leaders have frequently used the term 'Urban-Naxal' in their speeches. Addressing an election rally in Jharkhand in December 2019, PM Modi blamed the Congress and also the 'Urban-Naxals' for protests that were being organized in various parts of the country against the CAA. Earlier, on 16 November 2019, Union Home Minister Amit Shah had called for 'effective and decisive action' against 'Urban-Naxals' and terrorists operating in Jammu and Kashmir. And yet, in an RTI filed by *India Today* in February 2020 asking the Ministry of Home Affairs for information on these so called 'Urban-Naxals', who they are, in which areas they operate, etc., the response from the Left Wing Extremism Division in the Ministry responded that it had no information about 'Urban-Naxals'.

12. Article 370 was the basis of Jammu and Kashmir's accession to the Indian Union at a time when erstwhile princely states had the choice to join either India or Pakistan after their independence from British rule in 1947. The article, which came into effect in 1949, exempts Jammu and Kashmir state from the Indian Constitution. It allows the Indian-administered region jurisdiction to make its own laws in all matters except finance, defence, foreign affairs and communications. On 9 August 2019, the government revoked nearly all of Article 370, of which 35A is a part and which has been the basis of Kashmir's complex relationship with the Indian Republic. The government also moved to break up the state into two smaller, federally administered territories. One region will combine Muslim-majority Kashmir and Hindu-majority Jammu. The other is Buddhist-majority Ladakh, which is culturally and historically close to Tibet. Since then, the Indian government has cut off telecommunications to the region of Jammu and Kashmir, driven out tourists and journalists, and stationed approximately 35,000 additional troops there. The BJP had long opposed Article 370 and revoking it was in the party's 2019 election manifesto. They argued it needed to be scrapped to integrate Kashmir and put it on the same footing as the rest of India. After returning to power with a massive mandate in the April–May 2019 general elections, the government lost no time in acting on its pledge. Many Kashmiris believe that the BJP ultimately wants to change the demographic character of the Muslim-majority region by allowing non-Kashmiris to buy land there.
13. After years of legal dispute, violence and controversy, the final

judgment in the Ayodhya dispute was declared by the Supreme Court of India on 9 November 2019. The Court ordered the disputed land (2.77 acres) to be handed over to a trust (to be created by the Government of India) to build the Ram Janmabhoomi temple. The court also ordered the government to give an alternate five acres of land in another place to the Sunni Waqf Board for the purpose of building a mosque. Speaking after the court's verdict, Mr Modi said: 'The Supreme Court verdict has brought a new dawn. Now the next generation will build a new India.' There was a public outcry from many human rights activists after the verdict, although the Sunni Central Waqf Board accepted the verdict and declared that it will not submit a review petition for the same. The Supreme Court had concluded that while excavations by the Archaeological Survey of India at the site revealed the ruins of a Hindu religious structure dating back to the twelfth century, there was no evidence to suggest this structure still existed or was demolished when the mosque was built. The Court's judgment also states that the two events that served as the basis for Hindu claims—the supposedly miraculous overnight appearance of Hindu idols in the mosque in 1949 and the demolition of the mosque in 1992—were both criminal acts, the handiwork of Hindu fundamentalists. In light of its own conclusions then, the Court's verdict amounts to rewarding criminality. Hartosh Singh Bal, the editor of *Caravan* magazine remarked that 'The Supreme Court greenlighted the building of Rama's temple, in effect asserting the primacy of the faith of those who believe that the disputed site is the birthplace of Rama. As there is no evidence for the historicity of Rama, this must surely rank as one of the more remarkable legal justifications for deciding a case about ownership and possession of a piece of land'. See 'The Transformation of India is nearly complete', *The New York Times*, 11 November 2019.

14. Refer to the 2003 Citizenship (Amendment) Act (http://egazette.nic.in/WriteReadData/2004/E_7_2011_119.pdf, last accessed 28 July 2021).
15. Swami Vivekanand was an Indian Hindu monk, a chief disciple of the nineteenth-century Indian mystic Ramakrishna. He was a key figure in the introduction of the Indian philosophies of Vedanta and Yoga to the Western world and is credited with raising interfaith awareness, bringing Hinduism to the status of a major world religion during the late nineteenth century. He

was a major force in the revival of Hinduism in India, and contributed to the concept of Indian nationalism as a tool in the fight against the British empire in India. Vivekanand founded the Ramakrishna Math and the Ramakrishna Mission. For the full text of his famous speech at the World's Parliament of Religions in Chicago in 1893, see https://www.business-standard.com/article/current-affairs/full-text-of-swami-vivekananda-s-chicago-speech-of-1893-117091101404_1.html.

16. 'They threatened to kill us if we didn't leave India: Rohingyas', *Al Jazeera*, 23 January 2019.
17. 'U.N.'s top court orders Myanmar to take all measures to prevent genocide against Rohingya', *Time*, 23 January 2020.
18. '"Till now, no decision on nationwide NRC": Home Ministry's first official confirmation', *Outlook*, 4 February 2020.
19. 'Vajpayee-Advani imagined an all-India NRC and Modi-Shah added a Muslim filter', *The Print*, 23 December 2019.
20. 'Will identify and deport every illegal immigrant: Amit Shah', *India Today*, 17 July 2019.
21. 'Amit Shah in Rajya Sabha says no one to be marked "doubtful" citizen, no documents needed during NPR exercise', *Firstpost*, 12 March 2020.
22. 'Over 7 lakh Hindus among those excluded from the NRC, leaked data suggests', *Sabrang India*, 17 September 2019.
23. 'Citizenship Act: Protestors "creating violence can be identified by their clothes", claims Modi', *Scroll.in*, 15 December 2019.
24. 'India: Deadly force used against protesters', official website of Human Rights Watch, 23 December 2019.
25. 'Modi claims his government never brought up NRC—after a year of Amit Shah promising one', *Scroll.in*, 22 December 2019.
26. 'Who is linking Citizenship Act to NRC? Here are five times Amit Shah did so', *Scroll.in*, 20 December 2019.
27. 'PM Modi's claim that India has no detention centres is misleading', *The Quint*, 24 December 2019.
28. 'Amit Shah says govt "preparing in advance" for nationwide rollout of NRC amid reports of detentions camps in Karnataka, Maharashtra', *Firstpost*, 17 October 2019.
29. 'In Delhi riots charge sheet, police claim outsiders launched Shaheen Bagh', *Hindustan Times*, 25 November 2020.
30. In its earliest origins, the Hindu nationalist ideology assumed that India's national identity was summarized by Hinduism, the dominant creed which, according to the British census, represented

about 70 per cent of the population. Indian culture was to be defined as Hindu culture, and the minorities were to be assimilated by their paying allegiance to the symbols and mainstays of the majority as those of the nation (Jaffrelot, *Hindu Nationalism*). For Niraja Jayal, Hindutva ideology represents a distinct strategy of universalist citizenship. This classification might seem alarming considering the clear Hindu-majoritarian understanding of Hindutva, but it is exactly this majoritarian outlook that prompts Jayal to classify Hindutva as a 'distinctive, exclusionary, version of the universalist argument, a descriptive—as opposed to substantive—form of universalism' (Jayal, 'A false dichotomy?', p. 189). In an attempt to achieve complete confluence between religion and the nation, Hindutva employs two broad strategies in relation to religious minorities, assimilation into the project (through reconversion) or elimination from the State. See Jaffrelot, Hindu Nationalism; and N.G. Jayal, 'A false dichotomy?: The unresolved tension between universal and differentiated citizenship in India', *Oxford Development Studies*, vol. 39, no. 2 (2011), pp. 185–204.

31. Maulana Sayyid Abul Kalam Ghulam Muhiyuddin Ahmed bin Khairuddin Al-Hussaini Azad was an Indian scholar, Islamic theologian, independence activist, and a senior leader of the Indian National Congress during the Indian independence movement. Following India's independence, he became the first education minister in the Indian government.

PART ONE

Evolution of the Idea and Practice of Citizenship in India

FAYAJAL HAQUE

Shalim M. Hussain

On 29 January 2020 a 42-year-old manual labourer named Fayajal Haque left his home. He remained incommunicado for two days. His family, including his wife, Asiya Khatun, thought that he had gone to meet his other wife and were not worried. They were wrong. Two days later, some children found his body hanging from the crossbeam of the roof of their school building.

This was not the first time Fayajal had attempted suicide. According to his father-in-law, he had attempted suicide multiple times in the recent past. It all started with the publication of the final list of the National Register of Citizens (NRC) in Assam on 31 August 2019. The entire family had applied for the NRC but after multiple verifications and re-verifications, while Asiya found her name in the list Fayajal and both their daughters were left out.

According to both Asiya and her father, this is what caused Fayajal's mental breakdown. He kept losing his temper and started drinking heavily. Since August, he attempted suicide multiple times but his neighbours stepped in and foiled his attempts. 'He turned into a madman,' says Fayajal's father-in-law, 'sometimes he took poison, at others he would try to hang himself.'

Fayajal's anger turned to desperation. The family had acquired a house under the Pradhan Mantri Awas Yojana, an affordable housing initiative of the Government of India. During his last days, Fayajal would argue with his wife about

This is an excerpt from Shalim M. Hussain, 'Uncertainty Around NRC is Taking Human Lives in Assam', that appeared in *NewsClick* on 13 February 2020.

the futility of maintaining a house when he and his daughters had lost their citizenship and would possibly be thrown out of the country.

'People told him all sorts of things and scared him,' says Asiya. Fayajal once brought an axe to the house and began tearing down the walls. 'He didn't even spare the roof and ceiling,' she says. A few days later, he hanged himself.

Fayajal's is not the only case of suicide that resulted from the fear of losing citizenship. Over the years, people of Assam have been put on trial multiple times to prove their citizenship, NRC being the latest in a long line of bureaucratic measures to ascertain who in the state is a genuine citizen and who is not. Many have been driven to extreme measures faced with the horror of losing their citizenship, being evicted from their home and hearth, and possibly being thrown out of the country.

DEFINING CITIZENSHIP

Neera Chandhoke

At the turn of the twenty-first century, a number of influential scholars began to argue that the boundaries of the nation-state, nationalism and national identities had been transcended by the 'age of cosmopolitanism'. The concept of cosmopolitanism, which goes back to ancient Greece, signified a number of developments that had coalesced around the world in the period after *globalization* in the 1990s. Some of these developments were: the global movement of capital, migration of labour, strengthening of international institutions such as an international human rights regime, and the establishment of global organizations for the regulation of finance and trade.

At the same time, the belief that we have obligations to the rest of humankind, irrespective of which country they or we live in, caught the imagination of scholars in Western academia. The set of theories that related to obligations to 'distant others' came to be known as the global justice debate.

It was persuasively argued by political philosophers that the obligations we owe human beings in other countries may not be as strong as the ones we have towards our fellow citizens. But at least we should re-imagine ourselves as not only members of a nation-state, but also of a world community. Cosmopolitanism was critiqued as highly Western-centric by scholars of the global South, but this trend in philosophy contributed a great deal towards the expansion of the idea of what it means to be a citizen, and of the commitment we hold to fellow human beings.

A version of this paper first appeared in *Seminar*, no. 729: *Debating citizenship—A symposium on rethinking the link between citizenship and democracy* in May 2020.

If citizenship created a political community that shares a common fate, then globalization ensured that we were indeed citizens of a global community. A decision in one part of the world, on climate change for instance, would necessarily affect the future of people across the world. Citizenship could no longer be confined within the borders of the nation-state, it was bound to spill over into other societies and other cultures through interconnected processes such as financial and trade flows, interlinked legal regimes and the information revolution.

By the second decade of the twenty-first century, cosmopolitanism and the idea that we owe an obligation of compassion to fellow human beings wherever they might live and work had been banished to the margins. The advent and institutionalization of right-wing populist leaders across the world strengthened narrow, exclusionary and xenophobic nationalism, deliberately cultivated a deep suspicion of migrants and minorities, focused excessively on national security, fortified borders, and relentlessly emphasized the difference between 'insiders' and 'outsiders' even if the latter had been living and working in the country for years.

The former, it was held by populist leaders across the world, belonged to the nation, the latter did not. Whereas insiders were citizens of the nation-state, the latter were outsiders. Boundaries between citizens were hardened, and the open doors that exposed our vision to landscapes of solidarity and commitment to the well-being of others, were firmly closed, latched and locked.

Constricted notions of who belongs and who does not belong to the nation-state replaced cosmopolitan citizenship. Civic citizenship was replaced by ethnic notions of who is a citizen, the ethno-national State was substituted for the civic nation based on rights, belonging came to be conceptualized as ties of blood, populists stepped up the polarization of societies, and communities were sought to be divided. The natural constituency of the right-wing populist is an intolerant one.

And then a political miracle happened. People whose claims to citizenship were at risk, resisted. And others who were not directly affected resisted alongside their fellow citizens. Protests, occupation of public land, demonstrations and symbolic gestures of resistance have marked collective life in cities around the world. After a number of years, citizenship was propelled onto the centre of political agendas with a boom. Judiciaries have been snowed in with cases relating to who is a citizen and who is not. Citizenship has become a hotly contested concept and been destabilized. This has, however, taken its toll.

On the one hand, populist leaders encourage majority populations to flex their metaphorical muscles and declare ownership of, and monopoly over, the territory that is the site for the construction of a rigid and exclusionary nation-state. On the other, outsiders, migrants and minorities who have mixed their labour with resources and generated profit for the societies they live and work in, demand that they be given their due—the status of citizen and the rights of citizenship. Backed by fellow citizens in a rare gesture of solidarity, they refuse to accept exclusion, they reject the idea that their citizenship depends on a handful of documents—'paper citizenship' as the process of producing and showing documents is called. Those who are sought to be excluded have staked their claim to citizenship as a matter of right.

We witness, in the process, a major shift in the debate on citizenship; the shift from an emphasis on social rights as a marker of inclusion, to the troublesome concept of identity. For long, debates among academics concentrated on, at least, three dimensions of the concept. One, the notion of universal citizenship grants to each person (with justifiable exceptions to the principle) status as the bearer of rights, notably civil and political rights.

Two, these rights cannot but be compromised by social and economic inequality. If individuals are poor, if they lack access to the kind of economic and social resources their neighbours possess, it is painfully obvious that they cannot be equal. Universal adult franchise is no guarantee of social and economic equality and justice. These have to be fought for so that the project of universal citizenship can be realized.

Three, the notion of universal citizenship provides a touchstone against which lack of equal status can be evaluated. In sum, it was assumed that increased access to social and economic goods that people have a right to, at least in theory, would fulfil the presuppositions of universal citizenship. We saw the making of an inexorable connection between citizenship and class in most works on the subject following T.H. Marshall's significant work on *Citizenship and Social Class* (1949/1992).

The critique of social inequality and of discrimination meted out to people who were treated as unequal was made from the vantage point of universal citizenship. Increasingly, however, it came to be perceived that inequality, marginalization, and exclusion were a constitutive feature of citizenship not only for economic reasons, but also for reasons of identity. In India, the so-called lower castes, religious minorities, women, transgender persons, and Adivasis were treated as less than human, and therefore as partial- or even non-citizens. This was for purely arbitrary reasons: of birth into a community that has been typed as the enemy, the inferior, the outsider, in short as the 'other' with whom there can be neither truck nor transaction.

This perspective had nothing to do with 'insiders' who belonged and 'strangers' who do not. It concentrated on the plight of people who in theory possessed full citizenship rights, but in practice were discriminated against for reasons outside their control. None of us can choose which community we are born into, the language we speak, the belief systems we subscribe to, the rituals we perform and the customs we adhere to. Discrimination on the basis of factors not subject to our control is not only illogical, it is unjust. Justice implies that every citizen has an equal right to the benefits that a society offers to its members. She also has an equal obligation to bear an equal share of the burdens that a society imposes upon its members. It is unjust to exclude a member from an equal share in the benefits of society, and to impose excessive burdens on her just because she belongs to a community that is arbitrarily discriminated against.

Let us focus on religious minorities in this section of the argument. Injustice is compounded if our individual is targeted by hate speech, ritualized and repetitive violence and everyday humiliation. The police, it has been widely noted, come down heavily on religious minorities, and the judiciary does not offer enough protection to vulnerable sections of society, the media slots the community in perverse ways and social vocabularies deploy offensive language that no self-respecting society should tolerate.

Minorities cannot live in neighbourhoods of their choice, and workplace politics subject them to prejudice and bigotry. Each communal riot targets their property, person and livelihood disproportionately and in terribly vicious ways. Each riot leaves bleeding bodies and despairing hearts as we saw in the case of the Delhi riots that took place in February 2020. The riots left 50 people dead and hundreds injured, many with gunshot wounds.

It is clear by now that the equal status principle of democratic citizenship is deeply compromised by not only social inequality but also identities. In form, minorities are full citizens but in practice they have yet to cross over the threshold to a full membership of the political community. Theorists and historians of citizenship had hoped that the exercise of the franchise would at some point in time produce governments that were sensitive to internal exclusions and hierarchies, to governments that intend to transform relations. This was necessary to establish a correspondence between universal citizenship or the lack thereof, equality and justice.

The problem has now shifted—the contradiction was not only between the claims of universal citizenship and citizenship that is partially realized. The contradiction is between citizens and denial of the status to vulnerable sections of society. The notion of universal citizenship is a chimera, people are not only marginalized by social and economic disadvantage, they are excluded because they belong to 'this' religious community or 'that'.

The outburst of ethnic wars in the wake of the breakdown of actually existing socialist societies in 1989, the mobilization on the grounds of identity, and the phenomenon of waves of migrants flowing into Europe in a desperate bid to escape civil war and ethnic cleansing in their own countries foregrounded the issue of exclusion on the basis of criterion other than class. The insecurity and anxiety experienced by religious minorities in a majoritarian society like India was compounded by the entry of right-wing populist leaders that openly espoused an agenda which privileged the majority. The development bore serious consequences.

From 2004 to 2014, the United Progressive Alliance government led by the Congress at the Centre passed a number of laws that granted to citizens social rights, from the right to primary education to the right to work. Scholars began to wonder whether a social democratic revolution had found its way to India. The country had finally reclaimed social rights that had been granted by the Motilal Nehru Constitutional Draft in 1928, but which were relegated to the section on Directive Principles of State Policy in the Constitution in 1950.

In 2014, the Bharatiya Janata Party (BJP) took over. The party came back to power in 2019 with increased members in the popular house of Parliament. As members of the larger ideological brigade of the party, those who subscribe to Hindutva, began to unleash hate speech and mob lynchings of Muslims and Dalits, the biography of rights took a sharp U-turn. From 2004 to 2014 we spoke the language of social rights. The year 2014 heralded a return to the days of colonial rule, when leaders of the freedom struggle had to agitate for the recognition of civil and political rights. These were subsequently enshrined in the Constitution as fundamental rights possessed by every citizen.

We had thought that our civil and political rights were secure, guarded by a vibrant human rights movement in civil society, and an independent judiciary anxious to reclaim its image of impartiality after many silences during the internal Emergency (1975–77). After 2014 and the ascent of the religious Right to power, indiscriminate arrests of human rights activists, the clampdown on civil society organizations, the rapid erosion of the rule of law and judicial autonomy, in short, the curtailment of all institutions and practices that protect the individual against the State and that mediate between the citizen and the government, foregrounded the problem of civil rights. We had to turn our attention back to civil liberties that were gravely threatened by the flag-bearers of the Hindu Right.

On 23 June 2019, newspaper reports told us that the US Secretary of State had released the State Department's *2018 Report on International Religious Freedom* to the American Congress. It was released shortly after the BJP came to power for a second term in May 2019 with a massive majority in Parliament. The chapter on India in the report detailed mob-related violence, conversions of minorities, threats to their legal status and destructive government policies.

The Government of India, the report stated, had taken steps to challenge the legal status of minority educational institutions in the Supreme Court. As a matter of right, minority educational institutions have the freedom to hire faculty and to design their own curricula. Now things are different because the right-wing government seeks to interfere and regulate these institutions. Cities with Muslims names have been renamed, for example Allahabad has been renamed Prayagraj. The contribution of the Muslim community to India's art, literature, architecture, painting and music is sought to be erased. This, the report continued, has led to intensified tension between communities.

The report narrated incidents of religiously motivated killings, assaults, riots, discrimination, vandalism and restriction on the rights of citizens to practise their own religious beliefs and proselytize. 'Authorities have failed to penalize the perpetrators of killings in the name of the cow. Reportedly, the police, the administration and the judiciary are reluctant to act when it comes to mob violence against religious minorities. The ruling party has marginalized communities and attacked critics of the government. Senior officials of the Bharatiya Janata Party have made inflammatory remarks on the Muslim community. Authorities have protected speakers of abuse from prosecution. As of November 2018, there have been 18 such attacks. Eight people have been killed during the year, stated the report.'[1]

The ruling BJP, reported the same newspaper on the front page the same day, slammed the US for bias against the Modi government. In most such cases, the spokesperson stated, these instances are the result of local disputes and a criminal mindset against minorities and weaker sections of society. The spokesperson Mukhtar Abbas Naqvi continues to be the Minister of Minority Affairs in the second term of the government controlled by the BJP. He is reported to have said to *The Hindu* in an interview that Mr Modi had directly established contact with the minorities and exposed the hypocrisy of earlier modes of engagement with them. According to him, such reports were part of the '*baar ka horror show*', a horror show directed by political parties that were defeated in the 2019 elections.[2]

The statement exhibits indifference to our own people at best, and political cynicism at worst. The Minister should reflect on the sorry state of his fellow citizens who are subjected to vicious attacks, merely because they belong to another belief system that the religious Right is institutionally against. More significantly, when the Minister for Minority Affairs declares that lynchings have nothing to do with religious animosities, he engages in nothing but sophistry. He ignores a remarkable coincidence in our public life. Hate speech and crimes against minorities have risen since 2014 when the BJP came to power.

In October 2019, newspaper reports chronicled that Muslims were the targets of 51 per cent of violence related to the cow from 2010 to 2017. Out of 28 Indians killed in 63 incidents, 24 were Muslims, that is, they formed 86 per cent of the victims of violence leading to death. The website *IndiaSpend*, whose report the newspaper had drawn on, had carried out a content analysis of the English media on cow-related deaths. Ninety-seven attacks over bovine issues were reported after the Narendra Modi government came to power in 2014, and half of this cow-related violence, i.e. 32 of 63 cases, came from states governed by the BJP. More than 124 people were injured in these attacks and more than half these attacks were based on rumours.[3]

Muslims have been attacked in trains, on the road while legally transporting cattle, in agricultural fields, and even in their homes on the mere suspicion of carrying or storing meat. They have been publicly lynched and brutally killed. Lynchings continued in 2019 after the Modi government returned to power. Muslims are threatened by violence even when they perform their duties as citizens of India. On Republic Day, 26 January 2018, in Kasganj, western Uttar Pradesh, gangs of thugs riding motorbikes roared into the flag-hoisting area and attacked residents. It is Muslims that predominantly inhabit the neighbourhood. In the violence that followed, a 22 year-old youth, Chandan Gupta, was killed when a stray bullet hit him.[4]

The lynching of Muslims merely on the suspicion that they are engaged in transporting cattle has initiated a new trend of unspeakable intimidation and violence in Indian politics. Death by lynching in a public place where people stand around and watch or, worse, film the despicable event on their phones and upload it on social media, is the new normal. Violence has become a spectator sport, rivalling ancient Rome that had devised unique ways of putting men to death in public forums to storms of applause from the audience. In contemporary India, the audience claps even as their fellow citizens die painfully for no reasonable cause, except the assertion of brute power, or perhaps just sport.

Alongside violations of civil rights—the right to life and liberty—political rights that form the backbone of the status of citizenship began to be threatened by dire warnings of things to come, of tragedies that will be unleashed on the people of India in the near future. The government placed the onus of proving that we were citizens of India upon us. Now we have been forced to return to the basic question: Who is a citizen? Issues relating to social inclusion of all, irrespective of creed and belief systems, have been dismissed. Today, inclusion into the democratic polity of India depends on what religion you belong to. Legal activists are compelled to raise issues that we thought had been settled long ago. For long we had taken our citizenship for granted. Today, the government tells us that not all Indians are citizens, many are infiltrators. These will be detected, stripped of citizenship and of any rights that protect them against the State, and sent to desolate detention camps that are being constructed in various parts of the country. Here, people who are declared non-citizens, are expected to live bare lives in a space that is left undefined, but which hovers very close to the notion of statelessness.

In Europe, the debate has focused on the question of whether migrants from other countries should be granted citizenship. In India, the issue is different: that of reclaiming constitutional rights. The contradiction, as we noted above, is not that of universal citizenship and a citizenship that is partially realized; it is between citizens and denial of the status to vulnerable sections of society. The moment religion was introduced into the concept and procedures of citizenship, in the case of the Citizenship Amendment Act (CAA) forced through Parliament with the help of a brute majority in December 2019, minorities were in danger. According to the Act, refugees from the three Islamic countries of Pakistan, Bangladesh and Afghanistan will be granted Indian citizenship. Muslims are, however, excluded from this process. The government plans to administer a National Population Register (NPR) and a National Register of Citizens (NRC) in the near future to sift out who is a citizen and who is not.

Minorities are racked with anxiety, worried they will be declared non-citizens and illegal migrants if they cannot fulfil the requirements of government officials who scrutinize documents and decide on the legal status of the individual. Their anxiety is intensified by a hate-filled populism that relentlessly focuses on protest and dissent as anti-national. And we, confronted by a judiciary that refuses to take up civil liberty cases on an urgent basis, and a pulverized civil society, wonder who will confront those who have set themselves up as arbiters of citizenship.

And then our own political miracle took place. On 15 December 2019, students belonging to the Jamia Millia Islamia came out in large numbers to protest against the CAA. As the procession marched through the streets of an upper middle-class colony in South Delhi, students carrying banners that rejected the CAA demanded withdrawal of a legislation that connected citizenship rights with religion. The police attacked and shot young people, students were injured, the library was ransacked, and the campus destroyed. The violence inflicted on the student body set off a chain of protests by university students and citizens in the rest of the country. Thousands of citizens, particularly university students, marched and demonstrated against the inhuman treatment meted out to the students of Jamia Millia, Aligarh Muslim University and Jawaharlal Nehru University by right-wing elements and the police.

The objective of the demonstrations, that took everyone and particularly the government by surprise, was to protest against the imminent disenfranchisement of minorities. Protesters challenged the division of society on religious grounds, taking the Constitution of India as their referral. Public readings of the Preamble to the Constitution transformed the Constitution from a legal document into a political one. Never has India in the seventy-two years it has been independent seen the enactment of citizenship on this scale and with such fervour.

Student protests have been remarkably creative and imaginative. Singing revolutionary songs, young people carried posters expressing their determination not to allow the proposed National Register of Citizens to be implemented in their country. Women demonstrated in many parts of India, and the sit-in by women in Shaheen Bagh in South Delhi for more than three months has become a global symbol of protest against the denial of basic rights. Little children painted the national flag on their cheeks, and performances were staged against the backdrop of portraits of national icons—Gandhi, Ambedkar and Bhagat Singh.

Photographs in the morning newspapers and screened by television channels indicated the democratic nature of the protest: a young woman holding up an admonishing finger to the police, students offering roses to flummoxed police personnel, novel art forms that focused on the plurality of India and the determination to protect it, and chants of solidarity with Muslim fellow citizens. Thousands of citizens peaceably assembled on the streets and in public places to demand that the government observe constitutional morality. This was India's civil society moment.

In the period before the elections to the state Assembly in Delhi, BJP politicians engaged in hate speech and openly called upon their supporters to fire guns at the protesters. Protesters were met by threats of violence and there was perverse stereotyping of Muslim neighbourhoods that staged protests as so many mini-Pakistans. On 16 February 2020, communal violence that rapidly turned into ethnic cleansing led by mobs chanting slogans of death and destruction broke out in North East Delhi. Fifty people were killed, their bodies dumped in drains, showrooms plundered, houses, vehicles and human beings set on fire, small workplaces ransacked, and entire neighbourhoods destroyed.

The provocation for the onset of mob fury against the minorities was expectedly the democratic protest against the CAA and the proposed NPR and the NRC. In a democracy, civil society has the right to monitor acts of omission and commission of the government. The democratic protests that broke out in December 2019 were intended to achieve precisely this objective. The protesters opposed the targeting of minorities, and condemned the killings, abusive speeches and hateful acts that had rendered a vulnerable minority even more vulnerable ever since the BJP came to power in 2014.

These protests have brought forth an issue worth reflecting on. Citizenship gives us the authority to demand and benefit from the security and services offered by the State—passports, education, health, housing, post-retirement benefits, the right to travel, the right to employment and above all the right to vote. The right to vote gives us the capacity to hold accountable those in power. Citizenship embodies a democratic relationship between the State and its citizens.

But there is more to citizenship. Citizens of a political community owe each other an obligation of justice and solidarity against State repression. Citizenship, our young people reminded us, is not only about our status as a holder of rights, it is about membership of a political community. It is a relational concept that establishes a bond based not on blood but on belonging to a civic community defined by a Constitution. It is precisely this solidarity that a large section of Indians expressed towards their fellow citizens when they supported the latter's protest against draconian laws.

The protests fell into the category of what is called performative citizenship. Indians marched holding the national flag in one hand and a copy of the Constitution in the other, they assembled against the background of the national flag, sang the national anthem, read out the Preamble of the Constitution that promises liberty, equality, justice and fraternity, and transformed the Constitution into a publicly accessible and democratic document. The Constitution is the anchor of our identity, the protector of our rights, our legacy and our culture. The occupation of public spaces, the sit-ins on public roads, the coinage of innovative slogans realized, proclaimed and enacted its popular sovereignty.

Witness again the political miracle. For five and a half years the ruling party had appropriated the symbols of nationhood, collapsed the democratic State into the nation, and the nation into the government. Any protest against the government was typed as anti-national, those who moved petitions before the Supreme Court became Urban-Naxals, a term that is an oxymoron at best and absurd at worst. The protests enacted the basic rules of citizenship that rulers often forget. The paramount rule is that 'We, the People of India' are the repositories of power. The government is elected by us and responsible to us. The right to citizenship has been re-appropriated, popular sovereignty reclaimed and the government is sought to be put in its place.

Despite the bloodletting in Delhi, these protests continued to challenge and interrogate the power of the ruling classes. The entire concept of paper citizenship disseminated by the Government of India has been derailed, destabilized and rendered insecure. What we see today is citizenship as performance.

The rulers declare that the CAA will not take away citizenship from anyone. But as our young people recognized, the provisions of the Act will set the ground for further disenfranchisement of those who have lived and worked in India since birth, who possess rights as full citizens, who own the Constitution and the national flag, and who are citizens of India by virtue of membership of a territorially grounded political community. The second significant issue placed on the political agenda is that of solidarity with fellow citizens who may be stripped of full citizenship rights, deprived of the right to live and work in a location of their choice, deprived of the right to have rights, to protest, to assemble peacefully and without arms, and to share equally in the burdens and the benefits that a society has to offer.

These protests do not ask for the grant of citizenship to outsiders; protesters reassert their right as citizens and as insiders to hold an elected government accountable for acts that harm those who voted them into power. They demonstrate that the people of India will not accept any act that might deprive them or their fellow citizens of their rights in the near or distant future. They have reclaimed their basic constitutional rights.

In the process, an important question has been thrown up onto the political agenda. We have to, once again, articulate our relationship to the State and obligations to fellow citizens in the civic language of constitutional rights. We have to dismiss the implications of the CAA that India is a natural homeland for all Hindus wherever they live. That belief is dangerous, it will further divide the country; civic citizenship will unite us. We have to periodically reinstate our obligation to vulnerable citizens in the vocabulary of solidarity. We have to insist that civic obligations are grounded in the place we live, in common memories, and in the experience of sharing equally the benefits and burdens of a society. The notion of civic citizenship critiques the distinction between citizens on religious grounds as illegitimate and undemocratic. It informs us that there is a need to repeatedly side with our compatriots in the struggle against hierarchies and marginalization.

Till now the BJP has declared through words and deeds that any sort of dissent will not be tolerated and whoever disagrees with the government will be charged with sedition. Today, citizens tell the government that they will not tolerate the corruption of citizenship by the introduction of a religious criterion, that they will not allow any tampering with the Constitution of India which is our legacy.

Protesters proclaim that the right to citizenship is theirs by reason of birth, by reasons of belonging, by reasons of fidelity, by reasons of solidarity with fellow citizens, and for the simple reason that they bow their heads before the national flag and stand up in reverence when the national anthem is sung. This is performative citizenship, citizenship as enactment, citizenship as participation in the political decisions of a society, citizenship as articulation of popular sovereignty, citizenship as owing obligations to fellow citizens, citizenship as status and citizenship rights as a prized possession. What is the significance of paper citizenship before performative citizenship?

Notes

1. Shriram Lakshman, 'US report expressed concern on communal violence in India', *The Hindu*, 23 June 2019, p. 14.
2. 'BJP slams US for bias against PM', *The Hindu*, 23 June 2019, p. 1.
3. *Hindustan Times*, 12 October 2019.
4. Chaitanya Mallapur, 'Communal violence rose by 28 per cent from 2014 to 2017, but 2008 remains year of highest instances of religious violence', *Firstpost*, 9 February 2019.

CITIZENSHIP REGIMES, LAW AND BELONGING

Anupama Roy

Amidst the violence which accompanied Partition, the governments of India and Pakistan, which disagreed with each other on most things, agreed to exchange their 'lunatics'. In a powerful story about how this exchange unsettled the lives of 'lunatics' living in asylums, Saadat Hasan Manto wrote of Toba Tek Singh—a place name which became synonymous with a person and eventually became a trope for forced movement across the freshly crafted borders. The refusal of Bishan Singh or Toba Tek Singh—the man who stood on his feet for fifteen years—to be transported to India was not taken seriously by officials on the Wagah border. He was a harmless old man, confused in mind, they thought. No one could unequivocally tell him where his village was—in India or Pakistan. Bishan Singh died an anguished death in the no man's land between the two countries.

Another inmate of the same asylum climbed atop a tree, completely clear in his mind that he did not want to live in either country. He was going to make the tree his home. Yet another inmate, a person with an engineering degree—an otherwise pensive man in the habit of taking long walks by himself—was so perturbed by the prospect of being allotted to one or the other country that he took off all his clothes and thus shorn of all identifying accoutrements, ran into the garden.[1]

Defying the common sense that a lunatic asylum is not a

A version of this paper first appeared in *Seminar*, no. 729: *Debating citizenship—A symposium on rethinking the link between citizenship and democracy* in May 2020.

place where action is determined by 'reason', the responses of the inhabitants open up powerful moments of interruption of the custodial power of the State. They also tell us of the blurred zones that exist between law's distance and proximity, which are important for understanding the relationship between legal rationality and the *force* of law. In these zones, citizenship becomes entangled with the law's capacity to destabilize and recode ideas of belonging by affirming and simultaneously masking the power of the State to elicit obedience from citizens.

In this essay, I will attempt to bring the citizenship law in India to anthropological scrutiny by retracing the life of the Citizenship Act of 1955 to relocate it in the 'matrix...of historical experience'.[2] I will consider the citizenship law in India to be an accumulation of successive citizenship regimes which have in the contemporary moment culminated into a clearly identifiable tendency towards the association of citizenship with descent and blood ties. I argue that this tendency produces power-effect of the State through the deployment of the *force* of law.

With independence in August 1947, Indians were no longer British subjects under the British Nationality Act but citizens of a sovereign country. The passage to citizenship was part of a collective commitment to the democratization of power and the preservation of conditions of dignity and fraternity within the framework of constitutional democracy. The ethics and consciousness of citizenship were sought through democratic elections and a constitutional order which established popular sovereignty. This took place alongside state-formative practices, the structuring of institutions and the elaboration of democratic processes. The question—Who is a citizen of India?—became critical in two domains which involved different logics of sovereignty: the *identification of citizens as voters* representing the logic of democracy founded in popular sovereignty; and as *mapping and buttressing the territorial State* to control the movement of people across borders founded in the sovereign power of the State.

Citizenship at the commencement of the Republic was associated with birth, descent and domicile, so that anyone domiciled in India or born in its territory or outside it to Indian citizens, would be an Indian citizen. At the same time, the Constitution also recognized as citizens those who crossed the border from Pakistan or returned to India after having gone to Pakistan, with the intention of making India their permanent home. Interestingly, the physical borders were congealed instantaneously but remained temporally flexible to accommodate different kinds of movement of people across borders. If 19 July 1948 became the constitutional deadline for those who had made the decision to return to India to avoid having to apply for citizenship to an officer appointed by the government, anyone who had migrated to Pakistan before 1 March 1947 could return to India on a permit of resettlement and permanent return.

In 1986, an amendment to the Citizenship Act of India, 1955 made 24 March 1971 the cutoff date to identify those who had entered Assam from Bangladesh after 1 January 1966 to be eligible for Indian citizenship. Another amendment in the Citizenship Act of India in December 2019 introduced the cutoff date—31 December 2014—for persons belonging to the Hindu, Sikh, Christian, Jain, Buddhist and Parsi communities who had fled Afghanistan, Bangladesh or Pakistan before this date to escape religious persecution. These persons would no longer be considered illegal migrants and could apply for Indian citizenship.

In 2015, the 119th Amendment to the Constitution of India, following an agreement reached between India and Bangladesh, allowed the exchange of 51 Bangladeshi enclaves in the territory of India with 111 Indian enclaves in Bangladeshi territory. Indian citizens residing in the Indian enclaves in Bangladesh could either continue to stay on in the swapped territory and become citizens of the country which was now under the jurisdiction of Bangladesh or move to Indian territory if they wished to retain their Indian citizenship.

The Partition had ushered in a period of deep uncertainties about belonging. The legal rules and procedures to resolve them ranged from devising ad hoc rules to deal with contingencies, reciprocal arrangements and agreements for the exchange of people and property, to an exponential buttressing of the police force and bureaucratic apparatus of the State. The minutes of a meeting of the Standing Advisory Committee held in Delhi on 14 November 1949 under the chairpersonship of the Minister for Home Affairs, Vallabhbhai Patel, gives an insight into the policing activities of the State and the expenditure being incurred to augment them—the passport checkposts on the newly installed borders, the employment of extra police officers for the security of the sessions of the Constituent Assembly and additional police for the eviction of persons occupying evacuee property, the recovery of abducted persons[3] and the 'sudden expansion of Delhi and the increase in its population' (due to the migration from Pakistan), to mention a few.[4]

The legal ensemble pertaining to citizenship, as laid down in the text of the Constitution of India and subsequently the statutory framework constituted by the Citizenship Act of 1955, sought legibility through a range of identifiers such as duration of residence, facts about domicile, dates of entry and departure, birth and lineage/descent. These identifiers drew upon and corresponded to significant constitutive moments in the life of the nation, the imperatives of locating the legal sovereign who had the final say in matters of citizenship and state-formative practices which involved both the enactment of law to facilitate the identification of citizens and the designation of institutions responsible for implementing them.

Citizenship as a legal category was framed through two periods of interregnum between the formation of the Indian nation-state (1947) and the commencement of the Constitution (1950), and subsequently between the commencement of the Constitution (1950) and the Citizenship Act of India (1955). The interregnum between the enforcement of the Constitution and the enactment of the Citizenship Act of 1955 generated spaces of liminality in the closures brought in by the constitutional deadline. While the Constitution opened up the closures which came into existence with the drawing of territorial boundaries, the Citizenship Act of 1955 held out the promise of legibility to those who occupied the space of liminal and indeterminate citizenship between 1950 and 1955.

Nowhere is this more evident than in the manner in which the citizenship of people moving across borders in the period intervening the deadline set by the Constitution of India and the enactment of the Citizenship Act in 1955, returnees on resettlement permits and long-term visas, the minority population 'displaced' or 'evacuated' from Pakistan, and alien/ Pakistani wives of Indian nationals who needed to be registered as Indian citizens after the enactment of the 1955 Act, was resolved. Unlike 'abducted persons' which was a legal category put in place by the Abducted Persons Recovery and Restoration Act, 1949, 'displaced persons' was an administrative category, which figured in governmental files, opening up the possibility of new modalities of bureaucratic action. Their legal absorption into Indian citizenship was to be facilitated through their expeditious registration as citizens and their urgent inclusion in the electoral rolls.

The Ministries of Home, External Affairs, Rehabilitation, Law and the Election Commission of India acted in concert to complete the registration of displaced persons as Indian citizens expeditiously. Assurances were given in Parliament that the registration of such persons would be done with the least inconvenience to them. This meant making arrangements for their registration in all places where they resided in reasonably large numbers, e.g. towns, villages, refugee camps and settlements. A note on the instructions issued to state governments circulated for discussion among the officials of the Home Ministry directed that exceptions to the Citizenship Act and Rules must be made, and strict adherence to the requirement of documentary evidence waived, to treat the displaced persons as a separate category for registration under the Citizenship Act of India.[5]

Apart from the legal absorption of displaced persons as enfranchised citizens, laws were framed to transform the displaced into productive citizens. The Bihar government, for example, promulgated an ordinance—the Bihar Displaced Persons Rehabilitation (Acquisition of Land) Ordinance—'to provide for the speedy acquisition of land for the rehabilitation of displaced persons from Pakistan'.[6] This extraordinary legal measure was required to fulfil the commitment of the state government to 'receive and rehabilitate 50,000 displaced persons from Eastern Pakistan', about 50 per cent of whom were agriculturalists. Over the years, the legal absorption of displaced persons through administrative measures has given way to legal regimes of citizenship that have marked out specific patterns of migration as 'illegal' while congealing a notion of blood ties as the foundation of belonging in a '*national* order of citizenship'.[7] Yet, the installation of a national order has been contested where the articulation of citizenship, as in Assam, has taken recourse to non-national legacies of belonging.

In October 2019, Dulal Paul, a 65-year-old villager from Alisanga in Assam, who had been declared a foreigner in 2017 and had since been in detention in a camp in Tezpur, died in Gauhati Medical College Hospital. Paul's family refused to take his body home unless the government declared that he was an Indian citizen. How could they accept the body of a Bangladeshi man as their own family, they asked? Dulal Paul's name had not figured in the final National Register of Citizens (NRC), which was published on 31 August 2019. All his family members, including his son, found a place in the register. Despite possessing all his documents from 1965, his son claimed, Paul was declared an illegal migrant and remained in detention until his death.

The NRC and the Citizenship Amendment Act (CAA), 2019

represent contending tendencies in the contemporary regime of citizenship in India, which cohabit the legal assemblage of citizenship space, conjoined in their particularistic articulation of citizenship. The CAA 2019 purports to extend the protection of citizenship to those facing religious discrimination and simultaneously puts in place a regime which discriminates on the grounds of religion. The NRC is premised on the assumption that it is possible to distinguish between citizens and aliens on the basis of documents as evidence of citizenship. If the CAA has installed an exclusionary nationhood under the veneer of liberal citizenship, the NRC as it has unfolded in Assam has congealed together the relationship between legal status and blood ties.

The present regime of citizenship can be traced to the significant changes made in the citizenship law through an amendment of the Citizenship Act in 2003. The 2003 amendment constrained citizenship by birth, limiting it to only those whose parents were Indian citizens or one parent was an Indian citizen and the other was not an illegal migrant. The amendment also put in place the requirement of identification of citizens based on documentary practices which have long been associated with the structuration and standardization of State power, state-formative practices and the intensification and accentuation of State authority internally and externally.

While citizenship is understood as a condition of equality, it is dependent on a prior status of membership and the distinction, therefore, between citizens and non-citizens. The association of citizenship with legal status is a continuing legacy of passive citizenship of the absolutist States which were concerned with imposing their authority over heterogeneous populations. Yet, citizenship is also about identity and belonging which are both constrained and enabled by the understanding of citizenship as legal status, which is determined by the modes through which people acquire citizenship and the conditions in which they can retain, relinquish or lose it.

The idea that citizenship can be passed on as a legacy of ancestry and descent has become part of the contemporary legal landscape of citizenship in India. It transmits the idea of blood as an organizing principle of a bounded political community and citizenship as inheritance. These can be traced across generations and help establish ties with a homeland that holds the promise of return, generating ideas of belonging which construe citizenship as a natural and constitutive identity.

The responsibility given to the State to establish and maintain an NRC and issue national identity cards through the CAA of 2003 and the rules framed under it, require the Central government to carry out 'house-to-house enumeration' and collect particulars of individuals and families, including their citizenship status. Making an exception to this procedure, the NRC in Assam was prepared by *inviting applications* from all residents with particulars relating to each family and individual, including their citizenship status, which was based on NRC 1951, and the electoral rolls up to the midnight of 24 March 1971.[8] With the tracing of the pedigree of Indian citizenship to an Assamese legacy, the citizenship act opened up the possibility of hyphenated citizenship, hitherto alien to the vocabulary of citizenship in India.

The data of the 1951 NRC and the electoral rolls published in Assam up to 24 March 1971 cumulatively comprised the legacy data. Finding an ancestor in the legacy data to trace direct descent was made necessary for inclusion in the NRC for those who were not themselves part of it. The NRC 1951 was an outcome of a flawed and perfunctory exercise of enumeration confined to Assam. The rules devised for the preparation of the NRC gave the 1951 NRC legitimacy by inscribing it in a *national* identification regime and installing it as the core around which incremental electoral rolls could cluster. This process of establishing legacy involved a humungous bureaucratic exercise of compilation of legacy data by consolidating dispersed data into a single computerized database.

The statutory publication of the legacy data on 27 March 2015 inaugurated the process of updating the NRC in Assam plunging the state into a prolonged identification drill. Applications to be placed in the NRC were made on the basis of specified documents which alone could prove citizenship. The power of evidence assumed by documents drew from their capacity to establish linkage with the legacy data. After an ancestor had been traced in the legacy data, the computerized database assigned to the applicant an 11-digit number called the Unique Legacy Data Code that provided the applicant with a numerical link to the ancestor. The legacy code embodied a personal claim for verification for the applicant but also acted as a legacy trace linking the applicant with others who had been allotted the same code because of a common ancestry. The legacy trace could be authenticated only through 'linkage documents' carrying the names of the applicant and the ancestor who was present in the legacy data.

In an inversion of the relationship between documents and citizenship, the evidentiary paradigm invoked in the preparation of the NRC in Assam listed documents which would, under specified conditions, become proof of citizenship. The meaning of documents such as the voter ID card which are identity documents that can be obtained only by citizens changed as they became part of the identification regime associated with the NRC in Assam. These documents acquired evidentiary worth only by becoming part of a serialized link in relationship with other documents. Significantly, all these documents which were discrete in their origin and purpose were connected together to serve another purpose—to establish the lineage of the applicant which would henceforth constitute the proof of citizenship. Indeed, categories such as 'legacy', 'legacy documents', 'legacy data', 'legacy trace' and 'unique legacy data code', were innovations which made documents meaningful or irrelevant for the purposes of NRC.

In this process, documents got re-inscribed in a register

alien to their original inscription and purpose. When it was being prepared in 1948, the electoral roll came to be seen as an extraordinary and unprecedented 'act of faith'. It inserted 'the people' into the administrative structures of the State by linking the abstract text of the Constitution to their everyday lives as a popular narrative and prepared the ground for 'the conceptions and principles of democratic citizenship'.[9]

Writing about the first general election in India in a short story titled 'The Election Game', R.K. Narayan recounts the election fever that seized the people participating in what he called a 'large-scale rehearsal for political life'. No one, young or old, was left untouched 'as though a sense of sovereignty [was] aroused even in the most insignificant of us'.[10] The coincidence of citizenship with voting rights and universal adult franchise involved a governmental activity of identification different from any other such exercise since its objective was not the enhancement of the governmental power of the State, but the affirmation of popular sovereignty and transition to a democratic republic.

As a legacy document, the electoral roll was recalled on a different register which changed its authority from a text embodying popular sovereignty to a document providing legacy trace to serve the imperatives of the identification regime of the State. The worth of the legacy document depended on the extent to which it strengthened the regime of the legibility and evidentiary framework of which it was now a part. This was evident in a Gauhati High Court judgment that rejected a petition by Babul Islam against a Foreigners' Tribunal order pronouncing him a foreigner. Babul Islam had placed before the court his Electoral Photo Identity Card (EPIC) as proof of citizenship. While the EPIC is a voter identity card and not a citizenship card, the fact that only citizens can vote makes for a stable relationship between the two.

The Gauhati High Court refused to recognize the EPIC as evidence of citizenship on the grounds that it did not possess the attribute of 'due' proof which could make the EPIC 'admissible' evidence. The EPIC could be 'evidence' of citizenship only if it could be effectively inserted in the chain of validation linking it up with the pre-1971 voter list.[11]

Close on the heels of the judgment in the Babul Islam case, the same bench of the Gauhati High Court rejected a petition by Jabeda Khatun, a 50-year-old woman from Guwahari village, refusing to consider the 15 documents she had submitted as proof of citizenship. These documents included land revenue payment receipts, bank passbook, voter list and Permanent Account Number (PAN) Card but none of these could link her to her parents as legacy persons.[12] Both Jabeda Khatun and Manowara Bewa, whose citizenship claims too were turned down because of the absence of appropriate legacy documents, had submitted certificates by the *gaonbura* (village headman).

The Court, in the case of Jabeda Khatun, rejected the certificate on the grounds that it could be admitted as evidence only to prove that she had shifted after marriage to her matrimonial village as per the Supreme Court judgment in *Rupjan Begum vs Union of India* (1 SCC 579 2018). In the case of Manowara Bewa, the judge rejected the certificate issued by the village panchayat on the grounds that the petitioner failed to establish the authority of the documents through a corroborating oral testimony of the issuing authority in the court. In both cases, the Court had refused to accept the testimony of relatives as evidence of relationship with the legacy person.

It is significant that affirmation of blood ties according to the Court could only be done through 'public' documents. According to Section 74 of the Indian Evidence Act, 'public documents' are documents 'forming acts or records of the act—(i) of the sovereign authority, (ii) of official bodies and tribunals and (iii) of public officers, legislative, judicial and executive...as well as public records kept in any state of private documents'. Certificates by the gaonbura pertaining to relationships by marriage could not be considered public until they were also heard by the Court as an attestation of their veracity.

In the Manowara Bewa case, considering the legality of a certificate issued by the gaon panchayat secretary certifying that the applicant resided in the area within his jurisdiction, the Gauhati High Court ruled that the certificate of residence issued by the gaon panchayat could not be considered a 'public document' for a range of reasons. That the certificate was not issued from a record that the panchayat maintained under the provisions of the 1994 Panchayati Raj Act and Rules, was among the most significant. The certificate could, therefore, only be a 'private' document expressing *personal* knowledge. Its 'truthfulness' had to be attested to by the officer in court, and the officer was expected to take 'full responsibility' for the contents of the certificate. In case the officer of the gaon panchayat was not believed by the High Court, and the certificate holder was indeed a foreigner, the officer would be considered guilty of 'harbouring an illegal migrant' and guilty of 'gross misconduct' exposing him to 'departmental action' besides attracting penal consequences.[13]

The contemporary landscape of citizenship in India is an assemblage of tendencies that make for a practice of citizenship based on descent and an idea of national citizenship which for the first time makes religion a legal basis for making a distinction between citizens and aliens. Significantly, the ordering of citizenship on a national scale has been presented as necessary and indispensable for containing the 'dangerous consequences of large-scale illegal migration' from Bangladesh. The Joint Parliamentary Committee which gave its recommendations on the Citizenship Amendment Bill (CAB) argued against 'misconceived and mistaken notions of secularism' coming in the way of stopping this influx.[14]

Earlier, on 17 December 2014, Justice Ranjan Gogoi and R.F. Nariman of the Supreme Court of India had delivered a judgment in the case *Assam Sanmilita Mahasangha & Ors vs*

Union of India & Ors[15] laying down the modalities and the schedule for updating the NRC in Assam. In its administrative guidelines the Supreme Court followed its decision in *Sarbananda Sonowal* (2005) in construing the 'influx of illegal migrants into the state of India as external aggression'. The correspondence drawn between indiscriminate (illegal) immigration as an act of aggression against State sovereignty—its territory and people—is a trope commonly used across the world in election campaigns and for creating grounds for making changes in immigration and citizenship laws.

In November 2018, President Trump used 'invasion' as a metaphor to refer to the caravan of thousands of asylum seekers approaching the American borders along Mexico: 'It's like an invasion. They have violently overrun the Mexican border… These are tough people, in many cases. A lot of young men, strong men. And a lot of men that maybe we don't want in our country.'[16] The invocation of a crisis-ridden border, the need to deploy troops and to instal a wall at the border, along with the attack on birthright citizenship has been a common refrain by the President.

In her novel, *Home Fire*, Kamila Shamsie writes about the estrangement of young Muslim men and women born and brought up in England in the context of a post-9/11 world and the rise of ISIS.[17] Religious and cultural othering was, however, only part of the narrative of estrangement. Deeper and more pertinent were the complete withdrawal of State protection and the refusal of a right of return to a young man who joined the ISIS and subsequently wanted to exit. While Shamsie's fictional rendition of the conditions in which citizenship can be reduced to a privilege is evident in most countries, it is especially significant for the emphatic turn towards strengthening provisions that facilitate the deprivation of citizenship for public good and in the national interest. The loss of citizenship in such contexts relegates the political relationship between citizens and the State to a point where citizenship becomes a privilege that can be withdrawn.

A distinction can be made between those who deserve protection and those that do not depending on what is construed in contemporary contexts in India and elsewhere—the capability of a person to show sufficient and effective allegiance to the State and conformity to an idea of citizenship which is aligned with constitutive conditions of belonging, such as ancestry and culture. By forming a community of descent through citizenship, the State no longer establishes its authority as the primary source of universal membership by standing above and independent of other local communities of belonging, but itself becomes a community to which citizens are tied constitutively.

The insertion of legacy in the NRC in Assam has shown how citizenship has become a condition of constitutive belonging. Ranabir Samaddar has seen this constitutive power of citizenship unfold in two ways: as a procedure to arrest the power of the family through the construction of a legal myth called legacy, and the pruning of the power of the individual to claim citizenship as a *person*. Samaddar calls this a 'technical power' that drives a wedge in the 'broad continuum of the family reaching up to the state'.[18]

Following this argument, it is possible to see both these practices working through contradictory strands of logic—the substitution of the power of the family to absorb the 'awkward' citizen to make her inaccessible to the State and, on the other hand, reinstalling the order of the State through the power of legacy traced through the family tree verifiable by public evidence. The expulsion of the individual in the new identification regime reinforces the power of the State through its capacity to unsettle the family by exercising its power to summon individual members as nodes that make the family suspect.

Writing about the forms of legal and sovereign power in the colony, Achille Mbembe points at the manner in which colonial power was constituted as the colonizer's right to exercise absolute dominion over the native. Mbembe identifies three ways in which violence was imbricated in the imaginary '*command*' specific to State sovereignty in the colonial context—foundational violence which assumed a right to conquest, the legitimatization of violence through narratives of justification in terms of necessity and, finally, the sustaining of it as an enduring form of rule by everyday practices *in which the State does not stand apart from*, but has a specific relationship with society in a shared life. It was in this shared life that the colonized were required to subject themselves willingly. Anyone who desired another form of interaction, which challenged the authority of violence and questioned its protocols, was declared a savage and an outlaw, and treated accordingly.[19]

The invocation of 'crisis' in citizenship, generated by the spectre of indiscriminate immigration and the risks presented by 'strangers' among us,[20] has become the source for extraordinary legal regimes of citizenship. These regimes have recalled the sovereign's power to command by controlling the borders in the interest of a national community based on social cohesion, trust and shared interests. Yet, the moments of crisis are also ones of the iteration of constitutional moments—of 're-discovering' the set of principles that came to be adopted by 'We, the people'[21]—that have the power to 'break the causal chain of process and launch something unprecedented'.[22] These moments embody powerful acts of political courage that have the power to reiterate not just a constitutional order but a democratic one as well.

Notes

1. There are several English translations of 'Toba Tek Singh', a short story written by Manto in 1955. Among them is one available on www.sacw.net, February 1998 (last accessed 20 June 2021).
2. Ranajit Guha, ed., *Subaltern Studies*, Vol. I, Delhi: Oxford University Press, 1982.
3. Letter dated 29 May 1948 from the Home Secretary to the Chief

Commissioner of Delhi to the Secretary, Ministry of Home Affairs. File no. 16/44/48 Police (I), National Archives of India (hereinafter NAI).

4. Minutes of the Standing Advisory Committee, Ministry of Home Affairs, Government of India. File no. 16/31/49, NAI.
5. Note dated 18 July 1958, Ministry of Home Affairs (Indian Citizenship Section). File no. 10/1/56, MHA-IC, NAI.
6. Note of the PRO, Ministry of Agriculture, dated 23 August 1950. File no. 17/143/50 MHA-Judl, NAI.
7. Sanjib Baruah, 'The Partition's Long Shadow: The Ambiguities of Citizenship in Assam, India', *Citizenship Studies*, vol. 13, no. 6 (2009), pp. 593–606.
8. See 'Section 4A. Special provisions as to National Register of Indian Citizens in State of Assam' of the Citizenship Amendment Rules, 2009.
9. Ornit Shani, *How India Became Democratic: Citizenship and Making of the Universal Franchise*, Gurgaon: Penguin/Viking, 2018, p. 7.
10. R.K. Narayan, 'The Election Game', *The Hindu*, 3 February 1952.
11. Writ petition (WP[C] 7426/2019) by Babul Islam against an order of the Foreigners' Tribunal, where he was declared a foreigner of the post-1971 stream. See also, 'Gauhati High Court says electoral photo identity card not a proof of Indian citizenship', *India Today*, 17 February 2020.
12. Writ petition (WP[C] 7451/2019) before the Gauhati High Court. See also, 'Land revenue receipts, PAN card, bank documents no proof of citizenship: Gauhati High Court', *The Hindu*, 18 February 2020.
13. Judgment dated 28 February 2017, WP(C) 2634/2016.
14. *Report of the Joint Committee on the Citizenship (Amendment) Bill, 2016*, Lok Sabha Secretariat, New Delhi, January 2019, p. 12.
15. Writ Petition (Civil) No. 562 of 2012.
16. Meagan Flynn, '"An invasion of illegal aliens': The oldest immigration fear-mongering metaphor in America', *The Washington Post*, 2 November 2018.
17. Kamila Shamsie, *Home Fire*, New York: Riverhead Books, 2017.
18. Ranabir Samaddar, 'Migrants, NRC, and the paradox of protection and power', *The Wire*, 12 April 2019.
19. Achille Mbembe, *On the Postcolony*, Berkeley: University of California Press, 2001, pp. 6–7.

20. David Miller, *Strangers in Our Midst*, Cambridge, MA and London: Harvard University Press, 2016.
21. Bruce Ackerman, *We the People: Foundations*, Cambridge, MA: The Belknap Press of Harvard University Press, 1991, p. 5.
22. H.F. Pitkin, 'The idea of a constitution', *Journal of Legal Education*, vol. 37, no. 2 (1987), pp. 167–69.

WHERE DOES THIS STORY BEGIN?

Dr Hafiz Ahmed

Where does this story begin and where does it end? I do not know. These people, whose migration into India started in 1868, are still called 'foreigners' and 'immigrants'.

What did we not have? Lines after line of coconut and betelnut trees... I told my only son, 'Uproot and plant them on the embankment. If we cannot enjoy their fruits, hundreds will.' It could not be done. Now what do we have? Only the sand on our neck to lose, and the whole world to be conquered.

The people Amit Shah called 'termites', this story is about them. And it is unthinkable.

Sometimes they call us foreigners. Sometimes Pakistanis. Sometimes Bangladeshis. And then there are tussles over it. Neither does any political party intervene to help, nor anybody else.

FAITH-BASED CITIZENSHIP

THE DANGEROUS PATH INDIA IS CHOOSING

Niraja Gopal Jayal

The Indian idea of citizenship—as embodied in the Constitution and the law—is in the throes of a profound and radical metamorphosis. The twin instruments of this transformation are the National Register of Citizens (NRC) and the Citizenship Amendment Act (CAA). If the former is carving out paths to statelessness for disfavoured groups, the latter is creating paths to citizenship for preferred groups. While the first is, despite the looming threat of its extension across India, presently limited to the state of Assam, the second is designed to be pan-Indian in its application.

Not only do the two need to be read alongside each other, both of these in turn need to be read in the larger context of the government's policies towards minorities, whether in the forced 'amelioration' of Muslim women by the criminalization of the triple talaq or the clampdown, since early August 2019, in the erstwhile state of Jammu and Kashmir. They need also to be read in the context of the acceleration of violence against minorities over the past few years, especially by vigilante lynch mobs who have been thriving on the promise of legal impunity. An adequate understanding of both the NRC and the CAA depends on an appreciation of the ecosystem for minorities constituted by these twin phenomena, emanating from the State and society, respectively.

On the watch of the Supreme Court and under its unrelenting pressure for the completion of the NRC within a certain time frame, Assam has served as a laboratory for

This article first appeared in *The India Forum* on 31 October 2019.

a potentially dangerous experiment. Even though the results belied the expectations, the talk of sending those excluded from the register to detention centres has given credence to the fear that thousands of people are vulnerable to being rendered stateless and rightless. Existing detention centres in Assam are already populated, and new ones are being erected on an unprecedented scale. In Assam alone, there is the ongoing construction of a large detention camp, with a capacity of 3,000 detainees, with 10 others planned to fit a thousand people each. A detention centre in Nelamangala, near Bangalore, is being touted as a first in south India.[1] Meanwhile, the Global Detention Project has catalogued 10 existing detention centres in India, most of them in use since 2005 and 2006.[2]

The implications of these developments can be interpreted in multiple ways. From a legal perspective, they imply a foundational shift in the conception of the Indian citizen embodied in the Constitution of India, followed by the Citizenship Act, 1955. This is, first, a move from soil to blood as the basis of citizenship, from a *jus soli* or birth-based principle of citizenship in the direction of a *jus sanguinis* or descent-based principle; and second, a shift from a religion-neutral law to a law that differentiates based on religious identity. From the perspective of India's social fabric, they signal an ominous fraying and unravelling of what was a daring and moderately successful experiment in pluralism and diversity. From a political perspective, they point to a possibly tectonic shift from a civic-national to an ethnic-national conception of the political community and its terms of membership. From a moral perspective, they prompt us to confront the weakness of our commitment to human rights and to the moral and legal personhood of all human beings. From an international perspective, they remind us of, on the one hand, our longstanding aversion to signing international treaties on refugees and the reduction of statelessness and, on the other, our easy engagement in doublespeak with a valued neighbour.

I will elaborate on some of these aspects to show how they are collectively refashioning the fundamentals of our collective life.

In a sense, we are once again rehearsing the debates on citizenship in the Constituent Assembly. The chapter on citizenship in the Constitution was necessitated by Partition and is limited to the determination of citizenship for those extraordinary times. The debate on what became Article 7—relating to citizenship for the large numbers of Muslims who had fled India in the midst of the Partition violence but later returned—was fraught, the contention reflecting the communally charged atmosphere of Partition. Several members of the Assembly, who cast aspersions on the loyalty and intentionality of these returning migrants, called it the 'obnoxious clause'. Though the markers of religious difference were not openly displayed, they are easily spotted in the consistent use, in the Assembly, of the words refugee and migrant for distinct categories of people—Hindus fleeing Pakistan described as refugees, the returning Muslims described as migrants—subtly encoding religious identity in a shared universe of meaning. The Assembly eventually adopted what it called the more 'enlightened modern civilized'[3] and democratic conception of citizenship, as opposed to 'an idea of racial citizenship' and the Citizenship Act of 1955 gave a statutory basis to the idea of *jus soli* or citizenship by birth.

Over time, chiefly triggered by the political unrest in Assam, this conception has been moving slowly but surely in the direction of a *jus sanguinis* or descent-based conception of citizenship. Assam has a long and complex history of in-migration, mostly from Bengal, from the nineteenth century onwards. It witnessed substantial in-migration from 1947 onwards, peaking in 1971, and continuing steadily thereafter. It was no secret that many of the immigrants in recent decades had acquired forms of what Kamal Sadiq has called 'documentary citizenship' through 'networks of complicity' and 'networks of profit'.[4]

In 1985, in the wake of the gruesome Nellie massacre of 1983, the Assamese students' organizations that had led the agitation against the enfranchisement of migrants from Bangladesh, entered into the Assam Accord with the Rajiv Gandhi government, leading to an amendment in the provisions relating to naturalization in the Citizenship Act. This amendment created categories of eligibility for citizenship based on the year in which a person had migrated to India. All those who came before 1966 were declared citizens; those who came between 1966 and 1971 were struck off the electoral rolls and asked to wait 10 years before applying for citizenship; and those who came after 1971 were simply deemed to be illegal immigrants. Though these provisions were a response to the genuine grievances of the Assamese, they already contained the seeds of the politicization and incipient communalization of the issue of migrants.

Meanwhile, the gradual dilution of the principle of *jus soli* and the increasing recognition of elements of *jus sanguinis*—dependent on religious identity—was proceeding apace. Two amendments of 2004—one to the Citizenship Act and the other to the Rules under the Act—show how religious identity was gaining ground as the basis of legal citizenship. Both introduced religion into the language of the law, the first by implication and the second explicitly. The amendment to the Citizenship Act covertly introduced a religion-based exception to the principle of citizenship by birth. The amendment undercut the *jus soli* basis of citizenship, by stating that even if born on Indian soil, a person who had one parent who was an illegal migrant at the time of her or his birth, would not be eligible for citizenship by birth. Since most of the migrants from Bangladesh, against whose arrival there was so much political ferment in Assam, were Muslims, the term 'illegal migrant' signalled this religious identity.

The Citizenship Rules were simultaneously amended to exclude 'minority Hindus with Pakistani citizenship' from the definition of illegal immigrants. This amendment, firstly, destigmatized Hindu migrants (most of whom had come into the border states of western India from Pakistan) by dropping the label of 'illegal migrants' for them, and officially describing them henceforth as 'minority Hindus with Pakistan citizenship'. Secondly, it openly introduced a religious category into what was until then a religion-neutral law.

In the run-up to the Assembly elections in Assam in early 2016, the Bharatiya Janata Party (BJP) had made an electoral promise to 'free' the state from illegal Bangladeshi migrants by evicting and deporting them. This was a dog-whistle reference to a specific religion, as it simultaneously promised to give Indian citizenship to all Bangladeshi Hindu immigrants if it won the election. This promise would be fulfilled by the passage of the Citizenship Amendment Bill (CAB) (passed only in the lower house in January 2019) which will not only make explicit but also legitimize the inflection of the law on citizenship with religious difference.

The Bill essentially provided for fast-track citizenship by naturalization for migrants from the neighbouring countries of Pakistan, Afghanistan and Bangladesh who are religious minorities in those countries. It makes it possible for the preferred categories of Hindus, Buddhists, Sikhs, Parsis and Christians to obtain Indian citizenship in six years instead of the 11 it usually takes. Muslims are conspicuous by their absence in this listing, ostensibly on the grounds that they are not minorities in these three countries and cannot therefore be seen as persecuted. The fact that Muslim sects like the Ahmadiyyas and Rohingyas are also persecuted in these countries does not make them eligible for similar benefits. By introducing a religion-based difference in the presently religion-neutral law on citizenship by naturalization, this amendment would in effect create two categories of potential citizens: those professing the Hindu and other 'acceptable' faiths, and those professing Islam.

This was also the implicit objective of the NRC in Assam. The first National Register of Citizens for Assam was compiled in 1951 but remained largely dormant until political considerations gave it a new lease of life. In 2005, a meeting between the Centre, the Assam government and the All Assam Students' Union (AASU), chaired by the then Prime Minister Manmohan Singh, resolved to take steps towards updating the NRC to fulfil the requirements of the Assam Accord.

In 2009, a petition was filed in the Supreme Court by an NGO called Assam Public Works asking for the updating of the NRC to be started. The Court gave a direction to this effect, and the exercise began in 2015, with the objective of recording all those who have documentary proof of being Indian, and of them or their ancestors having been in India before midnight on 24 March 1971. In a society as historically undocumented as India, and in a region that is regularly visited by natural calamities like floods, there are many people who cannot produce documents to establish their ancestry. In fact, those who are native inhabitants for generations may be undocumented even as immigrants have acquired 'paper citizenship'.

The result of the NRC has demonstrated the very real possibility that undocumented nationals may be unfairly deprived of their citizenship status. At the end of its first round, four million people out of the 32.9 million who had applied were excluded. Fresh claims for inclusion were filed by 3.6 million people and at the end of this process, in August 2019, 1.9 million remain unauthenticated.

Champions of the NRC have been surprised and disappointed by this outcome, as large numbers of Hindus are unexpectedly among the excluded, and the percentage of exclusion was larger in areas inhabited by indigenous people, and lower in border areas where illegal migrants have settled. Those left out include people who have served in the Indian Army or the Border Security Force for decades, the nephew of former Indian president Fakhruddin Ali Ahmed, and even Syeda Anwara Taimur, the only woman chief minister Assam ever had. Ironically, a former anti-immigration activist and even a local BJP leader found themselves excluded. In some cases, children's documents were found to be acceptable but not those of their fathers. Notwithstanding the unexpected outcome of the NRC, public pronouncements from the ruling party continue to threaten the nationwide implementation of the register. It is of course another matter that the State capacity to 'sort' citizens in this manner is very doubtful.

As the factual outcomes of the process contradicted the political expectations of the enthusiasts of this exercise, the political messaging has sought to assuage fears by affirming that no Hindus would be deported. They could anyhow, on the basis of their religious identity, be reinstated after the CAA has become law. It is genuine but undocumented Indian nationals belonging to the Muslim faith who would be excluded with no recourse to the CAA, while documented (and possibly illegal) migrants who belong to other faiths would be included.

A legal challenge to the CAA could plausibly bring into question its constitutionality, specifically its contravention of Articles 14 and 15 of the chapter on Fundamental Rights. Article 14 guarantees that 'The State shall not deny to *any person* equality before the law or the equal protection of the laws within the territory of India'. This is not a right that is dependent upon such a person being an Indian citizen, it is available even to foreigners who happen to be within the territory of India. As such, differential treatment to individuals on the basis of their religious faith would appear to be in contravention of the Right to Equality. Article 15 prohibits the State from discriminating 'against any citizen on ground only of religion, race, caste...' and the introduction of religious identity as a criterion into a matter as fundamental as citizenship is certainly questionable. Placing people in detention centres is arguably also violative of Article 21 of the Constitution which guarantees the Right to Life and Liberty.

Experts have moreover questioned the legality of the NRC on the grounds that a provision under the Rules cannot contravene the provisions of the parent Act. Authorized by the Registration of Citizens and Issue of National Identity Card Rules, 2003, the NRC uses the cutoff date of 1971 (based on the Assam Accord) rather than the date of 1987 which is the defining criterion of citizenship by birth according to the Citizenship Act.

The NRC and the CAA are manifestly conjoined in their objectives. The first paves the way to statelessness and detention centres for many poor and vulnerable people, and most unjustly for those whose genuine nationality is repudiated *only on the basis of their faith*. The second offers a smooth path to citizenship for groups of migrants who are deemed acceptable *only on grounds of their faith*. In other words, faith is set to become the exclusive criterion for determining who is an Indian citizen and who is not, for inclusion as well as for exclusion. Together, the NRC and the CAA have the potential of transforming India into a majoritarian polity with gradations of citizenship rights that undermine the constitutional principle of universal equal citizenship; with privileges of inclusion being attached to some categories of citizens while others suffer the disabilities of exclusion.

Though the CAA ostensibly relates only to migrants seeking the legal status of citizenship, this is not just about migrants. The threat, rhetorical or otherwise, of a nationwide NRC shows that the fig leaf of illegal immigration is being used to bring the citizenship of *all* Muslim citizens into question. Migrants—beginning with those in Assam—are fast becoming a pretext to fabricate and advance a much more ambitious and nationwide project of 'othering'. The multiple identities that have historically been at play in Assam make it disingenuous to present the animosity towards migrants exclusively in terms of Hindu sentiments against Muslims. When it visited Assam in May 2018, the Joint Parliamentary Committee on the CAB was petitioned by hundreds of organizations agitating against the Bill, expressing not only the secular constitutionalist objection to introducing religion-based citizenship provisions, but also in many cases the fear of both Assamese-speakers as well as indigenous tribal communities becoming minorities in their own land. The attempt to extrapolate lessons for a national-level Hindu political consolidation from the Assam situation is based on a misrecognition of identities in that state, and on a flawed singularizing of its plural identity-related anxieties.

Not only does the CAA exclude Muslim migrants from the provisions for fast-track citizenship, Indian Muslims who are full citizens by birth have also been experiencing the abrogation of their constitutionally guaranteed rights of equal citizenship. Their endemic under-representation in India's public institutions and their abysmal education and employment indicators are well known. The unprecedented increase in incidents of vigilante violence against them over the last few years, and the impunity enjoyed by the perpetrators of such violence, signifies a systematic political and ideological attempt to render them second-class citizens.

The politicization of religious identity, finding articulation in and through the law, is a worrying portent for the founding vision of Indian nationalism which was emphatically civic-national in form. The march from a *jus soli* to a *jus sanguinis* conception of citizenship is also simultaneously a march from civic nationalism to ethno-religious nationalism, from a universalist and inclusive form of nationalism to an exclusionary form that renders difference as graded hierarchy. This is nothing less than a radical re-invention of the imagination of India that informed and inspired the freedom struggle and found embodiment in the Constitution. The context of the anti-immigrant discourse that underlies the NRC, and the selective acceptance of persons 'treated as illegal migrants' that underpins the CAA is important. It entails a substantive disenfranchisement of the Muslim minority, a normalization and justification of violence—both discursive and physical—against it, and a reconstruction of the Indian nation in the form of a Hindu Rashtra in which this minority lives on sufferance and must be prepared for everyday discrimination, legal and social.

In comparisons between the anti-immigrant and Islamophobic rhetoric of populist politicians across the world, it is rarely acknowledged that the 'other' in India is wholly, historically and organically Indian, and not a recent entrant or stranger as in Europe or the United States. It is the Sri Lankan Tamils, the Afghans and the Tibetan Buddhists who are relatively recent immigrants to India, but even before the CAA, India had no difficulty in assimilating them. In a society as plural and diverse as that encompassed by the territorial boundaries of the Indian nation, the quest to make the borders of religion and nation coincide is tantamount to opening up the scars of the Partition of 1947. This cannot be achieved without damaging the delicate balance in a society characterized by multiple heterogeneities of language, region, caste and even of religious sects.

At the same time, it cannot be denied that India has never had a spectacular record of commitment to human rights, or even to the idea that all human beings are entitled to moral and legal personhood. The conundrum before us recalls a contention most starkly identified by Hannah Arendt in her book *The Origins of Totalitarianism*. The supposedly universal and inalienable rights of man, Arendt argued, could not be invoked or claimed in contexts of statelessness. In the interwar years, there was no international body to which 10 million *de facto* stateless people could appeal for their human rights, because a human being who is not a member of some political community is without recourse to such rights. The loss of a polity is the loss of humanity, for only membership in a political community, i.e. citizenship, can give people what Arendt famously called the right to have rights. The deprivation of legality, of a juridical existence, is tantamount to the loss of moral personhood. Rights are meant to be enjoyed within a community, and the calamity of the rightless, said Arendt, is that since they do not belong to any community, no law exists for them, and nobody even wants to oppress them. This was why the Nazis first deprived Jews of their legal status of citizenship before conveying them to concentration camps.

In Assam, following the NRC, as of October 2019, 1,145 people have already been placed in six detention centres, living in sub-human conditions; 335 of these have spent three years in camps; 25 persons declared 'foreigners' have already died in the detention camps; and an estimated 33 persons have been driven to suicide by the fear of not possessing papers.[5] Although the Supreme Court has passed orders for the improvement of conditions in these centres, there is a genuine moral concern about the very idea of such detention centres which is at odds with India's constitutional values and more generally with the idea of human rights. Stripping people of citizenship (even of the merely documentary kind) and rendering them stateless is a clear violation of the duty, placed on States by the Universal Declaration of Human Rights, to avoid taking actions that result in statelessness and the deprivation of citizenship.

Bangladesh, meanwhile, has been persuaded at the highest inter-governmental level, that the political rhetoric of sending the 'termites' and 'infiltrators' back to Bangladesh is an internal matter, and that there will be no deportation. In fact, the impressive economic indicators of Bangladesh today give rise to the speculation that we could now be looking at less migration from Bangladesh to India than in the reverse direction. Already, with 1.1 million illegal Indian immigrants, Bangladesh is the fifth largest sender of remittances to India. Given the cross-border movement of people in both directions, the two countries could even consider devising a mutually acceptable arrangement based on guest-worker visas.

In the meantime, as the NRC converts legitimate citizens

into illegal immigrants and illegal immigrants into stateless people, both destined for the camp; as the CAA selectively legalizes illegal migrants; and as minorities are rendered second-class citizens by the insidious use of the law, India stands on the edge of a dangerous precipice where not only its constitutional values but also its moral compass is at grave risk.

Notes

1. These were described as 'movement restriction centres' rather than jails. 'NRC in Karnataka? Inside the detention centre for illegal immigrants 40 km from Bengaluru', *The News Minute*, 4 October 2019.
2. See 'India Immigration Detention', Global Detention Project (https://www.globaldetentionproject.org/countries/asia-pacific/india). Please note that some facts might have changed since the article was first published.
3. Constituent Assembly of India Debates (Proceedings), Vol. I, p. 424.
4. Kamal Sadiq, *Paper Citizens: How Illegal Immigrants Acquire Citizenship in Developing Countries*, New York: Oxford University Press, 2009.
5. Aditya Sharma, 'Passport to Kill', *News18*.

RECENT EXCLUSIONARY STEPS CAN ONLY BRING INDIA'S INTERNATIONAL IMAGE DOWN

Ashutosh Varshney

Right since 1945, up until recently, few democratic polities moved from inclusion to exclusion in their citizenship practices and laws. The big exceptions were mostly authoritarian, the Chinese treatment of Uighurs being the most recent. Some democratic polities might have remained as exclusionary as before but, by and large, when change came about, democratic polities edged towards larger inclusion. And when new exclusions were proposed, as in Trump's America or in the Le Pen version of France, political battles were launched by the forces opposed to such curtailments.

By its bi-focal citizenship move—one, excluding Muslim immigrants as citizens while accepting all other communities from Pakistan, Afghanistan and Bangladesh on grounds of persecution, and two, promising to introduce a National Register of Citizens, which will render stateless all those Muslims who don't have the documents to prove their Indian ancestry, even if they were born in India and have lived in the country for decades—Delhi is taking two of the darkest steps in the history of democratic citizenship since the European excesses of the 1940s.

The implications are so profound that one should pause to take a larger comparative and historical look. India's strengths and weaknesses are often better understood that way.

Citizenship is basically a legal code for the kind of political community a society is or would like to be. It says who can

....

This article first appeared in the *The Indian Express* on 16 December 2019.

be a member of the community—and with what bundle of rights. Since the American and French Revolutions of the late eighteenth century and the German Unification of 1871, the idea of citizenship has witnessed two models: Birth in a territory (*jus soli*) and blood-based inheritance (*jus sanguinis*). Ignoring ethnicity, race or religion, the former is often, if not always, built around the ideals of a society. The latter hooks citizenship to ethnicity or race, sometimes also to religion, especially in societies where religion is not viewed as a matter of choice, but as a bloodline, functioning almost like race or ethnicity. India is moving from the former model to the latter.

The voluminous literature on citizenship—and its cousin, nationhood—identifies the US and France as exemplars of the territorial model, and Germany and Japan as the epitome of blood-based citizenship. The consensus is that a community based on ideals is more inclusive—and harder to build—than one based on bloodlines.

Of course, even inclusive polities have their infirmities. The US is the best-known example of this. Formally embracing the ideals of freedom and equality in 1789, it kept Black slaves, who were neither free nor equal and, after the 1880s, it excluded Asians from its immigrant pool. It took the US until the 1860s to end slavery—and till the 1960s to de-link citizenship from ethnicity. Similarly, in France, questions about the loyalty of Jews existed right until the 1910s, and controversy has also marked the status of Muslims after the 1970s. But exclusions are challenged in such polities.

The blood-based models work differently. At the dissolution of the Soviet Union, Russian-speaking ethnic Germans, Soviet citizens until then, simply became citizens of Germany, once they demonstrated German ancestry. Non-ethnic members do exist in such polities, but they receive lesser citizenship, or an inferior bundle of rights. For some time, millions of Turks in Germany were 'guest workers', and naturalization of even Germany-born Turks was notoriously hard. But after becoming a member of the European Union, Germany also eventually moved in a more inclusive direction. Japan remains the great exception.

Where did independent India fit in? It was undoubtedly closer to the territorial model. In contrast, Pakistan was conceptualized as a Muslim homeland, where non-Muslims could be citizens, but would have fewer rights. India was never envisioned by Gandhi, Nehru and Ambedkar as a Hindu homeland. Furthermore, Indians in South and East Africa, or Southeast Asia, were not allowed to acquire automatic Indian citizenship. They were citizens of their adopted lands. In those foundational days, even Muslims returning from Pakistan could reclaim Indian citizenship.

The recent exclusionary steps can only bring India's international image down. India under Nehru was lauded worldwide for its constitutionally enshrined inclusive citizenship. If America's constitutive ideals were freedom and equality, India's founding values were equality, including religious equality, diversity and tolerance. Later, riots would often hurt religious minorities more, sometimes damningly so, but in the eyes of the law, there was no distinction between a Hindu and a Muslim. Even if politics deviated from the basic constitutional principles, the law did not follow suit.

Now, a fusion of law and an exclusivist political ideology is in the making. The government's claim that a modern polity must inevitably draw a distinction between *sharanarthi* (refugees) and *ghuspaithiye* (infiltrators) is mendacious. For, it is patently clear that if the existing Muslim citizens of India are unable to produce documents of Indian ancestry, the national register later, using citizenship amendments, can easily call them 'infiltrators', making them an object of internment, expulsion or disenfranchisement. In contrast, if the Hindus have a similar documentary deficit, they would neither be interned nor expelled, nor disenfranchised. They can claim they are welcome only in a Hindu homeland, not elsewhere in South

Asia, and thus acquire Indian citizenship. Assam is already burning, partly for this reason.

The government's second claim that the citizenship amendment is not anti-Muslim—for it will give refugee status not only to Hindus, but also to Christians and Parsis—is also political sophistry. Why should the refugee status, and therefore the possibility of citizenship, be reserved only for those persecuted in three Muslim-majority neighbours, not in the Buddhist-majority Sri Lanka or Myanmar? Both are India's neighbours and have a record of persecuting minorities. And what about the Ahmadiyyas, whom the Pakistani State, since the mid-1970s, has declared non-Muslim and oppressed? Is Delhi's heart really bleeding for the persecuted minorities?

After Kashmir, Delhi has yet again used brute parliamentary arithmetic for majoritarian ends. Democracy now urgently requires the judiciary and the streets. The Supreme Court may, or may not, act in a resolute manner—hence, protests are also necessary. Non-BJP state governments can exercise the option of non-cooperation, too. Most of the machinery for implementation of laws is, after all, with state governments. The threat of electorally and legally enabled exclusionary horrors is knocking at the door.

A TOOL KIT FOR HINDU RASHTRA?

Pamela Philipose

The Citizenship (Amendment) Act (CAA) of 2019, which fast-tracked Indian citizenship to non-Muslim migrants coming to the country from three Muslim-majority countries in South Asia—Afghanistan, Pakistan and Bangladesh—while denying the same concession to their Muslim counterparts, has upended the constitutional guarantee of equal citizenship in India. Once the Hindu-majoritarian party, the Bharatiya Janata Party (BJP), came back to power after the general election win of 2019 it ensured that the law came into force, and simultaneously set about expediting the *National Register of Indian Citizens* (NRIC)—which is an official record of citizens who are legally Indian and encapsulates their demographic and biometric data. This also entailed the intermediate step of putting together a National Population Register (NPR) to map the 'usual residents' of the country—defined as persons who have either resided in a local area for the past six months or more or who intend to reside in that area for the next six months or more—through house-to-house listing. The NPR exercise was expected to be conducted between April 2020 and September 2020, but could not take place because of the Covid-19 pandemic.

It is against this background that we come to the curious paradox of the seemingly contrasting stances on this law and its legal architecture adopted by the two most powerful men in India, Prime Minister Narendra Modi and Union Home Minister Amit Shah.

....

An earlier version of this article appeared as Pamela Philipose, 'A National Register of Citizens for India: A Tool Kit for Hindu Rashtra?' in *The India Forum* on 3 November 2019.

Shah's narrative on it was emphatic and insistent, with statements designed to strike fear in those being targeted, most specifically the Muslim community. In his election campaign of April 2019, to take one example, he observed that 'illegal immigrants' were 'termites...eating the grain that should go to the poor'.[1] This was a conscious repetition of a slur he had deployed during the state elections of 2018, which had created a great deal of unease among Muslims across India because the logical surmise they drew was that anyone from a Muslim background, without the necessary identity documentation, could be termed an 'illegal immigrant'. On 1 October 2019, a day before Gandhi Jayanti, Shah—now the Union Home Minister—in an address to the BJP workers in Kolkata, publicly renewed his pledge to implement the NRC/NRIC (National Register of [Indian] Citizens) across India so that 'each and every infiltrator' is externed. He continued to make references to the issue during his election rallies in Haryana in late 2019, even informing an election crowd in Gurugram that by 2024 India would be rid of all 'infiltrators and illegal residents'. The significance of the timeline was not lost on his audience: it signalled the intention to capitalize on the issue by the next general election.

By the winter session of Parliament in December 2019, the government was ready with its Citizenship (Amendment) Bill and it was Amit Shah, again, who tabled it in both houses of Parliament, framing it as the 'unfinished business of Partition'. He has also clearly linked the citizenship law with the NRIC. A YouTube video that the BJP put out on its official channel on 23 April 2019, a month before the general election, had Shah underlining the sequence: 'First the CAB will come. All refugees will get citizenship. Then NRC will come. This is why refugees should not worry, but infiltrators should. Understand the chronology.' This was reiterated several times, including in Parliament, after the BJP won its second term.[2]

In studied contrast Prime Minister Narendra Modi, once he

was back in power for a second term, was low-key on the issue. He may have referred to the NRIC occasionally while campaigning for the 2019 general election campaign but generally it was left to Shah to do most of the public articulation. The NRIC did not even figure in Modi's Independence Day address in 2019, nor did it make it to the innumerable speeches he made in the run-up to the Maharashtra and Haryana elections of 2019. In October 2019, four days after Shah's public pronouncement on it in Kolkata, he underplayed the concern during his interactions with his Bangladeshi counterpart, Sheikh Hasina, on her State visit to India, claiming that Assam's NRC process was an 'internal matter', 'a court-mandated process, which is ongoing' and one that will have no repercussions on Bangladesh.

After the unprecedented anti-CAA protests gripped the country for three months once the Bill was passed, the same seeming dissonance was apparent in the tones adopted by the two leaders. Shah's aggression in the face of the protests was overt. While inaugurating a mobile number to aggregate popular support for the amended Citizenship Act on 3 January 2020, for instance, he made it clear that his government would 'not go back an inch' to revoke the legislation even if all the Opposition parties come together and spread 'misinformation with all (their) might'.[3] The fact that protesters at Shaheen Bagh were demanding the rollback of the CAA was often the focus of his wrath during his electioneering for the Delhi elections. On one occasion he urged voters to press the 'EVM button of the lotus so hard that the current will force Shaheen Bagh protesters to flee'.[4]

Meanwhile, Narendra Modi consciously underplayed the issue. Ten days after the passing of the CAA, he attempted to assuage Muslim anxieties by claiming that 'no Indian Muslim will be sent to any detention centre'.[5] He also dialled down on the question of NRIC, claiming that his government has not taken any decision on it. Only rarely was this carefully crafted stance allowed to slip, as it did while he was delivering an election speech in Dumka, Jharkhand, when he attacked students protesting against the citizenship law with a communally overt statement that their clothes revealed their community.[6]

How is this policy of doublespeak adopted by these two men to be interpreted? Is there a genuine difference of political positions on the issue between the Prime Minister and the Home Minister, or is it a mere division of political labour for the longer term project of ushering in a Hindu-majoritarian State? The latter would seem the case. The Modi–Shah partnership has decisively transformed Indian politics, first at the Gujarat state level and later on the national stage. Together it spelt a rare unity of purpose and a cogent ideological vision developed through the long personal associations both men have had with the Rashtriya Swayamsevak Sangh (RSS). Lance Price, in his book *The Modi Effect*, characterizes Shah for good reason, as 'perhaps the only person that Modi trusts completely'.

In fact, theirs has always been a carefully crafted strategy to expand the BJP/RSS footprint across the country through the calibrated use of emphases and silences, ambiguities and certainties. In 1923, V.D. Savarkar had formulated the idea of the true Indian being 'someone who looked upon this land of his forefathers as his holy land; someone who inherited the blood of the race of the Sapta Sindhus; and one who expressed a common affinity to the classical language, Sanskrit...'[7] Both men are extremely aware that their ultimate goal is to promote these twin Savarkarite tests for full citizenship—*pitribhumi* (India as the citizen's ancestral land) and *punyabhumi* (India as the land of the citizen's religion). They also understand how central the CAA-NPR-NRC architecture is to the political consolidation of the Hindu community along the axis of citizenship.

Yet, despite the best efforts of Modi and Shah, there is an element of uncertainty to the CAA-NPR-NRC project they cannot afford to ignore. Precisely because it entails nothing less than the dismantling of the foundational principles of the Indian Constitution, it must for credibility's sake be seen as participative and democratic. Shah, for instance, has often claimed that the cutoff date for an all-India NRIC would be arrived at only after a nationwide consensus has been reached. Both men have iterated that no 'genuine' Indian citizen will be deported.

All this indicates the delicateness of the task in rolling out the NRIC nationally. While the citizenship law has been successfully enacted, its ramifications continue to pose serious challenges which had, incidentally, led to a delay in its enactment. The Modi government could have pushed through the law in its first term in office. It was the possibility that the move could negatively impact the party's prospects in the 2019 general election which had held its hand. Similar concerns could cloud future elections.

The challenges before the BJP and its two seniormost leaders are threefold. First and foremost is the anxiety within the Hindu community, both among those who are already living in the country and Hindu migrants who had arrived by 2014 and were eligible for citizenship under the new law. They nurse genuine worries that their lack of documentation could put their citizenship, or that of their children, in jeopardy. There is also concern among Hindu migrants seeking Indian citizenship that they may not be able to provide the necessary proof to indicate that they were victims of State persecution in their countries of origin. The scenario prevailing in Assam after the completion of the NRC verification process remains an ever-present warning: 12 lakh among the 19.6 lakh people[8] found ineligible for Indian citizenship happened to be Hindus. The angst this created among Hindus in the state was so deep that the BJP-led Assam government submitted an affidavit in the Supreme Court seeking re-verification of 20 per cent of the names in the districts bordering Bangladesh and 10 per cent elsewhere in the state.[9] Since the apex court has not issued an order on the matter, the situation continues to hang in the balance and could be potentially costly for the party.

The second challenge is widespread public anger in the eight north-eastern states over the passing of the CAA, given fears among local tribal communities of being swamped by resettled Hindu migrants, and being deprived of their rights—including the right to land and common property. In Assam, the largest state in the region, there was the additional argument that the new law violated the Assam Accord of 1985, which laid down that 1971 would be the cutoff year for Indian citizenship.

Here we need to note that the BJP, under the prime ministership of Narendra Modi, has been able expand its political footprint emphatically in the region. By 2020, it was ruling in four of the eight states that comprised the Northeast, and was part of, or linked to, ruling coalitions in the others. The possibility of this consolidation being undermined because of local resistance to the amended citizenship law led the Modi government to exclude states governed by the Sixth Schedule[10] and the Inner Line Permit[11]—administrative measures that give tribal communities of the region a degree of political autonomy—from the purview of the newly amended Act. While this step has helped to curb some of the resistance, it has by no means totally stemmed local disquiet.

In other locations of the country, the political dividends of CAA can always be exploited. When J.P. Nadda, who replaced Amit Shah as BJP president, speaks of the imminent possibility of CAA 'being implemented',[12] once the Covid-19 pandemic eases, it is intriguing that he chooses West Bengal to make the point. The calculation clearly is that easing restrictions on citizenship norms for Hindus from Bangladesh could prove a popular political trope in that state.

The third challenge is the scale of Muslim anger as already evidenced in the widespread anti-CAA-NPR-NRC protests that roiled the country. The new law was perceived as unconstitutional and violative of Article 14 that guarantees equal protection of laws. While a degree of resistance to the law may have been anticipated by its progenitors, they clearly had not imagined the sheer scale of these protests in terms of geographical dimension, persistence, outrage, passion and, most importantly, the solidarity they drew from non-Muslim groups, including students and young adults from a range of different religious backgrounds. By early January 2020, according to one source, there were 261 CAA-related protests across 24 states of which 230 were against the citizenship law.[13] Those protests played out for three months without let and, if it were not for the Covid-19 lockdown and the concerted repression mounted by the BJP government and its police, they may well have carried on.

What was also particularly distinctive about these protests was that it was driven by women. The reason they came in their hundreds to sit at protest sites across the country was succinctly summed up by one of them: 'The choice was simple: Either sit at the protest today or prepare to sit in a detention centre a few years later.'[14] Shaheen Bagh, a South Delhi neighbourhood, emerged in particular as a 'centre of solidarities; a place where people of different classes, faiths, ideologies, educational backgrounds, professions, gender identities, castes and regions stood together for the same cause: protecting the Constitution'.[15]

THE GOVERNMENT'S NEXT MOVES

To address these challenges the Modi government has adopted various strategies, two of which are highlighted here. The first is to create the necessary institutional infrastructure along with a data extraction regime. In the very first parliamentary session of BJP's second term, President Ram Nath Kovind in his address to the newly elected Members of Parliament of both houses, articulated the government's intent: '[it] has decided to implement the process of National Register of Citizens on a priority basis in areas affected by infiltration'.[16] The Modi government also passed—on the very day it was sworn back to power on 30 May 2020—the Foreigners (Tribunals)

Amendment Order, 2019, which decentralized decision-making with regard to the setting up of Foreigners' Tribunals. Earlier, only the Central government had the power to institute these tribunals; now even district collectors were empowered to do so.

If the Assam example is any guide, the functioning of Foreigners' Tribunals—quasi-judicial bodies which serve as the court of last appeal for those who stand deprived of citizenship—has been marked by not just blatant errors but strong communal biases. This is not surprising given that these bodies are presided over by poorly qualified people with no formal legal training. The Gauhati High Court has even had to strike down several of their verdicts for being legally flawed. Liberalizing the procedures for the institution of these tribunals, as the Modi government has done, is sure to compound such failures. But it demonstrates eloquently that it is ideological considerations rather than those of fairness and justice that are driving decision-making on citizenship.

Identifying those to be included and excluded is also crucially dependent on data gathered at levels ranging from the local and sub-district to the state and national, and encompassing not just the demographic but the biometric. Since its first term in office, the Modi government has displayed an inordinate appetite for aggregating the data of Indian citizens, despite strong pushback from concerned academics and activists alarmed about the possible emergence of a surveillance State. Shah's advocacy of a digitalized 'one nation, one card'[17] and the widespread use of the Aarogya Setu app are just examples of data harvesting by the Modi government which could well shape its citizenship project as well. The pandemic may have delayed the NPR process but it is only a matter of time before it is rolled out and for the first time additional data will also be sought, such as the names and places of birth of the parents of the respondent. As a group of civil servants observed in an open letter to the government, such exercises 'constitute an invasion of the citizens' right to privacy, since a lot of information, including Aadhaar, mobile numbers and voter IDs will be listed in a single document, with scope for misuse'.[18]

The second strategy of the BJP is to allow anti-Muslim-laced political and election rhetoric on citizenship issues proliferate in such a way that over time it emerges as the popular common sense. Already the idea that the country needs to be protected from 'infiltrators' ('*ghuspaithiye*')—an inappropriate military term that is now widely used—has been internalized by Indians over the years, and the widespread, random acts of vigilantism in the country also indicate rising hatred against the Muslim 'other'. But if the average citizen has to accept the NRIC, these attitudes, fears and hatreds within the Hindu community will have to be further deepened through living politics. What is required, in effect, is a conjuring trick. Rather like a magician pulling out one card and replacing it with another, the 'anti-migrant' card needs to be transformed into an 'anti-Muslim card', even as an 'anti-Muslim' card is miraculously made an 'anti-migrant' one!

The stock phrases about the NRC/NRIC circulating in the political domain are marked by a seemingly simple logic. Take for instance the colloquial statement that 'India is not a "dharamshala" for illegal migrants'. In August 2018, Raman Singh, then chief minister of Chhattisgarh who was fighting an election, had used it in response to a query put to him about Assam's NRC exercise. Strikingly, that very phrase was subsequently parroted by several BJP politicians, from Shahnawaz Hussain, former BJP spokesperson, to Anil Jain, BJP general secretary in charge of Haryana, and Kailash Vijayvargiya, BJP general secretary in charge of West Bengal, in their speeches. Public speech segues into ordinary conversations and goes on to influence everyday stances such as, for instance, the decision of middle-class flat owners in an apartment complex in Bengaluru to stop employing Bengali-speaking migrants as domestic workers.[19]

It is the ordinary Muslim that is paying the greatest price for such revanchist politics. Existential fears unleashed by the NRC exercise in Assam have now spread to every corner of the country and the three-month non-violent demonstrations in support of the Constitution and against the CAA-NPR-NRC was evidence of this. The struggle is not just for an individual's right to have rights in the country—which is what citizenship ultimately is about—but for their descendants in perpetuity as well. The law as it now stands deprives a child, even if born in India, of citizenship if one of its parents is an 'illegal immigrant', and there is no provision in the law which would allow such a child to become a citizen. Further, after the *Sarbananda Sonowal vs the Union of India* judgment of 2005 transferred the burden of proof of legality from the State to the person marked illegal, it is the accused who have to provide the necessary documentation to prove that they are bonafide Indians.

For a country of 1.35 billion, the looming crisis of citizenship is rife with dystopic consequences. With people marked as 'doubtful' citizens, the republic appears to be careening to a scenario of proliferating detention centres, divided families and the ceaseless search for the 'right' documents. With the nine-decade-old RSS and its Savarkarite vision firmly embedded in the country's politics, the CAA-NPR-NRIC tool kit would appear to be an extremely serviceable one for re-engineering India into a Hindu Rashtra.

Notes

1. 'Illegal immigrants are like termites, will throw them out if BJP comes back to power: Amit Shah', PTI/*India Today*, 11 April 2019.
2. Rohan Venkataramakrishnan, 'Who is linking Citizenship Act to NRC? Here are five times Amit Shah did so', *Scroll.in*, 20 December 2019.
3. 'We will not give an inch on CAA, says Amit Shah', *The Hindu*, 4 January 2020.
4. 'Vote for us to rid Delhi of Shaheen Bagh: Amit Shah', *The Indian Express*, 26 January 2020.
5. 'CAA, NRC have nothing to do with Indian Muslims: Modi', *The Hindu BusinessLine*, 22 December 2019.
6. 'Anti-Citizenship Act protests: Those indulging in arson can be identified by their clothes, says Narendra Modi', PTI/*The Hindu*, 15 December 2019.
7. Vikram Sampath, *Savarkar: Echoes from a Forgotten Past, 1883–1924*, Viking, 2019, pp. 416–17.
8. 'Exclusion of Hindu Bengalis from Assam NRC changing political [narrative]', *Business Standard*, 22 September 2019.
9. 'Congress says NRC Assam coordinator's directive to prepare list of "D-voters" is contempt of court', *News18*, 16 October 2020.
10. 'What is 6th Schedule & why it allows parts of Northeast to be exempt from citizenship bill', *The Print*, 6 December 2019.
11. 'Explained: What is the Inner Line Permit system, and northeast states' concerns over it?', *The Indian Express*, 5 December 2019.
12. 'CAA delayed by Covid, implementation soon', *The Indian Express*, 20 October 2020.
13. Mala Jay, 'Contrary to top BJP leaders' claims, anti-CAA-NCR protests are spreading, not losing momentum', *The National Herald*, 23 January 2020.
14. Ziya Us Salam and Uzma Ausaf, *Shaheen Bagh: From a Protest to a Movement*, Bloomsbury, 2020, p. xviii.
15. Harsh Mander, 'Shaheen Bagh and the politics of love', *Scroll.in*, 29 September 2020.
16. 'Address by the President of India, Shri Ram Nath Kovind to the Joint Sitting of Two Houses of Parliament', Official Website of the President of India, 20 June 2019 (https://presidentofindia.nic.in/speeches-detail.htm?683).
17. 'One Nation, One Card: Amit Shah proposes multipurpose card

with Aadhaar, passport, bank accounts and more', *Financial Express*, 23 September 2019.

18. 'India doesn't need CAA, NPR, NRIC, say over 100 former bureaucrats in open letter', *The Hindu*, 9 January 2020.
19. 'Apartments plan ban on migrant workers', *Deccan Herald*, 4 November 2019.

A WOMAN ON THE MARGINS

Varna Balakrishnan

Bear with me as we tell your story.
Let me introduce you.

Jamila Begum, forty-four years old,
from Barpeta, Assam.

I know this is not the best time—the monsoon is here; the river is furious and your village is flooded—but we also do not have much time left. The final NRC (National Register of Citizens) list comes out very soon. We met at your tin-walled house, built so for flood resilience. Your four children were there—a boy and three girls. Two of your daughters are married, the third engaged. Your son is still in school, which is now shut because of the floods.

The day we met, you told me that you have not been able to work in your small field ever since you have had to go around figuring out why your name did not appear in the NRC list.

This article first appeared as Varna Balakrishnan, 'The story of Jamila Begum from Barpeta, who is terrified she will be excluded from the NRC today' in *Scroll.in* on 31 August 2019. The illustrations are by Krishna Balakrishnan.

The village chief, *gaonbura*, says it is because your panchayat certificate was not accepted as proof that you are your father's daughter, that Jamila Begum is the daughter of Abdullah Islam, whose name was present in the 1951 NRC list. The notice says 'legacy person not parent or grandparent'. Never having been to school and married off before you could have documents like a voter's ID or a senior school certificate that 'link' you to your parents, the panchayat document was your last resort. Despite rules that attest to a panchayat document's validity, your name still stands excluded. Your son too was not included in the list. His name was spelt differently and carelessly by the officer who made your family tree. You tell me you could not have known of the error beforehand for you cannot read, as cannot the rest of your family. Notwithstanding, your fears have been compounded now that your exclusion has jeopardized the citizenship of all your children anyway.

I ask about your husband. You tell me that with income opportunities in your village dying out, he has migrated to Guwahati to be a construction worker. The police have picked him and his other Bengali-Muslim migrant friends up for 'questioning' a couple times. One of them was deemed a 'doubtful voter' one day. No one in your village knows why.

You have been hearing from your married daughters that with their citizenship under threat now, their relationship with their in-laws has soured. You had barely managed to gather the dowries during their weddings. Your third daughter's engagement is on the verge of breaking. Without education or a fortune to fall back on, she needs a marriage to ensure her social protection—but, 'Who wants a foreigner daughter-in-law?' you ask me. Foreigner, now that the government has insinuated so.

With the gaonbura's help, you filed a claim form against your exclusion. There is so much information that you wish you knew. How can you ensure that your documents are impeccable? How can you identify errors when you cannot

read? There have been rumours in the village that being asked to submit biometrics at the hearing centre implies that you will be sent to a detention camp. Is it true? What will the officer ask you? Who should testify for you?

You show me the notice stating your hearing date and centre. There are so many abbreviations in it—even the gaonbura does not have the answers. The centre is far away from your house and nine of your relatives are listed to testify. You tell me that the hearing day was a difficult one. Your siblings and you had to stay away from your fields and jobs for a long time, as did your children from their schools. Local buses did not go to the centre so you had to hire a minibus for your family. Luckily, a neighbour loaned you the money for it. The hearing was on a hot sunny day, but the centre had no shade for people to rest under. Your niece had to look around for hours to find a place to feed her baby and rest. The news of infants dying at hearing centres had terrified her.

The hearing was in a large room lined with desks. An officer sitting behind each of them. All of them men. There were people everywhere, going from one desk to another in no particular order. Some looking as lost as you did, some scrambling to find papers from their well-worn plastic bags of documents. For a woman who had spent most of her life interacting only with her family and neighbours and with very few men from outside, having to answer to all these strange intimidating men was daunting. When your turn to be heard finally came, you realized that the officer spoke only Assamese and did not understand the Bengali dialect your family spoke. When I ask you how the hearing went, you tell me that you do not know. They wrote down the testimonies from your family, but you are not literate so you could not read them and know what they said before you signed on them. You showed the officer the documents that you thought he was asking for—he seemed to be using different words for them.

'Are you confident about the results?' I ask. 'No,' you say. The officer joked with an insinuation that you were Bangladeshi. He was laughing, so you could not really tell what he meant. You are still worried about whether you had all the right documents. Nevertheless, the official hearing results have not come out yet.

Now we wait.

'Are you afraid?' I ask. 'Yes,' you say.

'Why?'

'They will take us to detention centres.'

You tell me about your neighbour who is a 'declared foreigner'. Although her parents and she have lived their entire lives in this area, she now lives in hiding, unable to work for a living or take care of her family. What happens to women when they are taken away? What happens to families when the sole breadwinner is taken away? What happens to families that have to spend years and money they do not have to challenge their disenfranchisement in the courts? After he was taken away from the market by the border police three years ago, your friend did not see her father until his body was sent back home for his funeral. The old man died in the detention centre. There is now a saying in the region—when they take you away, you are a foreigner; but when you die, your corpse is Indian to be interred.

~

Most social workers working with the Bengali-Muslims in the *char-chapori* region of Assam observe that a majority of those left out of the NRC are women (lack of transparency at the State's end prevents us from finding out the actual numbers). This State-created statelessness has brought about a combination of vulnerabilities to these women. While exclusion from the list disenfranchises them and erodes the already thin layer of social protection they enjoy, the process of fighting their exclusion itself is particularly challenging. The system's failure to take into account their realities—such as poor education and literacy, early migration due to marriage, and life in a fragile ecology that adversely affect the thoroughness of their documentation—has resulted in women being the primary targets of this project. The process further goes on to ignore the experiences of women (and other gender minorities and the disabled) during the claims process which makes it particularly arduous for those affected and is therefore systemically discriminatory over and beyond the exclusionary agenda of the NRC process.

This narrative is based on the information gathered during my fieldwork as part of the Karwan-e-Mohabbat from 1 to 6 July 2019, in Kamrup and Barpeta, Assam. All incidents in this narrative are based on true events and testimonials.

PART TWO

The Bitter Trail of Citizenship Contestation in Assam

CITIZENSHIP IN INDIA AND ASSAM

Mihika Chanchani and Varna Balakrishnan

There has been a flood of debate and interrogation around the changing nature of citizenship in India starting with the tortuous process of the National Register of Citizens (NRC) in Assam, which paved the way for the Citizenship Amendment Act (CAA), 2019.

The Assam NRC has embedded within it a reimagination of who is an Indian citizen, how they must prove this, as well as how their relationship with the State will play out in the future. It has become increasingly clear that these measures embody a move away from the holistic all-encompassing foundations of citizenship enshrined in the Constitution to a system that is exclusionary and imposes the burden of proof of membership to the nation on ordinary people, disproportionately impacting Muslims. The completion of the long, expensive and traumatic NRC exercise in Assam excluded 1.9 million people from the final list.[1] This then opens them up to an appeals process in the Foreigners' Tribunal (FT) and the prospect, hanging like the sword of Damocles over their heads, of even spending long years in a detention centre.

This background note attempts to briefly trace the evolution of citizenship in India, and specifically in Assam, to understand how the NRC process has caused a re-imagination of citizenship. Many articles in this volume draw on the evolution of citizenship through amendments to the Citizenship Act as well as the origins of the NRC in Assam to make various arguments. This piece is intended to serve as a brief explainer of the various developments so that readers may have some context that will enrich their understanding of the many analyses in this volume. It will first trace the changes to citizenship in India through the various amendments to the Citizenship Act, 1955, to show that there has been a steady contraction of the boundaries of Indian citizenship from its foundational imagination. Then we look at how citizenship was shaped in Assam. Finally, we will look at the idea of an 'illegal migrant' in India and what implications it has for ordinary people.

EVOLUTION OF CITIZENSHIP IN INDIA

Citizenship has been central to the understanding of a nation-state from its very inception. Citizenship or the lack thereof created the boundaries within which social and political life is governed. Everything from who was awarded protection within the State, to how different entities within the State would interact with one another, and whether a particular State was responsible for the well-being of a person would involve a question of that person's formal relationship with the State, their citizenship. Historically, citizenship was a mark of belonging and commitment to a specific place and the rights and responsibilities of citizenship were performed in this civic context.[2] However, the processes of globalization, modernization and the ways in which they have played out in specific contexts have led to a conflation of the boundaries between citizenship and nationality, between 'descent'/blood ties and civic and political membership, which has led to great terrors, historically and in our own time.[3] It is within this context that we must examine citizenship and its evolution in India. The process of post-Independence State formation in India, which was heavily influenced by the experience of colonization and Partition, had a significant impact on how citizenship was understood in the Constituent Assembly.[4] Similarly, further developments in the social, political, economic and electoral outcomes of India influenced the boundaries of citizenship.

It is worth mentioning here that 'citizenship', much like many ideas, is one of the most heavily debated and contested fields in the social sciences. Although the field of citizenship studies is vast and varied, the tensions of citizenship are often expressed through normatively loaded binaries, such as 'good' or 'bad' citizenship; active and passive citizenship; thin and thick citizenship; top-down and bottom-up citizenship, universal and group-differentiated citizenship; legal and substantive citizenship, etc.,[5] when, in fact, these categories are hardly clear-cut and the complexities of citizenship in India encompass all these categories at the same time. For this article, we are primarily focusing on how the legal boundaries of citizenship have changed through various amendments.

There have been many amendments to the Citizenship Act, 1955. In this section, we will only be talking about the most significant ones in terms of changing the basic criteria for citizenship. There were several amendments (for example in 2015) that are not mentioned here as they do not deal directly with the methods of being granted or acquiring citizenship.

Citizenship at the Commencement of the Constitution, 1950 and Citizenship Act, 1955

> 'The mere fact of birth in India invests with it the right of citizenship in India... We have taken a cosmopolitan view and it is in accordance with the spirit of the times, with the temper and atmosphere which we wish to promote in the civilized world.'
>
> —Govind Ballabh Pant, Home Minister, while introducing the Citizenship Bill in Parliament on 5 August 1955

Citizenship at the commencement of the Republic was an encompassing moment, rooted in the shared identity of a sovereign self-governing people having come together as a community of equals with an overarching 'national identity' which embraced the entire national community as well as each member of the political community. After long and heated debate in the Constituent Assembly, the distinction between the Indian citizen, as someone who enjoys certain rights and duties within the territory of India, and the non-citizen (alien) thus became effective on 26 January 1950.

The Indian Constitution doesn't prescribe a permanent provision relating to who is eligible for citizenship in India. It simply describes categories of persons who are deemed to be citizens of India on the day the Indian Constitution was promulgated on 26 January 1950, and leaves citizenship to be regulated by law made by the Parliament. Article 11 of the Constitution confers power on the Parliament to make laws regarding citizenship. The Indian Citizenship Act, 1955 was enacted in exercise of this provision.

The Citizenship Act formally came into force in 1955 and cited the claim to citizenship under the inclusive *jus soli* (by birth) principle, which meant anyone born in the territory of the country is an Indian citizen.

The Act provides for acquisition of Indian citizenship in the following ways:

1. *Citizenship by birth*. Anyone born in India on or after 1 January 1950 would be deemed a citizen by birth. This limit was further amended to include those born between 1 January 1950 and 1 July 1987.
2. *Citizenship by descent*. A person born outside India shall be deemed to be a citizen of India if either of the person's parents was a citizen of India at the time of his/her birth provided that the birth is registered within one year of its occurrence or commencement of the Act, whichever is later, at the Indian consulate.
3. *Citizenship by registration*. A person may be registered as a citizen of India, if the person is married to a citizen of India or has been a resident of India for five years immediately before making an application for registration.
4. *Citizenship by naturalization*. A person is granted a certificate of naturalization if the person is not an illegal migrant and has resided in India for 12 months before making an application to seek the certificate.

Of the 14 years preceding this 12-month duration, the person must have stayed in India for 11 years.

5. *Citizenship by incorporation of territory.* If any new territory becomes a part of India, the Government of India shall specify the persons of the territory to be citizens of India.[6]

It is therefore clear that at its outset, legal citizenship in India was envisioned as an open, all-encompassing system. Citizenship by birth, at least in theory, ensured that all within the newly created territory of India would be guaranteed equal protections and provisions by the State.

The Citizenship (Amendment) Act, 1986

> 'The time has come to tighten up our citizenship laws... We cannot be generous at the cost of our own people, at the cost of our own development.'
>
> —P. Chidambaram, Union Minister of State for Home Affairs, while introducing the Citizenship (Amendment) Bill in the Lok Sabha on 10 November 1986[7]

The social and political scenario had changed in India from 1955 to 1986. The specific history and context in relation to Assam under which this amendment was introduced will be discussed in the next section. However, it is important to note that the amendment in 1986 was said to have been introduced within the context of a large influx of 'illegal immigrants' from Bangladesh and Sri Lanka, Pakistan and some African countries that was causing cultural and political upheaval in India's border states.

The amendment completely altered the citizenship by birth or *jus soli* (right of soil) clause to citizenship by descent or *jus sanguinis* (right of blood). 'A person born in India on or after 1 July 1987 is a citizen of India if either parent was a citizen of India at the time of the birth.'[8] The Bill also tightened the screws further on other provisions of the Citizenship Act by raising, substantially, the qualifying periods of stay within India for grant of citizenship by registration, marriage or naturalization. It also changed the definition of 'Indian origin' by excluding from its purview those people whose grandparents, but not parents, were born in India.

The Citizenship (Amendment) Act, 2003

The 2003 amendment introduced two significant changes to the legal provisions of citizenship in India.

A person would be considered a citizen of India if they were born in India

- i) on or after the 26th day of January 1950, but before the 1st day of July 1987;
- ii) on or after the 1st day of July 1987, but before the commencement of the Citizenship (Amendment) Act, 2003 and either of whose parents is a citizen of India at the time of his birth;
- iii) on or after the commencement of the Citizenship (Amendment) Act, 2003, where:
  - a) both of his parents are citizens of India; or
  - b) *one of whose parents is a citizen of India and the other is not an illegal migrant at the time of his birth.*[9]

The 2003 amendment further reduced the accessibility of citizenship by encoding that neither parent could be an 'illegal migrant' at the time of birth. Citizenship by birth had been done away with already in 1986, but now citizenship by descent was tied to 'illegal migration'. This was a significant development, which will be further discussed in a later section of this paper.

The second significant development in the 2003 amendment was the introduction of a version of dual/transnational citizenship for Persons of Indian Origin (PIOs), in the form of 'Overseas Indian Citizenship'. Under the amended Act, an

Overseas Citizen of India (OCI) is a person who is of Indian origin and citizen of a specified country or was a citizen of India immediately before becoming a citizen of another country (on a specified list) and is registered as an OCI by the Central government. The categorization of OCI awarded a person with some special provisions though without being awarded political rights within the country.[10]

At the same time as the access to citizenship was becoming more exclusionary for large sections of India's population through the 'illegal migrant' clause, it was also becoming inclusionary for some through the OCI clause. Inevitably, for those whose parents had migrated from neighbouring countries, probably in search of better economic and social opportunities, the 2003 amendment set in stone their inability to access provisions and services from the State and set in motion a series of events that would eventually lead to the NRC in Assam and possibly in the entire country—the source of all their trauma and distress. Others, who had willingly chosen another country as their home, the Indian State was welcoming with open arms, revealing an underlying class bias on who is welcome and who isn't.

The Citizenship (Amendment) Act, 2019

The Citizenship (Amendment) Act, 2019 was passed by the Parliament of India on 11 December 2019. It amended the Citizenship Act, 1955 by providing a path to Indian citizenship for illegal migrants of Hindu, Sikh, Buddhist, Jain, Parsi and Christian religious minorities who had fled persecution in Pakistan, Bangladesh and Afghanistan before December 2014. Muslims from those countries were not given such eligibility.

It becomes clear from this brief glimpse into how citizenship evolved in India that over time the all-encompassing foundations of who could be considered Indian were slowly diluted to a formulation of a smaller and smaller community. How it turned from a State that accepted all born within its territory as citizens to one that placed the burden of belonging on ordinary people. From an inclusive citizenship model to a selectively exclusive one.

CITIZENSHIP IN ASSAM: AN OVERVIEW

The Contested Nature of the Region

The Citizenship Act of 1955, as we have seen, framed citizenship in India largely through the lens of birth within Indian territory, and it laid out the avenues through which one could become a citizen. However, the evolution of citizenship in the Assam context shows us how this understanding of citizenship became increasingly coloured not only by questions of descent but also by the identification of the non-citizen. Defining who the 'illegal immigrant' was had become crucial to identifying who the native Assamese was, and therefore who a legitimate Indian citizen was. The evolution of citizenship in Assam has also simultaneously been a contest between the Indian State and Assamese sub-nationalism. People believed that Assam state's 'relationship of dependency' with the Indian Union was affecting the state negatively.[11] To understand citizenship in Assam, therefore, it is imperative to look at its evolution since the Citizenship Act of 1955.

The geographical region of Assam has seen several waves of immigration since the nineteenth century, when the region was under colonial administration and the subcontinent was undivided. In the nineteenth century, the British settled farmers from the present-day regions of West Bengal and Bangladesh (among others) to the uncultivated regions in lower Assam. Further waves of immigration corresponded with the Partition of the subcontinent in 1947 and the Bangladesh Liberation War of 1971 when significant numbers of Bengalis—Muslims and Hindus—settled in the region.[12] This created space for a long-drawn-out political conflict on linguistic lines. In the late nineteenth century, the British efforts to promote Bengali as the official language of the region, and therefore the language of economic opportunity, was met with resistance from the Assamese intelligentsia and middle class, which grew into a form of ethnic sub-nationalism in the twentieth century. The modern-day discourse on citizenship in Assam, centred on linguistic sovereignty, migration and a movement to eliminate 'illegal immigrants' from the electoral rolls of the state, gathered momentum and organization in the 1979–85 Assam Movement.[13]

The Assam Movement

The Government of Assam website describes the Assam Movement, which began in 1979, as a 'historic' 'student-led' movement, primarily led by the All Assam Students' Union (AASU) and the All Assam Gana Sangram Parishad (AAGSP).[14] At the core of the movement was the issue of illegal immigration, particularly the government's policies on the admission and enfranchisement of migrants. AASU's call to action therefore was to mitigate 'continuous immigration' which had come to 'affect all walks of life' before it got too late. It demanded that the Central government take steps to identify and deport illegal immigrants.[15]

To this end, they further made a call to review the electoral rolls. The issue of illegal immigration created a sense of insecurity among the Assamese with regard to changes in demography, access to resources, language, land and employment. Increasing unemployment and poverty within the resource-rich state added to people's disgruntlement, too.[16]

During the period of agitation, Assam underwent significant political instability, with the previous state elections cancelled, the state put under President's rule and Lok Sabha elections cancelled retrospectively.[17] The period was also characterized by significant ethnic conflict where thousands were killed, including 3,000 people during the 1983 elections.[18]

It was in this context that the Illegal Migrants (Determination by Tribunals) (IMDT) Act, 1983 was passed, applicable for the state of Assam alone. The Act dictated that anyone who could not prove that they or their ancestors entered India before 23 March 1971 (the eve of the Bangladesh Liberation War), would be liable to deportation.[19] Under the Act, people could report suspected illegal immigrants to FTs, with the burden of proof falling on the person reporting (applicant).[20] It was therefore up to the person/state organization raising the report to prove that their suspicion of someone being an illegal immigrant was grounded in evidence. This was a long and tedious process, under which the Tribunals identified and declared very few people as foreigners.[21] This became a point of contention and dissatisfaction among the Assamese, considering it did not serve the demands of their agitation and because it was formulated by a Parliament in which they were underrepresented. On the other hand, members of the Muslim community believed that such a rigorous process was crucial to safeguard genuine Muslim citizens from the harassment which had become widespread as the Assam Movement gathered momentum.[22]

The largest political agitation to ascertain the nature of the true citizen in Assam was, in this way, defined by a quest to find out who it was not. The IMDT Act in practice altered the understanding of citizenship in Assam by making the 'illegal immigrant' central to the current and future formulations of the 'legal citizen'. The Assam Movement formally ended with the signing of the Assam Accord on 15 August 1985. This agreement, signed between Rajiv Gandhi and the leaders of the movement, demanded the expulsion and disenfranchisement of the 'foreigners'.[23] Beyond this, it promised 'constitutional, legislative, and administrative safeguards...to protect, preserve, and promote the cultural, social, linguistic identity and heritage of the Assamese people' and 'all round economic development' of the state.[24]

The Accord was crucial in changing the face of citizenship in

Assam. It introduced a hierarchized model of citizenship where a large number of immigrants who had come before 1966 were legitimized; those who came between January 1966 and 25 March 1971 could be naturalized after being disenfranchised for ten years; and those who had entered after 25 March 1971 were to be deported as illegals. Anupama Roy and U.K. Singh (2009) note that 'while the Assamese people, whose claim to citizenship was beyond any legal dispute, constituted the abstract universal citizen in the State, the migrant, marked out by her or his linguistic and religious difference occupied a residual zone of ambivalent citizenship'.

The ideologies championed by the Assam Movement and reflected in the Accord were finally legalized with the Citizenship (Amendment) Act of 1986, where a new part, Article 6A, was added to Article 6 of the Citizenship Act, which focuses on migration.[25] Article 6A is bespoke to Assam, reflecting the hierarchized citizenship enshrined in the Accord. The Act stipulated that to be a citizen of India, it was no longer enough to have been born in Indian territory—at the time of one's of birth, either one of the parents also had to be a citizen of India. A subsequent amendment to the Citizenship Act in 2003 gave lineage equal standing to place of birth, stipulating that to be an Indian citizen, one had to be both born in Indian territory and be the child of two Indian citizens, neither of whom are even doubted to be illegal immigrants.

Citing the 'inefficiency' of the IMDT Act in tracking and deporting illegal immigrants, several Assamese people campaigned for its repeal. This includes a petition filed by Sarbananda Sonowal, who argued that the provisions of the Act were so stringent that it made it practically impossible for it to deliver its end.[26] Finally, in 2005, the Supreme Court struck down the Act. With this, the duty of identifying illegal immigrants was transferred back to Tribunals functioning under the Foreigners Act of 1946—this meant that the burden of proof (of proving citizenship) now fell on the accused, and not the State. This in effect meant presumption of guilt, until proven otherwise—with the accused person having to furnish proof of their Indian citizenship. Apart from providing the basis for the process today, this judgment called illegal immigration a form of 'external aggression' to the Indian State, and thus amalgamated narratives of (in)security, criminality and national sovereignty with migration.

The current process of NRC verification and compilation and identification of illegal immigrants follows the 2009 Amendment to the Citizenship (Registration of Citizens and Issue of National Identity Cards) Rules, 2003 which added Section 4A specifically for Assam. The new rules direct the state of Assam to undertake processes to collect and verify documents from all residents of Assam to prepare the NRC, with the 1951 NRC and electoral rolls prior to 1971 as the basis.[27]

In August 2019, the Supreme Court further ruled that children born after 3 December 2004 are not eligible to be included in the NRC if either one of their parents are a 'doubtful voter' (DV), a 'declared foreigner' (DF) or a 'person with cases pending at the foreigner's tribunal' (PFT).[28] Along with the primacy given to lineage in the definition of citizenship, this order makes lineage crucial in the processes of disenfranchisement as well, highlighting the intergenerational effect of the NRC process.

How Do the People of Assam Become Indian Citizens?

The evolution of the idea of citizenship, as we have seen, is a combination of the complexities of Assamese ethnic identity and the perceived threat of illegal migrants. It is also a narrative of negotiation between the conception of citizenship for the Indian State and the sub-national identity of the ethnic Assamese. Given this, who is an Assamese citizen?

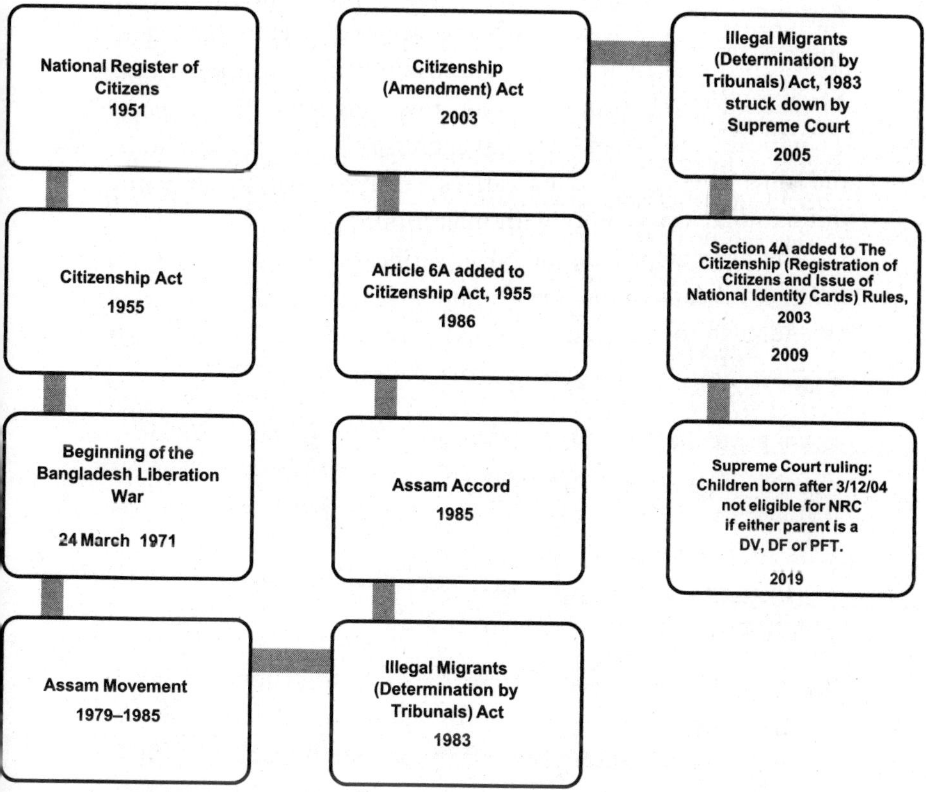

Figure 1. Chronological flow of events pertaining to citizenship in Assam.

1. One who has their or their parent's or grandparent's name in the 1951 NRC?
2. One who has their or their parent's or grandparent's name in the voter's rolls prior to 23 March 1971?
3. One who, if born after 2003, was born on Indian soil to two Indian citizens?
4. One who, if born after 3 December 2004, was born on Indian soil, and neither of their parents are currently a DV, DF or PFT?

This discussion about the evolution of citizenship in Assam lays bare one of the largest conundrums with respect to a pan-India NRC. Like Assam, several regions within the Indian subcontinent have a syncretic history marked by several flows of migration. If the quest to find the 'true Indian citizen' was justified at all, how would you still find them? Which events in history would determine it, who determines legitimate and illegitimate migration, and how do we create a uniform understanding of 'original ancestry' across a country so historically diverse as India?

The Citizen and the Migrant: The Citizenship (Amendment) Act, 2019

Even as these questions stand unanswered, the narrative of citizenship (and its lack thereof) in India continues to evolve through the changes engendered by the Citizenship Amendment Act, 2019.

In the Citizenship Act of 1955, 'illegal migrant' is defined as a foreigner who has entered India[29]

i) without a valid passport or other travel documents; or
ii) with a valid passport or other travel documents but remains therein beyond the permitted period of time.

The 2019 Act provides citizenship to persecuted members of minority communities like Hindus, Sikhs, Buddhists, Jains and Parsis coming from Afghanistan, Pakistan and Bangladesh.[30] It allows non-Muslim minorities who have entered Assam between 1 January 1966 and 24 March 1974 a chance of permanent citizenship by decreasing the naturalization period from 11 to six years.[31]

The discussion surrounding the Act exposes considerable inconsistencies in the Indian State's conception of a citizen, of migration and of asylum seekers, explored in various articles across this book. We have already seen how the boundaries of Indian citizenship have largely evolved from birth to descent and we have seen how the identification of the 'illegal immigrant' or the non-citizen was crucial to this. The CAA takes this further by relying on religion to determine which immigrant is to be welcomed and which to be turned away, and who can be naturalized as an Indian citizen, consequently mistaking the country's citizenship regime for its refugee and asylum policy. The Assam Movement, even though marked by ethnic sub-nationalism, was primarily not a movement based on religion. The question of religion, however, has a crucial impact on the NRC process, considering the fact that the majority of those who have been excluded so far are Muslims—the very group that the CAA also excludes. This positioning of religion as a determinant of citizenship and asylum is a reflection of the biases laden within the institutional structures.

At the time of writing this paper, around 19 lakh individuals stand excluded from the NRC in Assam, there are objections filed against the inclusion of nearly two lakh individuals, thousands are incarcerated in 'detention centres' and many have lost (or given up) their lives in the struggle to retain their citizenship. As they wait for the FTs to determine their fate, this process has clearly laid out that those defined as 'illegal immigrants' in India are not only those who have entered the territory of India without correct documentation, but also those who just do not have the documents or resources to prove their citizenship. Above and beyond failing to create an ethical and compassionate understanding of migration and refugees, we have also reduced the scope of Indian citizenship to one defined by documentation, and ignorant to historical complexities and social realities.

Notes

1. 'Assam final NRC list released: 19,06,657 people excluded, 3.11 crore make it to citizenship list', *India Today*, 31 August 2019.
2. L. Desforges, R. Jones and M. Woods, 'New geographies of citizenship', *Citizenship Studies*, vol. 9, no. 5 (2005), pp. 439–51.
3. Anupama Roy, *Mapping Citizenship in India*, New Delhi: Oxford University Press, 2010.
4. For a better understanding of the Constituent Assembly debates

around citizenship in relation to minorities refer to Anirban Bhattacharya's article in Part 3 of this volume.

5. Niraja Gopal Jayal, *Citizenship and Its Discontents: An Indian History*, Cambridge, MA: Harvard University Press, 2013.
6. Shruti Jain, 'Explained: The nuts and bolts of Indian citizenship', *The Wire*, 19 December 2019.
7. Tania Midha, 'Citizenship Bill: Tightening Act', *India Today*, 15 December 1986.
8. Citizenship (Amendment) Act, 1986 (see http://www.parliament.gov.sb/files/legislation/Acts/1986/THE%20CITIZENSHIP%20(AMENDMENT)%20ACT%201986.pdf, last accessed 20 June 2021).
9. Citizenship (Amendment) Act, 2003 (see https://indiankanoon.org/doc/949775/).
10. Ibid.
11. Anupama Roy and Ujjwal Kumar Singh, 'The ambivalence of citizenship: The IMDT Act (1983) and the politics of forclusion in Assam', *Critical Asian Studies*, vol. 41, no. 1 (March 2009), pp. 37–60.
12. Abhijit Dasgupta, 'On the margins: Muslims in West Bengal', *Economic and Political Weekly*, vol. 44, no. 16 (2009), pp. 91–96.
13. While concerns about illegal immigrants were present in Assam already, they were amplified and brought to the forefront with the revision of electoral rolls for the Mangladai parliamentary constituency by-election in 1979 which showed an extraordinary increase in the number of voters since the previous election. In the process of revision, objections were raised against 70,000 people of whom 45,000 were declared foreigners under the Foreigners Act, 1946 and the Rules of 1964. See Roy and Singh, 'The ambivalence of citizenship'.
14. 'Martyrs of Assam Agitation', Implementation of Assam Accord, official website of the Government of Assam (see https://assamaccord.assam.gov.in/information-services/martyrs-of-assam-agitation).
15. Sanjib Baruah, 'Immigration, ethnic conflict, and political turmoil—Assam, 1979–1985', *Asian Survey*, vol. 26, no. 11 (1986), pp. 1184–206.
16. Roy and Singh, 'The ambivalence of citizenship'.
17. The Election Commission cancelled the Lok Sabha elections of 1980 in 12 out 14 parliamentary seats, because of which Assam

was under-represented in the Parliament. With the annulment of the 1978 state Assembly elections in 1982, the state came under the administration of the Central government under President's Rule. The state election held subsequently in 1983 was largely considered illegal by AASU and others, since it was done under a wide clampdown on press freedom and the deployment of paramilitary forces. See Roy and Singh, 'The ambivalence of citizenship'.

18. Massacre in Nellie, a Muslim-dominated region in the southern banks of the Brahmaputra in Lower Assam. The Government of Assam currently provides compensation to the 'martyrs of the Assam agitation'. See Baruah, 'Immigration, ethnic conflict, and political turmoil'.
19. Sruthisagar Yamunan, 'How the Supreme Court's hardline stance on citizenship deepened the flaws in Assam's NRC', *Scroll.in*, 31 July 2019.
20. Under the Foreigners Act, 1946, under which this matter would have been otherwise, the burden of proof would have been on the person who has been suspected of being an illegal immigrant.
21. A special unit of the Assam police, a Special Branch Organisation under the PIP scheme (Prevention of Infiltration from Pakistan), the Border Police, instituted in 1962, with the sole responsibility of identifying and deporting illegal immigrants also plays a significant role in referring 'illegal immigrants' to the Foreigners' Tribunals. See Aman Wadud's chapter 'Understanding the Foreigners' Tribunal' included in Part 2 of this volume.
22. Roy and Singh, 'The ambivalence of citizenship'.
23. Baruah, 'Immigration, ethnic conflict, and political turmoil'.
24. Roy and Singh, 'The ambivalence of citizenship'.
25. Specifically, Partition induced migration.
26. Sonowal, a member of the Assam Assembly, was the former chief minister of Assam and also a former president of AASU. See Yamunan, 'How the Supreme Court's hardline stance on citizenship deepened the flaws in Assam's NRC'.
27. See Section 4A in The Citizenship (Registration of Citizens and Issue of National Identity Cards) Rules, 2003 (https://indiankanoon.org/doc/148758105/).
28. 'Assam: Children born after Dec 3, 2004 not to be included in NRC if any of the parent is a "D" voter, declared foreigner or pending case', *Live Law News Network*, 13 August 2019.
29. See Section 2(1)(b) of The Citizenship Act, 1955 (https://www.

indiacode.nic.in/bitstream/123456789/4210/1/Citizenship_Act_1955.pdf, last accessed 20 June 2021).

30. Proviso to Section 2(1)(b) of The Citizenship Act, 1955: 'Provided that persons belonging to minority communities, namely, Hindus, Sikhs, Buddhists, Jains, Parsis and Christians from Afghanistan, Bangladesh and Pakistan, who have been exempted by the Central Government by or under clause (c) of sub-section (2) of section 3 of the Passport (Entry into India) Act, 1920 or from the application of the provisions of the Foreigners Act, 1946 or any order made thereunder, shall not be treated as illegal migrants for the purposes of that Act: Provided further that on and from the date of commencement of the Citizenship (Amendment) Act, 2019, any proceeding pending against any person referred to in the first proviso shall be abated and such person shall be eligible to apply for naturalization under section 6.'
31. Proviso to Clause (d), Third Schedule of The Citizenship Act, 1955: 'Provided that for the persons belonging to minority communities, namely, Hindus, Sikhs, Buddhists, Jains, Parsis and Christians from Afghanistan, Bangladesh and Pakistan, the aggregate period of residence or service of a Government in India as required under this clause shall be read as "not less than six years" in place of "not less than eleven years".'

Land, Culture and Migration

WRITE DOWN, I AM A MIYA

Hafiz Ahmed

Write
Write down
I am a Miya
My serial number in the NRC is 200543
I have two children
Another is coming
Next summer.
Will you hate him
As you hate me?

Write
I am a Miya
I turn waste, marshy lands
To green paddy fields
To feed you.
I carry bricks
To build your buildings
Drive your car
For your comfort
Clean your drain
To keep you healthy.
I have always been
In your service
And yet
you are dissatisfied!
Write down
I am a Miya,
A citizen of a democratic, secular, Republic
Without any rights
My mother a D-voter,
Though her parents are Indian.

Write
I am a Miya
Of the Brahmaputra
Your torture
Has burnt my body black
Reddened my eyes with fire.
Beware!
I have nothing but anger in stock.
Keep away!
Or
Turn to ashes.

GROWING UP MIYA IN ASSAM

HOW THE NRC WEAPONIZED MY IDENTITY AGAINST ME

Abdul Kalam Azad

It has been more than a year since my three-year-old son started attending preschool. Like many other parents, I was nervous on his first day—I was worried that he might not be able to get along with his classmates—but as he spent more time without us, I slowly felt pride and then happiness. That first day, when he came out through the preschool's narrow gate, his eyes were teary and he looked frightened. I hugged him. His tears disappeared soon enough, and he began telling me about his day.

He has settled down now. He has many friends. Every day, he has a new story to tell. In the living room of our rented house he often plays with our landlord's young daughter. They sometimes sing together: '*Bilote halise dhunia podumi phool*'—In the pond a lotus sways. I never had the flawless Assamese pronunciation that he has already acquired in the first three years of his life. Listening to him, I feel immensely proud.

But when I look at him, I also feel immense fear.

I am reminded of my own childhood. My father never told me that the world outside his warmth and protection would be hostile to me. This only became apparent to me when I first visited Guwahati. It was here that I first realized that I have another identity, a subordinate identity—I was a *Miya*, a Bengali-origin Muslim, seen in Assam as an outsider, a suspected Bangladeshi.

Every year, a large number of people from my native place in Barpeta district of western Assam migrate seasonally to

This article first appeared in *The Caravan* on 23 September 2018.

Guwahati to work odd jobs in the unorganized sector. When I was 14 years old, I went to see the city and write a homework essay on how I spent my summer break. Late one afternoon, my uncle Sirajul Haque and I were waiting to cross a busy road in Guwahati's Lalganesh area. My uncle, who was then in his forties, had not been keeping well for two days, and had been unable to ply his rickshaw.

A group of young men stood nearby. They asked him to help push start a vehicle. My uncle began telling them about his health. The words had barely left his mouth when the young men began cursing at him. They called him '*Kela Miya*' and 'Bangladeshi' while kicking him. My middle-aged uncle pleaded for mercy with folded hands, but the young men did not relent. I was scared and fled the scene. I ran down a dark lane and disappeared, reaching the rented tenement where we were staying. Uncle too returned after a while. He didn't go to the pharmacy. As my other relatives prepared the evening meal, he lay in one corner and would not speak to anyone. He could not eat properly. I also kept quiet, and did not tell anyone about the incident. I could not sleep that night. Whenever I closed my eyes, the image of my uncle played again and again, like a motion picture.

I came back to my village with a heavy heart. I could not write that essay. For some reason, I resolved that day that I would continue to study, at any cost. I wanted to be Assamese—a better *Axomiya* then anyone else, whose identity could not be questioned by anyone. I learned the language. I imbibed the cuisine. I immersed myself in the tunes of *Bihu* songs. I did not realize when this became my life's biggest mission—from my classroom to my workplace, from my emotions to my imagination, my focus was to be Axomiya.

But every so often, I would be reminded that my efforts to be Axomiya were not enough. My accent was not pure—I was reminded that the dialect I spoke at home was 'filthy'. I was warned that my lungi could not be a part of Axomiya identity. I was reminded that my ancestors were not the sons and daughters of this soil.

Sometimes these warnings were violent—either verbal or physical—but sometimes, they were devoid of any action. I studied law for a few years at Assam University in Silchar, although I was unable to complete the course due to financial constraints. Silchar, a town in the Barak valley, is known as the heartland for Bengali nationalism in Assam. One day, I met an Assamese senior in the hostel. We introduced ourselves. When I told him where I lived—an address in the Barpeta district—he nonchalantly replied, '*Oh, tumi Miya?*'—You're a Miya? When I said yes, he silently walked away down the stairs, as if uninterested in talking to a Miya. I could not move for a few moments. I never had the courage to talk to him again.

I often wonder what makes him—and others like him—so powerful, and me so vulnerable. I ask myself why I felt subordinate in the first place. Why did I not revolt against the young men who punched my uncle? Why didn't I kick them back? What made me think the quality of their Assamese accent, the language and culture they possess is superior? What compelled me to think that without imitating their way of life, I could not be a dignified Assamese? Why can't my accent, my dialect, my costume and culture be a part of the greater Assamese identity?

The answer lies in the century-long histories of oppression, persecution and production of unlimited fear. Miya Muslims like me are not part of the Assamese vision which begins and ends with the indigenous Axomiyas. Though we have been living and working on this land for centuries—often for the so-called indigenous Axomiyas—we are not to be allowed in. This xenophobia has been formalized in the National Register of Citizens (NRC), which threatens to delegitimize any person who cannot prove their credentials to the satisfaction of the Axomiya state. It has weaponized all aspects of our identity, using them to keep us out of our own state and nation.

~

My uncle, who was abused by the so-called sons of the soil, has lost his soil to the erosion of the river Beki, one of the ferocious tributaries of the mighty Brahmaputra. Every year in Assam, thousands of people living on the *chars*—riverine islands—and along riverbanks, mostly Miya Muslims, get uprooted because of erosion. The Brahmaputra and its tributaries swell during the rains, swallowing parts of the chars and leaving their residents with no choice but to move inland. In any other part of the country, the victims of such erosion would be likely to receive compensation and rehabilitation from the government, or at least ask for it. In 1995, my uncle lost his land to the river and shifted to our village, hardly three kilometres from his previous home. Instead of a rehabilitation grant, he was served a notice by the Foreigners' Tribunal (FT), asking him to prove his Indian nationality.

He was not the only person in the family whose identity fell under suspicion after they moved inland. His elder brother, who also settled in our village along with him, was marked a D-voter—a 'doubtful' voter, suspected of being an illegal Bangladeshi immigrant and required to prove his identity before the Tribunal as well. Though our village is hardly seven kilometres from the district headquarters, it still does not have access to all-weather roads. Throughout the summer and monsoon months, our houses remain surrounded by water. Often, my uncle would call out my name in his loud voice, telling me to come to his house, or he would sail his banana raft across the water to come to ours. We would discuss the progress of their cases. In these conversations, he would appear confident in his ability to prove his Indian nationality. But I could see the fear and anxiety on his face.

One Monday, both my uncles went to the FT at the district headquarters to face trial. While they were on their way back, the elder brother suddenly collapsed from a stroke. He died before he could be taken to the hospital.

This is the cost my uncle paid to defend his Indian

citizenship—the life of his elder brother, then five *bighas* of land, which he sold to cover the court expenses. After his brother's death, my uncle became responsible for four more family members. He risked the abuse of being called a Bangladeshi once again and went back to Guwahati to pull a rickshaw so that he could feed his family.

My uncles are not my only relatives to be labelled D-voters. In 1997, nearly four lakh people across the state—mostly Miya Muslims and Bengali Hindus—were marked D-voters. Two members of my extended family made this list—a widowed aunt and another uncle. My aunt became a widow at a very early age. She was already having a tough time looking after her five minor children. Being designated a D-voter only made her more vulnerable, but with indomitable courage and resilience she looked after the family with the meagre income from labouring in the fields. My 'doubtful' uncle has a Master's degree in Economics from Gauhati University and teaches in a government school. During elections, he would perform the duty of a presiding officer, even though he was barred from exercising his voting rights for almost two decades.

'D' is not the only category that haunts my family members and me. A few years ago, personnel from the Assam Police's border unit—which has over 4,000 members, who have the power to ask anyone to prove their identity as Indians, and to refer any citizens to a Tribunal—raided a rented house in Guwahati's Dhirenpara neighbourhood, where residents of my village, who had travelled there to work in the informal sector, were staying. The police asked for their citizenship documents, noted down their names and addresses and took impressions of their fingerprints on blank papers. After almost a year, they started receiving notices from the FT, asking them to prove their citizenship. Among those who received this summons were two of my uncles, and one cousin who sells *jhaalmuri*—a savoury snack prepared with puffed rice—on the streets of Guwahati. My relatives were able to successfully defend their citizenship, but I cannot forget the looks of fear on their faces when they first received the notices.

Compared to many others, my family members were fortunate. Even aside from the D-voters, nearly 2.5 lakh people in the state—most of them poor like my uncles and cousin—have been referred to the FTs under suspicion of being illegal immigrants from Bangladesh. There are cases where government officials, including those from the army, the air force, the border security forces and the police, as well as schoolteachers, have been suspected and referred to the Tribunal. There are cases where one person has been referred to the Tribunal several times, even after the same Tribunal declared them an Indian citizen. The Border Police is never held accountable for such errors, or for inflicting this burden on citizens—it does this work with absolute impunity, guaranteed under the draconian Foreigners Act of 1946.

The Tribunals themselves have become houses of horror for Miya Muslims and Bengali Hindus. The institution is supposed to deliver justice, but has in reality worked like a slaughterhouse, snatching the citizenship and rights of rightful residents of Assam. Like the Border Police, the FTs are a one-of-a-kind system, plying only in Assam. The quasi-judicial body hears the cases of people whose citizenship is doubted by the state. The cases are decided not by judicial officers, but mostly by lawyers appointed as members of the Tribunal on a contractual basis. There are a hundred such tribunals operating across the state. Their members are appointed by the government, remunerated by the government, appraised by the government, and if found unsatisfactory, shown the door by the government. In 2017, 19 members of the Tribunals were removed from office. It has been reported that these members were removed in part because they did not declare enough people 'foreigners', as the Border Police that referred these cases had claimed they were.

According to government records, over 90,000 people have

been declared foreigners, of which more than 26,000 cases were decided by *ex parte* decree in the absence of respondents. Nearly a thousand of them are being held in six makeshift detention centres, housed inside jails across the state.

I visited several of these jails. I went to the detention centres as part of a research contingent—in January 2018, the activist and writer Harsh Mander, then the special monitor of the National Human Rights Commission (NHRC), invited me to join an NHRC mission to examine the due process through which a person is sent to a detention centre, study the centres, and assess the human rights situation of the detainees.

Over these visits, the little hope I had turned into despair. The detention centres are nothing but sections within district jails that have been cordoned off to house those who have been declared foreigners. The detainees are not allowed any formal communication with their relatives. The detainees do not have access to legal recourse such as appeals—the Tribunals do not hear appeals, so the detainees can only file cost-intensive writs in the High Court or the Supreme Court. Inside the detention camps, they live as convicted criminals.

At a camp in Kokrajhar, I met an elderly woman detainee, who couldn't stand straight. With her half-bent body, she crawled towards me, and tried to touch my feet. I stepped back. She rolled on the floor of the camp and began howling, with what seemed like all the might of her skinny body. She begged me for death—a mercy death.

I met a woman whose four-year-old son lives in the camp with her. She told me that when she was brought to the detention centre, he was 14 days old. Since then, the boy hasn't seen the world outside the four walls of the jail.

In the Goalpara detention centre, there were more than 50 actual Bangladeshis. Their circumstances showed how little concern the state has for those it deems foreigners. Some of the people we met had been there for nearly a decade, with little or no contact with the outside world. One of the detainees showed me a torn piece of paper with a Bangladeshi phone number. He had memorized the number five years earlier when he was first brought to the centre, and had now scrawled it on the paper, in the hope that he would one day get to call his family and inform them of his whereabouts. While my community is abused as illegal Bangladeshis on a daily basis, while lakhs of us are stripped of our citizenship rights, thousands arbitrarily declared foreigners and hundreds detained, actual Bangladeshis are dying to go back to their country. The government is taking no steps to make this happen.

~

After I returned from the detention centre, the innocent face of the boy continued to haunt me for a long time. Even now, I imagine my son in his place. The very thought sends a shiver down my spine.

I tried thinking of my visit as a privilege. After all, I had a first-hand experience of the horrors that people from my state were being subjected to. I became hopeful. I worked to document every important detail, so that when the report went to the NHRC and subsequently to my government, it could result in some positive change. My confidence was bolstered by various details that I was privy to—for instance, the mother of the four-year-old child was neither a Miya nor a Bengali Hindu, she belongs to the so-called indigenous Muslim community, a *khati*—pure—Axomiya. I was sure that my chief minister, Sarbananda Sonowal, who has built his political career on the campaign platform of protecting the rights of indigenous Assamese, would not tolerate this gross violation of their human rights.

But I was wrong again. Mander submitted the report to the NHRC, detailing the inhuman conditions of detainees and the procedural drawbacks of the process, as well as suggesting remedies. The NHRC—the highest quasi-judicial body in the country, which is mandated to protect the human rights of every individual, especially disadvantaged groups such as women, children and minorities—did not respond even after repeated follow-ups. This forced Mander to resign from the position of special monitor. He wrote a compassionate essay calling the detention centres 'the dark side of humanity and legality'.

In June, four special rapporteurs of the United Nations Human Rights Council (UNHRC) wrote a letter to the Ministry of External Affairs, expressing alarm and concern at complaints it had received about the exclusionary measures being taken by the NRC authority and the Election Commission. The measures, they feared, would exacerbate the discrimination faced by Miya Muslims and Bengali Hindus, 'who may wrongfully be declared as "foreigners" and consequently rendered stateless' or deprived 'of the right to political participation and representation'.

The letter cast the national spotlight on the NRC process. National and international media, which had so far paid little attention to the issues and concerns of Miya Muslims such as me, began giving us coverage. No doubt there were issues—an entire community, many members of which have lived in Assam for generations and have done everything within their power to assimilate into Assamese society and culture, was referred to simply as 'Bengali', whether Muslim or Hindu. These stories further highlighted the plight of the Assamese-speaking Miya Muslims, especially the role of the FTs and Border Police, or the pathetic conditions of the people living in the chars of Assam.

I expected that this would help bring some justice to the people fighting the biased Tribunals and languishing in detention centres across the state. But the Assamese nationalists had a different plan. A counter-campaign soon ensued in Assamese media, accusing imaginary vested interests of acting against the interests of the state, and attacking human-rights workers such as Mander for attempting to throw a spanner in the works of the NRC.

An error-free NRC is not the demand of only the so-called Assamese nationalists, but also for a Miya like me, whose Assamese identity has always been under question. In July 2010, along with three others, my wife's nephew was killed in police firing. They were protesting against the pilot project of the NRC being conducted. One of the columns in the form led to much anger as it asked for the country of origin. They were demanding an error-free NRC. My community viewed the NRC—a document that would officially grant us our identities—as a weapon with which to fight the humiliation and persecution we faced.

This belief was systematically destroyed as dozens of exclusionary filters were put into the updating process, including the clause of the so-called 'Original Inhabitants' to exclude Miya Muslims and Bengali Hindus. The issue of D-voters could have been solved along with the NRC updating process but excluding the descendants of people deemed foreigners by the Tribunals created more problems.

When someone raises these questions against these exclusionary and discriminatory processes, they become anti-Assamese even in the eyes of the so-called liberal Assamese intellectuals. My liberal Assamese friends accuse me of not being sensitive to the 'threat' they are facing from the supposed large-scale migration from Bangladesh. I almost want to feel this threat, but when I look back at my life, I realize that this threat is me—a Miya.

I think of my mission to be called Axomiya. If I lay claim to Srimanta Sankardev, the architect of modern Assamese society, if I prefer organizing Bihu over an Eid *mehfil*—we stopped celebrating the Bengali New Year over a century ago—if I feel proud when my son sings the songs of the revolutionary Assamese cultural icon Bishnu Rabha, then what threat do I pose? Why do the Assamese chauvinists question my identity despite me having a history of five generations living in this land?

I realize that my Axomiya qualities do not matter. What matters is that I am not them. They are not concerned about deporting illegal immigrants. The 'threat' is not about a threat to the Assamese language or the culture—Miya Muslims like me are a threat to their privilege and supremacy.

I do not know how to explain to them how I feel when I see my mainstream Assamese friends and their children being included in the NRC without having to produce a single document, while our credentials are examined thoroughly. If the NRC process is a test and everybody consented to participate, why is there not a level playing field?

Even our supposed allies appear not to understand. During the Assam Agitation in the 1980s, when the demand to update the NRC became a point of fierce contention, Hiren Gohain was one of the few intellectuals who described the agitation as hollow. An outspoken public intellectual, Gohain is also a fierce critic of the Bharatiya Janata Party's majoritarian rule. But even he couches his descriptions of the suffering of Assam's Muslims with the terms 'seems' and 'maybe'.

Although he said in an interview with *Al Jazeera* that everyone who came to Assam before 1971 should be termed natives of this land, Gohain clarified many things for the people of Assam, especially Miya Muslims, in a recent Assamese-language article. He suggested that Miya Muslims 'should not forget that seeking safety from platoons of police and CRPF [Central Reserve Police Force] is delusional. Their safety and the preservation of their basic day to day life is chiefly dependent on the trust and goodwill of the indigenous people'.

If I understand him correctly, I must console myself that my self-respect, my pride in being Assamese, or even my mere existence in this part of the world, is not only dependent on the trust and goodwill of the indigenous Assamese people but also on their kindness and grace. If the indigenous people do not trust us, Gohain appears to be saying that the world's largest democracy cannot provide us with security or protection.

Gohain is not just another intellectual—for our community, he was the epitome of courage and struggle. When he suggests that we not seek protection and justice from the state and surrender before the supremacy of the indigenous people, I understand why thousands of my community members massacred in Nellie, Nagabanda, Chaolkhuwa, Bahbari, and Khagrabari did not get justice.

Gohain's words, though hurtful, have a kernel of truth—I no longer trust the state to accept that I am Axomiya, to protect my rights. But I will survive. Swallowing abuse and humiliation has made me resilient. I have learnt how to live like a second-grade Axomiya. I only wonder how to prepare my three-year-old son.

THE CRISIS OF CITIZENSHIP IN ASSAM

Sanjay Barbora

Autonomy and social justice are often in a tense relationship in Assam. While the demands for autonomy reflect the desire for territorial control over land, demands for social justice reflect an insistence on citizenship and equality under constitutional law.

My first personal introduction to the flurry of activity that would be associated with the National Register of Citizens (NRC) in Assam was in June 2015. My partner and I were in Australia for a conference, when my father left several text messages for us to call him. He wanted the exact spelling of my deceased father-in-law's name, as well as the name of his village in Nagaland. 'Where have you both kept your school and college certificates?' he asked when I called. Thus it began, a scramble for documents that would prove that I was indeed a citizen of India, who was from Assam and had a formidable array of evidence as proof. My father explained that my partner's details would be sent to Nagaland and once the administration there verified the details sent to them, she too would be included in the NRC.

That evening, I caught up with an old schoolmate in a Sydney suburb. He, his wife and two primary-school-going daughters were Australian citizens. Over dinner, he told me that his father-in-law in Assam was very excited about the NRC and had been calling him to ensure that his documents were in place. My friend was born and raised in Shillong (Meghalaya) and had spent much of his adult life working outside India, so he was understandably curious about how this excitable rush for documents would play out.

This article first appeared in *The India Forum* on 14 February 2019.

On that chilly winter night in Sydney, he asked me if—like his father-in-law—I thought that the NRC would bring some closure to several decades of tumultuous politics in Assam. My response was non-committal and oblique. Fortified by our class and the fact that we had slowly become better travelled than our parents and Assamese surnames, we could afford to not find an answer to the question on that evening.

However, many others—especially women, indigenous groups, Muslims and those with no easy access to documents and papers—would find it difficult to be evasive about their futures and to avoid critically engaging with the collective future of political mobilization in Assam.

~

Since the announcement of the NRC draft on 30 July 2018, one has had to confront the fact that more than four million people had their names excluded from the list, leading many to commit suicide. This has divided civil society and public opinion vertically. Many student unions and political parties, as well as the administration, attempted to show that there would be no violence in dealing with the aftermath. Other members of civil society and political opinion have pointed out that the exercise itself was faulty and the rhetoric that pushed it was divisive in nature. Political commentators, advocacy groups and public intellectuals have spent considerable time and energy in persuading those who disagree with their view of the soundness of their positions.

To muddle matters for observers and activists outside the region, the Citizenship Amendment Bill (CAB) of 2016 that grants citizenship to all minorities from India's neighbouring Muslim-majority countries was passed by the lower house of Parliament on 8 January 2019. Organizations that welcomed the NRC came out in opposition to the Bill, while many who were opposed to the NRC, especially in the Barak valley, supported the enactment of the Bill. Civil society remained polarized along linguistic and regional lines even after the Bill was allowed to lapse in the upper house of Parliament on 13 February 2019. Bengali-speaking Hindus, especially in the Barak valley, felt betrayed by the government's cynical mobilization of communitarian politics, while most indigenous communities celebrated collective victory in the aftermath. But because the Bill failed to be passed in the upper house or Rajya Sabha, it lapsed when the term of the Union government ended in May 2019. However, after being re-elected, the Bill was reintroduced and passed by both houses of Parliament on 11 December 2019.

In Assam, the NRC was seen to be the legal and political way to address the two issues that have influenced political mobilization in the state since the mid-twentieth century: autonomy and social justice. The Citizenship Act, on the other hand, was seen as a reiteration of a peculiar colonial relationship between Assam and the rest of India, periodically emphasized by the disregard for political opinions of Assamese and indigenous people. While the demands for autonomy reflect the desire for territorial control over land, demands around issues of social justice reflect an insistence on citizenship and equality under constitutional law. Both issues have a very tense relationship with one another. They have led to decades of violent conflict, where the State has used a combination of military subjugation and co-optation of voices of dissent to deal with the situation.

Hence, political commentators and representatives of civic and political organizations have had a difficult time explaining to the rest of the country and the world why they have either supported or opposed a Supreme Court-monitored process to survey the legal status of every inhabitant of the state, even as they have differing positions on the Citizenship Amendment Act (CAA). When did they, or their ancestors make Assam their home? Could they prove their presence in the state going back to the partition of British India? Or did they come to Assam after the formation of Bangladesh in 1971?

Answers to these questions are entangled in colonial history, ethnic identity and control over resources in Assam. These three factors have been instrumental in defining the political discourse, anxieties and activism associated with the NRC process. As a British colony, Assam saw an unprecedented inflow of labour and capital that transformed the economic and political landscape of the region in the late nineteenth and early twentieth century. This transformation hinged upon extraction of resources and resulted in the politicization of ethnic identities. Radical political voices in Assam had frequently drawn from this mix to demand two seemingly contradictory guarantees—territorial autonomy (even secession) and differential citizenship rights—from the Government of India.

I have structured the remainder of this paper to elaborate on four interconnected areas of pertinence: (i) underlining the importance of colonial history, ethnic autonomy, resources and the NRC debates; (ii) taking a brief look at what exactly went into the NRC process; (iii) mapping the spectrum of reactions and the history of activism related to the NRC; and (iv) looking at the future of political discussions about citizenship within India.

ETHNICITY, RESOURCES AND AUTONOMY

The colonial period is key to understanding many of the enduring conflicts in Assam today. Adversarial positions on the NRC fall into a process that has been exhaustively researched and documented over the past few decades. The presence of the colonial State in Assam was limited to parts of the populated valleys where the government allowed people from East Bengal to settle on agricultural land for annual and decennial leases. The landscape, economy and society changed dramatically as cash crops like jute and tea, as well as minerals like oil and coal were grown or extracted in abundance from the area in the nineteenth and early twentieth centuries. This transformation also entailed a radical change in the demography of the region, as peasants and indentured workers from different parts of the British-controlled Indian subcontinent were brought to Assam. Tea plantations, in the central and eastern part of the Brahmaputra valley and in parts of the Barak valley, were given longer-term leases.

In the upland areas, however, the government followed a 'light-touch' policy and allowed indigenous communities to retain their traditional chiefs and heads, while making way for indirect rule by the colonial State. This policy continued after Independence and was reaffirmed by the Bordoloi Commission in 1949, when they proposed that the hills be governed under the Sixth Schedule of the Constitution.

Under the provisions of the Sixth Schedule, use and transfer of land between individuals was left to the discretion of the autonomous councils that allowed indigenous communities (defined as Scheduled Tribes under the Constitution) to govern certain areas where they were a numerical majority. The councils functioned as territorial enclaves within the larger state and in matters related to transfer of land and property reflected the light-touch administration during the colonial period.

While some territories and communities accepted this autonomy arrangement, others like the Naga and Mizo were less convinced. In both areas—Naga Hills (comprising the current state of Nagaland and parts of Arunachal Pradesh, Assam and Manipur) and Lushai Hills—demands for independent, self-governing territories brought together small, kin-based communities who were able to organize successful armed resistance to the post-colonial state and to settler communities.

The first territorial councils were elected in the autonomous districts around the undivided province of Assam in the 1950s and continue into contemporary times. Since then, the state of Assam has been reorganized and currently there are three territorial autonomous district councils—Bodoland, Dima

Hasao and Karbi Anglong—and six non-territorial councils—Deori, Mishing, Rabha Hasong, Sonowal Kachari, Thengal Kachari and Tiwa—in the state.

There is little doubt that Assam's long, complicated history of settlement and demographic change continues to play a dominant part in political mobilization in the region. This process was informed by tropes of identity, embodied in differences between groups, bureaucratic distancing of the state from people and the eventual centralization of power.

The post-colonial state has also held itself up as a neutral entity, claiming to uphold the rights of all citizens while simultaneously encouraging an incremental approach to demands for autonomy among indigenous and other communities who settled in the valleys during the colonial period. It continued after the partition of British India in 1947, as well as the formation of Bangladesh in 1971. It has predictably led to a polarization of opinion on the rights of the people of the region and those who have a right to call Assam their homeland.

Assamese and tribal activists often allude to demographic changes as the continuing legacy of colonialism, where the colonial State (and its post-colonial inheritor) wilfully used settlers in order to politically subjugate and economically exploit the region. This fact is reiterated through political mobilization along communitarian and ethnic lines, involving the formation of armed groups for almost all communities in Assam. Commentators argue that this is the precursor to attempts at creating majorities through acts of violence, causing large-scale displacement along India's north-east borders.[1]

The discourse on identity politics does not allow for certain communities to assert territorial rights in Assam.

This is particularly true for numerically large populations such as descendants of indentured workers in the plantations and subsistence peasants of the floodplains in the Brahmaputra and Barak valleys. Their presence in the region is tied to commodities, crops and a labouring history that places them in the point of contact between Europeans and pre-colonial society. This leads to a peculiar situation where radical political discourse on indigenous politics and rights over resources follows one that is similar to the cultural and political assertions of the First Nations communities in Canada, the United States, Australia and New Zealand.

In the 1990s and early 2000s, sections of the left-leaning advocates of autonomy made efforts to assert alliances that overcame ethnic identities. However, over time, as successive Central and state governments began to negotiate with radical voices of dissent, ethnic territorial autonomy was foregrounded as a possible resolution. This allowed a section of people to remain outside the scope of political mobilizations and as outsiders in particular districts and regions.

The relationship between Assam's realities as a colonial province and the possibility of its existence as a nation separate from India was often raised in the Assam Association formed in the early part of the twentieth century. The lack of an unequivocal answer has been one of the major sources of political mobilization, forming an ideological underpinning for movements for autonomy and secession throughout the second half of the twentieth century, until contemporary times.[2]

RIGHTS OF MARGINALIZED PEOPLE

There is a second order of issues linked to social justice that is linked in turn to such politics in Assam. They have to do with securing equal rights for marginalized people, regardless of their ethnic identity and based more on their social position within the political economy of the region. As mentioned earlier, the working class for Assam's tea plantations were forced to migrate from other parts of India, while many peasants in the Brahmaputra and Barak valleys were Muslims from East Bengal. Their conditions were markedly different from the white-collar workers, merchants and traders who were Bengali- and Hindustani-speaking Hindus from the Gangetic plains.

Historians and political scientists who have written about colonial Assam's referendum in 1947 that resulted in the Muslim-majority district of Sylhet joining (East) Pakistan and the rest of the province becoming part of India allude to the anxieties of local politicians in Assam when it came to colonial policies on immigration.

Assamese nationalists of the early twentieth century often differed from their counterparts in the Congress and also the Muslim League on the issue. The League's best-known politician in Assam, Syed Saadullah, who has been portrayed in history texts as the person responsible for encouraging immigration from East Bengal in the 1930s in his time as the prime minister, was actually castigated by peasant leaders like Maulana Bhashani for creating impediments in the acquisition of land by settlers. Similarly, Congress leaders like Ambikagiri Raichoudhury and political commentators like Jnanath Bora frequently reminded the party leadership (and Nehru, in particular) of the similarities between Assam and Palestine on the immigration and settler question.

Hence, when the Indian subcontinent was eventually partitioned, peasants and workers who were tied to the land and work in Assam were faced with difficult choices even though there did not seem to be much evidence of widespread violence (as in Punjab and Bengal). In the colonial province of Assam, religion was not the only factor that determined the decision people made to stay (or move). Language played an equally important role, especially for those who were going to become religious minorities within India. For a section of Assamese nationalists of the time, it was even more important than religion.

Coincidentally, two recent books—both anchored in colonial Burma—have appeared to allow one to make sense of what is going on in contemporary Assam (and its transnational neighbourhood).

Amit Baishya's translation of Debendra Acharya's novel

Jangam: A Forgotten Exodus in Which Thousands Died (2018),[3] detailing the harrowing escape of Burmese-Indian peasants from Burma into Assam during the Second World War, shows how twentieth-century decolonization was a violent process that disrupted the lives of many and led to a transfer of population from one part of the British Empire to another.

Anthropologist Anand Pandian and his grandfather M.P. Mariappan's evocative book, *Ayya's Accounts: A Ledger of Hope in Modern India* (2014),[4] on the latter's life journey, part of it as an evacuee from Burma, also details the trials of ordinary people caught up in extraordinary times and circumstances.

Both books are remarkable for their ability to depict the grainy details of uprooted lives that began with the unmooring of the British Empire. These events predated the formation of post-colonial nation-states and yet, almost 70 years hence, we find ourselves at similar crossroads again. Both books about Burma are memorable in the lack of rancour that the protagonists display for their Burmese neighbours, realizing that they were all caught up in circumstances beyond their control. It was almost as though anti-colonial movements in the region would bring closure to these divisive political events.

Unfortunately, they did not and as the current NRC process in Assam shows, the government added yet another layer of oppression to the lives of a large section of people who had placed their faith in the law.

Novelist Parismita Singh's thoughtful and reflective pieces on the fallout of the NRC allude to the difficulties that such people have had to endure, as well as the potential for violence that the fallout has brought in its wake.[5] These conditions force one to assess the future of debates around citizenship, not just in Assam but also in parts of the wider region that includes other states of the Indian Union and countries such as Bangladesh, Bhutan, Myanmar and Nepal. After all, discussions about citizenship and belonging have been central to the wider region and the fallout of conflicts has been significant as well.

The data collection process for the NRC tended to disaggregate citizens on the basis of property and lineage. It also collated on the basis of ethnic identity, gender and religion, leading to almost four million individuals scrambling for more documents and filing objections on how the process was carried out. In the following section, I address the evolution of the NRC and the kind of governmental resources that went into it. What was it? Was it like a census but with disciplinary consequences? Or was it a toothless exercise meant to pacify agitated opinions?

WHAT WAS THE NRC AND HOW WAS IT ROLLED OUT?

The NRC has an interesting timeline in the history of modern Assam, especially after 1947. It followed the 1951 census and appeared in government circulars issued to reassure agitating groups in Assam that the immigration issue would be addressed by the administration. This meant taking recourse to laws like the Foreigners Act, 1946 and the Foreigners (Tribunals) Order, 1939.

Such a process was in marked contrast to the upheavals of the tragic transfer of people between India and Pakistan in the west, where these laws were put aside to accommodate people escaping violence in West Pakistan. This difference between the two partitioned sectors of British India is important, as it alludes to the different ways regional governments responded to the humanitarian crisis.

Drawing attention to the government's unwillingness to address the movement of people in the east, as well as the persistence of civic efforts to raise the issue of immigration, Sanjib Baruah underlined the different ways in which the Partition narrative appeared in Assam and showed how it continues to have an impact on contemporary debate.[6] In his recent writings on the NRC, he has addressed the government's lack of preparedness in conducting such a process, drawing attention to the manner in which key neighbours were not adequately informed of the outcomes of this process, especially when political rhetoric was directed towards a historically specific population from Bangladesh.[7]

In 1951, people in Assam—especially Muslim cultivators and urban poor who lived along the East Pakistan border—were asked to fill out an enumeration form by the government as the initiation process of the NRC. As mentioned earlier, it was not for the first time since the country had attained independence from Britain that an enumeration process was being carried out. Ordinary citizens would have felt a sense of confusion, since the Census had just taken place. Moreover, those living along the Naga Hills were being asked a related set of questions regarding autonomy.

Hence, the idea of a government process involving various organs of the State but without much public debate, would have been seen as yet another administrative issue whose impact was not immediately tangible, especially since it involved the declaration of documents and evidence by individuals to the administration.

This was in marked contrast to the reaffirmation of independence after a plebiscite on the question of Naga territory and people being part of India that was undertaken by Naga leaders in the province of Assam. The referendum began on 16 May 1951 in the Kohima playground and involved only one ballot paper upon which every adult Naga was asked to stamp his or her view on the political future of the people. The plebiscite is central to the moral and political apparatus upon which Naga people continue to assert their independence and autonomy in India.

The 1951 NRC, on the other hand, was not central to the debates around citizenship for a greater part of the political history of Assam. No elected government took it upon itself to revise the NRC until 2010, a story that I deal with in the following section.

The capacity of the State to conduct such headcounts on

the basis of documents that attest to property, occupation and proof of residence has increased manifold since 1951. However, as anthropologist Matthew Hull has pointed out, there is no clear correlation between an administration's ability to document and how people respond to such demands.[8]

Most people who need to negotiate with the State know that there are theoretical (and practical) ways to create the kind of documentation in order to finish a job. In the recently concluded NRC in Assam, the government sought to minimize these shortcomings in two ways: (i) by throwing in the entire state machinery, including all departments of the Government of Assam, the Registrar General of India and the Supreme Court, into the process; and (ii) using technology to iron out 'wink-wink' deals that are attributed to the everyday workings of the State in developing countries.

2015 EDITION OF NRC

The 2015 edition of the NRC was more robust. It required individuals to show legacy data that included a family member's name in the 1951 NRC and/or having the individual (or a direct family member's name) included in the electoral rolls as of 24 March 1971, a day after the Bangladesh Liberation War was formally announced.

In case a person was unable to find her/his name in the legacy data, the administration allowed for 12 other documents that could be shown as evidence, provided they were granted before 24 March 1971. These were: (i) land tenancy records, (ii) Citizenship Certificate, (iii) Permanent Residential Certificate, (iv) Refugee Registration Certificate, (v) Passport, (vi) LIC Policy, (vii) government-issued License/Certificate, (viii) Government Service/Employment Certificate, (ix) Bank/Post Office Accounts, (x) Birth Certificate, (xi) Board/University Educational Certificate and (xii) Court Records/Processes.

These documents have an aura of middle-class respectability to them. They attest to a person having ownership of property, access to education, jobs and documents that allow her/him to travel at will. However, a vast majority of itinerant working people—most of whom constitute Assam's unorganized labour sector—were unable to produce these documents.

REACTIONS: A PLACE ON THE SPECTRUM

In this section, I map the range of positions that were articulated before, during and after the NRC process. In order to do so, I lay out the history of activism that informed the various parties that were intimately involved, including the tumultuous years of political violence that occurred during the 1990s and 2000s, centred on issues of territorial autonomy and sovereignty. Before one can make sense of the varying positions on the spectrum, one has to place the NRC within the context of radical activism that involved a wider range of actors than the ones frequently alluded to in Assam, namely the student unions and organizations that assert the rights of indigenous communities. In addition, as I will show, there was also a certain degree of advocacy and urgency shown by the Supreme Court of India, the Election Commission and the government in Assam in terms of addressing the issue.

In 1951, the NRC exercise was not extended to all districts of the state, which at the time included the current states of Meghalaya, Mizoram and Nagaland. A little more than a decade later, the Prevention of Infiltration from Pakistan (PIP) scheme was launched in 1962 and its enforcement to identify and deport was entrusted to the Assam Police. The Foreigners (Tribunals) Order was passed in 1964 to further enable local state officials to deal with undocumented migration from across the border, especially from erstwhile East Pakistan.

These legal measures affected the lives of Muslim communities living along the border areas, who were often pushed back into East Pakistan. They also extended an incommensurable level of power to local functionaries of the state at the block and village level when it came to determining matters related to citizenship.

Perhaps the legal measures were not able to identify undocumented immigrants since in 1969 the government—headed by Bimala Prasad Chaliha—put an end to the PIP scheme. In all this while, the NRC of 1951 was not revised, nor was there a concerted effort made by civil society organizations to call for its revision.

A key moment in the reappearance of the NRC in its current form goes back to 1979 and the by-election following the death of Hiralal Patowary, a Member of Parliament from Mangladai constituency in the north bank of the river Brahmaputra. Prior to the by-election, the Election Commission of India announced that there were more than 40,000 names of 'fake' voters on the list.

ASSAM AGITATION

Following this, Assam experienced over four years of civil unrest, a period popularly called the Assam Agitation (or anti-foreigner agitation, by some). It was during the agitation that the Government of India enacted the Illegal Migrants (Determination by Tribunals) (IMDT) Act, specifically for the state of Assam in 1983. Until then, suspected foreigners were identified and made to leave the country under the Foreigners Act that was enforced by the Foreigners' Tribunals.

The IMDT was specifically aimed at migration from East Pakistan/Bangladesh and inserted 1971 as the cutoff year for undocumented immigrants to be considered for deportation from Assam. The implications of analysing this law in contemporary times are twofold: (i) it laid the conditions for amending the laws for citizenship in India in 1985 from one that was based on naturalization to one based on birth; and (ii) acknowledged the need for diplomacy in addressing politics and history between India and Bangladesh. The second implication is important to bear in mind. It lays out the fundamental difference of opinion between those involved in the study and practice of Indian foreign policy and a populist political opinion on immigration within Assam.

The IMDT, until its repeal, was a cause for concern for representatives of both immigrant and indigenous communities, who viewed it as a problematic piece of legislation. For people of East Bengal heritage, it signified the persistence of doubt and accusations about their status. For indigenous communities, the law signified double standards in determining and bestowing citizenship rights on individuals in the country, placing the burden of proof on private individuals instead of the State.

The Assam Accord was signed in 1985 between Rajiv Gandhi (then Prime Minister of India) and representatives of the All Assam Gana Sangram Parishad (AAGSP) and All Assam Students' Union (AASU) to end the conflict and civil strife. It had several clauses built around the detection and deportation of undocumented immigrants, especially in the riverine areas, invoking the pre-Independence Foreigners Act, 1946 and Foreigners (Tribunals) Order, 1939.

It is interesting to note that there were no legislative efforts within Assam to find an alternative to the old colonial laws upon which much of the administrative exercise of detection and deportation was taking place. However, there was no mention of the NRC even though its current exercise is seen as a promise made as a part of the Assam Accord.

When the IMDT was finally repealed for being at odds with constitutional provisions for granting citizenship in the rest of the country in 2005, Sarbananda Sonowal (chief minister in the Bharatiya Janata Party-led government from 2016 to 2021) and leader of the All India United Democratic Front, Badruddin Ajmal, appeared as primary protagonists in the oppositional politics around the law. The repeal also elicited the involvement of the Supreme Court of India in the issue to come up with an alternative that could assuage demands for harder borders and controls over immigration in Assam. It was only after the repeal of the IMDT that updating the NRC appeared as a concrete proposal from the state to repair a relationship that had been marked by bloodshed, mistrust and antagonism between itself and civil society organizations in Assam.[9]

I shall explain the origins of this conflict in the subsequent section, but it would help to foreground violence in underlining the spectrum of positions and advocacy around the NRC.

An important organization in the activism around the process was Assam Public Works. It had come into existence in the year 2000 mainly to draw attention to the tensions arising from the armed conflict in Assam. In terms of political positions, it was squarely on the side of the government, making public pronouncements about the futility of the demands for self-determination and autonomy.

In 2009, the organization filed a petition (WP[C] 279/2009) demanding that the NRC of 1951 be updated and undocumented migrants be deported from Assam. The Government of Assam, then under the control of the Indian National Congress, attempted a pilot project in 2010 using the old 1951 forms that had references to Pakistan as place of origin, leading to protests by the All Assam Minority Students' Union in many parts of western Assam during which four persons died on 21 July 2010 in Barpeta town.

Media reports of the incident talked about the protesters burning effigies of Tarun Gogoi, who was then the chief minister of Assam and Samujjal Bhattacharya, who was the advisor to AASU. Both figures have seldom been on the same side of the spectrum on identity politics in Assam. The former Chief Minister's party was seen to be sympathetic to immigrants, partly due to the role that it played in opposing the Assam agitation in the early 1980s. The AASU advisor, on the other hand, was associated with a more robust nativist position on the matter.

The deaths in Barpeta forced the Government of Assam to set up a cabinet sub-committee to decide on matters pertaining to the updating of the NRC in the state in 2012. Until that time, the issue had not become as divisive, or even publicly debated, as it would become only a few years later.

SUPREME COURT INTERVENTION

In 2013, the Supreme Court of India intervened in the project. Justice Ranjan Gogoi, then a judge in the Supreme Court, instructed the state government to update the Court on the NRC, beginning a series of interventions that border on judicial advocacy. This nudge included demands for a timeline for completion of the process, a budget for undertaking the process, the immediate release of Rs 400 crore to the state government by the Centre and the appointment of IAS officer Prateek Hajela as the person to oversee the NRC update.

Operations, however, began in 2015, after the change in government in New Delhi. Two thousand five hundred *seva kendras* were set up across the state to help people understand the process for filing their applications.

In the process, many non-governmental, community- and student-based organizations were co-opted into aiding the government to ensure a smooth end to the NRC. Several commentators had brought up this issue in their defence of the NRC process.[10] However, others pointed out the disturbing realities associated with the behaviour of local state representatives on the ground, especially in their ability to make it difficult for Muslims of East Bengali heritage to engage in the process.[11] Bengali-speaking people and organizations from the Barak valley also protested against the NRC process, saying that it was designed to exclude them.

The United Nations Special Rapporteur on minority issues, Fernand de Varennes, also wrote a cautionary to the Government of Assam stating that any government-aided process that wilfully sought to deny citizenship rights to a section of the population based on religion, language or other social markers was tantamount to rendering them stateless. This view was endorsed by several non-governmental organizations working on minority rights within India and outside but was subjected to severe criticism by student bodies and commentators in the Brahmaputra valley.

Amidst the various student and political organizations weighing in on the issue, NGOs such as the Prabhajan Virodhi Manch (Forum Against Infiltration) led by senior advocate Upamanyu Hazarika have called for direct participation of citizens concerned about the rise of immigration from Bangladesh. The organization's website prominently displays the percentage of Muslim-populated districts in Assam as evidence of undocumented immigration and has been critical of the NRC's inability to be more forthright in its mission to identify foreigners in Assam.

Ugandan anthropologist Mahmood Mamdani draws one's attention to the weight of history, politics and the colonial encounter in the kind of views one asserts about brutal, polarizing events. In his book *When Victims Become Killers* (2001), he shows how routine matters of governance have the ability to be twisted to malicious extents. Those who advocate such intent are able to bestow some kind of warped political logic on atrocities that are committed by one section of people upon another.

Perhaps there is something similar happening in India, where the example of Assam is pertinent. People, ideas and political positions swerve towards selective readings of the past, especially when it comes to the disruptions caused by colonialism. In this process, some histories are privileged, while others are relegated to the margins.

In the following section, I look at the manner in which colonial history has created different political spaces for communities in Assam. I do so in order to underline the importance of ethnicity in the control over resources and territory, since all three are very important to understanding the NRC process. I discuss some of the possible outcomes of the citizenship debate, specifically within Assam, but also in relation to its impact on a wider region. This is particularly important in the light of protests against the Citizenship Amendment Bill in the Brahmaputra valley by organizations and individuals who were supportive of the NRC.

Interestingly, those who opposed the NRC in the Barak valley, especially organizations representing Bengali-speaking Hindus, came out to support the Bill. Therefore, when angry Assamese students shout slogans like 'Bangladeshis, go back!', they confuse many outside the region who wonder why then they are opposed to the Citizenship Bill. It is hard to explain that 'Bangladeshi' is not a religious category, but a sociological shorthand for a historical process that has muted regional specificities in nationalist debates.

CITIZENSHIP DEBATES

Against this bleak backdrop is what Irish poet Seamus Heaney in his Nobel acceptance speech called 'the abattoir of history', with a past full of violent expressions of identity. The triggers for the episodes of violence are many. Regardless of the spectrum of causes of conflict in the region, the recurring binaries that operate (in the conflict) are those of the *migrant* and the *native*; or *settler* and *indigenous*; or *citizen* and *foreigner*, or the generic *insider* and the *outsider*.

At the centre of the contestations is the process of migration or, more precisely, of mobility of human beings forced to move by the sheer force of geographic and political considerations not entirely of their making.

Such political predicaments are not unique to Northeast India. The evocation of fear of the outsider, hence the evolution of a narrative to 'drive out' those who are seen as the mirror opposite is similar to what transpires in other parts of the world. As different actors use the mediated public sphere to articulate their grievances against migrants/outsiders/foreigners, they simultaneously point to perceptions of anarchy among the actors themselves.

Mobility (across national borders) in this case is seen as a weakness of the State to police its boundaries.[12] If the features pages and editorials of vernacular dailies are anything to go by, migrants are seen to have an undue advantage in the mobility narrative.[13] This implies that the host populations are most likely to react to strategies they feel aid migrants and the conditions that aid migration in a manner that is confrontational (rather than reconciliatory).

Whether it is the dominant narrative of the AASU (in the 1980s), or the campaign for recognition of rights of the people of Terai in the new Nepali constitution, movements in the region have always tested existing notions of citizenship.

Sometimes, movements have used the dominant narrative of constitutions, while there have been times when constitutional language has been rejected in favour of innovative alliances that defy prescribed political possibilities. These processes are best captured in the manner in which the national constitutions and laws reflect the concerns of the inhabitants of the region.

In India, the government has used the political events and discourse in Assam to amend the Constitution and push through a version of citizenship that is marked by blood ties and cultural ascriptions, where it has become harder for a person to be granted citizenship in India even if she has lived and worked in the country all her life, unless she can prove that she has parents or ancestors who were born here.[14]

However, it is puzzling to come to terms with the fact that some of India's most abused citizens, living in one of South Asia's most militarized regions, can in turn seek the disenfranchisement of those they see as their *other*.

This is why I often find myself making subtle alterations to my views on the NRC depending on the person I am speaking to. Even as I understand the anxieties of the indigenous political discourse, I find it odd that its proponents were unable to be critical of the statist discourse on citizenship, as they once did in their opposition to militarization throughout the 1990s and in the first decade of the twenty-first century. This is especially true given the manner in which they had come out in protest of the government's blatantly anti-Muslim Citizenship Amendment Bill. It has forced me to engage with ideas that I dislike and disagree with.

Ranabir Samaddar expresses a melancholic view of this predicament.[15] In positing citizenship and statelessness as inseparable twins, he concludes that the voices of support for the NRC are emblematic of a collective revulsion towards an imagination of mixed lives.

MYRIAD WAYS TO CO-EXIST

Yet, the political discourse, framed as it is around notions of identity and history, does not do justice to the myriad ways in which people have managed to live with each other in Assam. These pathways of coexistence are evident in mundane spaces like weddings, funerals, village festivities during the harvest season and other events that allow for more layered lives to evolve.

For those trying to make sense of the contentious politics surrounding the NRC, there seems to be little hope for reconciliation between communities that see each other in adversarial positions over a government-sponsored, advocacy-driven process. It is true that a focus on the NRC process alone can lead one to the conclusion that its supporters displayed a monochromatic view of society, history and culture in Assam.

I recall asking a lawyer friend in Guwahati about the dogged defence of the NRC among left-nationalist Assamese commentators in August 2018. He and I agreed that the manner in which our friends and colleagues were defending the NRC was somewhat anachronistic and belonged to twentieth-century nationalist politics. It had alienated the *Miya* (Muslims of East Bengali heritage, most of whom speak a variety of regional dialect) people, many of whom had embraced the Assamese language and culture over the decades. My friend had spent much of his life fighting cases against the state's human rights violations during the brutal years of counterinsurgency in the late 1990s and early 2000s. He was presciently convinced that trusting the state to resolve the immigration issue was a mistake. We both agreed that the NRC was a distraction from other pressing matters that confronted the people of Assam.

As the streets of Guwahati were filled with angry young women and men protesting against the Citizenship Amendment Bill and later the Act, we felt vindicated by our analysis but disturbed by the manner in which this anger was being used in social media and on the streets.

The Government of India cynically used the CAA to iron over any pretence of non-partisanship on the matter of resolving conflicts arising from demands for autonomy and social justice. If anything, the sense of collective ennui, even after it was allowed to lapse, is a reminder that the militarization of politics and civil society in Assam has led to an untenable reality. Today, it is easier for middle-class Assamese men to reminisce about home and culture in distant places than it is for working-class Miya women who have been born and raised in the *chars* (seasonal riverine islands along the Brahmaputra in Assam and Bangladesh) to find their names in the NRC. Yet, asserting secular ethics and quotidian examples of tolerance will be left to those who have been systematically excluded by the government.

The NRC involved colossal expense for the State and civil society in Assam. It has disrupted relationships and forced people and organizations to revisit old colonial debates about autonomy and social justice. As the protests against its sinister cousin—the CAA—gain ground, one needs to imagine an alternative discourse that is built on dialogue and diplomacy. Such a discourse could start with conversations between governments and exchanges between writers, students and artists in the wider region that incorporates our transnational neighbourhood.

Notes

1. Paula Banerjee and Anasua Basu Ray Chaudhury, 'Introduction: Women in Indian borderlands', *Journal of Borderland Studies*, vol. 27, no. 1 (2012), pp. 27–29; Nel Vandekerckhove '"We are sons of this soil': The endless battle over indigenous homelands

in Assam, India', *Critical Asian Studies*, vol. 41, no. 4 (2009), pp. 523–48.

2. Sanghamitra Choudhury, *Women and Conflict in India*, New Delhi: Routledge, 2016; Rajendranath Saikia, 'Assam Association as the forerunner of Congress movement', *Proceedings of the Indian History Congress*, vol. 46, 1985, pp. 393–99.
3. Debendra Nath Acharya, *Jangam: A Forgotten Exodus Where Thousands Died*, trans. Amit R. Baishya, New Delhi: Vitasta Publications, 2018.
4. Anand Pandian and M.P. Mariappan, *Ayya's Accounts: A Ledger of Hope in Modern India*, Chennai: Tranquebar Press, 2014.
5. Parismita Singh, 'NRC: BJP is on a collision course with Assamese "nationalists" over citizenship bills', *Huffington Post*, 10 December 2018; and 'NRC sketchbook: As court and state haggle over documents, Assam prepares for a season of appeals and objections', *Huffington Post*, 30 August 2019.
6. Sanjib Baruah, 'The Partition's long shadow: The ambiguities of citizenship in Assam, India', *Citizenship Studies*, vol. 13, no. 6 (2009), pp. 593–606; and 'Assam: Confronting a failed partition', *Seminar*, no. 591, *Battle for the States* (November 2008).
7. Sanjib Baruah, 'Stateless in Assam', *The Indian Express*, 19 January 2018.
8. Matthew Hull, *Government of Paper: Materiality of Bureaucracy in Urban Pakistan*, Berkeley and Los Angeles: University of California Press, 2012.
9. Hiren Gohain, 'Debate: The NRC is what will allow Assam to escape from the cauldron of hate', *The Wire*, 13 August 2018.
10. Hafiz Ahmed, 'NRC: E cham buddhijibi e jothilota briddhi korise' [NRC: A few intellectuals are making it more complicated], in *Asomiya Protidin*, 31 July 2018; Bedbrata Bora, 'NRC-t xohai korok, jatiyotabadi xongothon e' [Nationalist organizations should help with the NRC], *Janasadharan*, 2 July 2015; and Ajit K. Bhuyan, 'Asolote NRC Kune Nibisare' [Who doesn't want the NRC, in reality], *Amar Asom*, 7 April 2018.
11. Ananta Kalita, 'Jatir Asistto Rokhyar Axro Xudhro NRC' [A fair NRC to safeguard national identity], *Dainik Asom*, 10 August 2018.
12. Mikhail A. Alexseev, *Immigration Phobia and the Security Dilemma: Russia, Europe and the United States*, Cambridge: Cambridge University Press, 2006.
13. Makiko Kimura, 'Conflict and displacement: A case study of

election violence in 1983', in *Blisters on their Feet: Tales of Internally Displaced Persons in India's Northeast*, ed. Samir Kumar Das, New Delhi: Sage Publications, 2008, pp. 150–63.

14. Anupama Roy, *Citizenship in India*, New Delhi: Oxford University Press, 2016.
15. Ranabir Samaddar, 'The NRC process and the spectre of statelessness in India', *The Wire*, 25 October 2018.

NRC in Assam and Constitutional Processes

NANA, I HAVE WRITTEN

Shalim M. Hussain

Nana, I have written attested countersigned
And been verified by a public notary
That I am a Miya
Now see me rise
From floodwaters
And float over landslides
March through sand and marsh and snakes
Break the earth's will draw trenches with spades
Crawl through fields of rice and diarrhoea and sugarcane
And a 10% literacy rate
See me shrug my shoulders curl my hair
Read two lines of poetry one formula of maths
Read confusion when the bullies call me Bangladeshi
And tell my revolutionary heart
But I am a Miya

See me hold by my side the Constitution
Point a finger to Delhi
Walk to my Parliament my Supreme Court my Connaught
Place
And tell the MPs the esteemed judges and the lady selling
Trinkets and her charm on Janpath
Well I am Miya.

Visit me in Kolkata in Nagpur in the Seemapuri slums
See me suited in Silicon Valley suited at McDonalds
Enslaved in Beerwa bride-trafficked in Mewat
See the stains on my childhood
The gold medals on my PhD certificate
Then call me Salma call me Aman call me Abdul call me
    Bahaton Nessa
Or call me Gulam.

See me catch a plane get a Visa catch a bullet train
Catch a bullet
Catch your drift
Catch a rocket
Wear a lungi to space
And there where no one can hear you scream,
Thunder
I am Miya
I am Proud.

CITIZENSHIP BETWEEN THE EXCEPTIONAL AND THE MUNDANE

Mohsin Alam Bhat

The Indian government has framed the question of citizenship in India as a curious mixture of the exceptional and the mundane. It tells us that the creation of the National Register of Indian Citizens (NRIC) is critical for national interest. 'We will have to implement NRC,' Home Minister Amit Shah has told Indians, 'to ensure the country's safety and security.'[1] There is a spectre of foreigners coming into India in hordes, destroying the social fabric of the country and economic opportunity for the people.

And as in the case of Assam, the government proposes to address this through an assortment of mundane procedural rules. If the 2003 Citizenship Rules are anything to go by, it will prepare a National Population Register (NPR) and ask those who it feels are doubtful citizens to prove their citizenship.[2] There is an abundance of banal legal jargon. Documents, particulars, evidence, family trees, linkage and legacy data, certification and burdens of proof. The government has appealed to this web of legality to claim legal legitimacy. Everything will be conducted, we are told, as per the law. Only foreigners need fear, not Indians.

None of this has allayed the anxieties of the country's vulnerable communities, most of all India's Muslims. They have come out on the streets for fear of being rendered precarious citizens, where their citizenship becomes perilously contingent on everyday arbitrary official discretion and whim.

This essay is a revised and expanded version of the paper titled 'Twilight Citizenship' that appeared in *Seminar*, no. 729: *Debating citizenship—A symposium on rethinking the link between citizenship and democracy* in May 2020.

The blending of the exceptional and the mundane in the contemporary politics of Indian citizenship, I propose, plays a very specific role. Citizenship is meant to be a guarantor par excellence of political status and rights. The proposed citizenship procedures—the NRIC and the NPR, in the context of the 2019 Citizenship Amendment Act (CAA)—not only harm those who are most vulnerable to precarious citizenship. They threaten to dismantle the fundamental features of Indian citizenship. They push it to its very brink by turning citizenship into an instrument of targeting and surveillance. They turn citizenship, I argue, into *twilight* citizenship.

THE EXCEPTIONAL

To understand what the triad of the NPR, NRIC and CAA means for citizenship, we need to turn towards Assam. In the last three decades, the Indian State has created a multitude of legal norms for identifying foreigners in the state. The NRC published on 31 August 2019 excludes 1.9 million persons, who now stand on the verge of statelessness. Assam's Foreigners' Tribunals (FTs) have already declared more than 100,000 persons as foreigners. Thousands more await their fate as they attempt to establish their citizenship in these Tribunals or in appeals to higher courts.

Starting in late 1980s, the Indian State created a matrix of legal procedures to identify foreigners in the state. The public basis for much of this was the 1985 Assam Accord. Coming on the heels of the Assamese nationalist mobilization led by the students, the Accord was a tripartite political agreement among the Central government, the All Assam Students' Union and All Assam Gana Sangram Parishad. The Accord offered a way to resolve the long conflict in the state that had become toxic and violent. Under the Accord, the immigrants who entered Assam before 24 March 1971 were given a route to citizenship.

The Central government made a political commitment to identify those who came to the country after the date, delete them from the electoral rolls, and 'expel' them in accordance with the law. While the legal infrastructure of tribunals and the Border Police was already in operation, the state considerably expanded and strengthened it. But this did not mitigate the anxiety about foreigners.

The contemporary character of the state's approach to suspected immigration in Assam began to emerge in the late 1990s. In 1997, the Election Commission of its own accord and without any transparent process marked 370,000 voters as 'doubtful'. The state asked these voters to prove their citizenship in the Tribunals. The year after in November, Governor Lt Gen S.K. Sinha sent an unprecedented report to the President arguing that the Central and state governments had failed to address the influx of illegal Bangladeshi migrants that threatened the identity of the Assamese people and national security.[3]

Sinha's report was seeped in the vocabulary and imperative of war. According to him, immigration was a 'silent demographic invasion', which would rapidly proliferate Islamic fundamentalism and split the region from India. 'There is an imperative need,' Sinha insisted, 'to evolve a national consensus on this all-important threat facing the nation.'

While the consensus took some time to evolve, it was the country's Supreme Court that led the way. As recommended by Sinha, the Court struck down the Illegal Migrants (Determination by Tribunals) or IMDT Act, 1983 in the 2005 case of *Sarbananda Sonowal*. It noted that by placing the burden of proof—the obligation to provide evidence—on the State rather than the person claiming to be a citizen, the Act had made the detection of foreigners 'not only difficult but virtually impossible'. This was certainly not true. Government data showed that the Tribunals under the Act had declared thousands as foreigners. The Court justified this on the basis of a large statistic of foreigners in Assam. These numbers have since been discredited as inflated and baseless.[4]

Behind the Court's hyperbole was the desire that more persons be declared foreigners. The foundation of the judgment was the imperative of war it borrowed from Sinha's report. The Court gave the imperative a clearer constitutional status. It held that illegal migration from Bangladesh amounted to external aggression against the country. The rising number of Muslims in the state indicated a demographic invasion. It was causing an insurgency among the state's residents. The IMDT Act was unconstitutional because it failed to protect the state against external aggression and internal disturbance, which was the core obligation of the Central government under the Constitution. The burden of proof was to be shifted onto the claimant. Extraordinary circumstances deserved extraordinary legal remedies.

CULTURE OF MASS SUSPICION

The spectre of national security and national interest in the *Sarbananda Sonowal* judgment reflects and further deepens a culture of mass suspicion. Any Muslim or any Bengali can be a foreigner. This mass suspicion has come to justify extensive procedures that provide wide executive discretion and legitimize sacrificing core values of due process.

This language of exceptionalism—mostly subterranean in judicial decisions—often bursts out in the open. For instance, the law requires that once a court settles a dispute, the principle of *res judicata* would bar other courts from hearing the same matter. Among the thousands who have been referred to the Tribunals, many have had to prove their case repeatedly even after being declared citizens in previous proceedings. In 2018, a two-judge bench of the Gauhati High Court refused to extend this principle to FTs.

Invoking *Sarbananda Sonowal*, the bench held that the proceedings before the Tribunals were '*sui generis*' because Assam was facing external aggression and internal disturbance.[5] National security and the integrity of the nation demanded that the state 'preserve the demographic balance of a part of India'. All principles of public policy stood 'subsumed' under this 'overarching public policy governing a sovereign nation'. The 'large-scale illegal migration of foreigners' threatened the character of the sovereign people. It was an existential crisis that demanded exceptional State action. Even if a person had to prove her citizenship many times, she must do so in the national interest.

PROCEDURAL VIOLATIONS

The *Sarbananda Sonowal* judgment lays down questionable standards of evidence. The judgment results in a presumption of non-citizenship. This is a starkly ill-suited policy for a value like citizenship, which is the very basis of legal personality within the constitutional community. The serious consequences for an individual—that include the possibility of being rendered stateless—would mandate higher legal standards for the State, and not the other way around.

The Court placed unrealistic—even cruel—evidentiary demands on people who are often poor, illiterate and without access to government documents. Since the judgment, thousands have been declared foreigners in *ex parte* proceedings—without their presence in the Tribunals. Many declared foreigners have complained that they never received notices. Others were unable to meaningfully participate in the proceedings. Daily wage workers could not risk missing a precious day's remuneration. Many others could not afford lawyers to represent them.

The practices of the FTs have further deepened the crisis. The Border Police officials who refer a case to the Tribunal must have grounds for suspecting someone to be a foreigner. The Tribunals rarely if ever permit lawyers representing precarious citizens to cross-examine them. By doing so, they preclude the only line of legal defence.

It is also becoming evident that the Tribunals are far from independent. The Ministry of Home Affairs employs the Tribunal members. The appointments are contractual, and their renewal depends upon the assessment of the government. It is a public secret that performance is measured in the number of declared foreigners.

REPUBLIC OF DOCUMENTS

Since the *Sarbananda Sonowal* judgment, India's institutions have turned citizenship into merely a question of evidence. Citizenship status—despite its fundamental importance for a polity—is now a mundane inquiry of facts in individual cases. It is now to be solely weighed in documents.

The Supreme Court's initiation of the NRC in 2014 was but a reflection of this trend. The process demanded that all the residents of Assam submit documents from a list of authorized public documents. The State essentially operated with the assumption that all the residents were foreigners unless they succeeded in establishing their citizenship.

This turning of citizenship into a mere question of evidence has come to reshape society. On the one hand there is the problem of legal vacuums. Assam's detention centres continue to function without clear legal guidance, as if they are outside the constitutional framework. On the other hand, there is too much law. In fact, there is an excess of it. Foreigners Act, Foreigners Rules, the FTs, Foreigners (Tribunals) Order, Citizenship Act, Amendment Act, the NRC, Supreme Court, linkage and legacy, family tree, SOPs, burden of proof. One can go on. This excess of law has overtaken people's lives. Complicated legal phrases and words have seeped into ordinary parlance. They have colonized language and imagination. People laminate their legal documents, secure them in polythene bags, keep them close. They are more precious than lives. There is a banal legalization of their lifeworld.

Legal institutions have maintained this legalization by keeping legal controversies unresolved. Take the *Assam Public Works* judgment in which the Supreme Court initiated the NRC in December 2014. The petitioners in the case had challenged Section 6A of the Citizenship Act that provided a route to citizenship to foreign migrants in Assam. The provision was meant to operationalize the Assam Accord. The petitioners argued that it discriminated against the people of Assam because it carved out an exception only for the state. The Court referred this question to a larger bench, which has still not decided the matter. And, in the same decision, it ordered the NRC, which was based on rules whose legality was undetermined. The Court has still not decided this either.

Or take the question of whether birthright citizenship applies to the state of Assam. Section 3 of the Citizenship Act unambiguously states that anyone born in India on or before 1 July 1987 is an Indian citizen by birth. Despite this, there has been a controversy over whether those who were born in Assam to foreigners would get the benefit of this provision. The Supreme Court in August 2019 left this question for a larger bench of judges, while asking the NRC to continue, perhaps assuming that Section 3 would not apply to children of foreigners. By not deciding the question, the Court left the fate of thousands of precarious citizens in the balance even as they may themselves have invested substantial time and money in the NRC process.

The excess of banal law in the citizenship process offers a veneer of legality. It suggests that the processes are bound by the rule of law. But beyond the appearance of legal form, these processes have only undermined concerns of justice. More worryingly, the aura of legality continues to mystify and obscure the unfolding tragedy. The debates around detention centres, for example, are quite often framed in terms of legal authorization. The question of legal authority has exhausted the question of humanity.

MELTING DOCUMENTS

Paradoxically, State institutions have also simultaneously robbed documents of all their evidentiary value. During the Tribunal proceedings, precarious citizens have to provide public documents to establish that they were either born in or immigrated to Assam, on or before 24 March 1971. If not, they have to establish ancestral linkage with those who did. Thus, precarious citizens are invariably required to procure old and inaccessible documents, many of which have been recorded and maintained by the State.

This hasn't stopped the FTs from relying on technicalities like minor errors in spellings and dates to declare persons foreigners. They often provide little or no time for procuring certified copies of public documents. They have often refused to accept public documents without the issuing government authorities testifying to their authenticity in person. While they place this demand on precarious citizens, the Tribunals refuse to issue summons to government officials to mandate their presence.

This pattern of undermining evidence has had the most severe impact on women. Most women before the Tribunals are illiterate and poor, and by implication without documents like school certificates or property deeds. They are also married at a young age, and hence separated from their parents and places of birth. Certificates drawn by the village councils or gram panchayats are often the only viable documents that they can produce to establish their citizenship.

In February 2017, the Gauhati High Court refused to recognize these documents 'in national interest', threatening the status of more than 100,000 women in the state. The High Court noted that the creation of new documents contradicted the imperative of resisting 'external aggression' and 'internal disturbance'. Within months, the Supreme Court reversed the decision, holding that the certificates may be accepted as linkage documents provided the authenticity of the document and its contents is confirmed. Despite this, the High Court, and the Tribunals by extension, have undermined their evidentiary value. They continue to demand that the authors of the certificates depose before the Tribunals and prove them on the basis of contemporaneous record.

This reveals the paradoxical nature of the citizenship process in Assam. The Indian State has made citizenship contingent on documents. But the documents appear to melt away under the intensity of the bureaucratic gaze. It has made evidence and fact peremptory, just as these practices have undermined their integrity and reliability.

CULTURE OF FEAR

Mass suspicion of foreignness and a complete disregard for ordinary due-process protections has engendered a pernicious culture of fear. There are numerous cases where family members have refused to testify for their relatives for fear of being targeted.

Take an example of what an FT lawyer from Bongaigaon district in Assam recently told me. He was representing a very old person in Tribunal proceedings, who passed away before the case was decided. The lawyer filed for closure of the case. Rather than concluding the case, the Tribunal member ruled that he had suspicions about the citizenship of the deceased. Hence all his family members must be brought before the Tribunal to prove citizenship.

This unhinged desire for declaring people foreigners, coupled with the uncertainty associated with the process and result, has created a graded order—a caste system—of precarious citizenship. People do not want to socially associate with persons labelled D-voters, or those who belong to families with declared foreigners. Marriages are out of the question because, for the State, foreignness is passed through bloodlines.

TWILIGHT CITIZENSHIP

The Central government's intention of creating the National Register of Indian Citizens will be the culmination of this transformation of citizenship—from normative political membership to scales of documentary evidence. Assam's example makes vivid what this process looks like. We are already witnessing a paranoia of foreigners taking over the country. The CAA entrenches the understanding that some among us are more amenable to suspicion than others. NPR and NRC offer the legal tools of filtering the *other*.

Until now, State institutions have directed the citizenship process only against certain sections of the population. It has marked the Bengali and the Muslim as the suspected foreigner, and hence most vulnerable to precarious citizenship. But the State may weaponize citizenship against the others. The fact that Assam's NRC excluded many other communities—women, the poor, transgender persons, the tribal, the Gorkhas, internal migrant workers—proves that no one is outside the pale of vulnerability.

Where does this leave citizenship? If these are the legal standards of citizenship, can any citizen meet them? The answer is an unsettling one: No. The web of legality has made some more vulnerable to precarity. But in the process it has rescinded citizenship altogether. The Indian State and its institutions have asserted an existential threat against the state of Assam. And then used the imperative of war to create a regime of exceptionalism where citizenship itself appears to be withering away.

It is obvious why none of this is only a matter of fairness of procedure. Procedure is but a symptom of what the Indian State has done to citizenship. When equal membership is a product of nothing but banal rules—in service of exceptional politics—we are staring at the twilight of citizenship.

Notes

1. 'NRC necessary for national security, will be implemented: Amit Shah in Kolkata', *The Wire*, 1 October 2019.
2. See Harsh Mander and Mohsin Alam Bhat's article 'Why the NPR is More Dangerous than the Assam NRC' included in Part 4 of this volume.
3. *Report on Illegal Migration into Assam*, submitted to the President of India by the Governor of Assam, 8 November 1998 (https://web.archive.org/web/20160308102548/https://www.satp.org/satporgtp/countries/india/states/assam/documents/papers/illegal_migration_in_assam.htm).
4. Debarshi Das and Prasenjit Bose, 'Assam NRC: Govt clueless about how many illegal immigrants actually live in India, RTI shows', *HuffPost India*, 31 January 2019.
5. *Amina Khatun vs Union of India*, WP(C) 7339/2015, order dated 19 April 2018.

THE JUDICIAL PRESUMPTION OF NON-CITIZENSHIP

Gautam Bhatia

On 17 May 2019, in a very short hearing, a three-judge bench of the Supreme Court—the Chief Justice of India, Ranjan Gogoi, and Justices Deepak Gupta and Sanjiv Khanna—decided a batch of 15 petitions under the title *Abdul Kuddus vs Union of India*. Innocuously framed as resolving a 'perceived conflict' between two paragraphs of the Schedule to the Citizenship (Registration of Citizens and Issue of National Identity Cards) Rules, 2003, the judgment—little reported in the media—nonetheless had significant consequences for the ongoing events in Assam surrounding the preparation of the National Register of Citizens (NRC).

TWO PARALLEL PROCESSES

What was the issue in *Abdul Kuddus*? In short, it involved the status of an 'opinion' rendered by a Foreigners' Tribunal (FT), as to the citizenship (or the lack thereof) of any individual. The issue arose because, in the state of Assam, there are two ongoing processes concerning the question of citizenship. The first includes proceedings before the FTs, which have been established under an executive order of the Central government. The second is the NRC, a process overseen and driven by the Supreme Court. While nominally independent, both processes nonetheless bleed into each other, and have thus caused significant chaos and confusion for individuals who have found themselves on the wrong side of one or both.

The petitioners in *Abdul Kuddus* argued that an opinion rendered by the Foreigners' Tribunal had no greater sanctity

This article first appeared in *The Hindu* on 23 July 2019.

than an executive order. Under the existing set of rules, this meant that an adverse finding against an individual would not automatically result in their name being struck off the NRC. Furthermore, the Tribunal's opinion could be subsequently reviewed, if fresh materials came to light. This was particularly important because, as had been observed repeatedly, citizenship proceedings were riddled with administrative (and other kinds of) errors, which often came to light much later, and often by chance. And finally, the petitioners argued that if the opinion of the FT was used to justify keeping an individual out of the NRC, then that decision could be challenged and would have to be decided independently of the decision arrived at by the Tribunal. In short, the petitioners' case was that the two processes—that of the FT and that of the NRC—should be kept entirely independent of each other, without according primacy to one over the other.

FLAWED TRIBUNALS

The Supreme Court rejected the petitioners' arguments and held that the 'opinion' of the FT was to be treated as a 'quasi-judicial order' and was therefore final and binding on all parties including upon the preparation of the NRC. There are, however, serious problems with this, which will severely impact the rights of millions of individuals.

To start with, neither in their form nor in their functioning do FTs even remotely resemble what we normally understand as courts. First, FTs were established by a simple executive order. Second, qualifications to serve on the Tribunals have been progressively loosened and the vague requirement of 'judicial experience' has now been expanded to include bureaucrats. And, perhaps, most importantly, under the Order in question (as it was amended in 2012), Tribunals are given sweeping powers to refuse examination of witnesses if in their opinion it is for 'vexatious' purposes, bound to accept evidence produced by the police, and, most glaringly, not required to provide reasons for their findings, '...as it is not a judgment; a concise statement of the facts and the conclusion will suffice' (although the Court, as an offhand remark, also added 'reasons' to 'facts' and 'conclusions'). Subject to provisions of this manner, Tribunals are left free to 'regulate [their] own procedure for disposal of cases'.

Unsurprisingly, glaring flaws in the workings of the FTs have come to light. Questions in Parliament showed that as many as 64,000 people have been declared non-citizens in *ex parte* proceedings, i.e. without being heard.

Testimonies reveal these people are often not even served notices telling them that they have been summoned to appear. Alarmingly, an investigative media report featured testimony by a former Tribunal member who stated that his compatriots competed to be what was jokingly referred to as 'the highest wicket-taker', i.e. the one who could declare the highest number of individuals 'foreigners'.

When adjudicating upon a person's citizenship—a determination that can have the drastic and severe result of rendering a human being stateless—only the highest standards of adjudication can ever be morally or ethically justifiable. But in further strengthening an institution—the FT—that by design and by practice manifestly exhibits the exact opposite of this principle, the Supreme Court failed to fulfil its duty as the last protector of human rights under the Constitution.

UNWELCOME DEPARTURE

The Court attempted to justify this by observing that 'fixing time limits and recording of an order rather than a judgment is to ensure that these cases are disposed of expeditiously and in a time bound manner'. This, however, is the reasoning of a company CEO, not that of the highest Court of the land, adjudicating upon a matter that involves the rights of millions of people. When the stakes are so high, when the consequences entail rendering people stateless, then to allow such departures from the most basic principles of the rule of law is morally grotesque.

The Court's observations in the *Abdul Kuddus* case and, indeed, the manner in which it has conducted the NRC process over the last few months, can be traced back to two judgments delivered in the mid-2000s, known as *Sarbananda Sonowal I* and *II*. In those judgments, relying upon unvetted and unreviewed literature, without any detailed consideration of factual evidence, and in rhetoric more reminiscent of populist demagogues than constitutional courts, the Court declared immigration to be tantamount to 'external aggression' upon the country; more specifically, it made the astonishing finding that, constitutionally, the burden of proving citizenship would always lie upon the person who was accused of being a non-citizen. A Parliamentary legislation that sought to place the burden upon the State was struck down as being unconstitutional.

What the rhetoric and the holdings of the *Sonowal* judgments have created is a climate in which the dominant principle is the presumption of non-citizenship. Apart from the absurdity of imposing such a rule in a country that already has a vast number of marginalized and disenfranchised people, it is this fundamental dehumanization and devaluation of individuals that has enabled the manner in which the FTs operate, the many tragedies that come to light every week in the context of the NRC, and judgments such as *Abdul Kuddus*. It is clear that if Article 21 of the Constitution, the right to life, is to mean anything at all, this entire jurisprudence must be reconsidered, root and branch.

Foreigners' Tribunals

I BEG TO STATE THAT

Khabir Ahmed

I beg to state that
I am a settler, a hated Miya
Whatever be the case, my name is
Ismail Sheikh, Ramzan Ali or Majid Miya
Subject—I am an Assamese Asomiya

After forty years of independence
I have no space in the words of beloved writers
The brush of your scriptwriters doesn't dip in my picture
My name left unpronounced in assemblies and parliaments
On no martyr's memorial, on no news report is my name
printed
Even in tiny letters.
Besides, you haven't yet decided what to call me—
Am I Miya, Asomiya or Neo-Asomiya?

And yet you talk of the river
The river is Assam's mother, you say
You talk of trees
Assam is the land of blue hills, you say
My spine is tough, steadfast as the trees
The shade of the trees my address...
You talk of farmers, workers
Assam is the land of rice and labour, you say
I bow before paddy, I bow before sweat
For I am a farmer's boy...

I beg to state that I am a
Settler, a dirty Miya
Whatever be the case, my name is
Khabir Ahmed or Mijanur Miya
Subject—I am an Assamese Asomiya.
Sometime in the last century I lost
My address in the storms of the Padma
A merchant's boat found me drifting and dropped me here
Since then I have held close to my heart this land, this earth
And began a new journey of discovery
From Sadiya to Dhubri...

Since that day
I have flattened the red hills
Chopped forests into cities, rolled earth into bricks
From bricks built monuments
Laid stones on the earth, burnt my body black with peat
Swam rivers, stood on the bank
And dammed floods
Irrigated crops with my blood and sweat
And with the plough of my fathers, etched on the earth
A...S...S...A...M

UNDERSTANDING THE FOREIGNERS' TRIBUNAL

Aman Wadud

FOREIGNERS ACT, 1946

Section 2(a) of the Foreigners Act, 1946 defines 'foreigner' as a person who is not a citizen of India. According to Section 9, the onus of proving whether a person is a foreigner or not lies on that person. The Foreigners' Tribunal (FT) furnishes opinion on the question of whether a person is a foreigner or not within the meaning of the Foreigners Act, 1946 whenever such a reference is made to them. The Tribunals have the powers of a civil court while trying a suit under the code of civil procedure with respect to summoning and enforcing the attendance of any person and examining her/him on oath, requiring the discovery and production of any document and issuing commissions for the examination of any witness.

SETTING UP OF THE FOREIGNERS' TRIBUNAL

Exercising the powers conferred by Section 3 of the Foreigners Act, 1946 (No. 31 of 1946), the Central government on 23 September 1964 issued a notification for a Foreigners (Tribunals) Order, 1964 and the creation of a Foreigners' Tribunal under Clause 2 of the Order. Tribunals were created by executive order of the Ministry of Home Affairs.

A tribunal is a quasi-judicial body created by the legislature—through a statute. Article 323B of the Constitution states that the 'appropriate legislature' may 'by law' provide for adjudication of matters by tribunals. This is limited to a specified category of matters, listed in the Article itself. Citizenship is not one of them. Even assuming that citizenship can indeed be decided by a tribunal, that tribunal still has to be created by the legislature.

APPOINTMENT OF TRIBUNAL MEMBERS

Rule 2(2) of the Foreigners (Tribunals) Order states that 'The Tribunal shall consist of such number of persons having judicial experience as the Central Government may think fit to appoint'. But subsequently the eligibility was relaxed to advocates with the minimum age of 45 years and 10 years of legal practice/legal experience in addition to sitting/retired District Judges/Additional District Judges. The eligibility has been further reduced to advocates with a minimum of seven years of practice. Earlier the Tribunal members were on a two-year contract but in 2019 it was reduced to one year.

When the question of delegation of power to set up a Tribunal came up before Hon'ble Gauhati High Court in WP(C) 4989/2016, the Court in its judgment dated 8 March 2018 stated that:

> 13. Article 258 of the Constitution deals with the power of the Union to confer powers, etc. on States in certain cases. Clause (1) of Article 258 starts with a non-obstante clause. It says that notwithstanding anything in the Constitution, the President may with the consent of the Government of a State entrust either conditionally or unconditionally to that Government or to its officers, functions in relation to any matter to which the executive power of the Union extends. Clause (3) provides for making of payment by the Government of India to the State concerned such sum as may be agreed upon or in default of agreement through arbitration in respect of any extra-cost of administration incurred by the State in connection with the exercise of powers and duties of the Govt. of India conferred or imposed upon a State Government.
>
> 14. Ministry of Home Affairs, Government of India had issued notification dated 19.04.1958 which was extracted in the case of Anwar (supra). The said notification was issued by the Central Government in exercise of the powers conferred by Clause (1) of Article 258 of the Constitution whereby

> the President with the consent of the State Government concerned entrusted to the Governments of each of the States mentioned therein, including the State of Assam, the functions of the Central Government in making orders of the nature specified in Section 3(2)(c), (cc), (d), (e) and (f) of the Foreigners Act, 1946 and under the Foreigners (Orders) [*sic*], 1948. While extracting this notification, the Supreme Court held that this notification was a complete answer to the objection raised that it was the Central Government alone which could make a lawful deportation order under Section 3(2)(c) of the Foreigners Act, 1946.

The judgment further stated:

> 17.1 Thus, we have two Central Government notifications, one dated 19.04.1958 and the other dated 17.02.1976, entrusting the Government of Assam, Superintendents of Police and Deputy Commissioners (in-charge of Police) to make orders of the nature specified in Sections 3(2)(a), (b), (c) and (cc), (e) and (f) after obtaining opinion from the Foreigners Tribunals by making reference under Paragraph 2(1) of the Foreigners (Tribunals) Orders, 1964.
>
> 18. Thus, there can be no dispute as to the legal foundation or basis for establishment and functioning of Foreigners Tribunals in the State of Assam. As a matter of fact, the Supreme Court in Sarbananda Sonowal vs Union of India reported in (2005) 5 SCC 665 after declaring the Illegal Migrants (Determination by Tribunals) Act, 1983 as unconstitutional, issued further directions that all cases pending before the Tribunals constituted under the aforesaid Act would stand transferred to the Tribunals constituted under Foreigners Act, 1946 read with the Foreigners (Tribunals) Order, 1964 and should be decided in the manner provided in the Foreigners Act, 1946 and the procedure prescribed under the Foreigners (Tribunals) Order, 1964. Further direction was issued to the State to constitute sufficient number of Foreigners Tribunals to effectively deal with the foreigners illegally entering into India (Assam) from Bangladesh. Such direction was

reiterated in the subsequent decision of Sarbananda Sonowal (II) vs Union of India reported in (2007) 1 SCC 174. While on Sarbananda Sonowal (II), we may note that the Supreme Court had noticed the uniqueness of the Foreigners Tribunals in Assam and observed as under:

> *26. The Foreigners Tribunal, it is said, has not been set up in any other part of India except the State of Assam. A different regime, therefore, exists in Assam from the rest of the country. If no tribunal has been established in the rest of the country, foreigners are identified by the executive machinery of the State. Thus, the province of Assam only has been singled out for adopting a different procedure. The problem in regard to illegal migration faced by Assam is also faced by other States including the States of West Bengal, Tripura, etc. It is, therefore, not in dispute that two different procedures have been laid down by the Central Government by issuing two different notifications on the same day.*

A Foreigners' Tribunal was first set up in the year 1964. By the year 1968, the number of Tribunals had increased to nine. The Tribunal gradually stopped being used between 31 December 1969 and 1 March 1973 as the government felt that they were no longer necessary as most of the 'infiltrators' had been deported. They were, however, revived again in 1979, and 10 Tribunals were constituted on 4 July 1979.

In 1983, Illegal Migrant (Determination) Tribunals were established under the Illegal Migrants (Determination by Tribunals) Act, 1983. Initially, 20 Illegal Migrant (Determination) Tribunals were established. In 2005, the Supreme Court declared the IMDT Act *ultra vires* and struck them down. As a result, the IMD Tribunals and appellate Tribunals ceased to function.

All cases pending before the Tribunals under the IMDT Act, 1983 were transferred to the Tribunal constituted under the Foreigners (Tribunals) Order, 1964 and are being decided according to the Foreigners Act, 1946 and the procedure prescribed under the Foreigners (Tribunals) Order, 1964 and later amended as Foreigners (Tribunals) Amendment Order, 2012. The Tribunal is required to discharge quasi-judicial functions. There is no appellate authority of the Foreigners' Tribunals. An order/opinion of the Tribunal is to be directly challenged before the Division Bench of the Gauhati High Court.

According to the seven-judge bench of the Supreme Court in *L. Chandra Kumar vs Union of India* ([1997] 3 SCC 261), all decisions of the Tribunals would be subject to scrutiny before the Division Bench of their respective High Courts under Articles 226/227.

While discussing the scope of interference with the Tribunal's order in a writ proceeding, the Hon'ble Gauhati High Court in a three-judge bench in *State of Assam & Ors vs Moslem Mondal & Ors* (2013[1] GLT[FB] 809) stated:

> Article 226 of the Constitution confers on the High Court power to issue appropriate writ to any person or authority within its territorial jurisdiction. The Tribunal constituted under the 1946 Act read with the 1964 Order, as noticed above, is required to discharge the quasi-judicial function. The High Court, therefore, has the power under Article 226 of the Constitution to issue writ of certiorari quashing the decision of the Tribunal in an appropriate case. The scope of interference with the Tribunal's order, in exercise of the jurisdiction under Article 226, however, is limited. The writ of certiorari can be issued for correcting errors of jurisdiction, as and when the inferior Court or Tribunal acts without jurisdiction or in excess of it, or fails to exercise it or if such Court or Tribunal acts illegally in exercise of its undoubted jurisdiction, or when it decides without giving an opportunity to the parties to be heard or violates the principles of natural justice. The certiorari jurisdiction of the writ Court being supervisory and not appellate jurisdiction, the Court cannot review the findings of facts reached by the inferior Court or Tribunal. There is, however, an exception

to the said general proposition, in as much as, the writ of certiorari can be issued and the decision of a Tribunal on a finding of fact can be interfered with, if in recording such a finding the Tribunal has acted on evidence which is legally inadmissible or has refused to admit admissible evidence or if the finding is not supported by any evidence at all, because in such cases such error would amount to an error of law apparent on the face of the record. The other errors of fact, however grave it [*sic*] may be, cannot be corrected by a writ court. As noticed above, the judicial review of the order passed by the inferior Court or the Tribunal, in exercise of the jurisdiction under Article 226 of the Constitution, is limited to correction of errors apparent on the face of the record, which also takes within its fold a case where a statutory authority exercising its discretionary jurisdiction did not take into consideration a relevant fact or renders its decision on wholly irrelevant factors. Hence, the failure of taking into account the relevant facts or consideration of irrelevant factors, which has a bearing on the decision of the inferior court or the Tribunal, can be a ground for interference of the Court or Tribunal's decision in exercise of the writ jurisdiction by the High Court.

WHY DO FOREIGNERS' TRIBUNALS SEND NOTICE?

The Assam Police Border Organisation has a presence in every police station in Assam. The Assam Police has this unique organization to deal with the so-called problem of illegal immigration from erstwhile East Pakistan—present-day Bangladesh. In 1962, the Assam Police established a Special Branch Organisation under the PIP (Prevention of Infiltration from Pakistan) scheme. Initially, the organization was headed by the Deputy Inspector General of Police, Special Branch. This special police unit was entrusted with detecting and deporting 'illegal foreigners' from what was then East Pakistan. Under the PIP scheme, nearly two lakh Muslims were forcibly deported to East Pakistan without any legal process.

Ideally, its job is to survey areas under its jurisdiction. If it comes across any 'suspected citizens', the Border Police is expected to ask for citizenship documents and give a reasonable length of time in which to submit such documents. If the person is unable to provide citizenship documents, the Border Police is empowered to send a 'reference case' (similar to a chargesheet) to the Foreigners' Tribunal against this person. But what actually happens is that the Border Police randomly picks up people and frames them as 'illegal immigrants' without any investigation whatsoever. In the reference case, they just write that they approached the concerned person and she/he failed to show any citizenship documents. In many cases, the Border Police approach poor and illiterate citizens, mostly daily wage labourers, rickshaw wallahs and even beggars, take their thumb impression on blank paper, prepare a reference case alleging such persons to be 'illegal immigrants' and refer the case to the Foreigners' Tribunal without any proper investigation. Many such unfortunate people allege that the Police ask for bribes and if the bribe is paid, the person in question is not framed as an 'illegal immigrant'. If, on the other hand, it is not paid, the case is referred to the Tribunal for trial. There are several cases where there was a dispute or rivalry between two private parties, and one party goes and bribes the Border Police to frame the other as an 'illegal immigrant'.

The Foreigners' Tribunal then issues a notice and asks the accused/'proceedee'/'opposite party' to appear before it and prove her/his citizenship, else she/he will be held a 'foreigner' by *ex parte* judgment. If you ask any investigation officer of the Border Police in private why they frame genuine Indian citizens as 'illegal immigrants', they will tell you they are pressurized from their higher authorities to frame more people as 'illegal immigrants' and complete targets. A police station is given a target of referring five, 10 or even 20 cases to the Foreigners' Tribunal every month. The lower-ranking police officers, therefore, arbitrarily and randomly frame as many people as possible as illegal immigrants without any primary investigation. This fact has been accepted before the National Human Rights Commission (NHRC) where senior police officer Louis Aind, DCP Crime, Guwahati, who was earlier in charge of the Border Police Unit admitted that a monthly target of six reference cases from each Unit was given to the police. This has been incorporated in the *Report on the NHRC Mission to Assam's Detention Centres*.

The Assam Police Border Organisation has also been granted discretionary powers to take fingerprints and photographs of anyone it suspects vide Government of Assam letter No. PLB.149/2008/Pt/8 dated 21 October 2009. There are allegations that those fingerprints and photographs are used to register reference cases against the suspects.

Apart from the Border Police, the Election Commission is also entrusted with the 'investigation' of the so-called doubtful citizens. Since 1997, the Election Commission of India has conducted 'strict scrutiny' of the voter list. If the Commission comes across any voters whose citizenship documents are inadequate, such persons can be marked as 'D' or 'Doubtful' voters. The D-voters cannot vote; they are disenfranchised; they are also deprived of the benefits of the Public Distribution System. In practice, however, the Election Commission officials have taken to framing citizens as 'doubtful' voters arbitrarily and randomly without even approaching the person in question and without conducting any kind of investigation at all.

The Commission has identified more than three lakh people as D-voters. The process of identification was dubious and it is alleged that junior officials of the Election Commission or officials from other government departments that were deputed were asked to mark at least 10 to 20 voters as D-voters in each village. There are many examples where one or two members of a family were marked as doubtful while others were spared. There are instances of government servants being marked as D-voters only because of their religious or linguistic identity.

Air Force officers, schoolteachers and other government servants who serve as presiding officers during elections are fighting legal battles to prove their Indian nationality; even police constables serving in the Assam Police were marked 'D', only because of their religion.

The 'D' from the voter list can be removed if the Foreigners' Tribunal pronounces the person in question as 'not a foreigner' or as an Indian citizen. The Election Commission sends such D-voter cases to the Superintendent of Police (Border) of the respective district, who in turn refers the case to the Foreigners' Tribunal for its opinion on the status of citizenship of the so called D-voter. The Foreigners' Tribunal sends notice to the concerned person to appear before it with citizenship documents and prove her/his citizenship.

Just because the Tribunal has held someone a foreigner does not mean he or she is actually a foreigner. Foreigners' Tribunals have been known to declare persons as foreigners because of minor anomalies of name and age in the voter lists and other citizenship documents, and also for not mentioning certain facts in their written statements, etc. Being held to be a 'foreigner' is, therefore, a result of minor technical errors and lack of competent legal support. In many cases, multiple notices are sent to members of the same family. It may even happen that one could be held as an Indian citizen at the same time as another from the same family with the same set of documents is declared a foreigner. Many people who have proved their citizenship once, have received notices again from the Foreigners' Tribunal to prove their citizenship. Even people from Uttar Pradesh and Bihar are being held as 'foreigners' or 'Bangladeshis'.

FOREIGNERS' TRIBUNALS AND THE RULE OF LAW

Accusing Genuine Citizens Without Investigation

The three-judge bench in *State of Assam & Ors vs Moslem Mondal & Ors* stated that,

Fair investigation and fair trial being the basic fundamental/ human right of a person, which are concomitant to preservation of the fundamental right of a person under Article 21 of the Constitution, there has to be a fair and proper investigation by the investigating agency before making a reference to the Tribunal. In such investigation the attempt has to be made to find out the person against whom the investigation is made, so that the person concerned is given the opportunity to demonstrate at that stage itself that he is not a foreigner. In case the person concerned could not be found out in the village where he is reported to reside or in the place where he ordinarily resides or works for gain, the investigating agency has to record the same in presence of the village elder or the village headman or any respectable person of the locality, which in turn would ensure visit of the investigating officer to the place where such person ordinarily resides or [is] reported to reside or works for gain and making of an effort to find him out for the purpose of giving him the opportunity to produce the documents etc., if any, to demonstrate that he is not a foreigner. The investigating officer, as far as practicable, shall also obtain the signature or thumb impression of the person against whom such investigation is initiated, after recording his statement, if any, provided he makes himself available for that purpose. There are also instances where the person against whom such investigation is initiated, changes his place of residence, maybe in search of livelihood or maybe to avoid detection. To ensure proper investigation and also having regard to integrity and sovereignty of the nation, once investigation relating to the nationality status of a person starts he must inform the investigating agency in writing about the change of residence, if any, thereafter. In case such person has failed to intimate the investigating agency in writing the subsequent change of his place of residence, the investigating agency has to mention the same in his report with his opinion relating to the status of such person on the basis of materials collected at the place where he earlier resided. That will ensure a fair investigation and submission

> of a proper report on such investigation to the authority. Needless to say, such investigation need not be a detailed or an exhaustive one keeping in view the nature of the proceeding before the Tribunal and the object sought to be achieved. Hence it need not be equalled with an investigation conducted in criminal cases.

But the Election Commission of India and the Assam Police Border Organisation randomly accuse genuine citizens of being doubtful voters and illegal immigrants, respectively, without conducting any investigation whatsoever. The verification forms meant to be filled in by the investigating officer are often empty with just the names and addresses of the proceedees. The grounds mentioned in the verification report state that 'the proceedee could not provide any citizenship documents'. The result is, even decorated Army and Air Force officers end up being randomly accused of being illegal immigrants.

Main Grounds Not Mentioned in the Notice

According to Sec 3(1) of the Foreigners (Tribunals) Order, 1964,

> The Tribunal shall serve on the person to whom the question relates, a copy of the main grounds on which he is alleged to be a foreigner and give him a reasonable opportunity of making a representation and producing evidence in support of his case and after considering such evidence as may be heard, the Tribunal shall submit its opinion to the officer or authority specified in this behalf in the order of reference.

This section was amended in the Foreigners (Tribunals) Amendment Order, 2012 which states:

> 3. Procedure for disposal of questions (1) The Tribunal shall serve on the person to whom the question relates a show cause notice with a copy of the main grounds on which he or she is alleged to be a foreigner. This notice should be served as expeditiously as possible and, in any case, not later than

> ten days of the receipt of the reference of such question by the Central Government of any competent authority.

The three-judge bench in *State of Assam & Ors vs Moslem Mondal & Ors* stated:

> The proceedee shall be served with the notice, together with the main grounds on which he is suspected to be a foreigner, as far as practicable, personally, whose signature/thumb impression, as proof of service, is to be obtained.

The Supreme Court in the *Sarbananda Sonowal vs Union of India* ([2007] 1 SCC 174), or *Sarbananda Sonowal II*, stated that,

> Having regard to the fact that the Tribunal in the notice to be sent to the proceedee is required to set out the main grounds, evidently the primary onus in relation thereto would be on the State. However, once the Tribunal satisfied itself about the existence of grounds, the burden of proof would be upon the proceedee.

But despite the statutory provisions and categorical guidelines by the Supreme Court and Gauhati High Court cited above, the Foreigners' Tribunals act with utter disregard, uniformly issuing notices to proceedees without any grounds for such action. Therefore, in the absence of any 'main grounds', a situation akin to the plaint of a civil case, the proceedee is unable to rebut the accusation convincingly. This clearly prejudices the case of the petitioner since they need to submit a written statement in the absence of clear-cut and tangible main grounds.

According to the Foreigners (Tribunals) Amendment Order, 2012 every case should be disposed of within a period of 60 days after the receipt of the reference from the competent authority. The 2012 Order further states that the Tribunal shall have the power to regulate its own procedure for disposal of cases expeditiously and in a time-bound manner. Such provisions have created unimaginable problems such as in the cross-examination by a Tribunal member.

In many Foreigners' Tribunals, government pleaders are either not appointed at all or are appointed at the last minute. In the absence of a government pleader, the Tribunal members cross-examine the proceedees themselves, thereby taking on the role of both judge and prosecutor.

POST-NRC

People whose names are excluded from the National Register of Citizens (NRC) get 120 days to file an appeal before the Foreigners' Tribunal. There are 100 Tribunals functioning in the state. An additional 221 members were selected to start working from the first week of September 2019. As discussed previously, according to the 1964 Foreigners (Tribunals) Order, a member should have judicial experience. This rule was relaxed to lawyers with 10 years' experience and then further relaxed to lawyers with seven years' experience.

To deal with the cases of exclusion from the NRC, the government issued a Gazette notification on 30 May 2019 amending the 1964 Order. The new amendment is called the Foreigners (Tribunals) Amendment Order, 2019. It is worthwhile to look at several of the rules contained therein in some detail.

According to Rule 2(A)(a), the state government or the Union territory or district collector or the district magistrate can now refer cases (or accuse anyone of being a foreigner) and constitute a Foreigners' Tribunal. Earlier, only the state of Assam was empowered to refer cases to the Tribunal. Although the Home Ministry has clarified that for all practical purposes the Foreigners (Tribunals) Amendment Order, 2019 will be applicable only to the state of Assam for the time being, as the Order empowers the state/UT/district magistrate (which means every state and every DM) to refer cases and constitute Foreigners' Tribunals, it is very possible that NRC may be implemented outside Assam. Or, even without implementing the NRC, just about anyone can be accused of being a 'foreigner' now.

While Rule 3A allows for someone excluded from the NRC to file an appeal—to be filed within 120 days from the date of order of rejection—before the Tribunal along with the certified copy of the rejection and grounds for appeal, let's look further.

Rule 6 states,

> In case no appeal is preferred under paragraph (8) of the Schedule appended to the Citizenship (Registration of Citizens and Issue of National Identity Cards) Rules, 2003, the District Magistrate may refer to the Tribunal for its opinion as to whether the person is a foreigner or not within the meaning of The Foreigners Act, 1946 (31 of 1946) in terms of sub-paragraph (1) of the paragraph 2.

It is pertinent to note that before the deadline of 31 December 2018, more than three lakh objections were filed against people who were included in the final draft of the NRC. Almost all of these objections were filed on the last day of 'Claims and Objections'. Before the last day, the number of objections was less than 800. However, many suspect that the number of objections actually filed was much higher than 800. From five-year-old children to the old and ailing, notices were sent to all the people against whom objections were filed including their family members for deposing as witnesses. According to the SOP, both objector and objectee had to appear at the hearing. But the presence of the objector is almost unheard of and almost every objection hearing was decided *ex parte*.

Most people against whom objections were filed have been included in the NRC final list. According to paragraph 3(b) of the order, 'if an objector does not file an appeal within 120 days, the district magistrate has the opportunity to file a reference against the person who had been objected upon, but his name appeared in the NRC because the objection was rejected'.

Rule 10 of the Order gives arbitrary power to the Tribunal, as it will issue notice to parties only if it *finds merit*. Merit is not defined in the order and this omission only increases the arbitrariness employed. Witnesses can be produced only after a notice is issued. But a case can be dismissed by the Tribunal even before producing witnesses and evidence.

And among the most damaging provisions, Rule 17 confers on the Tribunal the power to regulate its own procedure, a provision that was also there in the 1964 Order. This means that while other judicial forums are regulated by the Civil Procedure Code and Criminal Procedure Code, a quasi-judicial forum (Tribunal) which decides the most important constitutional right of citizenship has been given unchecked powers to regulate its own procedure. Unsurprisingly, Tribunals often abuse this power. Very often they don't even issue summons to witnesses stating that the burden of proof is on the accused. Moreover, after declaring a person a foreigner, many Tribunals don't provide certified copies of the relevant documents for the person to challenge the FT order. Simply put, the Tribunals act arbitrarily because they have the power to regulate their own procedure.

The end result of such unfair and arbitrary procedures, only made worse and ever more exclusionary with the passage of time, is deprivation of nationality. It is *Indian citizens* who lose citizenship and become stateless. What is more, immediately after losing citizenship, such a person can be detained in a detention centre—forcefully separated from kith and kin. The people declared as 'foreigners' by the Tribunals not only lose citizenship, but any and all rights enshrined in the Indian Constitution to a dignified life. This denial of the right to a life of dignity will not end merely with the person in question stripped of citizenship. Potentially, generations to come are in danger of being rendered stateless in perpetuity—left to a vulnerable and undignified life.

IN ASSAM, A SICK MAN WAS NOT SPARED DETENTION AND A HEALTHY MAN DID NOT SURVIVE IT

Arunabh Saikia

Phulbanu Nessa remembers clearly: It was the first day of the holy month of Ramzan in 2016.

A jeep full of policemen arrived at her home in Barpeta district's Balavita village. They asked for her husband, Amir Ali, then 53, sick and partially paralysed. 'They told us they were taking him for treatment,' said Nessa. 'One of them said, "We will bring him back once he is well."'

Instead, the police took Ali to a detention centre in neighbouring Goalpara district. Around twenty days later, his body arrived wrapped in plastic, his family recalled. Prison records, however, are at odds with the family's account: Ali died within a day of being put in detention on 23 May 2016, according to the official files.

Nearly two years later, Subrata Dey was brought to the same detention centre by the police. He was 37 years old when he was picked up from the eatery he ran a few kilometres from his home in Goalpara district's Krishnai area on 27 March 2018.

Less than two months later, on 26 May, his family was informed that he had died of a heart attack. Dey's family members and acquaintances were shocked. He had no history of coronary troubles; his wife and mother had visited him less than a week earlier on 21 May and he had not made any health-related complaints to them. 'He was sad, but not unwell,' said his mother Anima Dey.

~

This article first appeared in *Scroll.in* on 29 August 2019.

The National Register of Citizens (NRC), an updated list of Indian citizens in Assam, was released on 31 August 2019. Before the list was released, there was no clarity on what happens to those left out of it. No one knew for sure. The authorities said they will have to stand trial in Assam's Foreigners' Tribunals (FTs). In the past, those declared foreigners by these tribunals have been interned in six detention centres, which share space with overcrowded district prisons.

Detainees who subsequently secured freedom from higher courts recall their internment with horror: they were deprived of rights available to even murder convicts. Without access to legal aid, most detainees were subject to indefinite incarceration, until the Supreme Court in May ruled that those who had spent three years in detention centres may be released after furnishing bonds worth Rs 2 lakh.

In July, responding to a question raised in the state Assembly, the Assam government for the first time released a list of people who had died in detention. The list of 25 people included a 45-day-old child and an 85-year-old partially immobile man. *Scroll.in* met the families of six of them. Almost all of them claim to have documents to prove that they are Indians.

AMIR ALI, 53, BARPETA DISTRICT

Ali, a daily wage labourer, was first suspected of being a foreigner in 2012. He had employed a lawyer to defend him at the FT. 'We had paid him over Rs 20,000 in several instalments,' said his daughter-in-law Diljan Nessa.

Only those who can establish they or their ancestors lived in Assam prior to 1971 are counted as Indian citizens in Assam. The name of Ali's father, Aijuddin, featured in the 1970 voter list. To prove his link to his father, Ali had submitted a document issued by the village head. But the Tribunal ruled against Ali, stating that it was not entirely convinced that he was Aijuddin's son.

After his failed attempt to defend his citizenship, Ali had

been lying low, staying at relatives' and neighbours' homes, on the advice of his lawyer. The family, meanwhile, was preparing to approach the Gauhati High Court for relief. 'In the middle once, the local *thana* summoned him through the *gaonbura* [village head],' said Diljan Nessa. 'When they saw his condition, they said: "You are an old and paralysed man, go get your name cleared soon."'

It was around three months after that encounter that the police picked Ali up in May 2016.

Prison Diaries

Ali's illness, which his family is unable to clearly identify, worsened in prison. 'Three days after he was picked up when we finally got to see him, he told me: "There is no guarantee I will come out alive out of here; take care of everyone at home,"' Amir Ali's son Julhas Ali said.

The second time Julhas Ali met his father, around a week later, he looked even sicker. He had to be held by prison guards as he struggled to keep standing on his own. 'He just said one thing that day, "I will not survive this," and sat on the floor,' recalled Julhas Ali.

Around 10 days later, the family received word that Amir Ali had collapsed and died before he could be taken to the hospital.

The post-mortem report says Ali died of 'coma as a result of intracerebral bleeding of the brain'. According to a letter written by the superintendent of the detention centre to the local police apprising them of Ali's death, he had 'suddenly felled [*sic*] down the field'.

A Cross to Bear

Phulbanu Nessa said she did not know who to blame for her husband's fate. 'I do not know what killed him: the law, the state or Allah himself,' she said. 'But I do know that he died days after he was picked up.'

The tag of 'illegal' migrant still haunts Amir Ali's family. As descendants of a 'declared foreigner', none of his children and grandchildren have made it to the NRC—they are all 'illegal migrants' liable to be deported until they clear their names in the FT.

'All we want is for our names to come in the NRC and be counted as Indians,' said Julhas Ali. 'We have all been born here and so have my father and grandfather.'

SUBRATA DEY, 37, GOALPARA DISTRICT

Subrata Dey had been declared a foreigner in 2009 in an *ex parte* judgment pronounced without hearing his side of the case. His wife, Kamini Dey, said her husband had employed a lawyer who had cheated him. 'He would go to the court, but the lawyer would keep sending him back,' she alleged. 'He is singularly responsible for my husband's plight. All he did was milk us dry.'

It is likely Subrata Dey would have been acquitted had he got to present his side of the case. His late father, Krishnapada Dey, features in the 1966 electoral rolls; his grandfather, Manoranjan Dey, is part of the 1951 NRC.

According to Kamini Dey, the lawyer kept them in the dark about the status of the case. 'He would say things like, "Don't worry—nothing will happen to us Hindus,"' she said. The lawyer, she alleged, did not even provide them with a copy of the order declaring Subrata Dey an 'illegal migrant'.

When she confronted the lawyer after her husband's arrest, she claims he assured her that he would get Subrata Dey released in less than two weeks. 'Just keep the money ready,' he apparently told Kamini Dey. Her husband had already paid more than Rs 50,000 to him, she said. 'We had sold our cows to pay that fellow.'

But Kamini Dey said her patience ran out soon after. 'I told him, "Just give us back our documents, we will look for a new lawyer,"' she said.

When *Scroll.in* got in touch with the lawyer, he said he was only assisting another lawyer in the case.

'How Does a Healthy Man Die Like That?'

By the time Kamini Dey could arrange a new lawyer and file an appeal in the Gauhati High Court, her husband died—a death that no one in the Dey family has quite been able to come to terms with. The post-mortem report cites 'chronic coronary insufficiency'—heart failure—as the cause of Subrata Dey's death.

'How does a healthy man die like that?' Kamini Dey asked. 'Before putting him in jail, they had performed a medical test on him—if he was not well, why was he not given treatment?'

After his death, Kamini Dey has started selling jute bags to raise her two children, 17-year-old Biki and nine-year-old Sweta. There is another expense: an ongoing case at the Gauhati High Court to get her husband's name cleared, even if posthumously. For until that happens, Biki and Sweta would also not be counted as citizens.

'I have to do it,' says Kamini Dey. 'My children's futures depend on that.'

Detention Centres

IN THE NAME OF MY DEAD MOTHER

Ashraful Hussain

When our poems strike their hearts
They scream so loudly it's as if
Their pain is greater than ours.

Should we remain silent then
Or let their high-voltage drama
Stifle the fires in our heart?
Should we let go of the thread that binds
Our century-old heritage?

When my mother takes to the street
With an old rag around her waist
With an old bag of old papers
One on which is written
The history of fourteen generations

When my sister has her children
In a detention camp
When I grovel for my rights
Before the man in a black suit
Then no one is left for me except
My mother, father and sister.

I have grown a bud and two leaves on my hands
I have learnt to write two lines
I have learnt to open my mouth and say
That they bit me and that
I will squeeze the poison out of their teeth.

They say, rein it in man
No, I won't rein it in.
In the name of my mother who died
In a detention camp, I swear
That this voice in my throat will grow louder
And someday rustle the folds in your ears.
I swear, sir, I swear by my dead mother.

THE DARK SIDE OF HUMANITY AND LEGALITY

A GLIMPSE INSIDE ASSAM'S DETENTION CENTRES FOR 'FOREIGNERS'

Harsh Mander

As special monitor for the National Human Rights Commission (NHRC), I visited two detention centres in Assam in January 2018. I was among the first non-officials who entered these centres. This is my account of what I found.

~

As many as 1.9 million people have been excluded from the National Register of Citizens (NRC) in Assam, as the penultimate stage of a tortuously extended process of updating the NRC to determine who among the residents of Assam claiming to be citizens of India are foreigners draws to a close. Once they are given reasons in writing for their exclusion, they will have one last chance to establish their Indian citizenship in the Foreigners' Tribunal. If they fail, and their claims are rejected in the High Court and Supreme Court as well, their status as 'foreigners', or the more politically salient term 'infiltrators', will be confirmed. The Citizenship Amendment Act (CAA) has cleared the way for all people who were unable to prove their citizenship to still be accepted as Indian citizens, except those of Muslim identity.

The question looming like a gathering tempest, laden with momentous legal and humanitarian concerns, is: what will be the fate of those deemed to be foreigners? These may be a

This article first appeared in *Scroll.in* on 26 June 2018.

few thousand women, men and children, or tens of thousands of them, or hundreds of thousands. Since there is no formal agreement between the Governments of India and Bangladesh for India to deport persons they deem to be Bangladeshi foreigners, what will be their situation in a country they have treated as their home for generations? This is where they have family, friends, cultural and emotional ties, employment and, sometimes, farmlands. What will be their status, their future, their destiny if this country is now declared overnight a foreign, alien land to them?

These people face the threat of being rendered stateless, thrust into a predicament similar to that of Myanmar's Rohingyas—with India claiming they are illegal Bangladeshi immigrants and Dhaka not open to accepting deportation.

The only other clue we have about the possible future of these persons who will be judged to be aliens is the sombre experience of the past decade of several thousand persons who have been deemed to be foreigners by the statutory Foreigners' Tribunals in Assam. These persons, both men and women, have been kept in detention centres carved out of jails, sometimes for close to a decade, in appalling conditions, with no prospect of release. Little is known even in Assam, and even less outside it, of the condition of these detainees, of the provisions under which they were detained, and how the state has treated them.

UNENDING HUMAN TRAGEDY

These detention centres have not been open to human rights and humanitarian workers, so the conditions of their inmates has never come to public attention. Last year, I accepted an invitation from the NHRC to serve as their Special Monitor for Minorities. One of the first missions I sought was to make a trip to these detention centres in Assam. After many reminders, the Commission finally agreed to let me visit the centres with two of its officers. I visited Assam for this mission between 22 January and 24 January and took the assistance of two researchers—Mohsin Alam Bhat, who teaches at Jindal Global Law School, Haryana and Abdul Kalam Azad, an independent researcher formerly with the Tata Institute of Social Sciences, Guwahati. We visited two detention centres in Goalpara and Kokrajhar and spoke at length with the detainees. We were probably the first non-official human rights workers to gain access to these detention centres in the 10-odd years since they have been established. We also met jail and police authorities, district magistrates and senior officials in the state Secretariat, and civil society groups in Goalpara, Kokrajhar and Guwahati. We found that these detention centres lie on the dark side of both legality and humanitarian principles.

I was profoundly dismayed by what I saw and heard at the detention camps. I worked with my researchers on a detailed report, which describes the enormous and unending human tragedy of the detainees, and the extensive flouting of national and international laws, seeking urgent corrections. However, despite repeated reminders to the NHRC, I did not receive any communication about action taken by the Commission or the state and Central governments on my report. Now, with the prospect of possibly lakhs of people being deemed foreigners after the conclusion of the NRC process, I felt the only recourse for me was to resign from the office of special monitor of the NHRC and bring my report to the public domain.

CONDEMNED WITHOUT A HEARING

My first finding was that the majority of persons deemed to be foreigners and detained in the camps had lacked even elementary legal representation and had not been heard by the Tribunals. They were mostly detained on the basis of *ex parte* orders, or orders passed without hearing the accused person because they allegedly failed to appear before a Tribunal despite being served legal notices. Many claimed they never actually received the notices: we saw omnibus notices to large numbers of persons, sometimes naming some persons and simply adding a number for the others. Many were migrant workers working far from home, sometimes in another town or even another state, or were not at home, or for a variety of other reasons did not receive the notice.

For those who did get the notices, we learned that, typically, a huge panic set in and many sold their meagre properties and took large loans to hire lawyers to steer them through this process. Many of the lawyers were poorly qualified or deliberately let them down.

Even the Deputy Commissioner we spoke to said that every time he visits the detention centres, the detainees complain to him that they did not get proper legal representation and that they actually did possess the required documents, but there is no one to whom they can appeal. The officials admitted that many a time when the person is not found at home, the notice is served to relatives. They also said that people are unlikely to evade receiving notices because they know that this will limit their chances of proving their citizenship.

While listening to the detainees, it became clear that many of their cases had been decided *ex parte* and that they had not been given a fair chance to prove their Indian nationality. As a humane democracy, we provide legal aid even to people accused of heinous crimes like rape and murder but these people are languishing in detention centres without even committing a crime because they cannot afford legal services.

Overall, I am convinced that for a process that can result in the disenfranchisement, indefinite detention or expulsion of a person, the state government needs to ensure due process and, with it, compassion and an understanding of the predicament of persons that are poorly educated and lack economic resources and social or political capital. It needs to ensure that people are actually served their notices and given legal advice and support, and that much greater transparency is employed.

WORSE THAN PRISONERS

On our visit to the two camps—the one in Goalpara for men and the facility in Kokrajhar for women and children—we encountered grave and extensive human distress and suffering. Each centre has been carved out of a corner of a jail. Here, the detainees are held for several years, in a twilight zone of legality, without work and recreation, with no contact with their families save for rare visits from relatives, and with no prospect of release. In a jail, inmates are at least permitted to walk, work and rest in open courtyards. But these detainees are not allowed out of their barracks even in the day, because they should not be allowed to mix with the 'citizen prisoners'.

A jail for women is anyway far more confined than one for men and, within the Kokrajhar jail, the women's detention centre is even more cramped. Think of a situation in which these women—many barely literate homemakers, some aged widows—have not been allowed to move outside a confined space of maybe 500 square metres for close to a decade. In the women's camp, in particular, the inmates wailed continuously, as though in permanent mourning.

We were informed by officials that they have no guidelines or instructions from the Centre or state about the rights of the detainees. The detention centres are therefore *de facto*, if not *de jure*, administered under the Assam Jail Manual. We found that the state does not make any distinction, for all practical purposes, between detention centres and jails, and thus between detainees and prisoners charged with or convicted of crimes. In the absence of a clear legal regime governing the rights and entitlements of detainees, jail authorities selectively apply the Assam Jail Manual to them but deny them the benefits—such as parole and waged work—that prisoners are entitled to under jail rules. Thus, the detainees are treated in some ways as convicted prisoners, and in other ways deprived even of the rights of prisoners.

We found men, women and boys above six who had been separated from their families, adding to their distress. Many had not met their spouses for years, several not even once since their detention. In a moving representation to the NHRC Chairperson, detainee Subhash Roy asked, 'Which country's Constitution [on] earth separates husband from wife and children from their parents?' The detainees are not allowed legally to communicate with their family members but, occasionally, the jail authorities facilitate communication on humanitarian grounds on their mobile phones. Parole is not allowed even in the event of sickness and death of family members. In their understanding, parole is the right of only convicted prisoners, because they are Indian citizens.

Difficulties for families to meet are compounded because only a few jails in the state have been converted into detention centres. Many family members who have loved ones in the camps but have not been detained themselves do not have the money to travel to the detention centres, especially if these are in another district. There are at present six detention centres attached to jails in Assam. Until 2014, there were only two. The Goalpara centre houses detainees from eight districts. While the Kokrajhar centre is for women and children, Tezpur, Jorhat and Silchar also have small enclosures for women detainees.

There has been worldwide condemnation of the United States Government's policy to separate the children of illegal immigrants from their parents at the border. But this has been standard practice for detainees deemed to be foreigners in Assam for nearly a decade, without comment or censure by the larger human rights community. We found that because of the separation of families, a particularly vulnerable situation has been created for children. There have been situations in which the child has been declared Indian and both parents foreigners. In such cases, the State takes no responsibility for the child, who is left in the care of distant family members or the community. A child under six can stay with the mother in the detention centre. But the legal handling of children above six who are declared foreigners is even more unclear and shaky.

FAMILIES TORN APART

Halima Khatun, a middle-aged woman, has been detained in Kokrajhar for 10 years. Her four children live with her husband, who works as a chowkidar in a government school in Nagaon district. All her children, parents and six siblings are Indian citizens, and she alone was deemed an illegal Bangladeshi immigrant. When she was detained, her oldest son was 16. Her youngest son lived with her at the centre for some time. This assuaged her loneliness. But the authorities later handed the boy over to his father. Khatun's family has been working tirelessly but unsuccessfully to win her freedom, even raising money to hire a lawyer and approach the Gauhati High Court.

Fellow inmate Haliman Bewa, an elderly widow, was declared an illegal immigrant by a Foreigners' Tribunal and sent to the detention centre. Her only son has sold all their property, including their small house, to fight her case. He has still not been able to file an appeal in the higher courts.

Arti Das from Nagaon has been lodged at the centre for the last three years while her husband is detained in Tezpur. But their two sons are Indian citizens. Das does not have the money to hire a lawyer and fight to establish her citizenship. For 32-year-old Jalima Khatun, her son was just 14 days old when she was detained. It has been four years since and he has never once seen the outside world. At the men's detention centre in Goalpara, we met Ananta Sarma, 77, who had migrated from Tripura to Assam's Nalbari district to work as a cook at a roadside eatery, commonly called a 'line hotel'. His family, including his children, stayed back in Tripura. He married a second time in Assam and raised another family. More than six years ago, Sarma and his wife were arrested on the basis of an *ex parte* decree by a Foreigners' Tribunal that deemed them to be Bangladeshi nationals. Sarma said he had no idea how and when the case was instituted and tried. He did not receive a notice from either the police or the Tribunal. After their arrest, he said the police took them to the India–Bangladesh border in Mankachar in Dhubri district and tried to push them into Bangladeshi territory, only to be thwarted by the neighbouring country's border guards. They were driven back, separated and lodged at the detention centres—his wife in Kokrajhar and he in Goalpara. In these six years, Sarma said, he has met his wife only once, for a few minutes, at the Kokrajhar centre after receiving special permission from the detention authority. He was luckier than most others. When Sarma and his wife were arrested, their two children were in their teens—the boy was 14 and the girl 17. They have not met their children since their detention; they do not even know where they are or what they are doing.

Nur Mohammad, who is 63, ailing and with his hearing impaired, has been detained since January 2010. He was too weak and disoriented to speak clearly with us and had to be helped by his fellow inmates. A daily wager, he was served a notice to prove his citizenship at his home in Goalpara district. Though he claims he produced sufficient documentation to establish his Indian nationality, he could not convince the Foreigners' Tribunal. He feels he failed because he could not afford a lawyer. Since his detention, he has not met a single member of his family and has no means to approach the higher courts for his release.

RIGHT TO A LIFE OF DIGNITY

My paramount recommendation to the NHRC was to urgently establish a clear legal regime in conformity with Article 21 of the Constitution and international law to govern the condition of detainees. The State, under Article 21, must ensure a transparent procedure and respect the right to life and liberty of detainees. Their right to a life of dignity, even in detention, cannot be compromised. Detaining them as common criminals within jail compounds, without facilities such as legal representation or communication with their families, is a violation of their right to live with dignity and the right to procedural due process.

International law also explicitly lays down that immigrants cannot be detained in jails, and that their status is not that of criminals. According to the United Nations High Commissioner for Refugees' guidelines, detention is permitted only in officially recognized places of detention. The guidelines say States are obliged to 'place asylum-seekers or immigrants in premises separate from those persons imprisoned under criminal law'. In a 2012 report of the UN Working Group on Arbitrary Detention, Principle 9 states, 'Custody must be effected in a public establishment specifically intended for this purpose; when, for practical reasons, this is not the case, the asylum-seeker or immigrant must be placed in premises separate from those for persons imprisoned under criminal law.' The UNHCR also says that detention should not be punitive in nature. The use of prisons, jails and facilities designed or operated as prisons or jails should be avoided.

Humanitarian considerations and international law obligations also require that families of persons deemed to be illegal immigrants must not be separated under any circumstances. This leads to the requirement for open family detention centres not housed within jails.

Indian juvenile justice laws are also applicable here. The safety and care of children in situations in which they or their parents are deemed to be foreigners must be the direct responsibility of the State through the Child Welfare Committees established under the Juvenile Justice Act. The law applies to both children who are detained and those who are free while their parents are detained.

Detainees who suffer from mental disabilities must be given due support under Indian mental disability laws. The State's obligation in relation to mental disability also flows from Article 21, which is applicable irrespective of nationality and covers foreigners. Also, detainees above a certain age should not be detained.

Indefinite detention is a violation of Article 21 and of international human rights standards. The UN Working Group on Arbitrary Detention notes that detention 'must not be for a potentially indefinite period of time'. Guideline 4.2 of the United Nations Human Rights Council (UNHRC) says detention can only be resorted to when it is determined to be necessary, reasonable in all the circumstances and proportionate to a legitimate purpose. The authorities must not take any action beyond the extent strictly necessary to achieve the pursued purpose. According to the UNHCR, the test of proportionality applies in relation to both the initial order of detention and any extensions. Indefinite detention for immigration purposes is arbitrary as a matter of international human rights law. To guard against arbitrariness, maximum periods of detention should be set in national legislation. Without these, detention can become prolonged and, in some cases, continue till death.

NEEDED: A CLEAR, COMPASSIONATE POLICY

The fundamental right to life guaranteed by the Constitution applies not only to citizens but also to those whose citizenship is contested or denied. Their detention without due process and adequate, free legal representation violates their fundamental right to life. The Indian State must be compelled by the courts and by humane public opinion to formulate and announce a clear long-term policy on how it will treat a person declared a foreigner. This is crucial, because if the NRC declares thousands, even lakhs, of people foreigners, does the State want to detain all of them indefinitely? The policy must also clarify what happens to those whose appeals are rejected. With Bangladesh unwilling to take them in, are they then to be detained in these camps for life, with no relief? Is this lawful, constitutional and just?

On 11 June 2018, four United Nations special rapporteurs

wrote to the Indian government expressing concerns similar to those raised by me with the NHRC. In their letter, they quoted an Assam Minister stating that 'the NRC is being done to identify illegal Bangladeshis residing in Assam' and 'all those whose names do not figure in the NRC will have to be deported'. They said 'that local authorities in Assam, which are deemed to be particularly hostile towards Muslims and people of Bengali descent, may manipulate the verification system in an attempt to exclude many genuine Indian citizens from the updated NRC'. They also observed that 'members of the Bengali Muslim minority in Assam have experienced discrimination in access to and enjoyment of citizenship status on the basis of their ethnic and religious minority status. We are particularly concerned that this discrimination is predicted to escalate as a result of the NRC'.

India's policy must measure up to many tests. The first of these is India's constitutional morality, and national and international laws. But it must also be compassionate. We must defend the right to justice and public compassion of large numbers of mostly impoverished and very powerless people who may overnight find themselves treated as foreigners in their own land, and unwanted in any other. We must find ways to protect maybe tens of thousands of hapless people being condemned to the same fate the inmates of Assam's detention camps have been forced to endure. Indefinite incarceration of men, women and children in conditions worse than those of convicted prisoners, only because they were unable (or not enabled) to prove their citizenship, greatly diminishes India—its government, but even more its people.

POSTSCRIPT: TRUE JUSTICE

It is extremely unusual for an incumbent Chief Justice of India's Supreme Court to publicly declare his views about issues which are highly politically fraught, and which are still being considered in his Court. It is even more unusual for him to publicly disparage, using the harshest language, those who contest his views.

This is what Justice Ranjan Gogoi chose to do a few days before he remitted office. In a public function in Delhi, he vigorously defended the updating of NRC in Assam, an exercise which he had supervised and driven. He described the NRC as 'a base document for the future' which musters facts about 'illegal immigration', in order 'to remedy the wrongs and omissions'. This would end the 'turbulence whose effects changed the course of life of not only individuals but of communities and cultures across the region'. He described the critics of this process variously as 'armchair commentators', 'careless', 'irresponsible', contributing to 'worsening the situation', people who are 'playing with fire', who 'thrive through their double speak', are 'far removed from the citizenry' and have 'vile intentions'. Many of these critics are litigants in his Court.

I am one of those who challenged aspects of the NRC, particularly the detention centres, in the Supreme Court. I also later sought, unsuccessfully, the recusal of Chief Justice Gogoi from hearing the petition. Since he himself has pulled the debate outside the Court, I feel it is only fair for me also to respond to him in the same public space.

I was not opposing the idea of the NRC in Assam. This was envisaged as an instrument to end a decade of violence in Assam and to address the legitimate anxieties of vulnerable communities about culture, land and migration. We combatted the way it was implemented—mostly under the watchful eye of the Supreme Court—because it violated constitutional guarantees and due process and caused severe and avoidable suffering to recently immigrant communities.

The violations of elementary justice began over a decade earlier when the Supreme Court in its judgment in the *Sarbananda Sonowal* case deployed dangerously inflammatory sentiment based on false data to describe illegal immigration as 'external aggression' and an 'invasion' on India. It used this formulation to reverse the constitutional guarantee that any person is innocent until proved guilty, to shift the burden of proof instead to the person who claims to be a citizen, and not the State which accuses the person of being a foreigner.

The injustices of the process mounted through the period when the judiciary directed the NRC process. A People's Tribunal which included many respected retired judges and thinkers, held on 7 and 8 September 2019, illuminated several of these grave flaws. It maintained that the Supreme Court in the NRC case between 2014 and 2019 (a great part of this was under Justice Gogoi) resembled more an executive than a judicial forum. In the normal course of things, it observed, 'administrative processes are managed by the executive, and in cases of rights violations, the remedy lies before the courts. However, when the courts themselves "take charge" of such processes (and in executive-style fashion, as indicated by the opacity and use of sealed covers...and by the Court's insistence on setting deadlines despite the scale of the exercise and the potential injustices that might follow), the entire system of remedies is taken away, as there can hardly be an appeal against the Supreme Court's own devised procedures'.

This resulted in 'huge burdens on millions of impoverished and unlettered people because the burden of proof was shifted to the resident to prove that they were citizens, based on documents such as of birth, schooling and land-ownership which impoverished and unlettered rural residents anywhere would find hard to muster. Even when residents succeeded in producing these documents, these were often rejected for small discrepancies such as in the English-language spelling of Bengali names, or in ages even though it is well known that most rural people do not know their dates of birth. Many do not have legal land records. And in the middle of the NRC process, an arbitrary category was introduced of "indigenous" Assamese, who were treated much more leniently even when they could not produce the required documents'.

The Supreme Court also facilitated the creation of Foreigners' Tribunals of doubtful legality, presided over often by people without judicial experience, with enormous powers to decide citizenship of powerless people. It overlooked evidence presented before it of the arbitrariness, opacity and bias with which these Tribunals function.

I had approached the Supreme Court questioning the constitutional legality of detaining persons deemed 'foreigners' by these processes indefinitely in inhuman detention centres. I had visited these centres and found them akin to hell, violating international law and humanitarian principles. Detainees are housed in prisons within prisons. Families are separated, with husbands in one detention centre and wives in another, not allowed to communicate for several years. Children are often alone outside. Detainees have no work and recreation. Most of all, they have no hope of release, because there is no question of Bangladesh accepting them.

However, as the proceedings in my case transpired, I was deeply dismayed by remarks made by Justice Gogoi during the hearings, reported also in the press. For instance, he said to the Chief Secretary of Assam, 'The existing centres are housing 900 people as against the so many who have been declared foreigners. Why are there not thousands?' This created further panic among Bengali-origin Assamese people, and my colleagues from Assam reported a drive to detain more people. Instead of ending the violation of the Constitution and international law by releasing existing detainees from their endless suffering, I could see my petition resulting in further detentions.

I therefore sought the recusal of Justice Gogoi from hearing this matter. Justice Gogoi ruled that there was no question of him recusing himself. Instead, he took the singularly unorthodox step of removing me as petitioner from my own petition.

Arguing in person, I had said to him, that as a citizen approaching the highest court of this land, I do so in quest of justice. I am convinced that true justice is always tempered with compassion. And it is compassion above all which I found conspicuously absent in the actions of Chief Justice Gogoi in this matter. It is this same compassion that I find missing in his now public remarks about the NRC. He makes no mention of the profound and avoidable train of human suffering of millions of our most impoverished and vulnerable people which the NRC process has left in its trail.

Human Cost

D-VOTER, DE-NESTING AND DESPAIR

THE 'D COMPANY' OF ASSAM

Shah Alam Khan

Memisa Nishan was declared a foreigner under the Foreigners' Tribunal (FT) process in Assam—now enmeshed with the National Register of Citizens (NRC)—and has been incarcerated at a detention centre in Kokrajhar in Assam for the last ten years or so. She has a family.

Correction: she *had* a family.

Her three kids—two sons and a daughter—now live with her aged parents. Her husband passed away two months ago. His cause of death being myocardial infarction, or heart attack in common parlance. I was told that the stress of not being able to arrange a release for his wife led to his death. He had stopped interacting with people before he died. If noises can make you go mad, silence can kill even more viciously.

Memisa's youngest son was two years old when she was jailed. He is now 12 and has seen his mother only twice in all these years. He has forgotten the face of his mother and tells us that he cannot recognize her now. The brutality of a child not recognizing his mother is a little difficult to understand. Across the animal kingdom, nature has kept the mother–child relationship as simple as possible. It can be anything but complicated. But not in Assam, where a child can forget the face of his detained mother. I suppose the power of the State is greater than the power of nature.

Memisa's son is looked after by his elder sister, who is around 20 and works as a maid to support the family. She once went to school but dropped out after her mother was jailed. The other son is 16 and works as a mason in Meghalaya. He

This article first appeared in *The Wire* on 26 November 2019.

visits the family infrequently. The three kids and Memisa's parents cannot afford to visit her at Kokrajhar, as the sum of Rs 75 per person for the bus ride is too steep for the family.

If that wasn't enough misery, Memisa Nishan, we are told, has lost her eyesight in detention. The children allege that their mother lost her eyesight because of excessive crying. Memisa has not been informed of her husband's death, yet. Some tears still await to wash off her remaining vision.

The white sand beaches are not always a bright and happy topography. The *chars* or the river islands of the Brahmaputra in Assam are expelled by the mighty river from its deep blue heart as easily as they are engulfed back when the river erodes and cuts through its tracks as it majestically flows across the heart of the state. The life on the chars is thus fleeting, dependent on the mercy of the Brahmaputra.

We are told that there are 2,251 chars in total, supporting a population of more than three million people. These are the most deprived regions of the world, with literacy figures of around 15 per cent or less. Female literacy in some of the chars is less than five per cent, the lowest in any part of the planet. But still, people survive. They survive despite no health care, schools, roads, permanent houses, safe water, regular food supply! They survive despite the country looking away. Emily Dickinson had once written that to live is so startling that it leaves little time for anything else. Nothing could be truer than these words for the wretched of the chars.

On the Panpara char, I met a woman in her nineties. She will remain unnamed because the State has declared her a fugitive. She was a fugitive who could barely walk, shuffling with every step. I suspect she had a movement disorder, probably Parkinson's disease, of which the world has become more aware through celebrities like Muhammad Ali and Michael J. Fox. Her unsteady self was very much like the unsteady life which had unrolled in front of her. She said that she had voted in the very first elections in 1957. She had documents supporting the same. She too was a victim of the process of getting enrolled in the NRC. A leg injury prevented her from attending the Foreigners' Tribunal a few years ago and she was declared a foreigner without any further enquiry. The Magistrate at the Tribunal was told of her injury. He allegedly said that even if someone has died, the dead body has to be presented to prove their nationality! When it comes to the NRC in Assam, the dead are more trustworthy than the living.

The unnamed lady, like Memisa Nishan, was first declared a D-voter, a common action preceding the final act of detention by the FT. The arbitrariness of the process of being declared a D-voter is phenomenal. The onus of proving citizenship in the NRC rests solely with the people. The basic route to prove citizenship involves two main processes: drawing out an extensive family tree through an elaborate set of documents and proving your legacy to that family tree through a different set of innumerable and even more complex documents.

People on the char are thus obsessed with collecting documents which fulfil requirements of both the processes. In fact, the obsession with such documents even surpasses the obsession with life. As the Brahmaputra floods through a village or engulfs a char, people are more interested in saving their documents than their lives. No wonder suicides on the char happen when people are not able to collect enough documents to prove their 'Indianness' to the authorities.

In the Dumerguri Part 2 char I met Bobby Deol (yes, that's his name[1]), a seven-year-old whose father killed himself on 6 July after realizing that his name might not appear in the NRC list. Bobby Deol's 13-year-old brother had to be sent to Delhi to work as a ragpicker. After all, someone had to take up a 'job' to support the family. The lives of Bobby, his mother and two more siblings now hang by a thread. The process of enrolling in the NRC is hence one of extreme difficulty, bringing in despair, de-nesting homes and tearing families apart.

As we embark on our search for the 'new' India, more

and more people will meet the fate of Memisa Nishan and the unnamed woman. More people will hang themselves like Bobby Deol's father. More miseries will fill the chars. More children will leave their nests prematurely to earn a living for their starving families. The Brahmaputra will keep eroding its banks. It will keep filling sand into the homes of the char dwellers. That is nature and we have to respect its wrath.

But what about the sand in our tender hearts? Why do we, the lawful citizens of this land, have to look away from the despair of fellow men, women and children? How does that make us a strong republic? How does that define our idea of India? I wonder.

Notes

1. The child was indeed named after the actor. However, in Bengali, the pronunciation is somewhat altered and is rendered 'Bobbydul'.

WHY BOBBYDUL IS NOT IN SCHOOL

Abdul Kalam Azad

Mamiran Nessa is back home but lives in constant fear. Released a little over a week ago from a detention centre in Assam's Kokrajhar, the 40-year-old mother of two can't forget her 10 years in detention.

Pregnant when she was forcibly taken to the centre, she lost her foetus in its eighth month. Her husband fell into depression and died four years ago.

Her elder son Muktar Hussain, now 17, could meet her only thrice during those 10 years; her younger son, Mijanur, just once. 'When I first saw my mother after six years, I didn't recognize her,' Mijanur says.

Mamiran does not know how to rebuild her life. Her house was washed away in a flood, while her parents sold their land to fund her legal fight. She is still seen as an 'illegal Bangladeshi' and has to report to the police every week. 'Since I am not allowed to go outside the jurisdiction of the police station, I can't even go out in search of a job,' she says.

The stories of people in detention camps across Assam are harrowing. In January 2018, I was part of a National Human Rights Commission (NHRC) mission set up to study the condition of the detention centres. The mission was led by activist Harsh Mander, the then special monitor of the NHRC. The mission prepared a detailed report and submitted it to the NHRC, which took no cognizance of it. In June 2018, Mander resigned from the Commission and filed a petition about the centres in the Supreme Court of India.

Based on the petition, the Supreme Court in May 2019

This article first appeared in *The Hindu BusinessLine* on 27 December 2019.

ordered the government to release detainees who had spent more than three years in such centres. According to the media, over 300 detainees have spent more than three years in different centres across Assam, and many even 10 years. The government, however, has identified 56 detainees for release.

Assam has been at the centre of a violent storm over the presence of Bangladeshi nationals said to have crossed over illegally over the years. The border unit of the Assam Police and the Election Commission of India have identified over half a million people as 'suspected foreigners' and referred their names to Foreigners' Tribunals (FTs)—quasi-judicial courts that determine a person's citizenship, according to data released by the state government in the state Assembly. The Tribunals have declared more than 1.17 lakh people 'foreigners'.

In 2009, the Gauhati High Court ruled that those declared foreign nationals by the Tribunals be kept in detention centres until they were sent back to their own countries. The then Congress-led Assam government created two detention centres within jail premises—one in Goalpara for males, and the other in Kokrajhar for females. Later, four more detention centres were set up in the Dibrugarh, Silchar, Tezpur and Jorhat jails. The government says that those detained are illegal migrants who have no papers; human rights activists hold that many of the detainees are Indian citizens.

Assam's Bharatiya Janata Party government, with financial support from the Centre, is constructing a detention centre in Goalpara district in western Assam. Ten more detention centres are on the anvil. According to reports, the number of FTs is also being increased from the current 100 to 1,000.

In the old centres, created within the jail premises, the detainees are kept in dormitories, sometimes 35–40 to a room. Half open toilets are attached to the dormitories, leading to a foul stench throughout the day, not to mention the very real fear of disease.

In the last few years, at least 28 detainees have died at these centres. Many others have committed suicide fearing that they will be detained. As of now, more than 1,000 people are in these camps. There are hundreds of cases of mothers separated from their children, husbands from wives.

Over the last two weeks, I met some of those who had been released. Besides Mamiran, I also met Sabiya Khatun (45), a resident of Shimlabari village in Bongaigaon district of western Assam. She was released from the Kokrajhar detention centre after four years. She was freed under the SC's order, on two surety bonds of Rs 1 lakh each and on the condition that she would not go beyond the jurisdiction of her police station and appear at the designated police station once every week.

She has enough documents to prove that she is Sabiya Khatun. But a Tribunal had declared her a foreigner because the panchayat secretary, who provided a certificate to prove her parental linkage, failed to appear before it to testify that he had issued the certificate.

'I am ill and my feet shake when I walk,' says Khatun, seated at the back of her 16-year-old son's cycle. 'But we can't afford to hire a vehicle, and I am afraid of being sent back to detention.'

The officer in charge of the border unit says she will have to appear before it every Monday without fail, even if unwell. If she doesn't, she may be sent back to the detention centre, he tells me.

Khatun recalls how her family collapsed while she was detained. Her husband, she says, was a healthy and cheerful man before she was taken away. 'The neighbours say that after that, he stopped plying his rickshaw, stayed home almost all day and would suddenly cry out aloud,' she says.

Her family members and villagers requested the Border Police to allow her to meet her husband when he was critically ill. She was denied permission. His health deteriorated, and the money for his treatment, she rues, went to the court case for her release. He died, and their children dropped out of school and started doing manual work. She was not given permission to see her husband's body, she adds.

It is not just physical detention that is destroying families; the fear of detention is wreaking havoc too. In 2018, I met a 10-year-old boy called Bobbydul Islam in Dumerguri village, about 40 km from the Bongaigaon district headquarters. I counselled the boy's father about the need to educate him and ensured his admission in a government school.

Last month, I went to the village to meet members of a bereaved family. The head of the family had committed suicide because his name did not figure in the final National Register of Citizens of Assam and he feared that he would be locked up in a detention centre. When my colleague, rights activist Suman Das, took me to Bobbydul's house, I realized it was his father—with whom I had shared the dream of educating Bobbydul—who had committed suicide.

'He thought he would be arrested and sent to detention. He thought about his own fear but not about who would look after our children,' his wife says.

Bobbydul has dropped out of school again.

Gendered Exclusions

MY MOTHER

Rehna Sultana

I was dropped on your lap, my mother
Just as my father, grandfather, great-grandfather
And yet you detest me, my mother,
For who I am.
Yes, I was dropped on your lap as a cursed Miya, my mother.
You can't trust me
Because I have somehow grown this beard.
Somehow slipped into a lungi
I am tired, tired of introducing myself
To you.
I bear all your insults and still shout,
Mother! I am yours!
Sometimes I wonder
What did I gain by falling in your lap?
I have no identity, no language
I have lost myself, lost everything
That could define me
And yet I hold you close
I try to melt into you
I need nothing, my mother.
Just a spot at your feet.
Open your eyes once, mother
Open your lips
Tell these sons of the earth
That we are all brothers.

And yet I tell you again
I am just another child
I am not a 'Miya cunt'
Not a 'Bangladeshi'
Miya I am,
A Miya.
I can't string words through poetry
Can't sing my pain in verse
This prayer, this is all I have

STANDING OUTSIDE THE POLITICAL BORDERS OF 'WE, THE PEOPLE'

GENDERED EXCLUSIONS OF THE NRC

Varna Balakrishnan and Navsharan Singh

What does claiming citizenship mean if you are a woman, a *Miya* woman, in Assam today? Citizenship is a troubling question in Assam with deep fault lines. The question of who belongs and who does not, who is a native and who an alien has been an open sore on Assam's body politic. Assam was among the territories ceded to the British by the Burmese after the First Anglo-Burmese War in 1826 and it was home to hundreds of communities—among them Bodos, Cachari, Mishing, Lalung, Ahomiya Hindus, and Ahomiya Muslims—each with its own language and customary relationship to the land. It was a multi-lingual society with multiple sovereignties and different tracts in the region inhabited by different tribes, independent and sometimes in conflict with one another.[1]

Assam, a border state, also has a long history of in-migration, even before British colonialism expanded to the region. With British establishing control, the colonial State followed a policy of encouraging immigration to Assam and the subsequent waves of migration were linked to the prospects of enhanced revenues for the British.[2] In the early decades of the nineteenth century when tea plants were discovered in Assam, the British migrated women and men from various regions of India to Assam to work in tea gardens established by them. The spectacularly lucrative tea plantation was systematically feminized, and it grew on the most exploitative labour regime tied down by the harshest physical conditions with large-scale deployment of female and child labour at cheap rates. It was an industry where local people were unwilling to toil, so a large population of tribal people were transported by the British colonial planters from central India to Assam as indentured labourers during the 1860s–90s in multiple phases. Today, the plantation workers of Assam make up 15 to 20 per cent of the state's population, a majority of them women, and they continue to live on the plantations, on a starvation wage, at the mercy of plantation owners. They are not a single ethnic group but consist of different ethnic groups speaking dozens of languages and have different sets of cultures.[3]

By the late 1890s, as the tea industry matured, the British encouraged Bengali Muslim peasants—men and women—who were hard working and skilled in farming but had no land, to migrate to Assam. They came in large numbers and made the shifting islands of the Brahmaputra, known as *chars*, their home. They toiled on the difficult forest land, turning marshes into farmland and contributed to British revenue collection. There were also educated Bengali-speaking Hindu migrants who were encouraged to migrate as they were acquainted with the British administrative method. The educated Bengalis were recruited as clerks, supervisors and tax collectors and soon they came to dominate the local bureaucracy and had the major share of government jobs.

This history of waves of migration forms a very complex backdrop replete with anxieties over assimilation, culture, language, religion, ethnicity and jobs. In the failure of an inclusive political resolution, it often surfaced in violent forms bringing Assam to a point where Assamese identity—Assameseness—came to be based on the exclusion of the 'other'. It is not the borders that are ringed with wires, but the ethnic Assamese community rings itself to exclude the 'other'. So, what does claiming citizenship mean in this context? For the *Miya* 'who turned waste, marshy lands to green paddy fields',[4] whose mother and foremother toiled on the soil of Assam but who could never claim this land as motherland, what does citizenship mean? And, for the Miya woman, who was 'dropped on the lap of mother, just as her father, grandfather, great-grandfather, and yet was detested'.[5] For the Miya women who are part of a community that are not 'full members',[6] but whose own membership to their community is not complete, what does citizenship mean? Citizenship is perhaps most comprehensible from the position of those who are asked to proffer proof of their belonging. But what about those who must first gain the social standing to be counted for staking a claim to belonging?

These are troubling questions, for which no easy answers exist in the legal lexicon. Citizenship is about belonging and its associated rights, a legal status, which is gender neutral—but how the disadvantage of certain genders hides beneath the neutrality of the concept remains untouched. The social and legal differentiations that make citizenship gradational exist not only *between* communities, but also *within* the communities. This is, however, rendered invisible in a blind conception of citizenship. Consequently, not much exists by way of understanding how the process of inclusion and exclusion on which citizenship operates works for women. For the National Register of Citizens (NRC), the terms of inclusion are laid out unambiguously—it is through ties to land, lineage to family and identity in State records. But how do these terms play out for women? Women know that their only link to land is their labour; in the family, their identity is transformed as they turn from someone's daughter to someone's wife, taking on new names, moving to new locations; and for inclusion in State records they struggle to make sense of their belonging to the families. How do they claim citizenship?

Over many years past, for a large majority of Assamese people of Bengali origin the experience of claiming formal citizenship through the NRC process has turned into an ongoing ordeal. The aggressive gatekeeping to exclude these people from membership to the Assamese political community, worked at several levels: creating a threat perception and invoking the metaphor of war and silent attack by the 'infiltrators', sectarian movements, use of data which had little integrity, and court judgments.[7] Women and men who migrated to tea plantation areas and later to the shifting islands of the Brahmaputra, farmers from regions in present-day West Bengal and Bangladesh who came, encouraged by the British to cultivate regions in lower Assam, and migrants from the partition of the subcontinent in 1947 and the Bangladesh Liberation War of 1971 which further encouraged the movement of Bengali Muslims and Hindus into Assam, all toiled on the soil of Assam and learnt to endure the fury of the mighty Brahmaputra. They were Assamese, of Bengali origin.

The contemporary discourse of eliminating 'illegal immigrants' from the electoral rolls of the state gathered momentum and organization in the Assam Movement of 1979–85. Although this movement, the Assam agitation, when it started in the year 1978, was a movement against *foreigners* staying in Assam—a movement for 'driving out' all so-called illegal immigrants—all Bengali-speaking Hindus, Muslims and Nepalese were targeted. However, slowly, the perception about foreigners changed and only the Assamese Muslims of Bengali origin were targeted as Bangladeshi infiltrators. In the midst of the agitation, Assam saw the worst anti-Muslim carnage since Independence, in 1983, known as the Nellie massacre. In a matter of a few hours more than two thousand people were hacked to death. Built on the notion of a pure Assamese-ness, this movement pushed the politics of identity and language to construct an 'other' based on language, religion and class. The 'other' had no place on the soil of Assam.

The Assam Movement formally ended with the signing of the Assam Accord on 15 August 1985 between the Union government and the leaders of the movement, demanding the expulsion and disenfranchisement of the 'foreigners'. The Accord also promised 'constitutional, legislative, and administrative safeguards...to protect, preserve, and promote the cultural, social, linguistic identity and heritage of the

Assamese people'. This meant an entire community of people not perceived to be *Assamese enough*—Muslims and Hindus of Bengali descent, various indigenous groups, and transgender persons became the 'other'. The 'common culture' defined by the movement worked to their exclusion despite them possessing the common rights of citizenship. The merging of identities and citizenship rights thus created an environment for hierarchies of citizenship. Within this environment, the reality of unequal power on the basis of gender, rendered women and transpersons subject to twofold discrimination.

Women's citizenship has a deeply troubling gendered dimension even in a context where the whole community to which they belong is deemed illegal and external. In Assam, women outnumbered men in the category of 'doubtful voters'. These include the cases that were referred to the Foreigners' Tribunals and those who have been directly declared illegal migrants. Socially, the women of Bengali origin, the women of the chars, are the carriers of their own communities' culture with their distinct attire, language and markers of religious identity. They are also labouring women, their material context defined by sheer hard labour, critical for the process of accumulation, nonetheless, not enough to prove their belongingness to Assam. These women struggle amidst their poverty-stricken lives to carry the additional weight of claiming citizenship through a range of documents and burdens of proof.

India's conception of citizenship is gender neutral, providing all persons the right to citizenship and pass it on to their children. However, seemingly gender-neutral ideas of citizenship and nationality do not always imply a gender-just experience of this citizenship. This paper uncovers the layers in the gendered process of claiming citizenship in the experience of women and transpersons.

The paper develops in three parts. The first part describes in detail the evidentiary proof required to stake a claim to citizenship. The second part shares the testimonies of women in the chars. The five testimonies included here were collected during the visits of Karwan-e-Mohabbat to the chars in 2019. The final section concludes with reflections on the implications of the evidentiary proof as drawn from the testimonies.[8]

THE TYRANNY OF DOCUMENTS

In 2014, in the court of Ranjan Gogoi, the Supreme Court ordered that an updated list of the NRC be produced within a year where citizens were to produce proof of their citizenship through a specified set of 14 documents. The NRC process asked every person to provide one document each from two lists of documents—Part A, commonly understood as *legacy documents*, and Part B, commonly understood as *linkage documents*. Legacy documents were expected to prove one's long-term association with the land, where 'long term' was defined by an arbitrarily set date of the beginning of the liberation war in Bangladesh in 1971 or, if you have the privilege of recorded memory, of the NRC of 1951. Given the fact that not everyone applying for the NRC would have been alive in 1971 or 1951, 'linkage documents' are meant to undisputedly establish yourself as a direct descendant of someone with credible legacy documents.

In preparation for this, the Assam government issued the 'legacy data code' (LDC), referring to an official database of people whose names are present in the NRC of 1951 and/or in the electoral rolls up to 1971.[9] This legacy data was expected to be the most commonly used legacy document. In the absence of an LDC, persons could provide one among a list of 14 documents to establish the history on one's family.

Along with 1951 NRC and voting records, these include land and tenancy records, citizenship certificate, permanent residential certificate, refugee registration certificate, passport, LIC policy, any government-issued licence or certificate, government-issued service or employment certificate, bank or post office accounts, birth certificate, board or university educational certificate, and court records. All of these documents, unless stated otherwise require to be dated before the midnight of 24 March 1971—the eve of the war that led to the creation of Bangladesh.

Two supporting documents were also approved for the process. A circle officer/gram panchayat secretary certificate in respect of married women migrating after marriage. This can be of any year before or after 24 March (midnight) 1971. The second was a ration card issued up to the midnight of 24 March 1971. These two documents can be accepted only if accompanied by any one of the 14 documents listed above.

The further requirement arises if the name in any of the documents of Part A is not of the applicant themself but that of an ancestor, namely, father or mother or grandfather or grandmother or great-grandfather or great-grandmother (and so on) of the applicant. In such cases, the applicant shall have to submit documents as listed in Part B to establish relationship with said ancestor, i.e. father or mother or grandfather or grandmother or great-grandfather or great-grandmother, etc., whose name appears in any of the Part A documents. Such documents shall have to be legally acceptable ones which clearly prove such relationship. They include birth certificates, land documents, board or university certificates, post office records, electoral roll records, ration cards or any other legally acceptable documents.

At the outset, the combination of these two lists seems expansive, even benevolent, giving people enough avenues to furnish what the government wants. If such is the case, what explains the epidemic of the fear of being locked up in detention centres, especially among women? Are there really such large numbers of 'illegal immigrants' in the state to warrant such action, or is there more to it than meets the eye?

We can only understand why a person, or a group of people do not have the said documents in acceptable formats if we explore the implied meaning of the demands made by the NRC process. The ask for legacy documents such as land, electoral and educational records dated to over half a century before the present implies a demand that a true citizen of India would have to have undisputed and provable long-term relationship with the land. The ask for lineage on the other hand, demands a similar relationship with a heteronormative family structure. This is to say, to claim that a woman is an Indian citizen, she should either have proven ownership of land, or needs to prove beyond doubt that she directly belongs to a family that has consistent records to prove that they have inhabited Indian soil for over fifty years. The demands for documents imply that during this time, there also should have been a continuous and formal relationship with the State which allows for the existence of official documents that mark any major change or achievement in people's lives. It is paradoxical that the State is asking people to present documents, many of which are already part of State records.

It is this triad of proof of long-term relationship with the land, the family, and the State (via State records) that forms the cornerstone of the NRC process, and in turn defines the present-day understanding of citizenship. These are punishing asks for women who have ambivalent relationships with all three. Women outnumbered men in the category of 'doubtful voters'—these include the cases that were referred to the Foreigners' Tribunals and those where people have been declared illegal immigrants *de facto* because they failed to produce the relevant legacy documents. Women have faced more exclusion because in a hostile political environment, the authorities who are determined to exclude more people found women easier to exclude. What does this say about the idea of citizenship in India? Who is seen worthy of inclusion, and what renders someone 'unworthy' of it and hence fit for exclusion? Who is likely to be able to meet the triad of demands—prove that they are unmistakable children of the land, with documents to show?

WOMEN SPEAK OF THEIR RELATIONSHIP WITH LAND, FAMILY AND THE STATE

Khairun Nisha

Khairun Nisha of Mulagaon district (name and location changed) was all of 15–16 when she was married off. She went to live with her husband in his village which was a few kilometres away. They lived in the village for about two years where she delivered a baby girl at home, and when their home was washed away in the floods, she came to live with her natal family with her husband and the baby girl. They stayed on there. She had two more babies born to her in her parents' home, both boys. When her youngest was two years old, and she was 26 years old, she was declared a D-voter. She didn't know how it happened because none of her siblings were marked 'D' nor was her husband. Perhaps the Border Security Force people went to the husband's village and no one could verify a young girl Khairun Nisha as a resident of that village.

Her grandfather had been a resident of Rangapani from the late 1930s and the family had all the records to show that they were inhabitants of the village. The legacy documents were all there and with some effort they were also able to furnish documents showing the linkage. Mind you, it is not easy, as we might think, for women to prove that they are their father's daughters. How can you? You are never required to have a legal or civic identity—Khairun didn't have a birth certificate nor a school certificate which mentioned 'Khairun Nisha, daughter of Md...who was the son of Md...the son of Md...' whose name is included in the Nazul record of 1938. Her *nikah* was never registered and the *nikahnama* given by the village maulvi is not admissible as proof of residency in the NRC list of documents anyway.

But the family made a valiant effort and were able to get a document which identified her as a daughter of her father, as all her other siblings were. Armed with this proof, they started representing her case in different offices, but the newly acquired document was not deemed a proof of her residency, and in 2009, the Foreigners' Tribunal declared her a foreigner and she was sent to the detention centre in Kokrajhar, at a distance of approximately 125 kilometres from her village.

It's been 10 years and Khairun Nisha, an 'illegal Bangladeshi infiltrator', continues to languish in the Kokrajhar detention centre. Her little boy is now 12—she has seen him only twice in these ten years and he did not recognize her. The other son is 15 and works in Meghalaya's notoriously exploitative construction sites. Her daughter who was married off two years ago and has been bringing up the two boys by working as a domestic help, has also seen her mother only a couple of times in these years. As for the father of these children, the husband of Khairun, he couldn't cope with the disaster that befell the family when Khairun was arrested. He became sick, neither eating nor sleeping well. In the ten years that Khairun has been in the detention centre, he did not visit her even once. He couldn't bear to see her there, he confessed. And this man died a month ago. Khairun has not been told of his death. As it is her eyes have rotted from crying endlessly all these ten years—perhaps she has been crying for all of us, because we did not shed any tears when she, the opposite party, OP, as they are called in official language, was taken away by the police from the Foreigners' Tribunal.

Khairun is now 35 or so and, following the recent Supreme Court order that those who have done three years in the detention centre should be released, would soon be coming home. But when Khairun, the alleged foreigner, the illegal Bangladeshi, finally does come home, after ten long years, and is reunited with her family, one might imagine everyone would feel relief. But we will only have to hold our breath longer, more deeply. Because she will realize that she had only made it to the starting line of another long, arduous and volatile legal process that is difficult to predict or prepare for. She will be released on conditions which include two sureties of one lakh each, weekly police reporting, and, perhaps a magnetic tracking bracelet or anklet, which the Chief Justice proposed in a discussion on the matter. The family has arranged for the two sureties but for the last two months have been waiting for the permission from the state Home Department. When asked about the tracking band, the family was very upset and thought that it would only add to the distress of all of them.

Because of her detention, despite the family presenting the full family tree and legacy and linkage documents, 52 members of the family did not find their names in the NRC list which was declared on 31 August 2019. Besides her release, they are running around preparing to file an appeal. An arbitrary and callous stamping of 'D' on Khairun's voter card has led to a monumental crisis for the entire family.

She will learn that her two sons born after 3 December 2004, to her, a 'declared foreigner', according to Chief Justice Ranjan Gogoi's order, will also not be entitled to have their names included in the NRC and they will also be declared foreigners—illegal immigrants.

We met Khairun's family on 17 November 2019 in their home in Mulagaon district. Khairun's mother didn't stop crying the entire time, as if asking us why? Why did it have to be this way? The sad thing is, it didn't have to be that way, nor should it.

Habiba Nessa

Habiba Nessa (name changed), 80-something, remembers voting in the very first elections in the state in 1957. She was married and had a voter card. She even remembers the name of the MLA who she voted for in 1957. However, 40 years later, in 1997 she was declared a D-voter and her hearings began at the Tribunal. This was a very difficult process for her as she lives in a char and going to the Tribunal is tough. It involves walking several kilometres from her village to travelling in the rickety boats to the town, walking again to the town centre and then taking a shared taxi to the nearest Tribunal office. During one of her dates at the Tribunal, it had rained heavily and the two ponds in her village had overflown flooding the narrow path which they take to cross the village; so a water draining machine was brought to drain out the water. As she was crossing the flooded path to appear before the Tribunal, her saree got stuck in the machine and she fell, her leg twisted and she fractured her foot. She couldn't appear before the Tribunal on that day. Other people who were with her went ahead and informed the officers at the Tribunal of Habiba's fracture. The officer reportedly said that even if she was dead, the dead body should appear because whoever had a date must appear; there was no excuse. The Tribunal gave an *ex parte* order and she was declared a foreigner. The old woman is now a fugitive, hiding from char to char fearing arrest and life in a detention centre.

We met her in a village on the banks of Brahmaputra, she looked pale and terrified, her one leg weakened from the injury constantly shaking out of anxiety. Her lips were parched, and her eyes mournful. Habiba's husband died a long time ago. She has no land, no income and no paper to prove her legacy or linkage; her voter card was lost in the floods and her word doesn't count. She is an old woman and court battles are expensive, so no one filed an appeal in the court against the Tribunal order. Her sons' names appeared in the NRC because they claimed linkage with their father who had a legacy document. Habiba's name never appeared in any record and Habiba, a senior citizen, who voted in Assam's first election in 1957, disappeared from the records, erased from the family tree, her life a testimony to the utter meaninglessness of this policy and practice for women like her.

We met her in village on a char on 18 November 2019.

Jamina and Rehana

Jamina and Rehana (names changed for both) are strangers to each other, but they are both in a similar legal limbo. Both of them have been declared foreigners, and are currently in hiding, hoping that the day when the Border Police comes knocking to take them to a detention centre never comes. Jamina is a middle-aged mother of six, and the second wife of her husband, who is now too old to work. The sole earner of her family, she is a farmer whose farming fields and house are located on the banks of Brahmaputra, on lands that are often washed away by the river. Her house is a preciously constructed tin hut, with a small curtained toilet on the outside. When we met her, she was living in her nephew's house. Rehana too used to be a farmer who lived on the frequently eroded bankside, but unlike Jamina, she is over sixty years old. Her children have grown up and have their own families.

Five years ago, the Border Police brought a notice to Jamina's house, claiming that she, Joitan, is a D-voter. Jamina and her husband argued that the 'Joitan' in the notice is not her; her name is Jamina, as her voter ID also ascertained. An argument ensued, but the police did not budge and the couple was eventually coerced into accepting the notice. With the *gaonbura's* (village headman) help, they reported this to the local police station. Nevertheless, not so long after, they received a court notice for Jamina's hearing at the Foreigners' Tribunal. After a legal battle that stretched for five years, six months before our meeting, the Gauhati High Court declared that Jamina was a foreigner, even though her parents and siblings are included in the NRC.

In 1997, Rehana was disenfranchised after being deemed a D-voter. Even though she had her name in the 1985 voter list, for over 20 years, Rehana has not been allowed to exercise her franchise. Rehana's nephew, who was also our translator, insisted that the family has documents going back to 1890, when a land survey was conducted under British rule. Rehana was born in the 1950s, but she does not have a birth certificate as such facilities had not reached her community unit then. The nephew, who was born in 1974 also was not issued a birth certificate. However, he and others in the family are on the NRC. Rehana was married off at the age of 15, which means that any government documentation that she had as an adult refers to her marriage to her husband, and not to her lineage from her parents. She is now a 'declared foreigner'.

Jamina does not know why she has been declared a foreigner. Her grandmother's name was in the 1951 NRC list. Despite his high fees, her lawyer failed to keep Jamina up to date with the case proceedings and to inform her when her notice came. Being illiterate, she was completely reliant on the lawyer to navigate through the legal proceedings. On realizing that her first lawyer was unreliable, she found another one for the High Court case, but he was no different either. During the course of the five years that she fought her case, Jamina had to sell all her land to pay the legal fees. Yet she strongly believes that she was declared a foreigner due to the incompetence of her lawyers. Rehana, however, has been comparatively lucky in this regard. While Jamina was the sole earner of the family, Rehana is retired and her son was able to afford the legal bill. Rehana's nephew noted that their costs were significantly reduced because they personally knew the lawyer. Both women, however, had the same results in their hearings.

Now that they have been declared foreigners, both Jamina and Rehana are in hiding. In an environment of great fear of the detention centre, this seems to be an instinctive decision to them. However, living in hiding in other people's houses has meant that Jamina is not able to tend to her fields, or even work in someone else's. Fighting her disenfranchisement has led her to losing any little wealth that she had, while also being unable to earn new income. Her teenaged son works as a labourer in Guwahati to help the family out. While she is in hiding, her 17-year-old daughter runs the household while attending school by herself. Her youngest, a toddler, goes wherever she does, but he demands to go home very often. Jamina knows that she cannot promise him anything.

After she was declared a foreigner, Rehana moved away from her house in the char-chapori and has been living with her nephew and his family. She does not know much about the official processes that have declared her a foreigner or about what happens inside a detention camp. She, however, knows that if one's name is not on the NRC, they can be taken to the prison-like detention centre. At many instances during our meeting, Rehana broke down in tears. Even though she is very safe and taken care of in her nephew's house, at over sixty years of age, the prospect of being separated from her family and jailed, for reasons she does not understand, is terrifying to her.

Jamina's life is also marked by anxieties. Every time she went to a hearing, she would lose her appetite, constantly worrying if she, an illiterate, would be able to answer the kind of questions the officers would ask. She would remain anxious, wondering if she would be detained at the court itself and taken to a detention centre permanently. As she lives in hiding in others' houses, her appetite remains low, partly because of the anxiety and partly because she feels ashamed to be imposing on her hosts. Jamina's husband is old and unwell. She is concerned for his health, but she is even more worried about what would happen to her children if she is incarcerated and he is unable to help. That her 17-year-old daughter is almost always alone in their house has also made Jamina very uneasy. She told us that her oldest daughter, who is married, is being ill-treated at her in-laws', for not yet fulfilling all the dowry demands after three years of marriage and for being the daughter of a 'foreigner'.

Women like Jamina and Rehana are easy to disenfranchise—their illiteracy, their poverty, their womanhood, all act against them. However, their disenfranchisement also implies that their children have also lost the security of their citizenship. Rehana worries about spending her old age alone, in a detention centre. Even though her children are no longer dependent on her, she knows that her 'DF' status has jeopardized their future. Jamina is already seeing the effects of her disenfranchisement in her children—being unable to attend school, having to live in poverty, the potential of physical threats, and coping with the stigma of being a foreigner's children. Even though she wants to take her case to the Supreme Court, she does not have resources for it. As she lives in hiding, Jamina has one additional fear—potential sexual assault at the hands of the Border Police personnel themselves, before even reaching the detention centre.

We met Jamina and Rehana in July 2019.

Noorunnisa

It is the July of 2019, a month before the final list of the NRC was due to be released. The NRC Seva Kendra in Goraimari looks like an old government school. We met Noorunnisa (name changed) at a shop opposite it. She came with a large folder containing all her papers and documents—we will realize in time that this folder, often a worn-out plastic bag, is ubiquitous in the region, almost an extension of the persons of the Bengali origin Muslims and Hindus here.

Noorunnisa is only 19 and a college student. Her name did not appear in the first draft, neither did her mother's. Her mother's linkage documents, which establish that she is the daughter of her parents, were deemed unfit—as has been the case with several married women in the state. When they went about their appeal processes through the hearing centres, they were informed that Noorunnisa is a 'declared foreigner'. Declared by whom? Foreigner from where?

She lives with her mother and two brothers. Her father lives with his second wife and family in another town. Although a full-time college student, Noorunnisa also works in the field with her mother and at other people's houses. She also takes tuition classes for local children.

She knows the weight that the 'DF' tag carries, for the whole region is plagued by the fear of being dragged into a detention centre by the Border Police on an unassuming dawn. To be a 'declared foreigner' one would have to appear before the quasi-judicial Foreigners' Tribunal, and undergo an often long and expensive hearing. Noorunnisa, however, has undergone none of that. Without any warning or procedure, she was simply a declared foreigner. 'What will happen to me now? If my name does not appear on the list, they will take me to the detention centre. How can I leave my mother alone like that?'

As a college-going woman, Noorunnisa is a rarity. Most women of her mother's generation are illiterate. Which is why, the biggest loss that she has had to face in this process, she says, has been her education. Her grades have dropped considerably since she became entangled in this process—a combination of anxiety and poor attendance has meant that she has fallen a year behind. After expertly explaining her situation, it was while talking about her educational loss that she broke into tears. The disruption of her education has cost her financially as well. She had to pay 60,000 rupees to re-gain her admission. 'If all of this NRC issue did not happen, I could have written my exams well. There would have been no need for all this money and re-admission.'

For a person like Noorunnisa, who works multiple jobs, time is currency. However, having to fight her disenfranchisement has meant that her time is now spent in a bureaucratic rut. 'I have to keep coming to the NSK [NRC Seva Kendra], then go here and then there.' The centre for her hearing is at the other end of her district and she has already had four hearings. For each of those hearings, all members of her family who share the same legacy person need to be present to testify. This means that they have had to hire a big vehicle to travel. Defending her citizenship has clearly been a time-consuming affair, but combined with its financial cost—that spent and that not earned—the NRC process has had a crippling effect on her life.

Within this rut, Noorunnisa realizes that the fact that she is a woman has been central. If she were a boy, maybe she would have been spared, or at least things would have been easier, she wonders. She is worried about the dangers and judgments she has to face, having to stay out and travel alone. While listening to Noorunnisa's story, it was easy to forget she was only 19. The disruption of her education, her fears about detention and her worry for her mother have taken a serious toll on her mental health. She says that she has even thought about ending her life.

Swati

Swati Bidhan Baruah, Assam's first transgender judge, and president of the All Assam Transgender Association, highlights the specific lacuna that trans people fall in under the NRC. 'Most of the transgender persons have been abandoned. What is more, the transgender person has to struggle with their own identity, in society and within the family. When a trans child has been thrown out or has been abandoned by their own parents and handed over to trans groups, a child comes within the culture of a matriarchal tradition or a transgender tradition. So, in such a situation, documents that prove lineage between the parents and the transgender person, that too from 1971, is very problematic.' This estrangement from the birth family and the adoption of a new family, under a *gharana* system, can often come with migration in search for a community. Under these circumstances, holding land and family documents become even more difficult for trans women. Baruah notes that returning to the birth family to collect documents and fulfil the demands of the NRC process forces many trans people back into abusive and hostile households and associated trauma. To many, going back to their birth families is not an option at all. Baruah estimates that nearly two thousand Assamese trans persons have been left out of the NRC, including those who have migrated and could be closeted.

However, Baruah asserts that being a trans person is not the immediate cause of their exclusion. Perhaps Baruah's own situation provides a telling contrast. Even though she has had to go through her own struggles of acceptance with family and society, Baruah's family lives with her today. She also has documents that assert her family's 200-year history and residence in Assam, and the privilege that comes with it. Most importantly, Baruah has the social capital of being a judge and an activist. For her, therefore, proving her relationship with land, family and the state was straightforward. These are luxuries that most trans persons from the state cannot afford.

Procedural inconsistencies within the NRC also add to the roadblocks. While registering as a trans person is possible in the first round of the NRC, trans persons against whom objections have been raised do not have the option to identify as trans in the hearing. This creates not only a problem of misgendering but also of potentially damning documentary inconsistencies. Direct engagement with bureaucracy and police often subject trans persons to further vulnerabilities and potential abuse. These engagements, more often than not, force trans persons to argue for and defend their gender identity over and over again. Baruah says, 'Rather than the person's identity, they are interested to know what is between the legs... Even if you see the various police harassment cases with respect to the transgender community you will find that most of the trans persons are being sexually abused by the police... Most of the officials are still not properly sensitized or well versed with the transgender factor.' As a result, many try to limit their direct engagement with the police and other arms of the State to the minimum. Many trans persons whose names did not appear in the first NRC draft, therefore, did not even file claims, to avoid putting themselves through the hearing process.

Designing an inclusive citizenship requires the acceptance

of the cultural and social realities of trans persons, looking beyond heteronormative imaginations of 'family'. Baruah argues that the NRC process would therefore have to recognize the legitimacy of the adoptive family structures of gharanas, accepting the lineage of the *guru–chela* tradition.

We met Swati in November 2019.

The Incongruity of Documentation and Everyday Lives

These testimonies demonstrate why establishing ties to land, family and the State is a near impossible task for a large number of women and gender minorities, especially if they are also economic and cultural minorities. The chars, where Muslim peasants from Bengal have been migrating since the late 1890s, are remote, unmapped, and constantly under threat as they disappear when Brahmaputra changes course. The nearly 2,500 chars are home to nearly three million, largely Muslims, who form roughly eight per cent of Assam's population. They emerge and are submerged every few years. Every time a char erodes, the people living there lose their belongings, have to dismantle their homes and move to the next closest char by boat. New sandbars appear constantly even as old, inhabited places are battered by the currents of the river. The shifting life has meant the absence of land records, and for married women particularly, loss of association with natal home and a particular piece of land.

The testimonies reveal that in their experience women in chars have been remote from the State; the State has never been present as a valid referent in their lives. The precarity of everyday life and the acute absences of any public service in the chars is stark. Women's right to public services is not protected by the State and social institutions (including families and communities) do not necessarily recognize women's right to have rights. The very absence of public services, and the low socio-economic indicators in the chars, reflect State apathy. Despite having executed her democratic duty of voting since 1957, Habiba Nessa, as her testimony revealed, did not have access to transportation or to a hospital when she was injured during the NRC process. And the State has now termed her illegal formally taking away her right to live in her impoverished community. What does the State hope to achieve by disenfranchising those like her, who have not had a chance to experience the privileges, or even services, that should have been their right?

There is an acute deficiency of schools, hospitals and public transport, and these absences further marginalize women and make it difficult to acquire requisite citizenship documents to prove their association with the land. Literacy rates in the chars are especially low; not even a small minority of women has school leaving certificates, and even if a small percentage of them had gone to primary schools, those documents are not valid under the NRC guidelines. Illiteracy and poor education mean that very few women possess a matriculation certificate, the first acceptable education certificate that shows birth and parentage.

Underage marriage is not an anomaly in India. Nearly half of the women in the char area get married before they turn 18—so they are not registered voters in their parents' village. Women do not deliver babies in hospitals and neither has registration of birth ever been a common practice. In the absence of these documents, married women, now in their husbands' village, are unable to establish their linkage with their parents and prove their citizenship lineage.[10] Women who get married before 18 get on the voter list only after marriage and the only linkage they have is that of their husband. In a patriarchal society, the identity of most women is entwined with that of their husbands, but the NRC process does not recognize this.

While panchayat certificates are officially accepted as alternative linkage documents—char women are under stronger scrutiny. A.K. Azad notes that of the 4.7 million women who submitted this certificate, 1.7 we given the status of 'original inhabitants'—but this did not include Muslim and Bengali Hindu women.[11] Nearly three million married women had to undergo stricter verification and many women were excluded from the final NRC list despite establishing linkage through a panchayat certificate.[12] Many women have also migrated to Assam post marriage—their citizenship documents such as school certificates therefore need to be sent back to their home state for verification. The *Economic Times* has reported that of the 140,000 documents sent to West Bengal for verification, only 15,000 were verified.[13] Having to constantly migrate due to flooding, women also report that maintaining and keeping a record of all their documentation is a difficult task for the people of the region.[14] In some cases, without literacy or property ownership women do not directly maintain their documents and finances and leave it to their husbands. Their legal identities are practically amalgamated with those of their husbands, and the NRC process does not recognize this grey area.

Heteronormative family structures fail to accommodate gender and sexual minorities—to many, therefore, 'family' does not mean a unit associated with bloodline. The place of kinship in the lives of trans persons and gender and sexual minorities does not always draw from the heteronormative family structure. These concepts of relatedness, kinship, group membership, and consequently law and citizenship are redefined and transformed. But the State processes choose not to acknowledge and consequently punish those outside the heteronormative family structure.

Historical marginalization, lack of political recognition or just physical inaccessibility can mean that the State and its manifestations never reach certain communities or individuals, rendering it near impossible for them to have any documents. Although these are only a very few reasons why these demands of the NRC are exclusionary in their design, it is possible to understand the scale of an individual or community's vulnerability to being excluded from the NRC through the lenses of land, family and governance. Furthermore, we have seen that it is possible for a woman or trans person being deemed a 'foreigner' by the arbitrary and legally precarious Foreigners' Tribunals despite proof of belonging to all three—land, family and State.

Beyond these identity markers, their working-class position as small-scale farmers, migrant and/or other informal labourers also adversely affects their experience. Having to fight the threat of exclusion requires families to undertake multiple, long trips to far-off hearing centres, seek the service of literate persons and other officials, and engage in long-drawn-out legal battles at the Foreigners' Tribunals and courts. Not only does this require families to spend more than they can afford, it also takes away crucial productive working hours from them. To many families, therefore, fighting for their citizenship is a clear debt trap.

CITIZENSHIP BEYOND THE PAPERWORK

The NRC process in Assam shows how the government can add layers of oppression to the lives of a large section of people who had placed their faith in the law. These legal measures have affected the lives of Muslim communities and they also extend an incommensurable level of power to determine matters related to citizenship to local functionaries of the state at the block and village level with their prejudices not hidden. Women have faced more exclusion because the authorities who are determined to exclude more people found women easier to exclude.

The testimonies and narratives in this paper show that while the NRC process claims to be gender neutral, the experience of it is deeply gendered and its failure to recognize the difference in how different genders are able to access and exercise their citizenship makes women and trans persons highly vulnerable.

Furthermore, displacement and statelessness affect different genders unequally—we have seen that the socio-legal precarity brought about through the NRC and D-voter processes presents unique challenges to gender minorities, alongside their increased vulnerability to be rendered so. The working-class Muslim women of the char-chapori region therefore exist at the crossroads of both patriarchal and anti-minority flows of citizenship. Their destiny from citizenship to statelessness is decided by local- and district-level officers, often in an arbitrary and unguided fashion. The implications are too disturbing and too many may get affected. This raises fundamental questions about women's citizenship rights. What do they do? And how do they claim their right to have rights, and identity?

Many of these questions exploded in the movements against the Citizenship Amendment Act, 2019 all over the country. Opposed to the common liberal notion of citizenship as a formal relation between the individual with documents and the State, in these movements it was clear that citizenship is a more complex relationship mediated by identity, belonging, and much more. The movement—in the form of women-led sit-in protests, Miya poetry, and a whole range of the Constitution-reclaiming actions where women came out, braving State hostility and oppression, to claim rights—showed that citizenship is an active concept, beyond mere status and formal rights. It is a relationship that upholds participation and agency and how people, pushed to exclusion, stake their claims to rights.

In Assam, within the oppressive structures surrounding the NRC, women from the chars and trans persons have emerged as leaders and activists engaging is relentless claim-making and expression of their politics and agency. The onslaught in the form of police cases, fake news and rape threats faced by poet and activist Rehna Sultana, for instance, is ironically testament to the socio-political impact her work with and for her community has had.[15] The nature of attacks and accusations levelled against her makes it clear that in this citizenship tussle, while it is difficult to be a working-class Muslim woman of Bengali origin, it is even more dangerous to add political assertion to the mix.

Through their engagement within their community as activists and social workers, and with the State and outside world as political actors, women like Rehna have been actively practising their citizenship, even when the very foundations of their citizenship are being questioned. The nationwide female-led anti-CAA protests, that also invoked the Constitution at its core, were perhaps among the most deliberate practice of citizenship, on such a scale, the country has seen in recent times. Not only did they actively resist regressive changes to the country's citizenship laws, but the act of their protest itself expanded what it means to be a citizen. The struggle for their rights was remarkable and just as important as the rights they were struggling for.[16] Women citizens who had been repeatedly flung outside the political borders of 'we, the people', staked their claims to full membership of the society of citizens for themselves and their community.

Notes

1. See for instance the insightful Introduction in Hiren Gohain, *Struggling in a Time Warp: Essays and Observations on the Northeast's History and Politics with Particular Reference to Assam*, Guwahati: Bhabani Books, 2019.
2. See for instance Sanjib Baruah, 'The Partition's long shadow: The ambiguities of citizenship in Assam, India', *Citizenship Studies*, vol. 13, no. 6 (2009), pp. 593–606.
3. See for instance Juri Baruah, 'The public versus private space: The feminization of work in tea plantation, *ANTYAJAA: Indian Journal of Women and Social Change*, vol. 3, no. 2 (2018); Banamallika Choudhury, 'Addressing gender-based violence in tea gardens in Assam, India', IDH, The Sustainable Trade Initiative official website, 25 November 2020 (https://www.idhsustainabletrade.com/publication/addressing-gender-based-violence-in-tea-gardens-in-india/); and Nitin Varma, 'Producing tea coolies?: Work, life

and protest in the colonial tea plantations of Assam', unpublished PhD dissertation, Humboldt University, Berlin, 2011.

4. See Hafiz Ahmed's poem included in Part 2 of this volume.
5. See Rehna Sultana's poem included in Part 2 of this volume.
6. T.H. Marshall, *Citizenship and Social Class* (1950). Marshall looked at citizenship as rights and essentially a matter of ensuring that everyone is treated as a full and equal member of society, and ensuring this sense of membership through according people an increasing number of rights.
7. Such as the *Sarbananda Sonowal* judgment in 2005, which struck down the earlier IMDT Act and in a very significant move shifted the burden of proving citizenship onto the people.
8. We would like to thank Rehna Sultana for her support with fieldwork and translation in Assam.
9. See 'What are the admissible documents?' (http://www.nrcassam.nic.in/admin-documents.html) and 'Who are eligible for inclusion?' (http://www.nrcassam.nic.in/eligibility-criteria.html) issued by the Office of the State Coordinator of National Registration (NRC), Assam.
10. 'Many married women left out in NRC', *The Economic Times*, 4 August 2018.
11. A.K. Azad, 'Assam NRC draft: How women in char areas were left high and dry, *News18*, 8 August 2018.
12. A. Gani, 'Women suffer most post NRC', *The Citizen*, 12 August 2018.
13. 'Many married women left out in NRC', *The Economic Times*.
14. 'Eroding Citizenship in Assam | Karwan e Mohabbat', *NewsClick*, 7 June 2019 (available here: https://www.youtube.com/watch?v=Lp-owKTRz0I).
15. P. Dasgupta, 'Assam: Fake news sent this woman scholar on the run from police', *HuffPost India*, 5 November 2019; 'This Muslim woman was hit with 4 FIRs, rape threats for writing poetry in her mother tongue', *HuffPost India*, 30 July 2019.
16. See Ruth Lister, *Citizenship: Feminist Perspectives*, 2nd ed. Basingstoke: Palgrave Macmillan, 2003.

THE WAY FORWARD

RECOMMENDATIONS FOR A BROKEN SYSTEM

Mohsin Alam Bhat, Abdul Kalam Azad and Harsh Mander

The National Register of Citizens (NRC) in Assam threatens to produce statelessness on a scale unmatched by any democracy. It caused, in Assam, enormous suffering and dread to millions of mostly poorly lettered and very impoverished people, who have squandered all their meagre belongings to pay lawyers' fees to help them negotiate the hostile and opaque maze of the NRC bureaucracy and the Foreigners' Tribunals (FTs).

Citizenship is a meta public good since citizenship status allows individuals and groups to exercise most other rights and entitlements. Citizenship status also forms an important aspect of what political philosopher John Rawls calls the 'social bases of self-respect'. In his account, a just political system must guarantee self-respect or self-esteem of individuals because this dignitarian element is central for a person to lead a good life. For Rawls, this can only be done if the just society guarantees equal citizenship to everyone, as a recognition of everyone's status as an equally dignified person.[1] Hannah Arendt has articulated another compelling variation of the relationship between citizenship and human dignity. According to Arendt, human dignity is possible only when a person is a member of a political community. Human dignity is the result of other members of the polity recognizing the individual's status and ability to be a free agent. Consequently for Arendt, when any person is bereft of citizenship, she is stripped of humanity itself. This led her to lament that without 'the right to have rights'—the right to be part of some political community as a citizen—human dignity could not be guaranteed for everyone.[2]

In its design and implementation, the NRC is an arbitrary and opaque system, which consequently weakens stable citizenship. It has introduced a lingering frightening uncertainty in their lives about whether they would remain Indian citizens, or be locked up for years in detention centres, or forced to live as doubtful or non-citizens without elementary rights to access a range of public goods including owning property or accessing social protection such as subsidized food grains, or indeed be deported. This debilitating and humiliating instability and uncertainty marks the lives not only of those who were ultimately excluded from the NRC, but also those who had to go through the maze of burdensome bureaucratic procedures to prove their citizenship.

This unstable citizenship—that has rendered innumerable residents of the state precarious—amounts to adverse exclusion, especially of those belonging to vulnerable communities. The precarious citizens of the state were subjected to overly burdensome and often discriminatory procedures. These persons were compelled to divert all their meagre resources, time and energy—away from pursuing their lives and livelihoods—towards establishing their citizenship. This process heightened their vulnerability and engendered fear, harming their dignity and freedom.

Now the political establishment threatens to drag these precarious citizens through this same process all over again. It has been demanding re-verification in minority-concentrated districts, with the aim of increasing the total number of excluded persons. The NRC authority is yet to notify the final list that would entitle the excluded to file appeals in the FTs. Instead, at the time of writing the chapter, it had issued circulars instructing its officials to revisit the inclusion of several persons.[3]

The path for those who were—or will be—ultimately excluded from the NRC is now riddled with steep challenges. They now have the right to appeal to the FTs, which are notorious for arbitrariness and disregard for ordinary laws of evidence. If the excluded persons fail at the FT stage, they can certainly approach the Gauhati High Court and the Supreme Court. But the expense of this would be an insurmountable barrier for scores of the excluded to access justice.

To make matters worse, the state has failed to announce its policy for those who are ultimately excluded after exhausting all the legal remedies. The gravest violation of constitutional justice of the entire NRC process in Assam, which now threatens to imperil minorities across India, is that to date the Union government has not clarified what will be the fate of people who are finally declared to be foreigners. Neither the Supreme Court nor Parliament have compelled the government to clarify what the destiny will be of possibly one to two million people in Assam if they are finally declared to be 'foreigners'? Home Minister Amit Shah has made amply clear his determination to give citizenship to people of every religious identity except Muslim. If he succeeds in doing this, what will happen to those Muslim residents of Assam who are unable to prove their citizenship of India?

There is no question of Bangladesh accepting those whom the Indian government declares to be foreigners, but who deny that they are Bangladeshi. Thousands have been detained over time in detention centres located within prisons.[4] The Assam government has reported that it is building ten detention centres in the state of Assam, one of them which is nearing construction in Goalpara will house 3,000 'declared foreigners'.[5] But what will happen to possibly half a million or more people declared by India's judicial system, such as they are, to be non-citizens in Assam? And possibly several million more if the NRC is actually extended to the rest of India? Will the Indian government detain them in massive concentration camps? If so, for how long? Will they—men, women and children—be confined there all their lives? Or will they continue to live outside detention centres in India but stripped of all citizenship rights? Stripped of the rights to vote, to own property, to enter government service? What kind of lives will they live in absence of citizenship? The spectre of intense existential uncertainty, thus, pervades the lives of millions.

The appreciation of citizenship as a public good reveals that the State must secure the guarantee of status through legal and institutional means. It must not subject a person's citizenship status to arbitrary targeting. It must also create a transparent legal architecture in case the issue of citizenship verification and authentication arises. It also follows that a person must not be subjected to arbitrary and overly demanding inquiries about their citizenship status. Arbitrary questioning of someone's citizenship—particularly in the absence of transparent, fair and reasonable institutional procedures—would introduce severe uncertainty in her life, especially considering the serious consequences of the loss of citizenship. Legal processes can make citizenship precarious by making it contingent on arbitrary official discretion and whim. Precarious citizens are compelled to invest all their human and material resources to preserving their status, and divert them from achieving any other public good. Thus, processes that engender precarious citizenship suspend normal lives altogether. Exclusion from citizenship as a public good is triggered not only when a person is *de jure* (or even *de facto*) denied or deprived of citizenship. It is also triggered when citizenship status is threatened by unfair and arbitrary procedures. They amount to indirect exclusion by creating a heightened form of vulnerability. Precarious citizenship is exclusion because it undermines the security of status and an important basis of self-respect.

1. THE ONGOING NRC PROCESS

It has been more than a year since the final NRC was published. The government has still to issue individual rejection orders specifying the reasons for a person's exclusion, for every one of those excluded from the final NRC list. It is this that would allow the excluded persons to challenge their exclusion in the FTs. It is also yet to formally initiate this appeals process. The Assam government on the other hand is trying to discredit the NRC and is advocating a fresh NRC along with the national NRC. This would be nothing short of calamitous for the linguistic and religious minorities of Assam. It would mean that even those among these intensely vulnerable people who had been through a trial of fire to prove their citizenship to a hostile bureaucracy against immense odds would have to start all over again, and would need to go through similar painful and traumatic processes once more. The first recommendation is that the authorities should immediately issue identity cards to all the people who are included.

Those who were excluded from the NRC list are living through an immense degree of anxiety and uncertainty. The authorities should immediately release to them the 'reason of rejection' and kickstart the process of determination of their citizenship in a fair and judicious manner.

The environment of hatred and discrimination against the vulnerable communities has been mounting in the fraught and highly polarized political environment of the state. The amended Citizenship Act that provides citizenship to excluded Bengali Hindus has actually made the community more vulnerable in Assam. On the other hand the Bharatiya Janata Party government in Assam has been propagating hatred against the Bengali-origin Muslims. In such an environment the active hostility both of the state and the majority community against these vulnerable communities are only increasing. Authorities should make all the officials involved in the processes of citizenship contestation and determination accountable. They should also be provided training on principles of non-discrimination, human rights and rights of vulnerable social groups like women, children and the trans community.

2. TRANSPARENT JUDICIAL PROCESS

The rights to fair trial and due process are fundamental human rights. They are equally constitutive of the right to equal protection (Article 14) and the right to life, personal liberty and due process (Article 21) under the Indian Constitution. Article 9(4) of the International Covenant on Civil and Political Rights (ICCPR)—that India is a party to and hence bound by—lays down that no person can be deprived of her liberty without recourse to a court of law. Article 14 of the Covenant also lays down that everyone has a right to a fair and public hearing by a tribunal. Such a tribunal must be competent, independent and impartial. These rights of fair trial and due process apply to the legal determination of citizenship status.

Since citizenship is undoubtedly one of the most significant rights under international law, and has the most valued status under India's constitutional scheme, there is an even greater need to secure fair trial and due process while dealing with the question of citizenship determination and verification.

From this perspective, it is an anomaly that citizenship determination in Assam is being conducted not before India's courts but through the FTs. While the FTs appear to have trappings of courts, they are executive-created bodies constituted not under a law of Parliament, but through the government's rule-making powers under the Tribunals Order. They are meant to give their 'opinions' to the government regarding whether a person is a foreigner. There is no parliamentary legislation regarding the qualifications of its members. In fact, the government has consistently diluted the need for judicial experience for someone to be appointed as an FT member. At present, in addition to retired judges, the government recruits former civil servants and practising advocates without any requirement of compelling judicial experience or training. Moreover, there are no formal provisions that secure the independence of the FT members. There are many anecdotal accounts of lawyers being selected for this office who are ideologically aligned to the ruling establishment. Currently, the FT members are appointed on a contractual basis, and any extension of tenure is left to the government's assessment of their performance. There are serious fears—borne out by numerous journalistic reports—that only those FT members have been given extensions who have indiscriminately declared people foreigners.[6] There is also compelling evidence to show that the FTs have adopted arbitrary procedures, often disregarding basic rules of evidence, to declare people foreigners.[7] This problem is further aggravated by the fact that under the executive rules, the FTs are free to lay down their own procedures.[8] These factors clearly reflect that the FTs are not competent, independent or impartial, and thus do not fulfil the criteria of courts and tribunals as required under the law.

It is also relevant to note that when the question of citizenship determination comes up in other countries, they leave it to the final determination by ordinary courts. The question of citizenship determination should be left *not* to administrative bodies but to courts, which are more adept at evaluating evidence. For example, under the Immigration Act, 1971 of the United Kingdom, while the State does exercise the right to deport non-citizens, the question of determining whether a person is a citizen or not involves ordinary courts. Similarly, revocation of naturalization in the United States under the Immigration and Nationality Act, 1952 also involves judicial determination by courts. French law requires courts to determine if a person is a citizen owing to the 'inherent difficulties in providing proof of French nationality'.[9]

Ironically, the Indian Supreme Court relied on the practice in the USA and the UK to shift the burden of proof onto individuals in citizenship determination cases in the *Sarbananda Sonowal* case. But both these countries leave citizenship determination not to bodies like the FTs that are created by the executive, but to the courts of law bound by respectable rules of procedure and evidence, and with laws and conventions securing their independence and competence.

In light of this, we recommend that all citizenship determination processes come within the purview of ordinary courts. The Indian Parliament may enact suitable provisions, as part of the Citizenship Act, 1955 if need be, to constitute independent, impartial and competent special courts to adjudicate such cases. These special courts must meet the criteria of due process and fair trial that are mandated by the Indian Constitution and international human rights law. The members should be recruited through Assam Judicial Services and employment be made permanent so that they do not have to feel insecure of losing their employment while involved in the administration of justice. Individuals must have a right to appeal to the High Court and the Supreme Court against the decisions of these special courts.

3. REFORM OF THE FOREIGNERS' TRIBUNALS

In the interim, the government must seriously reform the current operation of the FTs. Reforms are needed at the three levels of structure, membership and operation. Structurally, the FTs must be given complete independence from the executive. There should be a politically insulated system for the appointment of members, who must be given security of tenure to ensure independence. The current system of contractual employment, and extension based on State evaluation must be completely removed.

In terms of membership, the government must reinstate the requirement of judicial experience for the members of the FTs. Appointing lawyers or retired civil servants as members undermines the need for transparent and rigorous legal reasoning and appreciation of evidence.

The government must also reform the operation of the FTs. At present, the FTs are not bound by any procedural and evidentiary laws, because of paragraph 3 of the Tribunals Order. The paragraph must be amended to make the ordinary laws of the land applicable in citizenship determination proceedings.

One of the biggest concerns has been the vexatious—and often non-existent—police inquiries that continue to target genuine Indian citizens. The FTs must be reminded and empowered to take punitive steps against the police officers filing false cases. They must also ensure that they assess the substance of the grounds and allegations of suspicion before issuing notices to individuals. The government must appoint government pleaders in all the FTs, which is not currently the case.

4. FAIR LEGAL RULES OF EVIDENCE

Some of the biggest concerns about the FT process—and by extension, about the appeals after NRC exclusion—have been about the faulty appreciation of evidence. Since the FTs are not legally bound by the Indian evidence law, extensive documentation has shown that they rely on hyper-technicalities, minor contradictions and overly burdensome evidentiary requirements to declare persons foreigners.

The most worrying area of concern is the question of burden of proof. The *Sarbananda Sonowal* judgment placed the burden of proving citizenship on the individual rather than the State. If one is to adopt a generous reading of the judgment, the Court's ruling on the issue was based on the understanding that ordinary—and hence, reasonable, fair and just—principles of evidence law would continue to apply. Consequently, the State will also need to share the onus to showing why certain evidence presented by the individual is not admissible or persuasive. But since the judgment, this burden of proof has degenerated into unfair demands from the individual.

First, the FT proceedings are overly dependent on documentary proof. This is unfair simply because most Indians do not have access to viable documents like birth certificates, school certificates and property ownership documents. Individuals are forced to spend resources on getting certified copies of public documents, most of which are already in the possession of the State. To make matters more burdensome, the FTs require many of these documents to be corroborated by officials and witnesses. This forces the individuals—mostly poor and unlettered—to incur heavy expenditure. Moreover, many FTs refuse to summon officials, who are most unlikely to come to the FTs merely on the request of the individual struggling to prove her citizenship.

Second, most of the documents are often error-ridden, which is also often the fault of the State rather than the individual. For example, individuals often present voter lists as evidence of their citizenship. These voter lists invariably have errors because of the EC's machinery. The FTs regularly reject such documents during the proceedings.

Third, the FTs never make any evidentiary demands from the State. Government pleaders are often missing during the proceedings. In their place, the FT members cross-question the defence witnesses. The members also practically never require the State to argue why documentary and non-documentary evidence presented by the individual should not be accepted. Finally, the FTs almost never make the inquiry reports and grounds of suspicion available to the individuals, to allow them to satisfy their burden.

These problems demand a serious review of the FT process in relation to the appreciation of evidence. The FTs must apply ordinary principles of evidence law as a rule. They must accept both documentary and oral evidence. Grounds of suspicion and inquiry reports must be made available to the individuals the moment notices are issued. Individuals should also not be required to certify government documents in their possession. The State is better placed to authenticate and present these documents to the FT. The State must appoint government pleaders during all proceedings, and the FT members must ask the State—as is the case in any normal legal proceeding—to assert its own evidence and rebut the individual's evidence. The burden of proof should be shared, rather than be placed only on the individual. A good practice in this regard is the African Court on Human and Peoples' Rights, which in its jurisprudence has held that in citizenship determination proceedings, the burden of proof must be shared.[10] The Court has held that since citizenship has implications for the dignity of individuals, it is not proper for the burden to be only on the individuals. The State must share the burden if it seeks to prove that the documents that the individual is relying upon are inadequate or wrong. Finally, minor errors, especially in government documents, must never be used to declare someone a foreigner.

5. APPELLATE COURT SUPERVISION

At present, the higher judiciary has limited the scope of its review of FT decisions. This review does not occur in the form of appeals from FT orders since the Tribunals Order does not provide for it. Rather, individuals who are declared foreigners by the FTs can file writs in the Gauhati High Court under Article 226 of the Constitution, beyond which they can approach the Supreme Court. Through this mechanism, the High Court has consistently refused to interfere with the factual findings of the FTs. This is despite the FTs not following standard rules of evidence and procedure, and numerous instances of badly reasoned orders. From available evidence, it also appears that the High Court never assesses the procedural lapses—absent or poor inquiries, non-delivery of grounds of suspicion, inadequate opportunity to cross-question government witnesses or prove the case, and absence of government pleaders—that may have undermined due process at the FT level. In light of the serious problems with the FTs, the High Court must adopt a more searching and demanding model of review of FT orders.

6. DETENTION

Under Indian and international law, any detention that is without legitimate purpose and disproportional is illegal.[11] It is the duty of the State to identify less intrusive means in case there may be any justified reason to secure a person. Indefinite detention would always be illegal.[12] The Indian government has not made its long-term policy regarding the ends of detention clear. Nor has it raised this matter diplomatically with Bangladesh, despite the rhetoric of deportation. In these circumstances, detention—of any person excluded from the NRC or through any other route of citizenship contestation—would be illegal. The State must affirm that no person will be detained and create alternatives to detention.

7. NATURALIZATION OF EXCLUDED PERSONS

One of the most worrying features of the NRC process is the uncertain fate of the persons who ultimately are unable to establish their citizenship during the appeals from their exclusion. International organizations have already raised concerns about a crisis of statelessness, and potentially a refugee crisis resulting from the NRC.[13] In this light, there is a need to consider the best policy and legal measures to address this impending crisis.

We recommend that the Indian State must immediately clarify its position on the final consequences of the NRC. It must also make necessary changes in Indian law to ensure that no person is rendered stateless. Under international law, all States are bound by the obligation to prevent deliberately or inadvertently rendering their nationals stateless.[14] The persons left out of the NRC after appeals will have no other viable nationality. India has not raised this issue diplomatically with Bangladesh, which in any case will be reluctant—to say the least—to accept any Indians who may lose their Indian citizenship. Consequently, India would be violating its obligations under international law if it does not secure the citizenship of Indian nationals.

India must amend the Citizenship Act, 1955 in light of this obligation. It must provide a transparent mechanism for the naturalization of any person who may be finally rendered without Indian nationality.

8. PROTECTING CHILD RIGHTS

India is a party to numerous international conventions that bind it to the obligation of securing the citizenship of children born in its territory.[15] These include the obligation to provide citizenship to children who would otherwise be rendered stateless. This is reflected in best practices across the world. For instance, countries like France and Finland confer citizenship to any child born in the country to unknown or stateless persons, or to those who cannot transmit citizenship to the child.[16] Estonia grants citizenship to any child born in the country whose parents were resident in the country for five or more years, and who did not have access to citizenship of any other country.[17] Article 21 of the Indian Constitution, which guarantees right to life with dignity, must be interpreted in this light.

The best course for India to meet these legal obligations is to strengthen birthright citizenship based on the *jus soli* principle.[18] The dilution of this principle through the 1986 and 2003 amendments to the Citizenship Act, 1955 must be reversed.

Moreover, any detention of children would violate India's commitments under international law,[19] and also be contrary to the Juvenile Justice Act, 2015 that places the best interests of children at the centre of State policy.

9. ENACTING A REFUGEE POLICY IN CONFORMITY WITH THE INTERNATIONAL REFUGEE CONVENTIONS

In his historic address to the World's Parliament of Religions in Chicago in 1893, Swami Vivekanand declared, 'I am proud to belong to a nation which has sheltered the persecuted and the refugees of all religions and all nations of the earth.' It is ironic that the Indian government that claims allegiance to Swami

Vivekanand has enacted the Citizenship Amendment Act, 2019 restricting citizenship to people on the grounds of both religion and nation.

There is a moral imperative for India to adopt an expansive and humane refugee law. This must conform to what is finest in India's civilizational ethos, and to the morality of India's Constitution. In this light, India must sign and ratify the international conventions on refugees, including the 1951 Convention Relating to the Status of Refugees.

The Convention defines refugees as persons fleeing persecution on grounds of race, religion, nationality, social group or political opinion. Refugees get legal rights, most important of which are 'non-refoulement', which prevents States from sending back refugees to persecution in their home countries. They also get secondary rights, such as education, work and property. It also prohibits discrimination in accepting refugees.

Accepting these legal obligations would mean recognizing undocumented immigrants as refugees, based on evidence determined by due process of their persecution in their home countries. This would also assure them a set of binding rights. The most important of these is the guarantee that they would not be forced to return to the conditions of persecution, threatening their lives and liberty, which they escaped. The second is that they would be assured lives of dignity within India, with education, health care and livelihoods.

It cannot be our case that as long as States have borders, sovereign governments should not have the right to identify those who have illegally entered the borders and act against them. Our conviction is that the exercise of this sovereign right must be lawful, transparent, free from bias, just and, in the end, humane. The burden to prove one's legitimate and lawful citizenship must be restored, first of all, to the government if it claims that one is a non-citizen, and not to residents who claim to be citizens. The evidence presented by the State, and that mustered by residents to counter the State's allegations, must be tested by a strict adherence to principles of natural justice, by qualified judicial officers whose independence is secured, and by giving both fair opportunity and, where needed, free legal aid. Those found to be illegal after this due process should not be detained indefinitely, in jails, with families separated. Detention centres of the kind that exist today must be declared unconstitutional, and shut down forthwith. The State must announce transparent policies, supported by Parliament, for undocumented persons who are not accepted by any other country, that adhere to international law and constitutional guarantees. And finally, India should offer citizenship to persecuted minorities from other countries without discriminating on the basis of religion, country of origin, and indeed gender, language, race, ethnicity, caste, sexuality and political belief.

Notes

1. John Rawls, *A Theory of Justice*, rev. ed., 1999, p. 386. See also Joshua Cohen, 'For a democratic society', *The Cambridge Companion to Rawls*, ed. S. Freeman, Cambridge University Press, 2002, pp. 86, 109.
2. Hannah Arendt, *The Origins of Totalitarianism*, Harvest, 1973, pp. 296–99.
3. Abhishek Saha, 'Explained: Move to delete "ineligible" names from Assam NRC—who, and why', *The Indian Express*, 19 October 2020.
4. In May 2020, the Supreme Court passed orders for decongesting jails in the context of Covid-19. Among the ordinary prisoners who were released, the government also released 308 of the total 802 persons in foreigner detention centres. See Rahul Karmakar, '308 "foreigners" released from Assam detention centres', *The Hindu*, 20 May 2020.
5. Sadiq Naqvi, 'Assam seeks 10 more detention centres to hold "illegal foreigners"', *Hindustan Times*, 15 June 2019.
6. For a more recent example, see Poonam Agarwal, 'Assam NRC: We did not know that we had to declare foreigners, rightly or

wrongly to save our jobs, said former judicial officer of Assam's foreigners tribunals', *The Quint*, 6 October 2020.

7. *Designed to Exclude: How India's Courts are Allowing Foreigners Tribunals to Render People Stateless in Assam*, Indians for Amnesty International Trust, Bengaluru, 2019 (https://www.amnesty.be/IMG/pdf/rapport_inde.pdf, last accessed 20 June 2021).
8. T. Rahman, 'Identifying the "Outsider"', *The Statelessness and Citizenship Review*, vol. 2, no. 1 (2020), pp. 112–37.
9. Commentaire Décision n° 2013-354 QPC du 22 novembre 2013 (Mme Charly K), Conseil constitutionnel, quoted in p. 9 of 'Ensuring that no child is born stateless', UNHCR's Good Practices Paper Action 2, 20 March 2017 (https://www.refworld.org/pdfid/58cfab014.pdf).
10. *Anudo Ochieng Anudo vs United Republic Of Tanzania*, Application No. 012/2015, 22 March 2018 judgment; *Robert John Penessis vs United Republic Of Tanzania*, Application No. 013/2015, 28 November 2019 judgment.
11. 'Securing citizenship: India's legal obligations towards precarious citizens and stateless persons', Centre for Public Interest Law, O.P. Jindal Global University, 2020 (https://jgu.edu.in/jgls/securing-citizenship-report/).
12. UN Human Rights Committee, Views adopted by the Committee under article 5(4) of the Optional Protocol, concerning Communication No. 2233/2013, UN Doc. CCPR/C/116/D/2233/2013 (18 April 2016).
13. 'UN High Commissioner for Refugees expresses alarm at statelessness risk in India's Assam', UNHCR, 1 September 2019 (https://www.unhcr.org/en-in/news/press/2019/9/5d6a24ba4/un-high-commissioner-refugees-expresses-alarm-statelessness-risk-indias.html).
14. See *Human rights and arbitrary deprivation of nationality: Report of the Secretary-General*, UN Human Rights Council, A/HRC/25/28, 19 December 2013; and 'Securing citizenship: India's legal obligations towards precarious citizens and stateless persons'.
15. See Article 7(1), Convention on the Rights of the Child; Article 24, ICCPR; Article 18(2), CRPD.
16. 'Ensuring that no child is born stateless', UNHCR's Good Practices Paper Action 2, pp. 8, 10.
17. Ibid., p. 15.
18. See 'Guidelines on statelessness no. 4: Ensuring every child's right to acquire a nationality through articles 1-4 of the 1961 Convention

on the Reduction of Statelessness', UNHCR, HCR/GS/12/04, 21 December 2012 (https://www.refworld.org/docid/50d460c72.html); and 'Ensuring that no child is born stateless', UNHCR's Good Practices Paper Action 2. See also 'Securing citizenship: India's legal obligations towards precarious citizens and stateless persons'.

19. Article 3, Convention on the Rights of the Child.

PART THREE

The Citizenship Amendment Act, 2019 and a Pan-India NRC

QUIT INDIA, '83, BASBARI

Ashraful Hussain

I stand in the witness box and look at your face;
Are you the symbol of justice?
I shut my eyes and give you everything—
My birth certificate, records of my childhood, youth,
Senility, riots, Quit India, '83, Basbari.

You turn my worn-out moth-eaten papers
Your stamp goes thump, thump, thump
Your pen draws a long line—
The sounds fall on my ears
But my eyes are shut.
My heart shivers.

I open my eyes and my hands
Are in the hands of salaried gunslingers.
I am taken to my cell.
My days pass in fear and uncertainty
Like a common criminal
Lost to dignity, lost to justice.

Who I am is my crime
What I am is what I look like
And my crime of language is what makes me stateless.

CONTESTED CITIZENSHIP

WHAT CONSTITUENT ASSEMBLY DEBATES FROM 70 YEARS AGO REVEAL ABOUT INDIA TODAY

Anirban Bhattacharya and Azram Rahman Khan

In November 1948, as Z.H. Lari was making a case in the Constituent Assembly for statutory provisions for the minorities, he was constantly heckled. Some members asked the Muslim representative from the United Provinces what 'his leaders' were doing about the minorities in Pakistan.

Lari eventually took on their taunts. His hecklers, he said, wanted him to follow the footsteps of Pakistan but he was not going to do so. 'I have not mortgaged my rights to Pakistan,' he said. 'What Pakistan does or does not do is not my concern.'

He added that Indian Muslims 'are the children of the soil and as such we claim the rights of citizens of India'.

More than seven decades have passed since then but the public discussions in India today remain uncannily similar. India's Muslim community continues to be subject to similar heckling—and worse. As hundreds of thousands of Indians took to the streets to protest the Citizenship Amendment Act (CAA), which introduces a religious criterion into the country's citizenship law, some of the questions that engaged the Constituent Assembly that was framing India's Constitution are being debated all over again.

While there were many apprehensions, disagreements and criticisms about the document in terms of what India's destiny ought to be, a larger sense prevailed about what it ought not to be. The members of the Assembly decisively decided against making India a majoritarian State—though the advocates for that position were quite loud even then.

Reading the deliberations of the Constituent Assembly

could be useful for Indians to get a better understanding of the present debate around citizenship and minority rights. It would probably help illustrate as to why the collective wisdom of the Assembly rejected efforts to adopt a narrow, sectarian agenda at the time.

BLOOD OR BIRTH?

Among the most pitched battles in the Constituent Assembly was the one to determine the basis on which Indian citizenship rested. Clauses on citizenship were debated thrice in the Constituent Assembly given its importance as being fundamental to the nature of the Indian republic. It was discussed exhaustively for all its implications and a larger sense prevailed on the guiding principles of Indian citizenship. There were two diametrically opposing principles that contended.

As Alladi Krishnaswami Ayyar noted on 29 April 1947 when the citizenship clause was first moved in the Assembly, the two principles that determine citizenship were *lex soli* and *lex sanguinis*. *Lex soli* means 'the law of the place of birth', while *lex sanguinis* means 'the law according to blood'.

Some members said that everyone born in the Union should be considered an Indian citizen—part of 'We, the people', irrespective of religion.

Opposed to this universalistic idea was posed a definition based on race, bloodline and religion that was in vogue at the time in continental Europe and beyond. This notion suggested that no matter where they were born, people belonging to a particular race would get citizenship.

It is this principle that has been bottled and served to us in the form of the CAA. Prime Minister Narendra Modi and others have repeatedly stated that this Act is for those who have no other place to go except India. In this conception of citizenship, the minorities who do not belong to a particular race, or religion, do not have equal footing as they are not considered natural citizens of the land.

SECULARISM AN OFFENCE?

While B.R. Ambedkar, Jawaharlal Nehru and several others made an effort to divorce the question of citizenship from the subject of religion, there were those who were bent on linking the two. Many of them were members of Hindu supremacist organizations who were drawn to the racial theories of Nazi Germany and admired Fascist Italy.

When this issue of citizenship being universal and democratic as opposed to sectarian was again discussed in the Assembly on 2 May 1947, Alladi reiterated what had been adopted by the Advisory Committee on Fundamental Rights, Minorities and Tribal and Excluded Areas chaired by Vallabhbhai Patel. He said, '"Every person born in the Union and subject to the jurisdiction; every person either of whose parents was, at the time of such person's birth, a citizen of the Union, and every person naturalised in the Union", so far as that part is concerned, there can be no exception [to citizenship]... [W]e are all agreed and there is absolutely no difference of opinion. It was discussed threadbare by the Committee which was appointed by this House and we unanimously came to the conclusion that this should be adopted.'

The third and conclusive debate on citizenship took place in the Constituent Assembly on the 10th, 11th and 12th of August 1949 after the citizenship clauses relating to domicile, i.e. Articles 5 and 6, were moved as part of the Draft Constitution. The Draft Constitution moved by Ambedkar too conferred the rights of citizenship only on two principles, namely birth and domicile. However, by this time Partition had been in effect for nearly two years and there were attempts by some members to use this tragedy and people's suffering to incorporate a sectarian notion of citizenship into the constitution.

Among them was P.S. Deshmukh of Central Provinces and Berar who on 11 August 1949 introduced an amendment that read, 'Every person who is a Hindu or a Sikh by religion and is not a citizen of any other State, wherever he resides shall be a citizen of India.'

Deshmukh claimed that Ambedkar's universalistic definition would make India's citizenship 'easy' and the 'cheapest on earth'. The reason for such 'easiness', Deshmukh claimed, was the 'specious, oft-repeated and nauseating principle of secularity of state'.

He explained,

> I think that we are going too far in this business of secularity. Does it mean that we must wipe out our own people, that we must wipe them out in order to prove our secularity?... I do not think that that is the meaning of secularity and if that is the meaning which people want to attach to that word...I am sure the popularity of those who take that view will not last long in India.

Deshmukh's words found an echo in Narendra Modi's victory speech in May 2019. He said that secularism was a 'drama going on for very long', and that the resounding victory for his Bharatiya Janata Party (BJP) marks the end of the drama. 'In this election not even a single political party could dare to mislead the country by wearing the mask of secularism,' Modi claimed.

In a few months' time came the CAA which has, in effect, tied the question of citizenship to religion. Not surprisingly, the justification given by Amit Shah in the Lok Sabha for this Act was partition of India on religious lines. This is clearly an attempt to complete their unfinished task of 1949.

SECULARISM, A DEFENCE

Nehru was among those who was alarmed by the constant haggling around the word 'secular', which was being presented as the root of all of India's problems.

He did not mince words as he knew that India could claim to be a democratic republic only if it was secular:

> It is brought in in all contexts, as if by saying that we are a secular state we have done something amazingly generous, given something out of our pocket to the rest of the world, something which we ought not to have done... We have only done something which every country does except a very few misguided and backward countries in the world. Let us not refer to that word in the sense that we have done something very mighty.

While there were those who had the moral conviction to defend the idea of secularism even in the aftermath of the bloody Partition riots, that belief appears diminished today even among members of so-called secular parties. The vocal commitment of Hindutva parties to their divisive ideas is met with a hesitant, uninspiring defence of secularism. It was, in fact, the protesters against the CAA who revived secularism in political discourse.

MINORITY RIGHTS: RELATIVE OR ABSOLUTE?

Gandhi, who was not a member of the Constituent Assembly, believed that the test of a democracy was deeply tied to the manner in which a society treats its minorities.

But there were those who, much like today, disagreed with the above and yet called themselves followers of Gandhi. They advocated for a narrower Hindutva-oriented definition of citizenship that was inextricably linked to the project of 'otherization' and to curtailing the rights of minorities.

Among them was Congress member Mahavir Tyagi, who proposed the house to postpone any discussion around minority rights and leave the matter to be decided later. The rights to be accorded were regarding protection against discrimination on the basis of the individual's religion, language or community.

His attitude was echoed in comments in Parliament by Home Minister Amit Shah. Shah claimed that minorities do not have the moral right to oppose the CAA if they support special provisions for themselves.

Tyagi's ideas and Amit Shah's iteration of them had been dismissed conclusively in the Constituent Assembly by Ambedkar:

> The only reason in support of this proposal—one can sense—is that the rights of minorities should be relative, that is to say, we must wait and see what rights the minorities are given by the Pakistan Assembly before we determine the rights we want to give to the minorities in the Hindustan area... Now, sir, with all deference, I must deprecate any such idea. Rights of minorities should be absolute rights. They should not be subject to any consideration as to what another party may like to do to minorities within its jurisdiction.

WHO'S WELCOME, WHO ISN'T?

The question of Partition refugees that the Constituent Assembly debated is very similar to the questions being asked today about immigrants. Some wanted to grant citizenship status only to Hindu and Sikh refugees. Others argued that it would be unjust to be selective. After all, there were Muslims who may have had to flee India in the wake of the bloody massacres that accompanied Partition but who chose to return once the dust settled to be citizens of India.

While there were those who wanted to exclude all Muslim returnees, members like Congress leader Brajeshwar Prasad argued for India's borders to be open to anyone who wanted to live here.

Of course, there were those who said that the Muslim returnees could in fact be 'spies', and thereby, a threat to 'national security'. But Prasad reiterated Nehru's contention that a majoritarian Hindu sentiment, if it presented itself, would pose a greater threat to India than any minority.

Some argued that it was economically unviable to take in Muslim returnees from Pakistan. But Brajeshwar Prasad had an unequivocal response:

> We are not a nation of shopkeepers… Whatever the economic consequences may be, we want to stand on certain principles. It is only by a strict adherence to certain moral principles that nations progress. The material development of life is no index to progress and civilization. I do not think it is politics or statesmanship to subordinate sound political principles to cheap economics. I see no reason why a Muslim who is a citizen of this country should be deprived of his citizenship at the commencement of this Constitution, specially when we are inviting Hindus who have come to India from Pakistan to become citizens of this country.

THE WAR IS FAR FROM OVER

The votaries of a majoritarian State had lost the battle in the Constituent Assembly in 1949, albeit by forcing advocates for secularism to make several compromises. But the war between a racial idea and a more democratic idea of citizenship was far from over. The Rashtriya Swayamsevak Sangh and its branch organizations such as the Bharatiya Janata Party have strived to conclude the debate in their favour. The CAA, after all, is not intended to merely give citizenship to non-Muslim refugees from three countries. That could have been, and has been, achieved even without the Act. In fact, even the government has admitted in the Parliament that the previous United Progressive Alliance government had granted citizenship to 13,000 Sikh and Hindu refugees. Instead, it aims to give legal sanction to the idea that India is the natural home to some while others are still aliens.

Ambedkar's fears were real. 'Democracy in India is only a top-dressing on Indian soil, which is essentially undemocratic,' he said. 'Constitutional morality is not a natural sentiment. It has to be cultivated. We must realize that our people have yet to learn it.'

Each of the sites of struggles for equal citizenship, the many Shaheen Baghs that sprung up across the country in the winter of 2019, were in fact schools in which we were learning constitutional morality. With each recitation of the Preamble, with its exposition and reiteration, we were earning for ourselves what was given to us. After all, there is no real learning without earning our rights on the streets.

The protesters were conscious of the significance of the moment. They knew that citizenship is the necessary precondition through which most of the other fundamental rights such as the right against discrimination on grounds of religion, race, caste, sex or place of birth, right to equal opportunity, right to freedom of speech, etc., are ensured in the Constitution.

This certainly unnerved those forces that were always opposed to what the Constitution espoused. In the aftermath of the February 2020 violence in Delhi that saw 53 deaths (the majority of them being Muslims), it has been alleged by those in the government that the struggle against the CAA was a 'conspiracy' to orchestrate violence.

Sites of struggle against the CAA have now been declared as places where anti-India conspiracies were hatched. There were continuous attempts to delegitimize the protests as they were happening by leaders of the ruling party. There were slogans inciting violence, deliberate provocations and open threats that were made on record by several BJP leaders preceding the violence. But instead of holding them accountable for what followed, peaceful protesters and young voices of reason who spoke of peace and harmony, of equality and justice, have been put behind bars by concocting a fantastic tale of a 'conspiracy'.

The struggle against the CAA caused many disruptions in the dominant public discourse by presenting an alternate discourse in which Muslim women took charge. It presented us with a grammar of dissent long lost after the freedom struggle, in which thousands of people sat peacefully on the streets and public spaces for more than 100 days and filled the sites with music, poetry, paintings, placards and slogans. However, we are now presented with a different representation by the government, police and the big media wherein they attempt to change reality and thereby history itself.

But as history has shown time and again, this battle like many others in the past for a dignified existence, might appear to have been lost, but is far from over.

CAA-NRC-NPR AND ITS DISCONTENTS

Mihir Desai

The spontaneity, breadth, youthful energy and social composition of the protests against the Citizenship (Amendment) Act (CAA), National Population Register (NPR) and the National Register of Citizens (NRC) are unprecedented, at least in my living memory. In some states, there has been a brutal repression of these protests, but despite this the protests have continued. Those in support of these orders (the CAA is in fact now a law) have mainly argued along the following lines: First, that the CAA will not affect Indian Muslims since it is about giving citizenship and not about taking it away. Second, that no decision has been taken about the NRC. Third, the NPR has nothing to do with the NRC. Fourth, even if an NRC is carried out, Indian citizens will not be affected.

My basic argument in this article will be that the CAA is unconstitutional. Even if the amendment is held to be constitutional, the protests are justified and should continue. If the CAA is held by the Supreme Court to be unconstitutional, the NPR and NRC should still be objected to, since they are exercises that will be extremely detrimental especially to the poor and the marginalized.

The CAA widens and expands the pool of persons who can claim to be citizens of India. The NPR and NRC provide the data and procedure for determining the finalized list of citizens of India. Those not in this list will be treated as foreigners or stateless persons without substantial rights. While presently all three of these orders are linked, even independent of each other they are dangerous and need to be opposed.

This article first appeared in the *Economic and Political Weekly*, vol. 55, no. 7 (15 February 2020).

On paper, there seems nothing wrong with granting citizenship to persecuted groups, or with having a register of citizens. But, when one looks deeper into the matter, calamitous consequences can be discerned. To realize their true import, it is important to unfurl the impact this will have on the Constitution and on the lives of millions of ordinary people.

CITIZENSHIP (AMENDMENT) ACT, 2019

This controversial amendment changes the 2003–04 embargo concerning citizenship rights for illegal migrants. As per the 2004 amendment an illegal migrant cannot get Indian citizenship under any condition. Obviously not by birth, but not even by naturalization or registration. What the 2019 amendment says is that if such an illegal migrant has come into India from Bangladesh, Pakistan or Afghanistan, prior to 31 December 2014 and if such a migrant belongs to the Hindu, Christian, Sikh, Buddhist, Parsi or Jain communities they will be entitled to citizenship by naturalization if they have stayed in India for five years. Thus, all such persons would be entitled to citizenship by 1 January 2020.

Undoubtedly, there can be no grievances against persons from other countries who have crossed over being granted protection. Ordinarily, this is done not through granting citizenship, but by granting refugee status through long-term visas and other permits. This is how Tibetan refugees and Tamil refugees from Sri Lanka, among others, were granted protection. It is also agreeable if what is now being done to grant citizenship is done in a neutral and non-discriminatory manner. It would be unobjectionable if the State decided to conduct a study, chart out groups or individuals persecuted for various reasons, such as religion, social exclusion, political beliefs, etc., from all bordering countries and decide to grant citizenship to such persecuted persons. What the CAA does is, for the first time, make religion a ground for granting or rejecting citizenship. This was not done when the Constitution was framed, nor under the Citizenship Act, nor in its earlier amendments, nor even at the time of the Assam Accord.

This is in clear violation of the secular nature of the Constitution—which is held by the Supreme Court to be part of the basic structure of the Constitution—and also violates the fundamental rights guaranteed under the Constitution. Unlike some of the other fundamental rights, Article 14, which speaks of equality of law and equal protection of laws, is applicable even to non-citizens, that is, foreigners. The Supreme Court has, time and again, said that this provision is designed to prevent discrimination. However, Article 14 does not prevent classification, if such classification is based on legal and relevant considerations. Every classification in order to be legal, valid and permissible must fulfil the twin test, that is, (i) the classification must be founded on an intelligible differentia which distinguishes persons or things that are grouped together from others left out from the group; and (ii) such differentia must have a rational relation to the object sought to be achieved by the legislation in question. Both these tests have to be satisfied simultaneously. The Supreme Court has also laid down an additional test, namely if the provisions of a legislation are arbitrary, then irrespective of classification, it can be struck down.

DISCRIMINATORY AND ARBITRARY

There is no doubt that there is differentia being created at three levels. First, in terms of the countries, that is, the law is applicable only to migrants from Pakistan, Afghanistan and Bangladesh. Second, in terms of religious vis-à-vis other types of persecution. Third, even within religious communities, it deals only with the six named religious groups.

In terms of countries, there is no logic or reason why only illegal migrants from three countries have been picked. Partition cannot be a reason as Afghanistan was not part of undivided India at the time of Partition. Illegal migrants have come into India from other countries also. These include lakhs of persecuted Tamils who have come from Sri Lanka, at least 40,000 persecuted Rohingyas from Myanmar, persecuted Tibetan refugees from China, large numbers of Chakmas who have come in from Bangladesh (some of whom are Muslims and most Buddhists). Rohingyas have been prima facie held to be persecuted even by the International Court of Justice. There is no reason why illegal migrants who are given protection are only from these three countries. For instance, there seems to be a deliberate omission of Tamils from Sri Lanka because that would indicate that a Buddhist-majority country is also capable of religious persecution, which then not only applies to Myanmar, but also, by its logic, means there is no reason why a Hindu-majority (or Christian- or Jewish-majority) country cannot be guilty of the same to its religious minorities.

Second, it is not clear why only persecuted communities from religious groups have been included. Even according to the Refugee Convention, 1951 and Refugee Protocol, 1967, those requiring refugee status include not just persecuted religious groups, but also those persecuted due to race, nationality, membership of a social group or for their political opinion. While India is not a signatory to either the convention or the protocol, if classification is required to be made on the basis of persecution, all these categories of persons should have been included. These would include, for instance, atheists in three of these countries, those charged with blasphemy, Shias, persons belonging to the LGBTQ+ (lesbian, gay, bisexual, transgender, and queer) community, etc. There are also certain tribal groups who have been forced to come into India from neighbouring countries and require protection.

Third, there is no justification why only six religious communities are included. For instance, in Pakistan in 1974, Ahmadiyyas were constitutionally declared as a non-Muslim minority, and by an Ordinance in 1984, it was made a criminal offence for Ahmadis to refer to themselves as Muslims, to their religion as Islam and to publicly practise Islam. Similarly, Shias in Pakistan have been facing a large number of problems; more so the Hazara Shias who can be distinguished by their language and ethnicity. A report by Human Rights Watch states that more than 500 Shia Hazaras have been killed[1] since 2008. According to another report, by the United States Commission on International Religious Freedom, around 600 Shias were killed between 1999 and 2003 as a result of extremist violence, and approximately 500 Shia doctors fled the country as a result of the assassination of more than 50 of their colleagues[2] in Karachi alone. In October 2015, United Nations Secretary-General Ban Ki-moon urged the Pakistan government to protect its citizens, including Shia Muslims. In Afghanistan, a *fatwa* issued in 2007 declared practitioners of the Baha'i faith as a blasphemous deviation from Islam. The Hazaras, even in Afghanistan, have been persecuted for centuries. Nearly half of them were killed way back in the 1890s, and the Taliban declares that killing Hazaras is everyone's duty. Many of these persecuted persons have crossed over into India and are illegally residing here.

Look at it from any angle. The CAA has no intelligible differentia. The CAA is also bad in law because it is arbitrary. There is no rationale behind this pick and choose. One may not be able to dispute that the included groups have been persecuted or they had fear of persecution. But citizenship is an individual and not a group matter. So, each individual would have to prove that they were persecuted or had genuine fear of persecution at the time they entered India.

There is some confusion concerning whether persecution is at all mentioned in the amending act. Whilst the Bharatiya Janata Party's game plan has been clear since the A.B. Vajpayee government, the precursor to the present amendment are the amendments carried out in 2015 and 2016 to the Passport (Entry into India) Rules, 1950 and Foreigners Order, 1948. The Passport (Entry into India) Rules provide that anyone who enters into India without proper travel documents can be prosecuted and expelled from India. Foreigners Order, 1948 (which was passed under the Foreigners Act, 1946) also provides for similar consequences.

Under the National Democratic Alliance government, in 2015 and 2016, both these rules were amended for granting exemption to persons belonging to minority communities in Afghanistan, Bangladesh and Pakistan, namely Hindus, Sikhs, Buddhists, Jains, Parsis and Christians who were compelled to seek shelter in India due to religious persecution or fear of religious persecution and entered into India on or before 31 December 2014 without proper travel documents (that is, those who are illegal migrants) from the provisions of these laws.

Thus, such illegal migrants cannot be prosecuted or expelled. What the present amendment does is to provide citizenship to these very persons, provided they satisfy the conditions under the amended Passport Rules and Foreigners Order. The amendment to the rules prescribes persecution or fear of persecution as one of the conditions, and thus, even the CAA would be applicable to only those illegal migrants who satisfy the condition of persecution. These rules are also under challenge in the Supreme Court.

What seems to be obvious is that the purpose behind the amended act seems to be to emphasize that Islam, by its very nature, is fundamentalist, and persecutes non-Muslims and needs to be opposed. This is a totally communal act.

What is important to understand is that even if the NPR and NRC never take place, the Amendment to the Citizenship Act would still exist and allow the grant of citizenship to certain communities while excluding others. In combination with the NPR and NRC, it becomes even more lethal.

THE NPR AND NRC

The idea of an NPR and NRC comes for the first time with the 2003 amendment to the Citizenship Act and the passing of the Citizenship (Registration of Citizens and Issue of National Identity Cards) Rules, 2003. The rules were also issued under the Citizenship Act, 1955. Before this, there was no requirement for every citizen to register on any common list. Article 326 of the Constitution provided that voting rights were available only to citizens. Thus, if you are a voter, you are automatically a citizen. Similarly, passports under the Passport Act could only be issued to citizens. Again, agricultural land can only be owned by a citizen. Consequently, by a simple rule of thumb, if you are on the voting list, or have a passport, or own agricultural land, you are a citizen and so would be the children born to you in India. The need for a separate register was completely otiose. If the State suspected anyone to be an infiltrator or an illegal migrant, the police had the powers, under the Foreigners Act, to arrest, prosecute and extradite such a person. What is also important is that under the Foreigners Act, the burden of proving that they are not a foreigner was on the accused and not on the State. And many such prosecutions have been conducted across the country and many of them successfully. The need for documented citizenship did not exist.

If a proof of citizenship was required, it was, by and large, by birth. The primary proof of birth is the birth certificate. For those born before 1987, proving their own birth would be enough. For those born between 1987 and 2004, they would also have to prove citizenship of one of their parents, and for those born after 2004, citizenship of both the parents would have to be proved. The compulsory Registration of Births and Deaths Act was brought in 1969. Three in five children (62.3 per cent) under the age of five had their births registered and possessed a birth certificate in 2015–16, according to the National Family Health Survey (NFHS-4),[3] the latest data available. This is an improvement from 26.9 per cent in 2005–06. But the present data seems to be an overestimation. In any event, even going by the latest figures, nearly 24 million children under five did not have their births registered in the last five years, UNICEF

(United Nations Children's Fund) estimated. For those above five years, the figure would of course be much higher.

The non-registration would be more frequent among tribals, Dalits and poor communities. In addition, millions of people are migrant workers within India who have hardly any birth or for that matter any documentation. In a study conducted by UNICEF in 2001, it was found that overall birth registration in India was 34.7 per cent, and within this, Uttar Pradesh had a birth registration rate of 6.5 per cent and Bihar of 1.6 per cent. Even if these figures may have gone up in recent times, it is still a long way to go for all births to be registered. If the example of Assam is anything to go by, a large number of persons have been excluded because, in their documents, there was a slight discrepancy in the spelling. Women are the biggest victims here because there is often no documentation linking them to the villages in which they are born, and with respect to the village they are married into, the documentation, at best, will be from the date of marriage, and not birth. Besides, names are changed after marriage, and there is often nothing to connect the previous name to the new name as spouse. Problems will also arise for those belonging to the transgender community.

Let us have a brief look at how the Citizenship Registration Rules operate. Under these rules, a population register has to be first created through a house-to-house enumeration. This is the population registration which was planned to be undertaken nationwide between April and September 2020.[4] Under no other law is there a concept of a population register. You carry this out only if you want to follow it up with the NRC. For the government to now say that the two are not connected is a white lie. If one wants to carry out a survey for the purposes of determining the country's population size and its break-up even at the micro level, you carry out a census. A census has been carried out every 10 years since 1872, and since Independence, it is carried out under the Census Act, 1948. The precise purpose of the census exercise (apart from knowing the population) is to find out the socio-economic situation to assist the government in making welfare schemes.

The question then arises is: Why did the United Progressive Alliance government conduct the NPR in 2010? That is a mystery. But, one thing is clear—that it was not meant for determining citizenship. By 2010, the law was settled. For all those born after 1987, proof of citizenship of one or both parents was essential. The NPR, for the purposes of citizenship, would need this information. But this was not part of the questionnaire of the NPR in 2010. It appears that the NPR was done for linking it with the Aadhaar scheme, which had started at that time. Maybe, at that time, the plan was to use the Aadhaar card like a citizenship card. The Aadhaar Act was passed only later by the NDA government in 2014, and Section 9 of this Act says that the Aadhaar card is no proof of citizenship. But all this is at the level of conjecture. What is clear is that under the NRC rules, the only purpose of the NPR is to follow it up with an NRC. What is now sought to be done is the addition of questions concerning details of parents' birth. And, of course, Aadhaar card details, etc., which will lead to massive surveillance.

The manner in which it works is that the population register is prepared locally by collecting information by a door-to-door study, and after this, it is verified and scrutinized by the local registrar (the lowest level officer at the village or ward level) and in case the citizenship of anyone is in doubt, such a person or family will be given a chance to prove their citizenship. This is where the problem arises. Who will be treated as a doubtful citizen will be decided by the lower level officer. There is a strong possibility that such a person will be directed to declare as doubtful voters only persons of certain communities and castes. Or, it can lead to huge corruption, which obviously will act against the poor. In a country where even to get a ration card bribes are regularly paid, citizenship will have a much higher price. Anyway, if your name is still excluded you can proffer an appeal to the district registrar. Now, under the Foreigners (Tribunals) Amendment Order, 2019, an appeal can be filed before the Foreigners' Tribunal, which will take the final decision. If you are unable to prove citizenship, you will be declared a foreigner and placed in a detention camp till you are extradited to a country that may want to accept you. It is also possible that the person declared as a foreigner is not placed in a detention camp, but roams around as a stateless person without rights, unable to access education, food, employment schemes and available for doing slave labour for a multitude of corporates who may be preying on such persons who can demand basic rights only at the risk of being sent to detention camps.

If the example of Assam is anything to go by, the Foreigners' Tribunals are a disaster. Principles of natural justice are routinely violated; no legal aid is being provided; these are *in camera* proceedings; a large number of presiding officers have no judicial experience and hardly any experience as lawyers; and it is strongly believed that they are given targets for declaring a certain number of people foreigners, which, if not met, render such presiding officers liable to being removed. Also, the burden of proving citizenship is on the accused. The public in Assam has spent huge amounts of money in gathering documents, travelling to Foreigners' Tribunals and paying lawyers. Many have sold their land for this purpose, and some have been pushed to commit suicide.

While under citizenship rules one is not obliged to answer any questions at the time of door-to-door studies, under Rule 7, it is the responsibility of every citizen to get themself registered in the Local Register of Indian Citizens, and, under the same rule, it is the responsibility of the head of every family to provide all details about every family member during preparation of the population register. Violation of the rule can lead to a fine of Rs 1,000. Even if one is willing to pay the fine and not answer the questions, the consequence can be that such a person will be treated as a doubtful citizen and possibly treated as a foreigner. For non-cooperation to work effectively, it needs to be widespread and not merely sporadic.

IN CONCLUSION

The CAA is a completely unconstitutional amendment and should be scrapped. The NPR and NRC, apart from being a colossal waste of money, will also lead to an unprecedented nationwide tragedy, disenfranchising crores of people and rendering them stateless and without rights. It will also go a long way in profiling the population, and especially with the present political dispensation, this will lead to communal and caste-based targeting. This will also advance further the agenda of the dispensation to complete the transition to a surveillance State. While Muslims, undoubtedly, will be targeted, the NRC and NPR will not omit from its sweep Dalits, tribals, the poor and the marginalized from other communities either.

Notes

1. Phelim Kine, 'Pakistan's Shia under attack', *The Diplomat*, 5 July 2014.
2. *Searching for Security: The Rising Marginalization of Religious Communities in Pakistan*, Report of the Minority Rights Group International, London, 2014.
3. National Family Health Survey (NFHS-4), 2015–16, Ministry of Health and Family Welfare, Government of India, December 2017 (http://rchiips.org/nfhs/NFHS-4Reports/India.pdf, last accessed 20 June 2021).
4. The population registration planned to be undertaken between April and September 2020 could not be carried out owing to the Covid-19 pandemic.

PART FOUR

Contestations Around the CAA-NRC-NPR

THE CENSUS

Lina Krishnan

Today I got a call
From Didi, my
85-year-old
Sister-in-law
The oldest
Of us *boumas*
Bolo toh, Ranu
When was my *biye?*
When did I cross this threshold?
I don't know, Didi
I came years after you
But why are you asking?

It is not me, dear
It is those men
The census people
So many questions they have
How long have you lived here?
Is this land yours?
Do you have identity proof?
Impertinence!

But (helpless now)
How do I tell them?
All these things?
Our father-in-law
In those days
Would not let us
Go out of the gate
Without an escort.
We did not look around
We did not see the bazaar
Pro-per-ly

WHY INDIA SHOULD SHELVE THE NATIONAL POPULATION REGISTER

Shivam Vij

The Union Cabinet has approved a budget of Rs 3,941 crore to update the National Population Register (NPR) and Rs 8,500 crore for the 2021 Census. The separate budgets alone tell you how the NPR and the Census are two different things. The NPR is not a precursor to the Census, contrary to popular perception.

The Census has been around since 1872. The NPR first found mention in Indian laws in 2003—in an amendment to the Citizenship Act by the Atal Bihari Vajpayee government. The first NPR exercise began in 2010. Since the NPR requires going to every Indian and asking them questions, a job the Census of India does well, the NPR was assigned to the same agency that carries out the Census: the Registrar General of India. That is all. That doesn't mean India needs the NPR for the Census.

HOW NPR WAS BORN

India has long felt the need to issue verifiable identity documents to its citizens, particularly in border areas. The need was highlighted by the Kargil Review Committee. That's how the NPR was born as an idea in 2003. The need was evident again when India started worrying about coastal security after the 26/11 Mumbai attacks in 2008.

But the NPR does not issue identity cards. As enshrined in the Citizenship Rules issued in 2003, the idea was to collect everyone's details through the NPR, verify claims of citizenship according to the Citizenship Act, thus creating a National

This article first appeared in *The Print* on 27 December 2019.

Register of Indian Citizens, and lastly issuing all these verified citizens an identity card.

But the Vajpayee government lost the 2004 election and the Manmohan Singh-led United Progressive Alliance government came to power in 2004. This government decided it will carry out the NPR, and separately issue biometric identity cards under a new law. Hence, we have the Aadhaar card.

MAKE AADHAAR THE NPR

Today, nearly 125 crore Indians have an Aadhaar card/number, as against an estimated population of 130 crore. All that the Narendra Modi government has to do is to make it compulsory for every Indian to enrol for Aadhaar.

Currently, enrolment for Aadhaar is voluntary, but giving your details to the NPR is compulsory. Doing so will save us the money on the NPR, the Rs 3,941 crore sanctioned recently. This might help us save the Rs 3,000 crore we are currently slashing from the school education budget because the Government of India is facing a 'funds crunch'. There are other good reasons why we need to immediately shelve the NPR.

NPR COULD KILL

First, the NPR exercise being undertaken by the Modi government feeds directly into its stated claims to carry out an all-India NRC (National Register of Citizens), isolating those who may not have the right documents to prove their citizenship. We know from Assam that this would be a meaningless exercise endlessly causing harassment and suicides. When even a Kargil war veteran and the family of a former President of India couldn't prove their citizenship, do we really think this is a feasible idea?

To make a bad idea worse, the Modi government has amended the Citizenship Act to selectively grant citizenship to 'refugees' from three neighbouring countries on the basis of their religion. The ruling Bharatiya Janata Party has repeatedly made it clear it intends to use this clause to give citizenship to those who may be declared non-citizens, illegal immigrants or foreigners through the NRC. That would only leave Muslims to be declared stateless. The NRC has also driven people to suicide.

That the NPR 2020 (unlike the NPR 2010) wants to know the date and place of birth of both your parents is proof enough that the government wants to use this data to, later on, ask you to verify your citizenship claim. Verifying citizenship is not a practical idea since many of us won't be able to find documents showing where and when our parents or grandparents were born. If we are shelving the idea of the NRC, we won't need the NPR. Why do you need a toy if you don't want to play with it?

We don't need the NRC, and, so, we don't need the NPR.

The idea of the NPR as a live directory, as already discussed earlier, can be served by Aadhaar. All that will be needed is to amend the 2016 Aadhaar Act. For instance, Aadhaar numbers are already being issued for newborn babies[1] and recorded with death certificates.[2]

PRIVACY NIGHTMARE

There's a second reason why we need to shelve the NPR. As currently planned, the NPR has all the makings of an absolute nightmare. With the 2020 NPR, the government wants to know details such as your passport number, Aadhaar number, driving license number, and so on. It is supposedly voluntary to give these details. But how many enumerators will tell the masses that they don't have to give these details if they don't want to? We have seen how the public was forced to enrol for Aadhaar despite it being ostensibly voluntary.

The Supreme Court's privacy and Aadhaar judgments have placed a number of restrictions on government use of Aadhaar data. It is feared that the government is duplicating the Aadhaar exercise (the NPR will even issue a number for every person), so that it can find a way of skirting the restrictions around Aadhaar data usage.

One of the scariest misuses of personal data by any government is for potential voter targeting. With the delimitation exercise a few years away, just imagine the misuse possible. Constituencies could be demarcated on the basis of people's religious, class or other categorizations. And since Aadhaar will collect phone numbers too, easy targeting of voters for the ruling party would be a boon.

If that sounds like a conspiracy theory, note how the previous Telugu Desam Party in Andhra Pradesh allegedly stole Aadhaar, voter ID, caste, government scheme beneficiary and other data of some 3.9 crore voters. Such a breach of privacy is a great indignity and would have been a much bigger public scandal in any other country.

The NPR will only make such political misuse of public data easier. The Modi government is about to bring a privacy law that is in itself a scandal. It gives the government very wide-ranging powers to access private data. It does not have strong safeguards to prevent the breach of privacy by the government itself, or redressal in case such a breach is identified. The Bill is weak when it comes to the biggest culprit of violation of privacy: the government itself.

Given the situation, this is a very bad time for the Modi government to be centralizing a host of personal data in the NPR. There have been privacy concerns around Aadhaar due to the use of biometrics. Now imagine the government creating a 360-degree profile of you with your Aadhaar, including details such as your occupation, marital status, family tree and so on. The proposed NPR is a Himalayan threat to citizens' privacy.

Notes

1. 'Now, blue Aadhaar cards for newborns, kids below 5', *The Times of India*, 28 February 2018.
2. 'Aadhaar will be required for death certificates', *The Times of India*, 4 August 2017.

CAA-NRC-NPR

MAKING THE CENSUS UNRELIABLE

Devesh Kapur and Neelanjan Sircar

Amid the anger and acrimony over the Citizenship Amendment Act (CAA), the National Population Register (NPR) and a possible National Register of Citizens (NRC), which the government has said has not been finalized yet, there has been little thought given to another growing challenge—the quality of official data. In the last few years, official data has suffered from credibility issues and undermined confidence in the economy. The Indian statistical system, once the envy of the developing world, has fallen on hard times.

In 2020 and 2021, the government planned to roll out the 16th Census (the eighth after Independence), to be conducted in two phases—a house listing and housing Census to be conducted between April and September 2020, followed by the population enumeration in February 2021.[1]

The Census is the key source of primary data at the village, town and ward level, providing micro-level data on demography, housing, assets, education, economic activity, social groups, language and migration, among other variables. It also provides population data to the Delimitation Commission for the constitutionally mandated decennial delimitation of parliamentary and assembly constituencies and serves as a key input for many government policies and public services.

It is a massive exercise—and massively expensive. The cost of the 2021 Census is estimated at Rs 8,751 crore (and NPR at Rs 3,941 crore), involving about 30 lakh enumerators and field functionaries (generally government teachers and those

This article first appeared as Devesh Kapur and Neelanjan Sircar, 'CAA-NRC-NPR controversy throws up new challenge for Census 2021—collecting credible data' in *The Print* on 7 February 2020.

appointed by state governments). Concurrently, the NPR—first prepared in 2010 under the provisions of the Citizenship Act, 1955 and Citizenship Rules, 2003 and subsequently updated in 2015—will also be updated along with the house listing and housing Census (except in Assam).

News reports have been streaming in that data collection exercises like the National Sample Survey (NSS) are being hampered in states like Andhra Pradesh and West Bengal. Reports from Karnataka indicate that people are declining to share personal information with officials visiting households in connection with government welfare schemes, with residents turning away ASHA workers on a Pulse Polio visit, fearing that somehow some of their information might find its way into the NRC.

At its core, the fears of a tainted Census stem from the NPR breaking one of the cardinal rules in objective data collection—the preservation of anonymity. Anonymity must be maintained if people are to report information truthfully, especially information that can be used against them. Otherwise, people will report the information that is most likely to yield a beneficial outcome, whether minimizing risk or maximizing benefits, not what is true.

If respondents ascertain that truthfully revealing certain kinds of information in the NPR is more likely to result in a question mark over their citizenship, they may choose to obfuscate or misreport. Because the NPR and Census are to be run concurrently—and both are under the auspices of the Registrar General of the Ministry of Home Affairs (also the key architect and driver of the CAA)—this loss of credible information is likely to extend to the Census. Thus, if the CAA and NPR are perceived as targeting a particular community, measuring that community, however genuine the intentions, through the Census, will simply not work.

Notes

1. Both the NPR and the Census were postponed owing to the Covid-19 pandemic.

WHY THE NPR IS MORE DANGEROUS THAN THE ASSAM NRC

Harsh Mander and Mohsin Alam Bhat

Prime Minister Narendra Modi claimed to the people of India on Delhi's historic Ramlila Grounds on 22 December 2020 that his government had never since 2014 even considered implementing a nationwide National Register of Citizens (NRC). But the NRC was part of the President's address in Parliament in June and had been promised by Modi's Home Minister and closest lieutenant Amit Shah several times in Parliament and outside. It was therefore an obviously flagrant untruth spoken by a person holding the most powerful public office in the Republic.

But some took comfort from his brazen fabrication as they saw in it a signal that he was stepping down from this core agenda of his government and its ideological mentor the Rashtriya Swayamsevak Sangh (RSS). It appeared that, perhaps, unsettled by the largest spontaneous countrywide protests seen after Independence, the Prime Minister had decided to push the national NRC into cold storage, at least for the present.

However, within days, it became abundantly clear that his purpose was not to reassure the masses of dissenting Indian people, even less to respect their intense disquiet about a measure that so many saw as divisive and destructive of the Constitution. It served two other very different purposes. It gave a fig leaf—albeit a very flimsy one—to supporters of the government. And, more importantly, it was an attempt to deliberately build a smokescreen that would mislead and further confuse public opinion.

The Home Minister was quick to state on record that

This article first appeared in *Scroll.in* on 12 January 2020.

the NRC would not be implemented but only, he repeatedly underlined, for the present. Both he and the Prime Minister refused to rule it out. But there was another most unmistakable indicator, a deliberate signal, that the government remained determined to continue to thrust the country down the dangerous and divisive pathway that it had charted for the Republic. This was the highly visible and public Cabinet meeting that was held at the peak of the protests, announcing that the government would begin work on a National Population Register (NPR).

AMBIGUOUS MESSAGE

The Minister who made the announcement said that the NPR had nothing to do with the NRC. But public trust in our Prime Minister and his Cabinet has never plummeted as low as it is today, because of the calculated official mendacities unleashed regularly on the people around matters as critical as the state of the economy, jobs, growth and, most dangerously, about citizenship, which is the foundational right as it is the right to have rights. Without public debate, without any transparency, a regime is being unleashed in which every citizen will have to establish her citizenship if the executive chooses to doubt it. This is being rammed through processes which are intentionally clouded in official secrecy. The only unambiguous message the Union government continues to convey, amplified by the RSS, is that the State seeks to dismantle the citizenship of people of only one kind of religious identity.

Supporters of the ruling establishment argue that, despite the announcement, the widespread fears that persist about the implementation of the National Population Register, alongside the National Register of Citizens and the Citizenship Amendment Act and that they will together lead to a mass exclusion of Indians, particularly Muslim citizens, are fanciful, even mischievous, fear-mongering. The protesters, on the other hand, have the clear insight that the government is attempting to discriminate based on a person's religious identity, and that this strikes fatally at the core of the constitutional morality of the Republic. But by the explicit design of the Union government, by its silences and falsehoods and dog whistles, it may not always be easy for people to see clearly how the three policies tie together, and what they portend.

To understand this, we need to begin first with the Citizenship Amendment Act, 2003, which was introduced by the A.B. Vajpayee government, and was what laid the foundations for the process of targeted disenfranchisement which the Modi government has taken forward with such resolve. If the Bharatiya Janata Party (BJP) had been returned to power in 2004, it is quite likely that the NRC-NPR may have been initiated much earlier.

The Citizenship Amendment Act, 2003 laid down firstly that a person cannot claim citizenship, even if born and raised in India, if any one of her parents is an 'illegal immigrant'. It then prescribed the creation of an NRIC as an instrument by which to identify 'illegal immigrants'. How the NRC would be executed would be prescribed by rules under the Act. These rules would not be required to be approved by Parliament because the executive is authorized to make rules as part of subordinate legislation. It is the Citizenship Rules, 2003 that provide that the Central government, through the Registrar General, can start compiling a National Popular Register 'for the purpose of the National Register of Indian Citizens'.

Thus, contrary to the disingenuous insistence of senior government functionaries, this is integral to the NRC. Under the rules, the NPR amounts to an 'initialization' of the NRC. The Registrar General has already initiated this process through a notification in July 2019.

After the compilation of the NPR, local government functionaries will be permitted to identify persons whose citizenship is 'doubtful'. These powers will lie with junior officials at the level of tahsildar and upwards. Not only will the officials have complete unguided discretion to classify residents as 'doubtful' citizens, they can also demand information or documents from any person they choose, regardless of origin or papers.

POWER TO DISENFRANCHISE

It is important to underline that this is no ordinary power. It is the power to decide if a resident, any resident, should be required to establish their citizenship through a web of vintage documents that few of us, even those who enjoy a range of privileges, would be able to muster. The consequences of not being able to prove their citizenship with these ephemeral documents can result in a person being declared an 'illegal immigrant', banished for years to detention centres, and stripped of citizenship rights including the right to vote and to own property. To put it starkly, it is the power to disenfranchise people.

Even more worryingly, the government can then make the draft public and invite objections against the inclusion of individuals and families. Before finalizing the NRC, local government officials will consider these objections. Again, the rules provide no guidance whatsoever about what nature of objections can be accepted.

This process is obviously open to severe abuse. In fact, it appears to be practically designed for such abuse, to empower the executive to target, without due process, individuals and families of its choosing, to ultimately deprive them of their citizenship rights. The problem is not only that the rules do not specify which documents are required for establishing citizenship. Officials are free to adopt varying standards for different citizens, which could lead to capricious targeting of citizens.

The delegation of such unbridled power to the executive violates the rule of law under the Constitution, which requires the legislature to provide proper guidance and safeguards for the implementation of laws. Parliament must include clear criteria, standards and principles to the executive to implement the purpose of the legislation. If the powers given to the government are—in the words of the Supreme Court's *Hamdard Dawakhana* case (1959)—'uncanalized and uncontrolled', the legislation is unconstitutional. The vague—and excessive—powers in the NPR-NRC process clearly violate this principle.

These powers also practically allow the executive to victimize genuine citizens. The stakes of the abuse are high. Citizenship status, as we noted, is foundational because it is the very basis of an individual's legal personality. For something so fundamental to be left to the discretion of ordinary administrators is an outrageous and unconscionable violation of due process. In a country where an overwhelming number of people do not possess legal documents, this executive discretion will potentially make everyone's citizenship suspect. If the Assam NRC is anything to go by, even the most basic documents may fail to establish citizenship if minor errors have crept into them.

Equally disturbing is the element of public objections. The rules allow for sensitive personal data to be collected and stored by government officials without any data security. This by itself violates the Supreme Court's ruling in the Aadhaar case (2018) that required anonymity and encryption. In complete disregard of this, the rules require the government to maintain data at various levels of government and publicize them for objections from the public. This further enhances the possibility of malicious targeting.

Imagine these powers in the hands of the current Uttar Pradesh government, India's most populous state headed by Chief Minister Adityanath who openly flaunts his hostility to Muslims. It is not difficult to imagine which people he and his officials would mark as 'doubtful citizens'. Imagine the power of ordinary citizens to further question the citizenship of other citizens, using the well-oiled machine of the RSS and its myriad affiliates. This process could realistically become an instrument for the systematic hate-targeting of a community by the State executive and its ideological fellow travellers.

The NPR-NRC process will, in these ways, establish a living nightmare of rules, where any individual can be drawn into a maze of legal procedure and constantly asked to produce documents that may never satisfy the bureaucrats.

The Citizenship Amendment Act fits into, indeed crowns, this legal dystopia. The constitutional objections to the amendment are well known by now. The government claims that the law ameliorates the condition of persecuted minorities from India's neighbourhood. But it is inexplicably limited to Pakistan, Bangladesh and Afghanistan. It overlooks the persecuted migrants from China, Myanmar and Sri Lanka. The government has given no rationale for the special treatment of persecution based on religion, as opposed to other grounds like ethnicity, language, politics or nationality. The amendment excludes Muslims despite the abundant evidence of religious persecution of Muslim sects in the region. It even fails to be a fair refugee policy for Hindu migrants. It arbitrarily excludes migrants that came after December 2014, even if they may have suffered religious persecution. Each of these violates the Constitution's equal protection clause that guarantees rational, reasonable and non-arbitrary treatment to all Indian residents.

But once the amendment exists alongside NRC and can be turned into its companion, the impact will not remain limited to regulating the citizenship of migrants. The government is yet to prescribe how non-Muslim migrants will be expected to prove their country of origin, date of migration and proof of persecution under the amendment. But there is a good possibility that the government will push for extremely minimal requirements of evidence, or even simply a presumption. If, indeed, that is the case, if non-Muslim Indians fail to prove their citizenship during the NPR-NRC process, even they may be able to invoke the amendment. No such respite will be available to Muslims, making the implementation of the law sectarian.

By excluding Muslims, the amendment reinforces a background assumption that Muslims are less Indian and more likely to be doubtful citizens. This is bound to shape the behaviour of officials involved in updating and finalizing the NPR-NRC. The amendment will become a weapon against citizens who the government feels are undesirable.

In Uttar Pradesh, we have found uniformed policepersons rampaging Muslim homes, lawlessly destroying property and beating even children, women and old people with visceral hate, in the manner of rioters. The residents in many of these homes told us that the policepersons also told them that they as Muslims would have to leave their homes and move to Pakistan, because of the new law.

If this is the kind of understanding that the BJP government has imparted to its supporters and officials about the CAA-NRC-NPR trinity and what it will accomplish, it is chilling to think of what could take place. What the unbridled powers vested in the junior executive to separate citizen from non-citizen and strip those they think undeserving of their rights and freedom could lead to and whom it could be exercised against.

In summary, far from pushing the NRC to the backburner, the Union government, by announcing an NPR, which includes newly added questions about a person's parents' details, heralds an NRC even more dangerous than the Assam NRC. There were many injustices in the way that the NRC was implemented in Assam, and they took an enormous toll in terms of human suffering. But the Assam NRC was not a communal anti-Muslim project. All persons of all faiths were equally tasked to prove their citizenship by a list of documents. An NRC which is built on the NPR will allow the executive to pick and choose whose citizenship it wishes to interrogate. This will succeed in thrusting India's Muslim people—and a range of the other most disadvantaged people, including homeless persons, persons with disability, transgender persons, nomadic and denotified tribes, orphaned and abandoned children, circular migrants and millions of others—into years of dread and uncertainty about if, when and how they might be deprived of their citizenship and sent to detention centres (which again, Prime Minister Modi claims, do not exist).

The piloting of the NPR had already begun in Karnataka on 1 January 2020, due to commence across the country from 1 April 2020.[1] Unless all the non-BJP governments refuse to implement the NPR, they will be collaborating in a process of targeted mass disenfranchisement of the kind that Nazi Germany witnessed in the grim years leading to the Holocaust. History will find it hard to forgive them.

Notes

1. The exercise was postponed owing to the Covid-19 pandemic.

IN THE IDEA OF AN 'ALL-INDIA NRC', ECHOES OF REICH CITIZENSHIP LAW

Nizam Pasha

The Ministry of Home Affairs issued a notification on 31 July 2019 stating that the Central government has decided to prepare and update the population register in every state of India other than the state of Assam. This means that the exercise of updating the National Register of Citizens (NRC) in Assam will now be implemented throughout the country.

Much has been written about the flaws inherent in the NRC process. The very idea that every person who was born in the country and has lived here all of her or his life should be able to furnish documentary proof of residence and familial relations emanates from a privileged notion of home and family life.

For one, it does not accommodate the homeless. Assam, for instance, is a flood-prone state where every year, during the monsoons, the Brahmaputra and its distributaries flood the riparian areas. Each year, many who do not live in *pucca* houses lose all their possessions and escape with their lives to start afresh.

These persons are now required to produce papers to establish their residence before 24 March 1971, or their relationship with parents or grandparents who can so establish residence. If they fail to do so, they will be declared illegal immigrants. Similarly, the process does not take into account orphans, abandoned children or youngsters who ran away from home to escape abuse and built their lives elsewhere.

The idea that for every citizen, there is a loving parent who has maintained birth records is deeply flawed. Therefore,

This is an updated version of the article that first appeared in *The Wire* on 26 August 2019.

the NRC, at every stage, excludes the most underprivileged. While the process excludes persons without reference to their religion (although going by the Sachar Committee report, there is a disproportionate representation of Muslims in the weakest economic classes), the government has, through the Citizenship Amendment Act, 2019, made undocumented migrants who are Hindus, Sikhs, Buddhists, Jains, Parsis and Christians from Afghanistan, Bangladesh and Pakistan—basically anyone who is not a Muslim—eligible for citizenship.

Putting the two together, the overall effect is that Muslims who are unable to establish citizenship will be declared illegal immigrants.

The Supreme Court on 13 August 2019 passed an order clarifying certain queries raised by the state coordinator of the NRC and dismissing a batch of applications filed by affected persons on the same issue. The question before the Court was regarding the status of children born in India after 3 December 2004, one of whose parents was a 'doubtful voter' or 'declared foreigner' or whose case was pending before the Foreigners' Tribunal or some other court, though the other parent was validly included in the NRC.

Chief Justice Ranjan Gogoi, speaking for the Supreme Court, held that even if one of the parents of such children was unable to establish citizenship in the NRC process, the child would not be entitled to have his or her name included in the NRC. The Court noted that these very questions were pending before the Constitution bench and would be decided in that case. Meanwhile, the state coordinator could proceed based on the above understanding for purposes of the NRC exercise for the present.

PARALLELS WITH THE THIRD REICH

The entire NRC process, and particularly the 13 August order, is eerily reminiscent of the Reich Citizenship Laws passed by the Nazi government in 1935. Historians mark the passing of the 'Nuremberg Laws' on citizenship as the beginning of the series of events now known as the Holocaust. The Reich Citizenship Law defined a citizen of the Reich as 'that subject only who is of German or kindred blood'.

The status of a citizen was acquired by the granting of citizenship papers by the government of the Third Reich. All political rights were available only to citizens granted papers under this law. The regulations that followed these laws struggled to define who a 'German' was and differently classified individuals of mixed Jewish and German parentage.

1935 Chart from Nazi Germany used to explain the Nuremberg Laws which employed a pseudo-scientific basis for racial discrimination against Jews. Photo: United States Holocaust Memorial Museum Collection/Wikimedia Commons, CC BY-SA

To begin with, persons with one or two Jewish grandparents were classified as German while individuals with three or four Jewish grandparents were classified as full Jews. Gradually, the laws moved on to become less and less tolerant of persons of mixed parentage, termed '*Mischling*', and demanded purity of blood.

Children and grandchildren of Jews who had married Germans and, in some cases, had even converted to Christianity and who thus far had seen themselves as German found themselves unable to pass the test and were denied citizenship.

Under these laws, an *Ahnenpass* (literally, 'ancestor pass') was issued to those found to be of 'Aryan blood', which was a record of the family tree of the individual and entitled the holder to citizenship rights. This again bears a striking similarity to the NRC process, where the family tree of each individual is being constructed, which will be reflected in the NRC extract, and will show that the ancestors of the holder have been verified to be 'of Indian origin'. This will then entitle the holder to rights available to a citizen under the Constitution.

In Nazi Germany, since the question of who qualified as a German came to depend on religion (Jewish or Christian), the Nazis had to rely on birth, baptismal, marriage and death certificates for issuance of citizenship papers. People scrambled to obtain these certificates typically maintained in churches and government offices, to establish their relationship with German (meaning Christian) grandparents.

With the NRC in progress in Assam and now with the issuance of the notification by the Ministry of Home Affairs for implementation of a population register throughout the country, as people scramble to collect birth certificates, ration cards and other documents establishing their connection with Indian parents and grandparents, one cannot help but sense a glimmer of past events.

The only difference being that the Indian NRC does not identify persons 'of Indian origin' based on religion or ethnicity.

However, with the Citizenship Amendment Act those who are denied citizenship will solely be Muslims and all others will be granted refugee status and allowed to remain in the country.

What is most inexplicable about how the Supreme Court has conducted these proceedings is that—as the Court itself mentions in the 13 August order—questions that form the very basis of the NRC process have been referred to a Constitution bench and are still pending adjudication.

LACK OF JUDICIAL URGENCY

The fixing of 24 March 1971, as the reference date for the exercise of Section 6A of the Citizenship Act is itself the major plank of the challenge before the Constitution bench. So someday, after the entire population of the State is asked to demonstrate that they came to India prior to 24 March 1971 in an exercise that has taken years and hundreds of crores of the public exchequer and in which lakhs of people are likely to be declared stateless, the Supreme Court will sit to decide, in hindsight, whether that date had any constitutional basis.

Another question to be decided is whether, after over 40 years of living in India, a person can be displaced even if found to be an illegal immigrant. The constitutional validity of Sections 3(1)(b) and (c) of the Citizenship Act which form the basis of the 13 August order is itself under challenge in another writ petition and has again been referred to a Constitution bench, which again has not yet been constituted.

To put the Court's sense of urgency around the formation of that bench into perspective, of the many cases referred to five-judge benches of the Supreme Court, two cases, in particular, were jostling for a hearing in the summer of 2017. The Supreme Court decided that while the constitutional basis for the NRC exercise could wait its turn, the practice of triple *talaq* that persisted for 1,400 years could not be tolerated for another summer and the issue of the constitutional validity of the practice required the immediate attention of the Court.

And so, that challenge was listed for hearing before a specially constituted five-judge bench that held hearings over the summer vacations and pronounced the well-known *Shayara Bano* judgment that is now part of our recent constitutional history. Meanwhile, the NRC exercise—which is likely to render lakhs of people stateless—was allowed to go on without any examination of its constitutional basis.

The upshot of the above discussion is that the very basis on which the NRC exercise is proceeding is *still to be adjudicated upon*. Further, there is no clarity on what will happen to persons declared as illegal immigrants in this exercise. At present, there is no scope of deporting them since there is no existing agreement with Bangladesh to accept immigrants, nor is Bangladesh likely to suddenly accept lakhs of persons, that it has no record of—most of whom were born in India.

Many in Assam have languished for years in detention centres after being declared illegal immigrants by Foreigners' Tribunals. The constitutionality of indefinite detention in these centres located in jails, and of separating of families, had been challenged by activist Harsh Mander in the Supreme Court.[1] Ultimately, the Court ordered the release of detainees after three years though with some harsh conditions. These detention centres again remind one of concentration camps.

The homes of Jews who were taken away to concentration camps were looted and often occupied by their 'German' neighbours. Would the same not happen to persons who are declared illegal Bangladeshi immigrants and removed to detention centres? Should not an adjudication on the question of the consequences of exclusion from the NRC, therefore, be the focus of attention of the Supreme Court before declaring lakhs of people non-citizens and visiting the social consequences of statelessness on them?

Instead of discharging this judicial function, why is the Court expending its energies in issuing day-to-day directions regarding the implementation of the process like an administrative authority? Unfortunately, these questions cannot be asked of the Court, because while it may have taken upon itself to discharge executive functions, it is still not answerable to the people.

Notes

1. See Harsh Mander's article 'The Dark Side of Humanity and Legality: A Glimpse Inside Assam's Detention Centres for "Foreigners"' in Part 2 of this volume.

I DON'T KNOW MY NAME TODAY

Chan Miya

I don't know my name today
Lost: it's lost in misspellings, taunts, jeers
And the quagmire of your office papers, closets, cabinets.
From Fazr Ali born at dawn
To Fazal Ali the class captain
To Fazal Miya singer of Magun songs
To a nameless Bangladeshi labourer in Guwahati
I have lived many names, many lives
But none of my own.

While selling myself in the labour bazaar
I remembered how numbers were squared
While pulling sheaves of corn I remembered Magun and
    Magun soothed me
On my haunches at the detention camp
I thought—
Didn't I make this building?

I have nothing now
But an old lungi, a half-ripe beard
And a photocopied sheet of the '66 voters' list
With my grandfather's name burnt in it.

Yes, I have no name today
But don't dangle before my eyes the name you have
    given me.

Don't call me a Bangladeshi
I don't need your barbs
Don't condescend with 'Neo-Assamese'
Give me nothing
But what I own.

I will find a name someday
And you won't fish it out for me.

AT THE EDGE OF THE CLIFF

THE NATIONAL NRC WILL BE A TIPPING POINT FOR INDIA'S MOST VULNERABLE POPULATIONS

Mihika Chanchani

Beginning in November 2019, India witnessed a historic event—the largest spontaneous countrywide protest the country has seen since Independence. The passage of the Citizenship Amendment Act (CAA)[1] and the subsequent announcement of the National Register of Indian Citizens (NRC/NRIC) were the triggers for this. For the first time in India's recent past, thousands of people took to the streets, in large cities and small villages alike, to protest against the unconstitutional, draconian and biased law that is sure to have deep implications for the country's foundational constitutional values.

Several articles in this volume have detailed the glaring anti-Muslim bias in these laws and the blatant Hindutva agenda that is being pushed through. Until the CAA-NRIC came along, there was no large-scale movement against the systemic targeting of Muslims in India which is why the recent protests, largely led by Muslim women, are so critical in the history of resistance in India. But it was not just the Muslims who came out in large numbers. Others who belonged to various vulnerable groups and organizations also took to the streets to protest against the CAA and NRC. The movement was a powerful show of solidarity among the various marginalized groups of India to defend the secular principles enshrined in the country's Constitution.

The author acknowledges and is grateful for the support of Dr Suresh Garimella of the Centre for Equity Studies, Varna Balakrishnan of Karwan-e-Mohabbat and Dr Harsh Mander in conceptualizing and researching this paper.

Through the participation of these groups, it was evident that the CAA and NRIC were not just a 'Muslim issue' but rather one that will impact a majority of India's most marginalized people. 'Dalits, Adivasis, OBCs, women and minorities have been insecure ever since the Modi government came to power six years ago. Today, if the CAA-NRC is implemented, people of all marginalized communities will be filled with such insecurities,'[2] claimed a representative of the Alliance Against CAA-NRC-NPR in January 2020. The various forms of historical marginalization and socio-economic discrimination of Adivasis, Dalits, women, sexual minorities, persons with disabilities, etc., play out in the lives of the vulnerable in a multitude of ways, leading to the perpetration of immense structural violence and neglect on the part of the State and society at large. Endless years of marginalization and exclusion have already ensured that these communities live on the edge. The upcoming NRC will push them over it.

The systemic structures and life experiences of marginalization play out in different ways for vulnerable groups and the individuals within them. Furthermore, there is a significant intersection among these different groups that are hardly homogeneous. For example, a disproportionately large number of circular migrants are Dalits, Adivasis and Muslims. We make our assessment of the impact of the NRC on various groups in full acknowledgement of this. This paper seeks to examine the particular circumstances of each group that might render them more vulnerable when entering the NRC process. It does not, however, seek to explain these complexities in any comprehensive manner, it merely aims to expose some of the factors that might lead to these groups being excluded from the national NRC. The data for this paper has been collected through phone interviews[3] conducted with various activists, researchers, social workers and academics who worked either with or on each vulnerable group between February and April 2020, as well as secondary data sources.

BEHIND THE SMOKESCREEN

> 'We have promised in our manifesto that once Narendra Modi forms government once again, we will implement National Register of Citizens in the entire country. We will remove every single infiltrator from the country. And all the Hindu and Buddhist refugees...we will find each of them, give them Indian citizenship and make them residents here.'
>
> —Statement by Home Minister Amit Shah in an election rally in West Bengal on 11 April 2019[4]

> 'No nationwide NRC has been announced... If it is announced in the future, the rules would be drawn in such a way that no Indian citizen is inconvenienced.'
>
> —Government sponsored newspaper advertisement published 20 December 2019[5]

The government's constant flip-flopping on whether the national NRC is even going to take place, let alone exactly when, in what form, what documents will be required as proof of citizenship and what the consequences for not being included in the list would be, mean that many crucial questions remain unaddressed. During phone interviews, when various community organizers were asked what they were doing to prepare their communities for what was to come, their frustration and helplessness at the absence of reliable information was evident. 'Everything will depend on how the NRC is finally implemented. There is lack of clarity on the issues. It is hard to say how exactly the NRC is going to impact people without knowing how it is going to happen,' said Priyanka Jain of the Centre for Migration and Labour Solutions (CMLS) when asked about the impact on circular migrants.

The deliberate creation of a smokescreen around the particularities of the NRIC has crucial repercussions on the ability to make concrete assessments about the scale of damage this might cause, and on the ability of community organizers to mobilize and prepare people. In Assam, citizens and community organizers had anticipated the NRC some years before it was actually implemented, given the long-standing narrative around the presence of 'illegal immigrants' from Bangladesh and strong ethno-nationalist political traditions.[6] This anticipation allowed the workers to do much of the groundwork needed to educate and organize vulnerable populations around the documentary requirements of the process. Even so, millions of people were excluded.

OPPRESSION BY DOCUMENTS

During the NRC in Assam, which rendered 19 lakh people at risk of statelessness,[7] the state required people to have documents under two broad categories. The first, 'commonly understood as *legacy documents* were expected to prove one's long-term association with the land, where "long term" was defined by an arbitrarily set date of the beginning of the liberation war in Bangladesh in 1971 or, if you have the privilege of recorded memory, of the NRC of 1951. Given the fact that not everyone applying for the NRC would have been alive in 1971 or 1951, "linkage documents" are meant to undisputedly establish yourself as a direct descendant of someone with credible legacy documents'.[8] 'Legacy documents' could include anything from a list of 14 acceptable documents including land and tenancy records, citizenship certificates, permanent residential certificates, refugee registration certificates, passports, LIC documents, any government-issued licences or certificates, government-issued service or employment certificates, bank or post office accounts, birth certificates, board or university educational certificates, court records, etc.

At a glance, it seems as if the government had given people a broad set of documents that could be used to establish that they belonged to this land. The reality, however, was more complicated. Countless stories of people who had one or more of the required documents yet were left out of the final NRC list in Assam surfaced showing that the implementation of the process itself was flawed.

Apart from the problems with implementation, it is contested whether the mere presence of documents is a marker of 'belonging'. Within the broader framework of citizenship and statelessness studies, there is much debate on the understanding and use of identity documents or citizenship documents. Many countries, including India embody the complex contestations that come to the surface in relation to documents and belonging. Whilst the human rights approach may draw on a framework that understands documents as providing access to rights, for example the use of ration cards or Below Poverty Line (BPL) cards to access welfare services, a government may understand documents and registration as an effective way to govern, for example, mandating voter IDs to engage in the country's electoral process. Meanwhile, an authoritarian State may understand documents as crucial tools of surveillance and population control that embrace some populations and exclude others, as was strikingly evident in the use of national ID cards for the exclusion of Rohingyas in Myanmar;[9] the NRIC in India also has some traces of this.

As evidenced by the Assam experience, documents and the lack thereof, became the central tool through which the state decided belonging and citizenship. Given the government's deliberate obfuscation of the issue of the national NRIC, in this paper, I will use the two broad categories of 'legacy' and 'linkage' documents to examine the impact on a range of vulnerable populations in India. Through the various conversations with community organizers it is apparent that, even in its broadest form, the demand for 'legacy' or 'linkage' documents would be extremely difficult and traumatic for large sections of India's most vulnerable. Secondly, given the number of people who are at risk of exclusion, statelessness and, in the worst case, mass detention, we contest the very basis of limiting proof of citizenship to availability of documents which vastly expands bureaucratic control over individual lives.

Circular Migrants

The quantum of internal movement in India is large. While the official estimates provided by the Ministry of Statistics and Programme Implementation (MOSPI) suggest a number of 30 million per year,[10] sector-wise employment estimates show that more than 100 million people move every year from rural areas in search of livelihood. A majority of such migrants work in the informal/unorganized sector; a large number are daily wagers and very few have any form of valid identity, given their transient existence. It has been repeatedly noted by researchers and organizations who work on issues of migration that 'urban growth has been exclusionary and exploitative leading to the reproduction of poverty and socio-economic inequalities at the work destinations'.[11] In cities where they work, migrants lack voting rights. Stuck in a state of constant flux, moving between urban and rural locations, migrants miss out on participating in the only institutional mechanism in the country, the elections, to raise their political views/concerns. They also fail to carry with them the basic entitlements guaranteed by the State such as access to low-cost food, health, subsidized education and shelter.[12]

One of the biggest questions with regard to migrants and in relation to the NRC is about the process itself and where it will take place: *at the location where the migrants come from or at the location where they work?* Either way, Priyanka Jain, of the Centre for Migration and Labour Solutions, fears that it will be disastrous. If the NRC process is implemented in their source locations, a large-scale movement back to villages or towns will mean loss of income and livelihood for the potentially long and arduous duration of the NRC. As the large-scale 'de-urbanization' during the lockdown imposed as a result of the Covid-19 pandemic has shown, this is an extremely traumatic and violent experience.[13]

This could also take the shape of more frequent movements between home and work, often thousands of kilometres across the country, at great financial cost. If the NRC is implemented at the destination, then millions of people risk exclusion since they do not migrate with the vast range of documents that the NRC might demand. Furthermore, the fight for basic rights like safe, clean housing, sanitation, food, safety equipment at work, etc., in unforgiving environments is hard enough and more often than not a losing battle, even without the scramble for documentation that might formally recognize their presence, and therefore their ability to demand rights, in their destinations of work.

For municipalities and other vested interests, the NRC could be a way to permanently get rid of the semi-permanent labour who is trying to find a foothold in the city, living as it does under inhuman conditions in shanties or under flyovers. In fact, this is exactly what happened in January 2020 when a group of plainclothes policemen oversaw the demolition of around 200 makeshift settlements in Bengaluru's suburb claiming that the sheds were illegal and there were 'possible Bangladeshis present'.[14] That settlement housed people from all over the country who had come to the city to work on construction sites, as domestic workers and other informal-sector labourers. Even though several of them showed their identity documents, like Aadhaar cards, voter IDs and even NRC certificates in the cases of Assamese migrants to officials as their homes were being demolished, the officials paid no heed. An internal investigation by CMLS revealed that the Bangalore Municipal Corporation had been eyeing that land for a long time to build a mall.

Priyanka fears that millions of such migrants all over the country will be similarly treated if the national NRC is implemented. For a group that is already on the margins and facing many forms of exclusion, who have been viewed as 'useless' or 'criminal' by the city, the police and the administration, the possibility of statelessness could mean the perpetration of even more structural and physical violence against them.

Urban Homeless

In early February 2020, the National Coalition for Inclusive and Sustainable Urbanization (NCU) released a hard-hitting statement against the NRC. The activists, researchers, urban practitioners, lawyers, informal-sector workers, collectives and individuals that make up the NCU claimed that the national NRC would 'adversely impact the 1.77 million homeless people in India. Our own surveys in just five states (Andhra Pradesh, Bihar, Jharkhand, Maharashtra and Tamil Nadu) reveal that, on average, 99 per cent of all homeless people do not have their own birth certificates, which in the context of NRC-NPR-CAA, becomes a dangerous proposition. Moreover, 30 per cent of the urban homeless population does not have any identity proof'.[15]

The 2011 Census estimated that India has 1.7 million homeless people. However, organizations that work with homeless people recognize that they are hard to count and estimate the numbers of urban homeless to be at least three million homeless adults, adding half that number for homeless street children. It is generally considered that one per cent of a city's population (in large cities) are homeless. The urban homeless already live on the margins of society, neglected, without much by way of State support. Armaan Alkazi, who works with Hausla, a project that supports the urban homeless in Delhi, notes that homeless people daily face the struggle of staying alive, feeding themselves and getting a job. For women the situation is further compounded. Moreover, numerous communicable diseases like TB are prevalent among the homeless population. Without access to health care, rations and with very little bargaining power, the urban homeless are entirely dependent on the little work they are able to acquire and the few organizations who work with them. They are constantly faced with unsympathetic State officials, police and other institutions who see them as 'irresponsible' and 'unaccountable', mere squatters on the streets with no prospects.

The possibility of the NRIC could prove the last blow for this extremely vulnerable community. One of the biggest issues is that a large majority of the urban homeless do not have ties with families or were born and raised on the streets with no official record. Therefore, establishing linkage documents to ancestors is virtually impossible. Establishing 'legacy' documents like tenancy certificates, permanent residency certificates or passports is, again, virtually impossible as the urban homeless clearly do not have land ownership, any permanent residence or even voter IDs, let alone passports! An additional concern is the inconsistency in the spelling of names between different documents. On the off chance that a person was able to provide enough such documents, their names are often spelt differently in different documents. The lack of education and even basic literacy among the urban homeless means that they are reliant on the way each official chooses to spell their names when drawing up these documents. Without much support and caught in the unforgiving web of red tape, these seemingly small inconsistencies could mean the difference between belonging and exclusion.[16]

Armaan of Hausla is concerned that the NRIC could be the mechanism through which further violence is unleashed on the urban homeless. Already the victims of extreme structural violence through neglect and invisibility, the police and other institutions are likely to *increase the physical violence against them if they are deemed 'illegal immigrants' on top of being 'irresponsible homeless' people.* This double exclusion could prove to be very dangerous for a community that is already condemned to a daily struggle for basic needs and survival.

Trans People

> 'I left home on account of my identity and joined the community... I have not been excluded from the NRC, but my old identity has been included.'

Pinky, a trans person excluded from the final NRC list in Assam, further added that to challenge her old identity as a male, she would have to go back home to get the relevant documents which would be extremely traumatic for her. Swati Bidhan Baruah, who took on the issue of the exclusion of trans people from Assam's NRC and later became the first transgender judge in Assam, claimed that of the state's transgender population of close to 20,000, around ten per cent members had been excluded from the state's 33 districts due to a lack of documents. Those whose names had been included were mostly men.[17] This story of the exclusion of the trans community in Assam is indicative of how the NRIC might impact the large population of trans people all over the country.

Trans people have faced many levels of discrimination, stigmatization and marginalization for centuries. They have been victims of extreme physical and structural violence. The most recent evidence of this was the 2019 Transgender Persons (Protection and Rights) Bill. 'The Bill, ostensibly aiming to protect transgender persons' rights, has been drafted hastily, with no real understanding of gender identity and expression. This was made amply clear in the original draft, with the offensive and unscientific definition of a transgender person as someone who is "neither wholly male nor wholly female".'[18] After much protest, the definition was rectified to be more inclusive of gender identities but reflects the state's basic lack of understanding and empathy towards the trans community.

'Access to official documents like voter IDs, ration cards, etc., is extremely challenging and traumatic for the trans community,' says Ajita Banerjie who has worked with the LGBTQ+ community for many years. Much of the fight for trans people has been about their gender identification and the structural violence that is embedded in filling official forms. When registering for voter IDs or any other official documents, there are only three gender options: male, female and 'other'. People who refuse to identify within the 'other' category would therefore not be included in this process. With the lack of official documents, trans people are more likely to be excluded from the NRIC.

The 2019 Bill further accentuated this trauma. According to the Bill, a transgender person '"may make an application to the District Magistrate for a certificate of identity indicating the gender as 'transgender'" and a revised certificate may be obtained "if a transgender person undergoes surgery to change gender either as a male or female"'.[19] This is retained in the final Act as well. In the eyes of the state, in effect, a trans person must forego the right to self-determination of gender and must produce a medical certificate to acquire a document that correctly identifies their gender, or face exclusion altogether. This also means that trans people are likely to have different documents with different gender identifications. Ajita explains that trans people might have a birth certificate identifying them as 'male', and a voter ID identifying them as 'female'. While the government views this as an inconsistency, this is an indication of years of misgendering. The NRIC would, in effect, ensure that a trans person's own stated gender identification, for which they might even have undergone a medical procedure, would become the reason for their statelessness due to inconsistencies in their documents.

The harrowing experience of the NRC in Assam exposed fears over what the government might do next to the thousands of excluded trans people, given the seemingly impossible task of acquiring papers and the lack of resources for pursuing a legal course.[20] A similar fate awaits the millions of trans people across the country if the NRIC is implemented. Ajita additionally warns that the exclusion and possible detention of trans people puts them in graver danger than the average person given the abusive treatment they face in jails. The mass detention of trans people if excluded from the NRIC is a terrifying prospect exposing them as it will to bullying by other inmates, physical and sexual assault and deprivation of medical attention.[21]

Sex Workers

'*Documents ka sawal paida hi nahi hota*' [The question of documents doesn't even arise], claims Kusum of the All India Network of Sex Workers (AINSW) when talking about the NRIC in relation to sex workers. This clearly came out during the Assam NRC where a large number of sex workers from the Silchar red-light district in Assam found themselves excluded from the final NRC list. In Assam, sex workers failed the NRC test because their family members refused to share their legacy data.[22] What is more, in the unlikely event that they could acquire the necessary legacy data—the 'family tree'[23] data—another added measure for verification wherein members of one's extended family must add one's name to their family tree in order to verify a person's identity ensured that they would still end up being excluded. Due to the stigma around sex work, members of the extended family of sex workers refuse to add their names to their 'family trees' which of course means exclusion from the final NRC list. This also reflects the apathy and stigma of society and the State and is something that sex workers have had to endure for many years. In fact, one of the longest fights of sex workers in India has been that for visibility and recognition, of State entitlements and dignity of work. It is only now, after years of struggle and very little change, that sex workers are pursuing the electoral route to make their voices heard.

The Chouddo Nombor Galli in Assam is the largest active brothel of the Northeast, with close to 200 sex workers, almost all of whom are victims of human trafficking.[24] This is true of red-light districts in many parts of the country. Thus, the trauma of going through the NRIC wherein one has to prove one's lineage as a marker of citizenship is doubly traumatic for these workers.

For the thousands of sex workers who were born and grew up in red-light districts, as well as home-based sex workers, the stigma attached to their work makes accessing these documents even more difficult. Kusum says that although some sex workers might have voter IDs and be registered in their places of origin, excommunication from the family or community makes approaching their families for linkage documents almost impossible. Often, brothels don't serve as permanent residences for sex workers when registering for documents, and there is very little scope of landownership given that a majority of the sex workers are women. All of this makes it that much harder for them to come up with legacy documents.

Add to this the apathy, sometimes disgust, often abuse, with which State officials treat sex workers and you can see how many hurdles they will have to cross to even access the institutions through which they might be able to apply for and acquire documents and why they often fail to do so. Having to undergo the NRIC and all that it will entail is therefore going to make these workers even more vulnerable to statelessness and trauma.

Highly Stigmatized Caste Groups (Manual Scavengers)

Manual scavengers and septic tank cleaners, both in rural and urban areas, have long been invisible to the State and society at large. Even though manual scavenging has been outlawed, thousands of people continue to engage in this work without dignity or the option to leave. Having faced centuries of discrimination and marginalization, without access to education, it is no surprise that manual scavengers are excluded from electoral rolls as well.

Manual scavengers are entirely dependent on State officials for access to documents. In a system where caste discrimination is so much a part of people's everyday lives, when manual scavengers interact with agents of the State they are treated badly, abused, or, at best, ignored.

In field research conducted on manual scavengers in Dhanbad, Jharkhand in February 2020 by researchers from the Centre for Equity Studies, it was noted that the applications of these people are not taken seriously in government offices, even when they visit these offices. They are not given the time of day, made to run pillar to post and usually sent away empty-handed. They also have to deal with the enduring corruption; even if they receive residence certificates, they are only given '*Asthayi*' (temporary) certificates which require regular renewal. They have to pay bribes to the local officials to apply for/acquire the documents. Only people who can afford to pay these bribes upfront can even possibly think of getting their documents. Many reported that they felt too intimidated to approach government officers for anything.

It was further found by the field researchers that a majority of the manual scavengers do not have any documents, legacy or linkage, that might be needed for the NRIC. No birth certificates, almost no land ownership which is inherent in the nature of the caste system. Most don't have ration cards or BPL cards, either, and even face difficulty acquiring caste certificates due to the high levels of illiteracy and lack of awareness about these schemes. Given this, it is almost certain that a large section of manual scavengers and other highly stigmatized caste groups would face exclusion.

Adivasis

Adivasis constitute 8.6 per cent of India's total population. All indigenous peoples in India have faced countless attacks and threats against their rights—especially to land, self-determination and autonomy—for centuries. Forest-dwelling communities have faced a long-lost battle with displacement for the sake of development. Displacement and migration are a reality for most tribal groups around India. However, for those designated Particularly Vulnerable Tribal Groups (PVTGs), the situation is even worse. According to reports, these groups are either so invisible to the State or are so heavily discriminated against that accessing any documents at all is a major challenge.

Fifteen crore individuals better known as the Denotified

Tribes[25] (DNTs) of India, continue to be considered 'criminal by birth'. Nomadic and semi-nomadic communities continue to face harassment at the hands of law enforcement agencies. The repeal of the Criminal Tribes Act (CTA) after Independence has not changed the mindset of government officials or members of society who continue to reflect a colonial hangover when it comes to the treatment of DNTs. Given their centuries-old tradition of constant movement, they often do not possess any residential proof, which leaves them out of the majority of the government's development schemes as well as with no proof of address to register to vote.[26]

'These people are constantly migrating from one place to another. Because even the name of their village has been removed, it has disappeared. It is not in the system any more. Even if they name the village, where is it? Which district? This is a major issue,'[27] says Aloka Kujur, Jharkhand-based Adivasi rights activist. This poses very obvious and very serious challenges for the NRIC. How will DNTs, PVTGs and other tribal groups obtain legacy documents for landownership when their whole village has been obliterated for the sake of 'development'?

This was acutely evident during the Assam NRC, wherein a preliminary survey conducted by the Rights and Risks Analysis Group in 2019 found that 25,000 Bodos, 12,000 Reangs, 8,000 Hajongs and thousands of persons belonging to other tribes had been excluded from the NRC. As many as 25 per cent of about 36,000 Reangs in Hailakandi district were excluded. Furthermore, an overwhelming majority of the Reang women were excluded as they were not able to prove legacy from 1971. Once they are married, most of these women are deleted from family ration cards losing all proof of their identity/legacy.[28] A similar situation would likely obtain if the entire country were to undergo the NRIC. The cruel irony of this situation would be that tribals, who are in fact the original inhabitants of these lands, whose traditional lands have been taken away, would be excluded and rendered stateless as well.

Old People Without Care

Anupama Datta of HelpAge India who works with the elderly warns that the NRIC will bring 'untold misery and many avoidable existential problems'. Age and the lack of care in old age brings with it poverty and dependency. For the elderly, the unnecessary process and the various arbitrary measures in implementing the NRIC make the situation that much more difficult. There is often a sense that old people have 'given what they can to society and are not of use any more'; there are questions over the logic of providing for their sustenance. If the registration officer believes this then he is unlikely to include old people in the registration process.

Digitization itself has created problems for the elderly who might not have the knowledge to access these facilities. This was evidenced during the immense problems faced in the Aadhaar/UID process and such problems will be compounded hundredfold during the NRIC. According to Anupama, the old have difficulty understanding how systems work at government offices, especially the intensely bureaucratic and deliberately confusing NRIC, which will create trauma, psychological and economic stress.

During fieldwork in Assam, members of the Karwan-e-Mohabbat team came across several instances of old persons being asked extremely specific questions at the hearing centres and tribunals, and then reprimanded if they were not able to be accurate. In one case, harassment by the hearing centre official by building on existing fears about the collection of biometric information at the Centre, pushed a 97-year-old man to commit suicide.[29]

Even though people might have the ability to prove their legacy in terms of birth certificates and other documents, the elderly often only retain in their memory snippets of information—like the name of the village but no other details like district/state or the name of the then *sarpanch* or some other vague information (like first names of relatives/siblings), all of which would present only partial information and in most cases be impossible to retrieve/verify. Furthermore, the elderly might find accessing hearing and documentation centres extremely difficult given the fact that India's urban and rural transport systems are appallingly unfriendly to the elderly or disabled. The prospect, then, of detention of the elderly, especially the ill, is deeply worrying.

REIMAGINING BELONGING

> 'The government of India is talking about religious persecution that minorities in our neighbouring countries are facing. But it doesn't care about crores of Dalits and Adivasis who may not possess even the basic documents to prove their citizenship. Are you trying to push them into detention centres? Are you going to make them stateless?'
>
> —Prof N. Sukumar, Alliance Against CAA-NRC-NPR[30]

The NRC in Assam serves as a haunting warning for what is to come. It is clear from the harrowing experiences there, as well as an understanding of the ground realities of the communities mentioned in this paper, that the national NRC will cause unspeakable horrors. For the thousands of people who have been stigmatized either for their identity or profession (sex workers and the LGBTQ+ community) accessing linkage documents to their families who have likely disowned them will cause much trauma. For circular migrants who constitute a large majority of India's working population, and who are traditionally left out of State protection and all other such mechanisms as a function of their movement, the NRIC would add immensely to their suffering. For those communities whose plight is already invisible to the State and society like the urban homeless, manual scavengers, denotified tribes, old people without care and many more, the NRIC will, unfortunately, be just another layer in their already oppressive lives. It has become abundantly clear that the NRIC will push millions already at the margins and engaged in a daily fight for basic rights over the edge, to a life of acute distress.

The communities mentioned above are by no means the only vulnerable groups who would be pushed over the edge if subjected to the NRIC. Muslims, women (especially single women and widows),[31] persons with disabilities,[32] persons with mental illness,[33] and potentially millions of others who are uneducated and lack the resources to acquire such a vast range of documents would risk exclusion. The entire NRIC process seems to have been conceptualized without a single thought to the millions of people for whom the everyday struggle to survive is their only reality. It is then prudent to ask what purpose the NRIC would serve. Why has the government created it and why is it adamant about pushing forward a policy that will clearly be harmful to large numbers of the country's citizens? Why are the parameters of 'belonging' to this nation limited to the availability of some documents? These are all questions that were front and centre in the ongoing fight against the CAA-NPR and NRIC.

The solidarity exhibited by millions of people in support of the Constitution and its foundational principles represents a critical moment in the history of India. It invokes the need to reimagine our understanding of 'belonging'; to move away from systems that exclude and marginalize to systems that include and strengthen; to radically overhaul the current structures that keep millions of vulnerable people at the edge in the first place and to resist at every moment when our collective humanity is challenged.

Notes

1. 'Rajya Sabha passes Citizenship (Amendment) Bill', *The Wire*, 11 December 2019.
2. 'Newly-convened alliance underscores potential impact of CAA-NRC on Dalits, Adivasis', *The Wire*, 16 January 2020.
3. This research was limited to phone interviews due to the restrictions imposed by the nationwide lockdown in response to

the Covid-19 pandemic. We conducted 10 telephonic interviews with community organizers and members of various projects working with the vulnerable groups mentioned in this article.

4. Shoaib Daniyal, 'Modi government claims no all-India NRC announced. Here's why this is false', *Scroll.in*, 19 December 2019.
5. Ibid.
6. Refer to Varna Balakrishnan and Navsharan Singh's article 'Standing Outside the Political Borders of "We, the People"' included in Part 2 of this volume.
7. 'Assam NRC final list out: What will happen to the 19 lakh excluded people?', *Business Today*, 31 August 2019.
8. See Balakrishnan and Singh, 'Standing Outside the Political Borders of "We, the People"' included in this volume.
9. Natalie Brinham, 'When identity documents and registration produce exclusion: Lessons from Rohingya experiences in Myanmar', *LSE Blogs*, 10 May 2019.
10. National Sample Survey, 64th round, June 2008.
11. 'Unlocking the urban: Reimagining migrant lives in cities post Covid-19', Ajeevika Bureau, Udaipur, April 2020 (https://www.aajeevika.org/assets/pdfs/Unlocking%20the%20Urban.pdf, last accessed 20 June 2021).
12. 'Political inclusion of seasonal migrant workers in India: Perceptions, realities and challenges', Ajeevika Bureau, Udaipur, 2018 (www.aajeevika.org/assets/pdfs/Political%20Inclusion%20of%20Migrant%20Workers%20in%20India.pdf, last accessed 20 June 2021).
13. Tanushree Venkatraman, Saurabh Chauhan, Sanjoy Dey and Ritesh Mishra, 'In long walk back home, migrants battle hunger, scourge of Covid-19', *Hindustan Times*, 16 May 2019.
14. 'Bengaluru Police demolishes makeshift houses of migrants as CAA-NRC debate rages on', *India Today*, 19 January 2020.
15. 'CAA-NRC will affect homeless most, divert funds towards health, education instead: Urban planners', *NewsClick*, 4 February 2020.
16. 'In India's citizenship test, a spelling error can ruin a family', *The Economic Times*, 17 August 2018.
17. Gaurav Das, 'The NRC poses a two-fold predicament for Assam's transgender community', *The Wire*, 8 October 2020.
18. Ajita Banerjie, 'Against the mandate for inclusion: The Transgender Persons Bill 2018', *The Hindu*, 20 December 2018.
19. Ajita Banerjie, 'Transgender Persons Bill has let down the community's long struggle for self-respect', *The Indian Express*, 2 December 2019.

20. Das, 'The NRC poses a two-fold predicament for Assam's transgender community'.
21. Mrinalika Roy, 'Transgender prison inmates face abuse, neglect in Bengaluru', *Reuters*, 3 January 2017.
22. Anirudha Laskar, '200 sex workers in Silchar fail to enroll as citizens in the final NRC', *Northeast Now*, 16 September 2019.
23. 'NRC updation in Assam: 40% verification of family tree complete', *The Economic Times*, 2 April 2018.
24. Laskar, '200 sex workers in Silchar fail to enroll as citizens in the final NRC'.
25. Denotified Tribes (DNTs), also known as Vimukta Jati, are the tribes that were listed originally under the Criminal Tribes Act of 1871, as Criminal Tribes and 'addicted to the systematic commission of non-bailable offences'. Once a tribe became 'notified' as criminal, all its members were required to register with the local magistrate, failing which they would be charged with a 'crime' under the Indian Penal Code. The Criminal Tribes Act of 1952 repealed the notification, i.e. 'de-notified' the tribal communities. This Act, however, was replaced by a series of Habitual Offenders Acts that asked police to investigate 'criminal tendencies' of 'suspects' and whether their occupation was 'conducive to settled way of life'. The denotified tribes were reclassified as 'habitual offenders' in 1959.
26. A.P. Jitender Reddy, 'End this long trauma', *The Hindu*, 7 December 2018.
27. Ananya Singh, 'How will CAA and NRC affect India's tribal population?', *The Citizen*, 21 December 2019.
28. Prasanta Mazumder, 'Assam NRC: Rights body says over one lakh tribals excluded', *The New Indian Express*, 2 December 2019.
29. Aditya Sharma, 'Passport to Kill', *News18*.
30. 'Newly-convened alliance underscores potential impact of CAA-NRC on Dalits, Adivasis', *The Wire*.
31. Varna Balakrishnan and Navsharan Singh's chapter in this volume elaborates on the gendered dimensions of the NRC in Assam.
32. Varsha Torgalikar, 'Why disabled persons in India are opposing CAA-NPR-NRC', *NewsClick*, 20 January 2020.
33. Prasanta Mazumder, 'Most people left out of NRC are suffering from trauma and humiliation, finds survey', *The New Indian Express*, 3 August 2019.

NARESH AND JINU KOCH

Abdul Kalam Azad

Soon after Prime Minister Narendra Modi said that there were no detention centres in the country, Naresh Koch, a detainee in the Goalpara detention centre in Assam, breathed his last at the Gauhati Medical College and Hospital.

Naresh passed away on 5 January. He became the 29th person to have died at a detention centre in the state since 2014. The state has six detention centres housed inside district jails, while a Central-government funded exclusive centre is being constructed in Goalpara's Matia area.

Three days after his death, I visited his family at his home, located close to the well-known Archaeological Survey of India protected historical site, Surya Pahar, in Goalpara district. I have been meeting the families of those who have been kept in detention centres, those who have died by suicides out of fear of being sent to detention camps, those who have been excluded from the National Register of Citizens (NRC), those who have been facing litigations at the Foreigners' Tribunals, etc., on a regular basis. All the stories are living testimonies of institutionalized brutalities, of sheer injustice. However, Naresh Koch's story is one of the most disturbing stories I have encountered so far.

Naresh Koch belongs to the indigenous Koch tribe of Assam. His son and his brother were included in the final NRC released last year. He is neither a Muslim of Bengali origin nor a Bengali Hindu and doesn't belong to any of the other communities which are widely perceived to belong to the

This is an excerpt from Abdul Kalam Azad, 'The Tragic Demise of a "Declared Foreigner" at Goalpara Detention Centre', that appeared in *The Wire* on 12 January 2020.

category of people who could have migrated from Bangladesh. Naresh developed hypertension during the two years he spent in the Goalpara detention centre, suffered a stroke and finally died at the Gauhati Medical College.

Naresh and his second wife Jinu, who belongs to the Garo tribe from Meghalaya, used to work at a fish farm, a few kilometres away from his home. Two years ago, at the end of a hard day's work, Naresh went to a country liquor shop on the main road to have a drink. His wife said local police picked him up from there. They later learnt that, as per police records, he had been named a 'declared foreigner' by a Tribunal. He was declared a foreigner despite the fact that he and his ancestors did not have a connection with any foreign country other than the soil of Assam—the Koch dynasty once, under the reign of glorious kings like Nara Narayan and general Chilarai, spanned various parts of Assam and Bengal.

Naresh was a 'Declared Foreign National' (DFN), an abbreviation which implies rightlessness. According to Jinu, she and his son Babulal (from his first wife) didn't find out about this and Naresh's detention for a few days. A couple of days after Naresh had been picked up, they heard, from some villagers, that Naresh had been sent to the detention centre. Forget the costs of fighting Naresh's case in the higher courts, the family couldn't even manage to gather one hundred rupees to cover the expenses for transportation to visit him in the detention centre.

Due to Naresh's arrest, Jinu soon lost her job at the fish farm, as well as the pending wages. Babulal occasionally found work as a manual worker, which became the only source of income for the family. Naresh continued to remain in detention.

Two years passed by. Suddenly, this in December 2019, a police team visited Jinu and requested her to leave immediately for the Goalpara Hospital to see her husband. She was told that he was seriously ill. Since Jinu didn't have a penny in the house, the police team gave her Rs 100 so that she could rush to the hospital. However, before she could reach the hospital, her husband was shifted to the Gauhati Medical College, about 150 kilometres from her home.

This time, the local police gave Jinu Rs 1,000 and sent her to Guwahati. An uneducated tribal woman from Khardang village on the Assam–Meghalaya border, Jinu had never visited Guwahati before; she couldn't even speak Assamese fluently. 'I somehow reached the hospital but found him paralysed. I had not seen or spoken to him in the last two years. I wanted to speak to him. He tried speaking to me, but couldn't,' Jinu related. The stroke had paralysed his tongue as well.

Jinu spent the next 13 days at the hospital and looked after Naresh while two policemen guarded them day and night.

On 5 January, Naresh breathed his last. The police brought his body to his village from where he had been detained as a 'declared' foreign national. While he was alive the state treated him as a 'foreigner', his wife and son were separated from him. But death had finally brought them together.

Jinu said that the police cremated him that night itself in the presence of a group of five or six people and left immediately after the cremation.

When I reached Naresh Koch's home, it was getting dark. I found Jinu in the courtyard. The sound of the *azaan* could be heard from a nearby mosque. I noticed the green light from the government-subsidized electric meter attached to an exterior wall of the house twinkling. Jinu entered her Pradhan Mantri Awas Yojana-funded house. I presumed she had gone in to turn on the light. Instead, she came out with a kerosene lamp. Even though she had a free electricity connection from the government, she didn't have enough money to buy a bulb.

Jinu said that after Naresh's death, she had nothing to eat at home. She had to resort to begging and collected two hundred rupees to buy rice, potato and green chillies. Her biggest challenge now is to repay the seven hundred rupees she borrowed to cover the cost of firewood used in Naresh's funeral.

WHOSE BENEVOLENT STATE?
CITIZENSHIP, REFUGEE PROTECTION AND THE CAA-NRC

Varna Balakrishnan

The Indian State and its representatives have long argued for the merits of the Citizenship Amendment Act, 2019 by framing it as a humanitarian olive branch from the Indian State to refugees from neighbouring countries. However, a deeper examination into this claim is imperative to understand its implicit and explicit meanings, and subsequently, its credibility. In this paper, I will first be looking into what this State narrative on the relationship between the CAA and refugee has been, and how this narrative perceives the 'refugee' it claims to protect. I will be juxtaposing these claims with international law and policies that lay the ground for a good refugee protection regime. I will be making an argument that India is a long way from having a good refugee protection law not only because of legal inconsistencies but also because it fails to recognize the lived realities of refugees. With the National Register of Citizens also actively creating statelessness, the NRC-CAA regime is fundamentally antithetical to refugee protection. Therefore any such framing of the CAA is fallacious, to say the least.

STATE RHETORIC: WHO IS AN ILLEGAL IMMIGRANT AND A REFUGEE?

The CAA and NRC have long been framed by the State and the ruling Bharatiya Janata Party (BJP) as benevolent pieces of legislation and policy that will cleanse the country of 'illegal immigrants'. 'The government will *identify illegal immigrants* living on every inch of the country's soil and will deport them as per the international law,' Union Home

Minister Amit Shah claimed in the Rajya Sabha in July 2019.[1] The definition of an illegal alien/migrant is central to the understanding of citizenship as it defines its boundaries. In order to create in-group cohesiveness, for example to construct notions of nationalism or patriotism within a nation-state, it is integral to define the 'out-group' and who is excluded from the project.[2] Therefore, authorization and control of entry and movement of aliens—freedom of movement and residence being a right reserved for 'legitimate' citizens—is construed as a significant manifestation of State sovereignty.[3] This is clearly reflected in the primary objective of the NRC process, as established in many public statements—to identify and deport illegal immigrants, by giving most priority to areas affected by infiltration. The CAA is argued to act in conjunction with the NRC to provide protection to legitimate refugees (as opposed to infiltrators), which was promised in the BJP manifesto for the 2019 Lok Sabha elections:

> We are committed to the enactment of the Citizenship Amendment Bill for the protection *of individuals of religious minority communities from neighbouring countries* escaping persecution.[4] [Emphasis added]

It was confirmed not long after by Union Home Minister Amit Shah:

> I want to assure the refugees who have come to India that the Narendra Modi government will bring Citizenship Amendment Bill and after that, you will get *as many rights as me in this country*. The BJP government will get [*sic*] the right to each and every refugee the right to become the Prime Minister of this country. We will make each and every refugee [a] citizen of this country.[5] [Emphasis added]

Beyond Union Home Minister Amit Shah's claims of the objective of a pan-India exercise, government and ruling party representatives from different states have also made similar arguments in public. In West Bengal, where there is a strong history of contention along international borders, the CAA and NRC have been framed as a refugee protection mechanism that would enable Bangladeshi Hindu refugees to attain full Indian citizenship easily. That no Hindu will have to leave the country due to this process has been reiterated by several representatives of the government and the ruling party on multiple occasions. Here's BJP state president for West Bengal Dilip Ghosh:

> People of Bengal are being misled about the NRC... I assure *all Hindu, Buddhist, Sikh, Jain refugees they won't have to leave the country, they will get Indian citizenship* and enjoy all the rights of an Indian national.[6] [Emphasis added]

This has been explicitly clarified by Amit Shah as well:

> I want to tell you today that before conducting the NRC the BJP government will bring the Citizenship Amendment Bill or CAB. CAB means that all the Hindu, Sikh, Buddhist, Christian, Jain [*sic*] who have come to this country will get Indian citizenship permanently.[7]

These statements warrant crucial questions about India's legal and moral standpoint on who the illegal immigrant and infiltrator is, and who the refugee it aims to protect is. From the statements made by ruling party leaders and office bearers, it comes through that an 'illegal immigrant' is a Bangladeshi and/or Rohingya immigrant, an infiltrator. They are the 'majority community' of our neighbouring countries Pakistan, Bangladesh and Afghanistan, i.e. Muslims. As Kailash Vijayvargiya, national general secretary of the Bharatiya Janata Party argues:

> India is not a charity house that those who are the *majority community in Bangladesh, Afghanistan and Pakistan (Muslims)* can infiltrate, spread terror and take away the livelihood of our citizens.[8] [Emphasis added]

BJP leaders Kapil Mishra and Neelkant Bakshi let their imagination run riot:

> It is also possible that it is a conspiracy to save the *Bangladeshi and Rohingya infiltrators* and somehow obstruct the directions of Centre and Supreme Court in the process of identifying the infiltrators.[9] [Emphasis added]

The statements also identify illegal immigrants as those who live on the fringes of society, are homeless and who live outside the radar of everyday policing. As Uttar Pradesh DGP O.P. Singh asserts:

> Such people are often found *living in the outskirts* of every district, away from people who could identify them as illegal immigrants. New settlements will be marked, besides we will identify *homeless* people living on the roadside, as these are the possible places where illegal immigrants could hide.[10] [Emphasis added]

It has also been stated that 'no country will accept them'. This prompts a crucial question: Are the illegal immigrants really foreigners who have crossed an international border?[11]

Simultaneously, the 'refugee' has been placed as the moral opposite of the 'illegal immigrant'. The CAA and several public statements by the government and ruling party leaders mark them as individuals of minority religions (i.e. Hindu, Sikh, Buddhist, Christian, Jain) from neighbouring countries—Pakistan, Afghanistan and Bangladesh—who are escaping religious persecution. On multiple occasions, as we have seen above, BJP leaders have reiterated that refugees thus identified will be given full Indian citizenship, and, further, that no Hindu will be deported.

These statements consistently establish that what distinguishes an illegal immigrant (deserving of punishment) from a refugee (deserving of protection) is their religion, i.e. their Muslim identity. However, there are also clear inconsistencies in the rhetoric around the alleged purpose of CAA and NRC within the BJP itself. The 'illegal immigrant' in Karnataka has not been understood as Muslim—their criminality has been more defined by their poverty and their linguistic identity outside of Kannada. These definitions could also apply to migrants from within India, from 'other states'. BJP leaders in Bengal have, on the other hand, defined their 'outsiders' on the basis of their religion. In the public claims made by those in power, 'refugee' and 'illegal immigrant' have been terms passed around callously to speak to immediate interests, very rarely reflecting an actual official understanding of what it means to be either of them.

Understanding the impact the CAA and NRC could have on India's refugee policy calls for enquiry into who India legally considers a refugee, what a good refugee protection policy looks like and how India's refugee policy, combined with the CAA, really fares in meeting international standards of refugee protection.

BEING A REFUGEE

The 1951 Refugee Convention (Convention Relating to the Status of Refugees), a pivotal internationally recognized legal document on refugees, defines a 'refugee' as 'someone who is unable or unwilling to return to their country of origin owing to a well-founded fear of being persecuted for reasons of race, religion, nationality, membership of a particular social group, or political opinion'.[12] Currently, there are 26 million refugees across the world, of which 68 per cent come from just five countries: Syria, Venezuela, Afghanistan, South Sudan and Myanmar,[13] and 84 per cent of the total refugee population are currently hosted by developing countries.[14] The United Nations High Commissioner for Refugees (UNHCR) understands an asylum seeker thus: 'when people flee their own country and seek sanctuary in another country, they apply for asylum—the right to be recognized as a refugee and receive legal protection and material assistance. An asylum seeker must demonstrate that their fear of persecution in their home country is well-founded'.[15] The Convention recognizes someone as a refugee if they:

- have a well-founded fear of being persecuted because of his or her: race; religion; nationality; membership of a particular social group; or political opinion;
- are outside their country of origin or habitual residence;
- are unable or unwilling to avail themselves of the protection of that country, or to return there, because of fear of persecution; and
- are not explicitly excluded from refugee protection or whose refugee status has not ceased because of a change of circumstances.

Once these criteria are fulfilled, a person is a refugee, even if an official decision has not been made on their refugee status application. This implies that 'the recognition of refugee status is *declaratory*: it confirms that the person is indeed a refugee'.[16]

As the boundaries and nuances on refugee protection and citizenship laws are constantly being blurred, it becomes imperative to ask if an enquiry into citizenship in a refugee context is possible. The notion of citizenship identity, at the most basic level, derives from understandings of membership of a community (itself a contested concept), describing the relationship between individuals and the State, and between individual citizens within that community.[17] Academic and humanitarian literature on citizenship and refugees have long argued that it is possible to imagine citizenship within a refugee and even refugee-camp context. Talking about refugees' agency, Simon Turner asks whether a politics of the stateless is possible and if citizenship can be exercised by the stateless.[18] Ruth Lister argues that the 'vocabulary of citizenship' and its meanings vary with socio-political and cultural contexts.[19] She asserts that citizenship needs to be seen as a process, rather than just an outcome. The struggle to attain citizenship rights and expand existing ones should therefore be considered as important as the rights themselves. Within these understandings is also the stance that citizenship cannot be reduced to a legal status but should be seen as a discursive space that even those without the legal entitlement can engage with, involving 'practices of becoming claim-making subjects in and through various sites and scales'.[20] These discussions are pinned on an effort to expand the normative and legal understanding of citizenship, and recognize and strengthen people's agency. At the most basic level, it requires a sound framework of recognizing refugees and asylum seekers, and nowhere do they argue for limiting the scope of citizenship laws as a means to empower refugees.

Being a Refugee in India

Although India currently hosts over 200,000 refugees from Sri Lanka and Tibet alongside 40,000 refugees and asylum seekers from other countries registered with UNHCR,[21] India does not have its own national refugee or asylum policy. India is not signatory to the 1951 UN Convention on the Status of Refugees or to the 1967 Protocol Relating to the Status of Refugees—which lie at the core of the international refugee governance protocols. Neither does it have a specific domestic legislation, or even definition, for refugees that dictates a uniform treatment of asylum seekers and refugees.[22] However, through conventions such as the 1948 Universal Human Rights Declaration, India has international humanitarian obligations which require it to respect human rights. India is also a signatory to the non-binding Bangkok Principles on Status and Treatment of Refugees (2001).[23] The South Asian Association for Regional Cooperation (SAARC) has also agreed upon a Social Charter, as well as a Convention on Regional Arrangements on the Promotion of Child Welfare in South Asia.

Most recently, India became signatory to the New York Declaration for Refugees and Migrants, which was adopted by 193 countries in September 2016, which creates the ground for a new framework for refugee protection—the Global Compact on Refugees (GCR). The Compact is a 'coordinated effort to strengthen international response to protracted refugee situations and comprehensively addresses all stages of refugee protection, from reception to long-term solutions'.[24] This is, however, non-binding.

Given this, the governance of refugees in India comes under the Foreigners Act (1946), Citizenship Act (1955) and now the Citizenship Amendment Act, 2019, and refugees *de facto* stand in violation of the Passports Acts (1967). Under the Foreigners Act, a 'refugee' is a 'foreigner'—aliens who are on Indian soil either temporarily or permanently. The Citizenship Amendment Act (2003) defines all non-citizens who entered the country without a visa as 'illegal migrants', making no exceptions for refugees or asylum seekers.[25] Neither does the CAA 2019 make these distinctions.

The Foreign Regional Registration Office (FRRO), under the Bureau of Immigration, is the national governing body of the refugees. Although the UNHCR is the primary administrative body in refugee camps across the world, India's relationship with the UNHCR is ambivalent.[26] It is permitted to undertake registration and refugee status determination (RSD), and provide assistance for repatriation to those not recognized as refugees by the government.[27] Refugees' welfare is highly jeopardized because the FRRO does not distinguish between refugees and asylum seekers—the Foreigners Act is only an immigration determinant.

Laws governing refugees therefore largely depend on the bilateral relationship between India and their countries of origin.[28] This includes a series of ad hoc executive policies from the Ministry of Home Affairs such as the Tibetan Rehabilitation Policy, 2014[29] and the relief and rehabilitation policy for Sri Lankan refugees.[30] Refugees from neighbouring countries (except Myanmar) are directly assisted by the government, primarily due to security concerns, and those from non-neighbouring countries and Myanmar are assisted by the UNHCR. It is crucial to note that while the UNHCR undertakes an RSD process for each refugee, Indian laws do not give legal validity to this 'refugee' status, or to any documentation pertaining to it. Lawyer Roshni Shanker notes that while this system allows refugees to reside in India on a good faith basis, it leaves them vulnerable to any changes in this good faith.[31] As policies and politics of governments change, so do the rights and lives of the refugees. Unfortunately, in 2020, the Indian government reduced its budget for their relief and rehabilitation by over 80 per cent.[32] This cumulative absence of international law obligations and domestic laws have enabled the Indian government to leave the situation of refugees in a 'state of limbo' and provide space for arbitrary decisions and potentially unreported human rights violations in the camps and elsewhere.[33] Is the Citizenship Amendment Act, 2019 then the much-needed solution?

A GOOD REFUGEE PROTECTION LAW

Internationally, refugees and asylum seekers are subject to two sets of legal protections. The first includes international human rights laws, and the second, conventions and legislation determining and protecting the rights of refugees specifically. With these protections in place, what should a good refugee regime entail and ensure?

Refugee protection is grounded in the fundamental principle of *non-refoulement*, i.e. a refugee's right to be protected from forced return. It is contained in Article 33(1) of the 1951 Convention, which states: 'No Contracting State shall expel or return ("refouler") a refugee in any manner whatsoever to the frontiers of territories where his life or freedom would be threatened on account of his race, religion, nationality, membership of a particular social group or political opinion.'[34] All refugees, including those asylum seekers whose who have not yet been formally recognized as refugees, are entitled to this. In addition to the 1951 Convention, several international and regional human rights laws prohibit the forced repatriation of anyone, refugee or not, when they stand the risk of violence, torture and other human rights violations. The principle of non-refoulement is also a crucial aspect of customary law norms—this means that even States like India that are not signatory to the 1951 Convention must respect it.

Functioning hand-in-hand with the principle of non-refoulement is the right to *seek and enjoy asylum.* Countries across the world, including India, have had a rich cultural practice of asylum and sanctuary, even before international laws and covenants laid them down. Today 'asylum' is not defined in international law, but is generally referred to mean the larger network of provisions and protections, including but not limited to non-refoulement. It includes the right to have access to fair and effective processes, access to the UNHCR, and treatment upholding human rights. It holds the host States responsible for maintaining peaceful and humanitarian asylum systems, and refugees and asylum seekers to respect the laws of the host States.[35]

Given this, the UNCHR recommends that parliamentarians and lawmakers ensure that the principle of non-refoulement and the rights of asylum seekers are strongly enshrined in national legislation. It further recommends that countries accede to international treaties that protect the rights of refugees and displaced people, and consistently re-evaluate their decisions to not do so. This should be coupled with efforts to remove any restrictive interpretations of these laws at the national level. The UNHCR recommends that States should draw inspiration from the vast body of international standards established in this field, and even try to expand the criteria to be declared a 'refugee' in accordance with local needs (as has been the case with the 1969 Organisation of African Unity Convention).[36]

DO THE CAA-NRC MEET THESE STANDARDS?

Indian law recognizes that where international treaties are not in contradiction with national laws, they must be enforced. In the absence of a unified refugee policy, the Indian courts have, through several judgments, recognized the internationally mandated principles of non-refoulement, the rights of asylum seekers, right to a fair process as well as access to the UNHCR.[37] However, this does not imply that the Indian government has been able to fairly and consistently uphold international standards in practice. Senior lawyer Rajeev Dhavan (who also re-drafted a Model Refugee Law) argues that 'Indian courts and the Indian government have divergent views on refugees, persecution, and deportation'.

Roshni Shanker argues that there are three prominent myths about the CAA.[38] The first is that it expands the protection offered to refugees. This stands untrue when we take into account the fact that the two largest groups of refugees that the Act claims to benefit—Bangladeshi Hindus and Afghan Sikhs—were already eligible to claim citizenship before the CAA was passed. Besides this, the CAA does not bring about any practical progress to the refugee-citizenship process. The benefits offered in the CAA through the reduction of the naturalization period, from eleven to five years, are undercut by the tedious and long-drawn-out bureaucratic processes that need to be followed once the eligibility criteria are met. The argument that the Act only expedites the process of naturalization for certain minority groups, while allowing pre-existing processes for other groups to continue also does not hold much practical value. The refugee status determination carried out by the UNHCR is more often than not the only proof of residence that many refugees might have in order to access the benefits of the CAA. Moreover, without the government officially and legally recognizing them as refugees, this access remains a mirage. In the long term therefore the closest that they can get to citizenship is a discretionary long-term visa. The Act therefore does not add more nuance or efficiency to the existing practices or attempt to bridge the gap between international standards and Indian practice.

India's Poor Record

While the CAA fails to actually address or improve the possibilities and choices available for the refugees residing in India, the NRC process has actively worked towards creating stateless persons out of Indian citizens. International law recognizes the right to nationality as a fundamental right. While it recognizes that States have their right to determine who their nationals are, arbitrary deprivation of nationality is prohibited.[39] Changes in citizenship laws are among the primary causes for statelessness—they create a risk of citizens being rendered stateless if they are unable to meet the demands proposed in the new laws. The over 19 lakh people who have been left out of the NRC in Assam and the many who languish in detention centres currently exist in this limbo of actual statelessness, or the threat of it. The Indian State therefore is not only looking at refugees and asylum seekers from different countries, but also at manufactured statelessness within its borders.

Over and above the legal provisions, or the lack of them, India has also had a rather inconsistent record in upholding the rights of refugees, asylum seekers and stateless people. India's insistence on forcefully 'deporting' those determined as 'foreigners' to Bangladesh through a violent and arbitrary 'push back' procedure, in the absence of an extradition treaty that can indisputably confirm their country of origin and without any understanding with Bangladesh on the reception of the deportees,[40] is dangerously close to refoulement. India's violations of the principle of non-refoulement have been very pronounced in its treatment of Rohingya refugees from Myanmar. In August 2017, the government announced plans to deport 'illegal foreign nationals' including 40,000 Rohingya refugees. Kiren Rijiju, then Minister of State for Home Affairs, claimed that their registration with the UNHCR as refugees does not exempt them from being identified as 'illegal immigrants' and they would therefore will be deported.[41] Seven Rohingya men were refouled to Myanmar in October 2018 where the threat and persecution that they first escaped are far from gone.[42] This makes it clear that even the cursory power given to the UNHCR to conduct refugee status determination does not amount to actual protection for the refugees against arbitrary violations of their rights.

Refugees, asylum seekers and stateless persons also have a precarious life during their residence in this country. The National Human Rights Commission Special Monitor for Minorities, Harsh Mander, had found that the detention centres in Assam are rife with gross human rights violations, extreme mental health crises and are in a legal limbo.[43] Thirty 'foreigners', all of whom were either illiterate or barely literate and economically weak, have died within these detention centres since 2016.[44] Sri Lankan Tamil refugees in India have been subject to extreme surveillance and incarceration into prison like 'special camps' owing to an increasingly securitized approach to them since 1991.[45] Despite ongoing civil-war conditions through the early twenty-first century in Sri Lanka, the Indian government undertook several repatriation drives where the refugees' consent was either ill-informed or absent. This had brought India under severe scrutiny for violating non-refoulement at the time.[46] Today, even though multiple generations of refugees of different origins, many whom were born on Indian soil, reside within and outside camps in India, they lack the prospect of any long-term aspirations or politico-legal identity. The CAA makes no effort to address these gaping inconsistencies and injustices that characterize India's refugee regime.

CONCLUSION

Being a refugee is more than the legal identity it engenders—the social condition of being a refugee, of being a resident of a camp and of living in between traumatic times brings along a very specific historicity and identity that even the best of legal definitions fail to recognize. 'Refugee', while being a protective legal status, is also a special moral and political condition.[47] Refugee communities in India, despite being residents of the land and parts of its communities for decades, do not often share a relationship with the Indian State beyond that of benefactor-beneficiary, regardless of how extensive or insignificant the benefits have been. Reports from refugees, academics and humanitarian workers in the context of displacements induced by currently ongoing conflicts argue that most refugees just want to go home—but the nature of their community's persecution is such that this is rarely a viable option.

However, the majority of displaced people in the world are not in such emergency situations, but are trapped in protracted displacement—which are 'situations characterized by long periods of exile and separation from home...which have moved beyond the initial emergency phase but for which solutions do not exist in the foreseeable future'.[48] This includes the majority of the refugees in India. As communities of refugees exist within these socio-legal limbos, and as new generations of refugees are born and raised within protracted displacement situations, their needs, aspirations, and understanding and experience of the refugee identity evolve. India's refugee policy takes no account of these evolving challenges that have grown within its aegis—it does not take into consideration the fact that within its refugee protection regime there is very little room for claim-making or socio-political expression. To create a 'benevolent' refugee policy, as claimed, therefore would require the State to perceive refugees as much more than mere data points or security concerns.

We have seen that the NRC process actively works towards creating stateless persons, flouting multiple international covenants and human rights principles. The CAA on the other hand neither effectively counters this nor provides any additional protections—it only further contracts and misconstructs the parameters of who a refugee is. It is therefore clear that not only do the CAA-NRC not account for any real refugee protection mechanisms, but they are also fundamentally antithetical to the idea of refugee protection itself. Ironically, they work towards limiting the understanding of 'citizenship' in India, both constitutionally and within public discourse. The Government of India has also not come up with any new comprehensive refugee protection and asylum granting policies or checks and balances to its existing practices. It has failed to take into account the diverse needs of refugees currently on its soil, to adapt to respond to international standards and guidelines on refugee protection, and to establish consistent and comprehensive relationships with its neighbours in this regard. Sarah Ahmed, while looking at political speeches on asylum seekers notes that the distinctions between the genuine and the bogus asylum seekers refer to those who are welcome and those who are not. She argues, '[P]artly, this works to enable the national subject to imagine its own generosity in welcoming some others. The nation is hospitable as it allows those genuine ones to stay. And yet at the same time, it constructs some others as already hateful (as bogus) in order to define the limits or the *conditions* of this hospitality.'[49] Given the failings of the CAA and the perils of the NRC in these contexts, any argument that the CAA-NRC is a reflection of the Indian State's benevolence towards refugees in the face of an 'illegal immigrant' crisis is therefore a fallacious claim that betrays its sectarian intentions.

Notes

1. 'Will identify and deport every illegal immigrant: Amit Shah', *India Today*, 17 July 2019.
2. Joke Meeus, Bart Duriez, Norbert Vanbeselaere and Filip Boen, 'The role of national identity representation in the relation between in group identification and out group derogation: Ethnic versus civic representation', *British Journal of Social Psychology*, vol. 49, no. 2 (2010), pp. 305–20.

3. Anupama Roy and Ujjwal Kumar Singh, 'The ambivalence of citizenship: The IMDT Act (1983) and the politics of forclusion in Assam', *Critical Asian Studies*, vol. 41, no. 1 (March 2009), pp. 37–60.
4. 'Citizenship Amendment bill has become necessity for those left out of NRC: Assam BJP President Ranjeet Das', *The Economic Times*, 3 October 2019.
5. 'Before NRC, Citizenship Amendment Bill will be passed', *Deccan Herald*, 5 October 2019.
6. Tathagata Bhattacharya, 'Is Amit Shah planning to throw Muslim refugees in West Bengal into the Bay of Bengal?', *National Herald*, 2 October 2019.
7. 'Before NRC, Citizenship Amendment Bill will be passed', *Deccan Herald*.
8. 'NRC will be implemented in West Bengal: Kailash Vijayvargiya', *The Times of India*, 25 September 2019.
9. 'BJP files complaint against Kejriwal, MLA Saurabh Bharadwaj for comments on NRC', *Asian Age*, 26 September 2019.
10. 'Prepare list of illegal immigrants: UP DGP OP Singh orders district cops', *India Today*, 3 October 2019.
11. In the absence of any concern over repatriation or deportation mechanisms and corresponding foreign policy, is detention and criminality the only foreseeable fate of the 'infiltrators'? To what extent will this further criminalize poverty and homelessness? It is crucial to note here that the term almost always used is 'illegal'—ascribing criminality to what is essentially a question of civil-legal documentation.
12. 'Convention and Protocol Relating to the Status of Refugees', 1951, UNHCR (https://www.unhcr.org/en-in/protection/basic/3b66c2aa10/convention-protocol-relating-status-refugees.html).
13. See 'Refugee Statistics' (https://www.unrefugees.org/refugee-facts/statistics/) and 'What is a Refugee? Definition and Meaning' (https://www.unrefugees.org/refugee-facts/what-is-a-refugee/), official website of the UNHCR.
14. Charlotte Edmond, '84% of refugees live in developing countries', World Economic Forum, 20 June 2017 (https://www.weforum.org/agenda/2017/06/eighty-four-percent-of-refugees-live-in-developing-countries/).
15. 'What is a Refugee? Definition and Meaning', official website of the UNHCR.

16. Frances Nicholson and Judith Kumin, 'A guide to international refugee protection and building state asylum systems', Inter-Parliamentary Union and the UNHCR, 2017, p. 18.
17. Ruth Lister and Jo Campling, *Citizenship: Feminist Perspectives*, Macmillan International Higher Education, 2017.
18. Simon Turner, 'What is a refugee camp?: Explorations of the limits and effects of the camp', *Journal of Refugee Studies*, vol. 29, no. 2 (June 2016), pp. 139–48.
19. Lister and Campling, *Citizenship*.
20. Engin F. Isin and Greg Marc Nielsen, eds., *Acts of Citizenship*. London, New York: Zed Books, 2008.
21. 'Global Focus—India', official website of the UNHCR (https://reporting.unhcr.org/node/10314).
22. J. Xavier and A. Sharma, *Legal Rights of Refugees in India*. New Delhi: Indian Social Institute, Jesuit Refugee Service, 2015.
23. S. Bang, 'The status of refugee in India: Need for a domestic legislation for protection of their human rights', *Asia Pacific Journal of Management & Entrepreneurship Research*, vol. 1, 2012, pp. 21–31.
24. P. Saxena and N. Raja, 'The imperative to offer refuge', *The Hindu*, 20 June 2018.
25. Bang, 'The status of refugee in India'; and Xavier and Sharma, *Legal Rights of Refugees in India*.
26. Isin and Nielsen, *Acts of Citizenship*, p. 16; and Xavier and Sharma, *Legal Rights of Refugees in India*.
27. R. Shanker, 'India does not legally recognise a refugee', lecture at the Policy and Inclusion Debate Series: Towards an Ethical Refugee Policy in India, Centre for Equity Studies, New Delhi, 5 February 2020.
28. Bang, 'The status of refugee in India'.
29. 'Tibetan Rehabilitation Policy 2014', Exile Tibetans (website) (https://www.exiletibetans.com/countries/asia/india/tibetan-rehabilitation-policy-2014/).
30. 'Scheme for providing relief and rehabilitation assistance to Sri Lankan refugees', Ministry of Home Affairs, Government of India, 2018 (https://www.mha.gov.in/sites/default/files/RW-SL-1011.pdf/, last accessed 20 June 2021).
31. Shanker, 'India does not legally recognise a refugee'.
32. 'Tibetan Rehabilitation Policy 2014'.
33. S.P. Kodiyath and S. Padathu Veettil, 'Invisible people: Suspected LTTE members in the special refugee camps of Tamil Nadu',

Refugee Survey Quarterly, vol. 36, no. 1 (March 2017), pp. 126–45.

34. Nicholson and Kumin, 'A guide to international refugee protection and building state asylum systems', p. 20.
35. This is of course assuming that the laws of the host States do not fundamentally violate all rights of the refugees.
36. It is crucial to note that even though the most prolific refugee protection legislations have emerged from countries in the EU, today, a majority of refugees are hosted by middle-to-low income countries, often neighbouring to the refugees' countries of origin. See J. Wood, 'These countries are home to the highest proportion of refugees in the world', World Economic Forum, 19 March 2019 (https://www.weforum.org/agenda/2019/03/mena-countries-in-the-middle-east-have-the-highest-proportion-of-refugees-in-the-world/).
37. R. Dhavan, 'India needs a proper refugee law, not a CAA suffused with discriminatory intent', *The Wire*, 20 December 2019.
38. Shanker, 'India does not legally recognise a refugee'.
39. OHCHR's work on the right to a nationality and on statelessness, official website of the Office of the High Commissioner for Human Rights (https://www.ohchr.org/EN/Issues/Pages/Nationality.aspx).
40. P. Biswas, 'Statelessness in Assam', *The Statesman*, 20 May 2019.
41. 'India: 7 Rohingya deported to Myanmar', Human Rights Watch, 4 October 2018 (https://www.hrw.org/news/2018/10/04/india-7-rohingya-deported-myanmar).
42. '7 Rohingya refugees deported to Myanmar after Supreme Court refuses to intervene', *Hindustan Times*, 4 October 2018.
43. See Harsh Mander's article 'The Dark Side of Humanity and Legality: A Glimpse Inside Assam's Detention Centres for "Foreigners"' in Part 2 of this volume.
44. '30 "foreigners" dead in Assam's detention centres', *The Hindu*, 12 April 2020.
45. Abhijit Dasgupta, *Displacement and Exile: The State-Refugee Relations in India*, New Delhi: Oxford University Press, 2016.
46. K. Ananda, 'Politics after a ceasefire: Suffering, protest and belonging in Sri Lanka's Tamil diaspora', unpublished PhD dissertation, Columbia University, New York, 2016; and Abhijit Dasgupta, 'Repatriation of Sri Lankan refugees: Unfinished tasks', *Economic and Political Weekly*, vol. 38, no. 24 (2003), pp. 2365–67.
47. L.H. Malkki, 'Speechless emissaries: Refugees, humanitarianism,

and dehistoricization', *Cultural Anthropology*, vol. 11, no. 3 (1996), pp. 377–404.

48. M. Couldrey and M. Herson, eds., 'Protracted displacement', *Forced Migration Review*, no. 33 (September 2009) (https://www.fmreview.org/sites/fmr/files/FMRdownloads/en/FMRpdfs/FMR33/FMR33.pdf, last accessed 20 June 2021).
49. S. Ahmed, 'The Organisation of Hate', *Law and Critique*, vol. 12, no. 3 (2001), pp. 345–65.

'I WILL MISS MY HEARING. WHAT WILL HAPPEN TO ME?'

Parismita Singh and Shalim M. Hussain

It was an ordinary day like any other in the *char* area villages like Sontoli in Barpeta district, when the notices started coming in. A few had arrived on the 31st of July but the bulk of the notices were served in the village of Kamrup (Rural) on the 3rd of August. The hearings were scheduled for the NRC (National Register of Citizens) Seva Kendra in Upper Assam on the 5th and 6th of August.

Sahanur Ali, the *gaonbura* or village headman of Mohtoli village told us that he received the notices on the 3rd of August. He put together a team of 10 people to help him. They distributed hundreds of notices all through the night for the hearings a day or two later.

For many daily wage workers and farmers, this induced a state of panic as desperate people sold livestock, jewellery and crops to hire buses to travel hundreds of kilometres to these districts. The transport owners seized the opportunity and raised fares, a bus that could be hired for 10,000 rupees now demanded 35,000 to 40,000 rupees.

Activists like Rehna and Salma were at bus stops in Sontoli village till 1 am on the 5th of August assisting panic-stricken people who had NRC appointments for the next day in districts like Nagaon, Jorhat, Mariani, Sibasagar. These people were hundreds of kilometres away from their homes, places they had no idea how to get to.

In Dakshin Gudhoni char (Barpeta), an island in the middle

....

This is an excerpt from Parismita Singh and Shalim M. Hussain, 'NRC Sketchbook: Ahead of Deadline, One Final Rush for Inclusion in Assam', that appeared in *HuffPost India* on 30 August 2019.

of the river Brahmaputra, most of the villagers had already left for NRC verification when the notices for three people of a family arrived. It was afternoon and their NRC summons announced their hearing for Jorhat on the next day. This was not unusual. Sometimes, notices came in around midnight adding to the panic. Gaonburas worked round the clock serving these notices.

Ashraful, Rehna, Salma and others had put out their phone numbers as an impromptu emergency helpline for those seeking help for the sudden NRC summons, and the people of Dakshin Gudhoni char reached out to them.

Ashraful and his team decided that their boat should come to the Peradhora *paarghat* in Nalbari district because there was less rush for vehicles there. The family informed them that they would travel by night after arranging their papers and the boat would arrive by 1 am.

But at 1 am, there was no boat. Ashraful's team waited by the shore, fearful and unsure of what to do. All around was the dark river at night, no phone network to reach the people on a boat in the middle of the river. Where were they?

The boat finally arrived at 3 am. After going through the documents to make sure they had carried everything, the three people boarded a reserved vehicle organized by the team. These people had only a few thousand rupees, and eventually, Ashraful had to borrow money from a shopkeeper to make up the rest. In a few hours' time, they would have to make it to Jorhat, four hundred kilometres away.

But how would these people manage in Jorhat and Sibasagar? What would people who spoke little standardized Assamese with no links of kinship or familiarity do there?

Appeals were sent out to friends in Upper Assam for assistance. August is peak summer in Assam with very high humidity and unbearable heat. Bondita Acharya, a Jorhat-based activist with this network, speaks of the inadequate provisions and sheer callousness of the administration.

'Thousands of people poured in for NRC hearings on buses and trucks. The administration made no arrangements for drinking water, toilets, meals or places where these families could rest. People waited from 9 am to 10 pm. In one Jorhat centre, the hearing finished at 1.30 am!'

Women, she said, suffered particularly. Those who couldn't speak standardized Assamese were panic stricken by these proceedings, which could potentially see them removed from the NRC lists. On a visit to the Dhekorgora block, Acharya found three women collapsed from dehydration. There were mothers with infants, the whole situation was traumatic.

It was an impossible situation. But a network of organizations like local masjid committees, charities, feminist collectives as well as individuals across ethnicities and religions, stepped in to help.

Then there were the accidents.

Vehicles of all sorts: trucks, tempos, boats, buses hired at the last minute speeded through the night to make it to morning appointments. A little after midnight on the 5th of August a bus carrying NRC claimants from Sontoli to Golaghat in Upper Assam met with an accident at Khanapara, outside Guwahati.

A tipper truck carrying hot bitumen crashed into the rear of the bus and turned turtle. The tar burnt many of the passengers, with its thick black grains embedded in their skin. At the Gauhati Medical College and Hospital, where they were taken, the first impulse of the traumatized passengers was to huddle with their families and check if the valuable papers proving their citizenship had been spared by the bitumen.

The scene in the hospital was chaotic.

One woman in shock sat at the hospital, repeating to whoever was willing to listen, 'I will miss my hearing. What will happen to me?'

These accidents created more chaos. And once more, appeals on social media were sent out for basic assistance to those injured and languishing in hospitals in Gauhati. The people of Sontoli were fortunate enough to have not lost anyone. Four people died in two separate accidents in Sibasagar and Golaghat. Often family members, even in their grief, continued with their NRC verification in other parts.

But even in such dire times, the travails of these riverine people does not make for a narrative only of suffering and victimhood.

It is also one of resilience.

CITIZEN OF AN INDIAN STATE

Shalim M. Hussain

Miya poetry can be said to have started in April 2016 when Hafiz Ahmed, a leading public intellectual, academic and teacher from Assam wrote a poem titled 'Write Down, I am a Miya'. It was a derivative poem, the title and style taken from Mahmoud Darwish's 'Write Down, I am an Arab'. In a brilliant example of how themes and aesthetics translate across cultures, the poem received a lot of love on Facebook, where it was first published, and found great resonance. This was not the first time that the word Miya, used as a cuss word on the streets of Assam, found a place in poetry. Almost three decades ago, Hafiz Ahmed's contemporary, Khabir Ahmed, had written the poem '*Binito Nibedon Ei Je*' (I Beg to State That) in which he proclaimed, probably for the first time in Assamese poetry, '*Moi Ejon Miya*' (I am a Miya).

The word 'Miya' is used in a derogatory sense against a people who have, in more politically correct terms, been called 'Bengali-origin Muslims of Assam' or 'Bengali-origin Assamese Muslims'. This rather unwieldy term is used for residents of Assam whose ancestors migrated from parts of the erstwhile Bengal province of the British Raj (present-day Bangladesh) in the nineteenth century. Over the last four years, especially after Miya poetry started, the word 'Miya' has been used, a little cautiously, as a collective term for the community by members of the community and outsiders. There has been some debate on whether the term is acceptable at all. One journalist tried to use the abbreviation BOAM. I remember thinking how hilarious it would have been had the journalist abbreviated 'Bengali-origin Muslims of Assam' to BOMA. *Boma* is the Assamese word for bomb.

The reaction Hafiz Ahmed's poem evoked has more to do

with the kind of reach social media sites, particularly Facebook, allow. It was shared widely, commented upon and embraced by young people from the *char-chapori*[1] community of Assam as a much-awaited act of assertion. I wrote a poem titled 'Nana, I Have Written' as a response to Ahmed's poem, other poets wrote more responses and, very soon, we had a chain of Miya poems circulating on Facebook. After the fifth or sixth poem was written, M. Reyaz, who was then a journalist with *twocircles.net*, published an article on the website about our poems. It was here that the term 'Miya poetry' was first used as a collective term to refer to the poems. It was a convenient enough term and some of us didn't have a problem accepting it largely because, though it was used as a cuss word, the word 'Miya' was also used as one of the words with which the community referred to itself. Reaching a consensus on what our poems should be called or what themes we were supposed to write about, a manifesto was impossible because most of the Miya poets were not in touch with each other. Most of us were introduced to each other through our poems. A common ideology was not even necessary because every poet was writing in their own style largely about their lived experiences. This is why it is difficult to make a generalized argument about Miya poetry. Commentators have called it a movement, social media trolls have called it a divisive, counter-productive process and even well-wishers have questioned if we were trying to undo a historic process.

Miya poetry had a decent audience within Assam, but it had its detractors too. Towards the end of June 2019, there was a lot of discussion on Miya poetry. It started on social media forums, spilled over into newspapers and televised news shows and culminated in a series of police complaints against the Miya poets. The first complaint was filed by Pranabjit Doloi on 10 July 2019. Doloi's complaint began with '...one "Miya Poetry" is going viral on Social Media which is being circulated widely through National and international sites as well as in

Al Jazeera, The Wire.in, NE Thing, etc.' He then presented the poem and very meticulously analysed it, line by line, stanza by stanza, underlining why the poem is 'creating an image of our state as a barbarian state in the eyes of the world which is a threat to the security of the Nation in general and Assam in particular'. The other complaints that followed had almost the same content. The accusation was the same—the Miya poets had besmirched the reputation of Assam.

But let's return to the accusation that preceded the 'Miya poetry controversy' of 2019—'undoing a historic process'. The historic process we were sometimes accused of undoing was the unwritten agreement the char-chapori Muslim community had made in the middle of the last century when we decided to return to Assamese as our language in all official documents. A little clarity is required on this point. There is a wide, though not universal, consensus among the Miya community that we will continue to return to Assamese as our language. The rationale being that Assam is our homeland and we know of no other reality. Assamese is our language as much as it is the language of other communities who claim it as their own. We have done well by it and have tried to give back to it as well as we can. However, the reality is that we speak our own dialects in our private spaces—among friends, with family members, etc. There is no contradiction between using dialects and returning to a standard language in official documents. Furthermore, there is a possibility that with the spread of education in the community, standard Assamese will probably become our first language in the future. For all the students from the char-chaporis, Assamese is the first language we learn at school since the medium of instruction in an overwhelmingly large number of schools in the char-chaporis, barring a few English-medium schools that have come up in the last two decades, is Assamese. As far as Miya poetry is concerned, most of the poems are written in standard Assamese. Those that are written in the local dialects are translated into Assamese and English for better circulation.

The above argument therefore raises the question: is it necessary to speak Assamese to be Assamese? What emerges from this question is a set of questions: Is it not enough to be an Indian citizen resident in Assam? Does the Miya need to bear fealty to the Assamese language? Language is an important part of Indian political life. The states were organized on the basis of language, and as a component of culture, language is integral to group identity. In the poems written by the 'char-chapori' poets of the 1980s,[2] there is an overwhelming feeling of loss—of home, and also of language. This loss is balanced by the new home—Assam. The river islands and banks are tough, but hard labour finally makes them suitable for agriculture. The following lines from Khabir Ahmed's 'I Beg to State That' tell the story of migration and making a new place home:

I beg to state that I am a
Settler, a dirty Miya
Whatever be the case, my name is
Khabir Ahmed or Mijanur Miya
Subject—I am an Assamese *Asomiya*.
Sometime in the last century I lost
My address in the storms of the Padma
A merchant's boat found me drifting and dropped me here
Since then I have held close to my heart this land, this earth
And began a new journey of discovery
From Sadiya to Dhubri...

Since that day
I have flattened the red hills
Chopped forests into cities, rolled earth into bricks
From bricks built monuments
Laid stones on the earth, burnt my body black with peat
Swam rivers, stood on the bank
And dammed floods
Irrigated crops with my blood and sweat
And with the plough of my fathers, etched on the earth
A...S...S...A...M

This poem defined the tone of 1980s 'char-chapori' poetry and the new trend of Miya poetry. It also helps us understand the Miya poet's sentiment towards land, language and identity. The poet believes that the blood and sweat of his ancestors helped build the current state of Assam. As such, he has as much claim to it as any other 'son of the soil'. Moreover, there has been a complete disconnect with the land of his ancestors and this is a loss the poet has reconciled with. This is why Miya poetry is not a return to one's roots or the hankering for a lost identity. The Miya poet's ancestors built something new in the land they call home. It is an identity that can accommodate Assamese and 'Assameseness' and the language of one's forbears.

This is the reason why poems of lament are written when this sense of belongingness is challenged from outside. Consider the beginning of 'Write Down, I am a Miya':

Write Down
I am a Miya
My serial number in the NRC is 200543
I have two children
Another is coming
Next summer.
Will you hate him
As you hate me?

Write
I am a Miya
I turn waste, marshy lands
To green paddy fields
To feed you.
I carry bricks
To build your buildings
Drive your car

For your comfort
Clean your drain
To keep you healthy.
I have always been
In your service
And yet
you are dissatisfied!

The structure and style of the poem is obviously borrowed from Mahmoud Darwish but once Hafiz Ahmed situates the poem in contemporary Assam and questions the reduction of human beings to numbers, even the sentiment turns similar. The Miya community forms a major chunk of the unorganized labour market of Assam. They have their names in the NRC and yet they are looked down upon, considered outsiders, threats. Their national identity is suspect, or at least not enough. This fear of not belonging is aggravated by the memory of multiple accounts of actual violence against the Miya community.

Shajahan's poetry sublimates his personal experiences with a calendar-like recounting of the violence down the ages. Take for example his poem 'I Am Yet a Miya'. Here, Shajahan does a roll call of sorts of the history of violence the Bengali-origin Muslim community has seen. Built into the fear of non-belonging is the poet's self-image. In Shajahan's poem, the Miyas are the 'Dravidians in Pragjyotishpur' (Pragjyotishpur being the old name for the state of Assam) who have remained in the same grovelling state throughout history as 'kings and dynasties pass'.

Mine is the sacrificial offering of '61
Of blood screaming through
The binds of history
Mine is the story of '83, '90–'94, 2008, 2012, 2014.

Mine is the oppression, the ignominy
The deprivation of Dravidians in Pragjyotishpur

I am the colour of shame
Holding its ears, bending its knees
While kings and dynasties pass.

Abdul Kalam Azad's 'Every Day in the Calendar is Nellie' mirrors Shajahan's 'I Am Yet a Miya' in many ways. Like Shajahan, Kalam's poem also uses as its base a historical moment—the Khagrabari massacre of 2014. It is a very visual poem, a collection of snapshots, as it were, of people affected by the violence. There's the old man shivering in the cold, the mother whose child has grown up in captivity, the mother who has lost her child. All of these deaths are marked on a calendar whose pages refuse to turn. They all show one date—18 February 1983, the day of the Nellie massacre, the day that began the history of violence. Underlying the poem is a strong feeling of horror.

Nearby, Uncle Fajal trembles like a leaf
Uncle has a fever, hasn't eaten for two days
He sits on a bamboo bed the size of a calendar
Aunty trembles like a leaf
What if the waters rise some more?

The wet calendar dries
Fear drenches my mind
In a dark room my hands turn the pages

A damned fox, maybe a civet, stole my hens
The cacophony of chickens struts over
My calendar.

Regardless of the year in which the killings happened, regardless of whether they happened in '83, '90–'94, 2008, 2012, or 2014, the horror remains the same. All of us are inheritors of the horrors of the past. If the same horrors are visited upon a community again and again what good will it do to push the past under the carpet? Should the past not be confronted? Should it not be an edifice of what should not be done? Should it not be a memory of what went wrong?

For educated people in my community, Miya poetry is a novelty. It is also transgressive because the dominant mood of the poems, at least in the early stages, was angst. Angst makes people uncomfortable. Because some of the more popular ones are written in dialect, Miya poetry is also looked at as something that strains against the status quo. For communities like ours which value social mobility, maintaining the status quo is essential. If anyone breaks the status quo or questions it, the effects are felt not just by the individual who flouts the unspoken rules but by the community as a whole. This is why some of the strongest critics of Miya poetry belong to the community itself. In the game of looking at and being looked at from within the community and without, this is the position Miya poetry finds itself in—is it parody? Is it dangerous? Is it art? Is it, to use a wonderful Assamese phrase, *bouddhik bhondami*—intellectual fraud?

If one were to analyse the idiom of the Miya poems rather than the language in which they are written, one would find that it's a fresh local idiom. The tone is consciously commonplace—the language of the home and the street. There is no intellectual posturing but a refreshing directness—none of the postmodern deferral of meaning. Yet, in its challenge to what is usually considered standard Assamese or standard English, the poems retain the essence of postmodernism. It is difficult to get a sense of what the oeuvre of Miya poetry actually is. That will probably take some time and a few anthologies to assess. However, the claim the Miya poets are making over the language is simple—'Give us a place.' And this is a reflection of what is happening in the fields of education, health, politics, policy, etc. 'Give us a place,' the char-chapori community claims. Give us a place in the land which is also our own, the government we have helped elect, the language we also love and adore, the ethos which we also want to participate in. As the poet Siraj Khan says in his poem '*Amar Polayo Sikhse Shororer Gali*'—the language of humanity is the same the world over.

Notes

1. Another term used for the Bengali-origin Muslims of Assam. 'Char' means a riverine island and 'chaporis' are river banks. Hyphenated together 'char-chapori' refers to the geographical area of Assam where most of the Bengali-origin Muslims of Assam live.
2. Precursors of Miya poets.

AFTERWORD

RECLAIMING THE LAND

Navsharan Singh

This volume is being published at a time when the Covid-19 pandemic is still raging and India is limping back to a new normal after a series of lockdowns, beginning with the national lockdown that was imposed on 24 March 2020. At a notice of just four hours, and with no provision for relief to the crores of people whose livelihoods and security would be destroyed, the entire country was shut down. Workers who had come from the villages and small towns of India to earn a living in the cities suddenly found themselves abandoned by their government, and in sheer desperation started walking back home. They marched silently without food and water for hundreds of kilometres in peak summer, hounded and harassed by the police. Many died on the way of dehydration, exhaustion and hunger. The images of the exodus were reminiscent of the forced displacement of Partition. Home and belonging suddenly took on a new meaning in this experience, as did the very idea of the Indian State and democracy.

In the months prior to the pandemic and brutal lockdown, the country had gone through a momentous democratic movement, as lakhs of ordinary people took to the streets to defend the fundamental idea of citizenship and belonging that the BJP-led government was trying to extinguish. People had risen in protest against the Citizenship Amendment Act (CAA), as soon as the law was passed in December 2019. As the essays in this collection have shown, the law is blatantly discriminatory, making religion a basis for Indian citizenship—it offers refuge to persecuted religious minorities, barring Muslims, from three of India's neighbouring countries, Pakistan, Bangladesh and Afghanistan. After the National Register of Citizens (NRC) experience in Assam, many Indians were quick to read the links between the NRC and the CAA, and the looming threat of disenfranchisement of India's Muslims.

The mass protests saw vast mobilization of Muslim women; they staged sit-in protests, first in Delhi's Shaheen Bagh locality and then across the country—in Uttar Pradesh, West Bengal, Gujarat, Telangana, Punjab, Karnataka, Madhya Pradesh, Rajasthan and Maharashtra, among other places. Against the backdrop of the discriminatory law, the country saw a new vision for citizenship being articulated in these protests. As the protests swelled, women, who have always experienced differentiated citizenship rights, occupied the public sphere and engaged confidently with a deeply political national agenda. In fact, they provided leadership to the widespread and unprecedented protests.

Feminist analysis has been drawing attention to the fact that gendered citizenship, inherently and deeply unequal, is realized through the creation of a public-private binary, a strict parting of spheres, with the male belonging to the public and the female to the private. This binary was breached in the anti-CAA-NRC movement. Women claimed the public sphere in defence of their most fundamental right. They raised slogans, waved flags, read the preamble to the Indian Constitution, made speeches, and claimed the Republic. In the bitterly cold and wet winter of 2019–20, braving threats of violence by the police and right-wing goons, braving derision and accusations of being paid protesters and 'misled' women, they stayed firm, refusing to vacate the protest sites. It was a rare and extraordinary example of ordinary citizens asserting themselves, wanting to participate in deciding how collective rights are to be negotiated. They created a vibrant public space and marked their presence in the national public discourse. Many of these women had no previous experience of political engagement, but they jumped right into an intensely political challenge—that of citizenship, from which they had largely been excluded.

In Assam, where a national register for citizens was first created in 1951—and which is the only state of the Union yet with such a register—the terms of inclusion in the NRC are laid out unambiguously: ties to the land; family lineage; identity in State records. Women know that their only ties with the land are through their labour; in the family, their status and identity are transformed as their guardian changes from father or brother to husband and they take on new names, moving to new locations; and for inclusion in State records, they struggle to make sense of their belonging to their families, whether natal or those that they are married into. How then do they claim citizenship based on these ties and relationships? Besides, their citizenship is not a simple matter of a formal relationship with the State reflected in some documents; it extends to a range of institutions and lived realities—the family and the household, customs and practices, and other institutions that affect women's and men's lives and opportunities such as personal law, caste and religious codes and property rights, especially for women who marry outside their community. The experience of the NRC process, especially after the Supreme Court passed an order in 2015 for the citizenship register to be updated, had made women in Assam acutely aware of their vulnerability. Women in other parts of India understood this too when the Central government issued a notification in July 2019 to update the National Population Register (NPR)—which would form the basis for a National Register of Indian Citizens (NRIC)—across the *entire* country, and then brought in the CAA. Having understood what this implied, the protesting women in different parts of the country refused to submit to a citizenship status based only on the scrutiny of certain papers. The slogan '*Hum kaagaz nahi dikhayenge*' (We will not show any documents) found profound resonance in the protest sites. When the interlocutors appointed by the Supreme Court came to assist a rapprochement between the Indian State and the protesters, the women were clear in what they wanted: a complete roll back of the CAA, and no to NPR and NRIC.

The protests were initiated by India's Muslim women, but they also drew other women in an act of solidarity. The women were brought together by their common gendered-citizenship experience, where the private is regulated by the family and access to the public is regulated by men. The protest opened a new space to challenge the impunity with which this divide is preserved. Women, young women more specifically, worked on collective actions in support of each other. They learnt and shared their life stories; they spoke about their shared anxieties and the future of their children in the country. In contesting the CAA, women—Muslim and non-Muslim—pried open the very construct of citizenship.

Many observers have remarked on the fact that these women were out on the streets for a cause which was not even 'women specific'—they had not come out to protest rape, sexual harassment or domestic violence. Many asked the question: What have women to do with the 'political' question of citizenship? But women at the protest sites, who realized their deep vulnerability because of their gender identity, knew that the issue *was* women specific. In Assam, Muslim women have been routinely subjected to State violence for resisting the hardships and insecurities institutionalized by the State, and they are now paying a heavy price for being part of citizenship movements. Many women in other parts of India have also been intimidated, assaulted and arrested—a number of them under the draconian Unlawful Activities (Prevention) Act (UAPA)—as the anti-CAA protests have gained momentum and been termed 'anti-national' and seditious.

Women's protest movements have resulted in a fresh evaluation of the very concept of citizenship: What does it mean when even the private space granted to a woman as a citizen is not guaranteed and protected by the State? What does citizenship feel like for victims of the violence of the family, the *khap*, the *jirga*; for victims of the systematic violence against marginalized caste groups and religious and ethnic minorities in which the woman's body becomes the site of war? Women are seldom acknowledged as full citizens, as subjects with a right to bodily, emotional and intellectual autonomy and integrity. The political narrative is never, or hardly ever, about upholding the rights of women as free and equal citizens of the democratic nation. Policies and initiatives are instead oriented towards saving the 'honour' of mothers, sisters and daughters. These efforts are so designed that they lead to disempowering rather than empowering young women.

The anti-CAA-NRC movement laid bare the fault lines in the neutral concept of citizenship and revealed its gendered nature, which would now be overlaid with a religious bias. The meaning of citizenship was redefined in the movement through a whole range of Constitution-reclaiming actions where women came out, risking State hostility, to assert that citizenship is an active concept beyond mere legal status and formal rights, and beyond State sanction. It is a concept that can have no meaning unless it enables people pushed to exclusion to stake claim to their Constitutional rights; to absolute equality.

And then, at the peak of the anti-CAA-NRC movement, Covid-19 struck. While people were locked up in their homes, the State tightened its authoritarian grip. In the early hours of 25th March, the first day of the nationwide lockdown, massive police contingents, with bulldozers and professional demolishers in tow, cleared Shaheen Bagh and other protest sites. All art installations were dismantled and slogans and graffiti painted over. The Disaster Management Act (2005) was invoked and all gatherings were banned. Since a lockdown was already in force, this was a gratuitous move and its real purpose was clearly to persecute the defenders of democracy and the Indian Constitution. In Delhi and several other places, police began rounding up many of the women and men who had been involved in the protests, and arresting them under harsh anti-terrorist laws like the UAPA. To further intimidate ordinary citizens, several of those who had only visited the protest sites in solidarity were called for long custodial interrogation, and lists of 'suspects' were leaked to the press to vilify those who had taken a public position against the CAA. A peaceful democratic movement, led largely by women, which had successfully built a moral consensus against the dangerously partisan agenda of a majoritarian State was crushed with an iron hand, using the pandemic as both cover and excuse.

~

Assam published its updated NRC, meant to be a list of Indian citizens living in the state, on 31 August 2019. It left out about 19 lakh applicants, close to six per cent of the entire population of the state. But this did not make the BJP—the party in power both in Assam and at the Centre—happy. The number wasn't large enough to justify the scaremongering it had indulged in, raising the spectre of Bangladeshi Muslim 'infiltrators' swamping Assam and changing its demographic profile for ever. The list also put the BJP in a tight spot when it found that a large number of those excluded were Bengali-speaking Hindus, who are its traditional vote bank in Assam. The party rejected the revised NRC and declared that it would approach the Supreme Court for a re-verification.

The Assamese nationalists were also unhappy with the updated list. They had opposed the CAA because it would grant citizenship to all non-Muslims who claimed persecution in Bangladesh and had entered the country on or before 31 December 2014. They wanted *all* 'illegal' immigrants, regardless of their religion, to be kept out of Assam or deported. They, too, had always spoken of huge numbers of Bangladeshi migrants and the grave threat this posed to native Assamese. The 19 lakh figure didn't suit them either.

The demand for identification of illegal immigrants, deletion of their names from voter lists and finally their deportation had been going on since 1979, with the All Assam Students' Union

(AASU) spearheading a six-year nativist agitation which ended with the signing of the Assam Accord between the Indian government and leaders of the Assam Movement in 1985. It was agreed that all refugees and immigrants who had entered Assam after 25 March 1971 would be deported, and that the NRC, first prepared in 1951 (and only for Assam), would be updated based on the census conducted in the same year, 1951. The process of updating the 1951 list was delayed for years after that and eventually began in 2015 following directions from the Supreme Court, which acted on petitions seeking detection of 'illegal' immigrants, especially from Bangladesh. The updated list was to include all those persons, and their children and descendants (the court order did not include the word spouse), whose names appeared in the 1951 NRC or in any of the electoral rolls up to the midnight of 24 March 1971, when the liberation war for Bangladesh's independence from Pakistan began. Names of people with origins outside India found to be residing in Assam illegally after that date were to be excluded from the updated list. The 19 lakh who did not find their names in the 31 August 2019 list belong to this category of 'foreigners'.

The NRC rules outline that rejected persons can challenge their exclusion within a period of 120 days by filing an appeal before a Foreigners' Tribunal (FT). FTs are the quasi-judicial bodies that adjudicate on matters of nationality in Assam, and each FT is headed by a single judge designated as a 'member'. Each FT has the power to determine if a person is an Indian citizen or a foreigner according to the provisions of the Foreigners Act, 1946 and the Foreigners (Tribunal) Order, 1964. If the rejected person doesn't get relief from the FT, s/he can move the Gauhati High Court and then the Supreme Court for relief. But the excluded persons can challenge their exclusion only *after* they receive formal notices known as 'speaking orders', or rejection slips, citing the reasons for their rejection. In the meantime, they can be arrested and sent to detention camps for 'foreigners'.

As this volume goes to press, almost two years after the updated NRC list was published, the fate of the excluded is still uncertain. The process of issuing formal rejection notices is yet to culminate and the excluded are staring at possible statelessness if they fail to produce documentary evidence of their claim to citizenship and file appeals in the FTs and courts. But a lot has happened in the intervening two years. There is a new BJP government in the state under a leader who led the election campaign on an undisguised Hindutva plank. It was clear during the election campaign that the BJP in Assam had shunned politics that hinged on sub-nationalism. The party had built an anti-Muslim public sentiment during the campaign and the election result is being read as an approval for granting citizenship to all non-Muslim Bangladeshis. Himanta Biswa Sarma, who now became chief minister, had also publicly said that he was for changing the cutoff year for deciding citizenship to 1951 from 1971 as agreed upon in the Assam Accord. Amit Shah during his numerous visits to Assam had reiterated that refugees who come to Assam would be given citizenship rights, but infiltrators would not be allowed inside the state. 'The next BJP government will enact laws to tackle the menace of "love and land jihad" in Assam,' he had said.[1]

Post elections, in one of his first interviews as the incumbent chief minister, Sarma mentioned approaching the Supreme Court again for a reverification of the NRC—up to 20 per cent of entries in areas bordering Bangladesh and 10 per cent in the interior areas of Assam, adding to the growing environment of fear and uncertainty for those who are awaiting formal notices.

Assam had 100 FTs as of September 2019 and at least 20 of them were without members till early 2020. The state government had decided to set up 200 additional FTs to hear petitions of the huge numbers who had been excluded from the NRC. So, in September 2019, it appointed 221 retired judges and bureaucrats with experience of discharging judicial duties and lawyers with at least seven years of experience as members of the tribunals. But the setting up of additional FTs did not conclude for the next 20 months, and the 221 members who had been appointed to operate the new tribunals were attached to the existing tribunals. And the 1,600 people recruited as support staff were assigned work only in June 2021 after Himanta Biswa Sarma was sworn in.

The process of completing the NRC exercise remains stuck as a result of power politics and bureaucratic delays, but the ordeal of those excluded continues. Petrified people wait for the slips which will give them the reasons for their rejection. It is also becoming evident that the threat of statelessness is not only communal but also gendered in nature, aggravating existing gender inequalities. In November 2019, a team from the advocacy organization Women against Sexual Violence and State Repression (WSS) led a fact-finding mission in Assam to study how the NRC has affected women.[2] The report concluded that since proving citizenship under the NRC relies largely on documents pertaining to land, lineage and education, in a patriarchal society the entire process is weighted heavily against women. Women have historically and traditionally been excluded from entitlements to land and access to education and in most cases have almost no documentation to prove their existence as citizens. The WSS report found that a large number of married women found themselves excluded from the NRC because they didn't know whether to provide documents of the lineage of their in-laws or of their parents. The WSS survey also revealed that women from outside Assam who had married Assamese men have all been excluded from the updated NRC list. There are also many women who provided all the necessary documents and yet find themselves excluded. Before all of them looms the very real possibility of detention, deportation and separation from their families.

The excluded persons wait for 'speaking orders' even as their livelihoods have been ruined by the pandemic lockdown and by the floods which started engulfing their *chars* and villages in May 2020 and continued for over three months. Already affected by the citizenship verification processes, these people were brought to the brink of despair. First the lockdown prevented them from bringing their agricultural produce to the market, and then the floods washed away everything, turning them into climate refugees. In the middle of this immense human suffering, the fear and anxiety of approaching the FTs, presenting their case and new documents, moving the Gauhati High Court (if the FTs rejected their appeals) and organizing legal aid drove some of them to suicide. The delays in receiving the rejection slips only compounded the trauma.

News reports cite the effects of Covid-19 as the reason for delays in the process of issuing rejection slips, but this doesn't add up as the revised NRC list was out on 31 August 2019 and the lockdown began in late March 2020. Perhaps the delay is not an accident. The excluded people continue to face the stigma of being 'Bangladeshi infiltrators' even if they have demonstrated their family ties and ties to the land. People who had hoped that the updated NRC would put an end to the hostility they face, after their papers had been scrutinized and their citizenship established, feel betrayed as an inconclusive NRC process keeps the sword hanging over their future.

Meanwhile, the Assam government continues to reiterate its stand that there should be a re-verification of the names included in the final NRC—re-verification of 20 per cent of the names in the districts bordering Bangladesh and 10 per cent in the rest of the districts. So even those whose names appeared on the updated list are not assured of their belonging. And then there are stridently nativist organizations such as Assam Public Works (APW) that demand 100 per cent re-verification of the new NRC list.

This leaves the whole exercise conducted over five years—which cost over 1,500 crores of rupees and caused immense grief to millions of people—inconclusive, indeed meaningless. Not only this, there was also a shift in the citizenship discourse before the state elections. In November 2020, Himanta Biswa Sarma in an interview proclaimed that the fact that 5.56 lakh Hindus and 11 lakh Muslims were in the doubtful list was not the concern; the issue now is conflict of cultures: 'It is not a Hindu–Muslim [matter]. It is a fight between two cultures. The so-called migrants—Bangladeshi Muslims—have started a new concept in Assam. They call it Miya culture, Miya poetry...Miya language... We have to protect the composite Indian culture and more particularly Assamese culture...'[3] This shift in goalposts—from all outsiders being a concern to naming only the Miya as a threat to the composite culture of Assam—leaves a large number of people in limbo. It is unclear whether the 5.56 lakh Hindus not on the list now stand a better chance of being included; as for the 'Miyas', even if they are on the list, they face the new risk of being regarded as a threat to the 'composite' culture of Assam, only multiplying their suffering and humiliation. They can see that the NRC process will probably never be completed, it will be kept alive and unfinished in the service of electoral politics and to fan hatred against the Miya, a pejorative term for Muslims of immigrant origin which is increasingly being used to refer to the entire Muslim population of Assam. The Miya poets, who chose poetry as a medium to highlight and speak against injustice, indignity and discrimination in their own land, were criminalized and stringent cases were slapped against them4 for 'inciting hatred between communities'. These poets, that include both women and men, are Assamese of Bengali origin, many of them young students. One of them, Rehna Sultana, a 28-year-old scholar at Gauhati University and a social activist, also received threats of sexual violence for her poetry on the Miya community—about how Miyas must always keep proving their identity as Assamese.

~

Since the updated NRC was published in Assam, 13 Indian states and Union territories have opposed the current format of the nationwide NPR exercise that was set to begin on 1 April 2020 and had raised concerns that the information collected would be linked to the NRIC which, coupled with the CAA, could be misused by the authorities to rob Indian Muslims of their citizenship rights. Andhra Pradesh, Bihar, Delhi, Tamil Nadu, Kerala, West Bengal and Madhya Pradesh have opposed the NPR and NRC/NRIC in its current format. Rajasthan, Punjab, Kerala, West Bengal, Telangana and Chhattisgarh have passed anti-CAA resolutions too. The main concerns that these states and civil society have expressed are about the additional questions that have been introduced in the NPR form, including details about place of last residence, mother tongue, Aadhaar number, mobile number and, perhaps the most curious and alarming of all, the date and place of birth of parents. Many among India's minority communities, especially Muslims, fear that such an NPR would be the first step towards a nationwide NRC and their eventual disenfranchisement.

Members of the government continue to make conflicting or contradictory statements. Home Minister Amit Shah told Parliament in mid-March 2020 that people could choose to not respond to certain questions in the NPR. But when the non-NDA chief ministers and activists said that this was no guarantee that people would not face any problems in the future, there was no further clarification from the government. After having declared on several occasions inside and outside Parliament—through its Home Minister, Minister of State for Home Affairs and others—that there would be a nationwide NRC and that the NPR would form the basis for such a register, the Modi government did backtrack a little. But even then it dissembled—there was no unequivocal statement; a standing committee of the Parliament was told that 'till now no decision has been taken to create National Register of Indian Citizens'.[5] Neither the Prime Minister nor the Home Minister has ruled out the possibility of an NRC exercise in the future. If the government does not intend to weaponize citizenship and force millions of India's Muslims to live in fear of being rendered homeless and locked up in detention centres, it should be simple enough to make a clear, unambiguous statement.

The Home Minister also told the Rajya Sabha that 'No documents will be asked as part of the NPR…no one will be marked D [doubtful citizen]'. But as Shoaib Daniyal explained in an excellent piece in *Scroll.in*, this was 'a classic half-truth':

> The NPR is a list of residents of India. Once that data is collected by means [of] a door-to-door survey, a verification process will be carried out which will identify people whose citizenship is 'doubtful'. These 'doubtful' citizens will then have to prove they are not illegal migrants. Anyone who is unable to, will be legally marked an 'illegal migrant' and prosecuted under Indian law. Everyone else's name will be moved from the NPR onto the NRC and they will have the right to claim Indian citizenship.
>
> So, in a very narrow, technical sense, Shah is right. There is no process of marking citizens 'doubtful' during the NPR. Which is obvious: the NPR is a door-to-door survey to collect personal data on residents.
>
> It is *once* the NPR is collated that people are marked 'doubtful' as part of a verification process.
>
> Thus, residents will be not marked 'doubtful' during the NPR but *after* it. Moreover, the process of marking Indians 'doubtful' can only be done *if* the NPR is conducted. Without NPR data, the next stage—the verification process—cannot be carried out.
>
> Shah's statement was therefore a partial statement of facts that intended to conceal the overall truth.[6]

Responding to widespread concern about the new question in the NPR form that asks for the date and place of birth of a person's parents, the home ministry told a parliamentary panel in March 2019 that this was necessary data for government welfare schemes which are generally family-based. But as several leading economists, social scientists and public intellectuals have pointed out, the Census of India already provides a basic household and population listing based on anonymous data, which is perfectly adequate for making new social and economic policies or refining existing ones. What then is the need to introduce contentious requirements in the NPR?

As Harsh Mander and Mohsin Alam Bhat write in their essay in this volume, the NPR project is even more dangerous than the Assam NRC:

> [F]ar from pushing the NRC to the backburner, the Union government, by announcing an NPR, which includes newly added questions about a person's parents' details, heralds an NRC even more dangerous than the Assam NRC. There were many injustices in the way that the NRC was implemented in Assam, and they took an enormous toll in terms of human suffering. But the Assam NRC was not a communal anti-Muslim project. All persons of all faiths were equally tasked to prove their citizenship by a list of documents. An NRC which is built on the NPR will allow the executive to pick and choose whose citizenship it wishes to interrogate. This will succeed in thrusting India's Muslim people—and a range of the other most disadvantaged people, including homeless persons, persons with disability, transgender persons, nomadic and denotified tribes, orphaned and abandoned children, circular migrants and millions of others—into years of dread and uncertainty about if, when and how they might be deprived of their citizenship and sent to detention centres... Unless all the non-BJP governments refuse to implement the NPR, they will be collaborating in a process of targeted mass disenfranchisement of the kind that Nazi Germany witnessed in the grim years leading to the Holocaust. History will find it hard to forgive them.

WHERE DO WE GO FROM HERE?

As the State shifts the goalposts for the NRC, from making citizenship conditional on a list of papers to demanding absolute conformity; as hundreds of people are incarcerated for taking part in protests against discriminatory citizenship laws; as livelihoods destroyed in the pandemic remain precarious; and as the country suffers a regime that is using a health and humanitarian disaster as an opportunity to entrench itself in power and introduce majoritarian and pro-big business, neoliberal policies, what do the ordinary people do? Naomi Klein has written about the rise of disaster capitalism—how national disasters are used by governments to push through policies that may be anti-people as there is little chance of resistance from the people themselves. The Indian State has gone even further than this. It has cynically used the Covid-19 crisis not only to ram through policies and laws that are anti-labour, anti-farmer, and anti-poor, but also to centralize power, suppress dissent and incarcerate people who oppose it even with mere words; it is building 'disaster authoritarianism',[7] finding ever new ways of diminishing citizens' rights.

The Industrial Relations Code, 2020, for instance, introduces massive changes in the country's labour rights. It gives sweeping freedom from regulatory control to factory owners, strengthens the unequal bargaining power of employers and limits the role of trade unions. The Code was passed without any discussion inside or outside Parliament—in just three days an entire system of hard-won labour rights and guarantees, including minimum wages, regulated work hours and safe working conditions, was countermanded, all in the name of attracting foreign investment. The timing of the Code and the enormous changes it introduces make a mockery of the living realities of the poor and labouring classes, whose terrible precarity became so evident during the lockdown.

Almost in parallel, the government introduced three extremely contentious farm bills—the Farmers' Produce

Trade and Commerce (Promotion and Facilitation) Bill, 2020; the Farmers' (Empowerment and Protection) Agreement on Price Assurance and Farm Services Bill, 2020; and the Essential Commodities (Amendment) Bill, 2020. The bills were introduced in Parliament on 14 September 2020 and were passed in less than a week. The government ignored repeated demands by opposition parties to refer the bills to a parliamentary committee and used its brute majority to bulldoze them through both the Lok Sabha and the Rajya Sabha. Then, even as different sections of society appealed strongly for more discussion and reconsideration, the President gave his assent to the bills on 24 September and they became laws.

But while no nationwide opposition was mounted against the changes in the labour rules, the farm bills brought farmers on a war path with the Centre. Led by farm unions of Punjab who have been working for decades with different sections of the peasantry, and joined by groups from other states, lakhs of farmers marched to Delhi, where they were stopped at the borders by a massive police force. As the farmers refused to turn back, the Delhi police, which reports to the Central government, sealed the borders with barricades, concrete slabs and razor wire, and at one time plastered the roads with nails and metal spikes. As this Afterword is being written, the farmers are still protesting at the borders of the Indian capital, demanding a complete rollback of the farm bills which they are convinced will make easy way for corporatization of agriculture, turning small farmers into farm labour in their own fields and casual labour in unwelcoming cities.

Through the extreme agrarian distress and the crisis of livelihoods, the deepening class, caste and gender inequalities and the corporate sell-out, the Centre has been trying to pulverize basic rights and freedoms through the routine use of legislations like the UAPA. These draconian laws, which give governments exceptional powers, superseding basic tenets of the Constitution such as the right to life, liberty and equality, are used to arrest dissenting citizens and keep them incarcerated for months and years. The muzzling of all forms of dissent has added to the present crisis of the disenfranchisement of citizens not only in Assam but across the country. Since the BJP-led NDA came to power with a massive mandate, dissent has not only been opposed ideologically, it has also been criminalized. The chargesheet against the youth leader Umar Khalid, who was arrested for his alleged role in the anti-CAA protest and the violence that broke out in Delhi, for instance, mentions that Khalid put together a coalition of 'current government haters'. So hating the government is now a crime, to be mentioned in a police chargesheet.[8]

Protesting in a public space is also being criminalized. In the *Amit Sahni vs Commissioner of Police & Ors* case, the Supreme Court ruled that Shaheen Bagh-type protests are not acceptable and the administration is justified in taking action to keep public areas free of obstructions by protesting citizens. 'We cannot accept the plea of the applicants that an indeterminable number of people can assemble whenever they choose to protest,' the court said.[9] This ruling, in effect, restricts citizens' fundamental rights of freedom of expression and freedom to assemble peacefully. These rights, guaranteed by our Constitution, can be restricted reasonably only on the ground of public order and then too only when there is evidence that the protesters will resort to or incite lawless or disorderly acts. No such evidence was presented against the Shaheen Bagh protest; there was evidence only of its peaceful nature. So the Supreme Court order used 'inconvenience to commuters' as justification for invoking a threat to 'public order'.[10]

When there are laws and ordinances to prevent peacefully protesting citizens from 'inconveniencing commuters', roads are carpeted with nails and people are charged with sedition for disagreeing with governments, what do the people do? How do they even register their protest effectively? When farmers from Punjab and Haryana reached the Delhi border a senior police officer addressed them from the other side of the barricades and asked, 'Why are you here? Don't you know that we are facing a pandemic?' The farmers responded: Didn't the government know that there was a pandemic to be fought when it passed the three ordinances without any consultation? 'Who asked them for these laws?' asked a farmer. The police official said, 'There are 101 ways of getting your point across to the government, why did you come to Delhi?' The farmer responded, 'You tell us two ways of getting our point across and you can keep the remaining 99 to yourself. Just tell us two ways of telling the government that we do not want these damn laws which they are saying will benefit us.' The farmers were making a point central to the functioning of a democracy: When the State has no response to dissent other than to criminalize it, what do the aggrieved people do?

As the farmers' movement turns into a wider movement—receiving the support of different sections of working people, small traders, women's rights activists, poets, musicians and other artistes—it is becoming a platform to raise fundamental questions of justice and equity; it is expanding the idea and practice of democracy through citizens' activism and solidarity. The charter of the farmers lays down demands that are related not only to the peasantry but are also deeply linked with the demands of other urban and rural workers. The farmers are demanding the unconditional repeal of the new farm bills and the Electricity (Amendment) Bill, 2020. But they are also seeking implementation of the Public Distribution System (PDS) throughout the country. They are seeking immediate release of imprisoned intellectuals, democratic rights activists and student activists and withdrawal of the false cases registered against them. They are seeking withdrawal of all the restrictions imposed against the right to dissent in the country. Farmer leaders and activists speak as passionately and eloquently about why every Indian must oppose the farm bills[11] as they do about why we must all demand the release of political prisoners.[12]

The farmers have said that in order for them or anyone else to be able to participate in democracy, equity and justice and freedom of speech and expression for every single citizen is a non-negotiable right. They argue that when intellectuals and human rights activists are put behind bars, the right of a farm labourer to hold to account the State which has reneged on land reforms is also threatened. When food becomes a commodity to be traded only under market conditions, the urban and rural poor who still need food rations lose their right to food. These are important linkages that the farmers have been able to make and argue in favour of, which points to the transformative potential of their movement in building larger coalitions of all the people who are being forced to the margins by an unjust regime. The farmers' movement has provided continuity to and strengthened the vision of solidarity which was becoming evident during the anti-CAA movement when it was abruptly crushed. The anti-CAA-NRC movement forced mainstream India to think of active citizenship, to ask questions of the State. The farmers' movement is doing the same, forging links between issues of food security, livelihoods, human rights and democracy.

Over the last few years, the regime in India has disenfranchised the poor and the marginalized section by section, community by community, forcing them to fight their battles for justice in silos. The walls that divide people in our diverse, deeply layered society have made it difficult to build bridges between the oppressed. But when people's right to their Republic is being undermined so relentlessly, there is a growing realization that perhaps the only effective resistance is moral pressure built through broad alliances and democratic movements which can bring the interests of all the marginalized together. The defence of democracy demands that we stand with each other and mount a collective challenge to the repressive power of the State. Belonging is about fighting for justice together; about claiming the right to belong, and actively defending it.

Notes

1. 'Refugees in Assam will be given citizenship rights, infiltrators not allowed, says Amit Shah', *The Print*, 26 March 2021.
2. The WSS team travelled to the Barak valley region, home to several Bengali Hindus and Bengali Muslims, to the *chars* and villages in the districts of Jorhat, Sibasagar and Hojai, home to those who fled erstwhile East Pakistan in 1964 and tea plantations on which migrant workers from Jharkhand and the Chhota Nagpur plateau toil. See 'WSS fact finding on the updating of the NRC in Assam', press statement of the WSS fact-finding team, WSS website, 28 November 2019 (https://wssnet.org/2019/11/28/wss-fact-finding-on-the-updating-of-the-nrc-in-assam/).
3. 'Himanta Biswa Sarma: NRC, CAA no longer the discourse... Issue now is conflict of cultures, this claim of Miya identity', *The Indian Express*, 23 November 2020.
4. On 10 July 2019, a complaint was filed in a Guwahati police station accusing 10 people of indulging in criminal activities 'to defame the Assamese people as xenophobic'. These 10 people are poets, many of them young, and students who write Miya poetry.
5. 'MHA Says "No Decision Has Been Taken on Nationwide NRC"', *The Wire*, 2 February 2021.
6. Shoaib Daniyal, 'Did Amit Shah just scrap plans for an NRC? Not really', *Scroll.in*, 13 March 2020.
7. G. Sampath, 'The "Shock Doctrine" in India's Response to COVID-19', *The Hindu*, 15 June 2020.
8. 'Delhi violence: Chargesheet filed against Umar Khalid, Sharjeel Imam in conspiracy case', *Scroll.in*, 23 November 2020.
9. Sanya Talwar, '[Breaking] "Public places cannot be occupied indefinitely": Supreme Court on Shaheen Bagh Protests', *Live Law*, 7 October 2020.
10. V. Venkatesan, 'Supreme Court's Shaheen Bagh judgment will lead to fresh curbs on right of peaceful protest', *The Wire*, 8 October 2020.
11. 'Why every Indian needs to oppose the farm bills', *NewsClick*, 3 December 2020 (available here: https://www.youtube.com/watch?v=x1KcP9NJLM0).
12. 'Farmers demand release of political prisoners | #WeThePeople | Karwan e Mohabbat', *NewsClick*, 3 December 2020 (available here: https://www.youtube.com/watch?v=-VMPMEDviWM&feature=youtu.be).

LIST OF CONTRIBUTORS

ABDUL KALAM AZAD is an activist and independent researcher based in Assam. He was formerly with the Tata Institute of Social Sciences, Guwahati.

AMAN WADUD is a Guwahati-based human rights lawyer who has defended hundreds of people declared foreigners in Assam.

ANIRBAN BHATTACHARYA is a researcher and activist, and the former head of the research team at the Centre for Equity Studies, New Delhi. His work has centred around political justice, labour rights, issues concerning caste and gender-based discrimination, minority rights, social protection, migration, and democratic rights at large.

ANUPAMA ROY is the chairperson, Centre for Political Studies, School of Social Sciences at the Jawaharlal Nehru University, Delhi.

ARUNABH SAIKIA is a journalist currently working with *Scroll.in*. He has reported extensively on the citizenship crisis in Assam.

ASHRAFUL HUSSAIN is an activist, social worker and poet from Assam. He is currently the Member of the Assam Legislative Assembly for Chenga, Assam.

ASHUTOSH VARSHNEY is the Sol Goldman Professor of International Studies and Social Sciences, and a professor of political science at the Watson Institute for International and Public Affairs, Brown University. He is also the director of the Center for Contemporary South Asia at the university. He has previously taught at Harvard University and the University of Michigan, Ann Arbor, and has published many books including *Democracy, Development and the Countryside: Urban–Rural Struggles in India*; *India in the Era of Economic Reforms*; *Ethnic Conflict and Civic Life: Hindus and Muslims in India*; and *Battles Half Won: India's Improbable Democracy*.

AZRAM RAHMAN KHAN is a research scholar at the University of Delhi.

CHAN MIYA is a poet based in Assam.

DEVESH KAPUR is the Starr Foundation South Asia Studies Professor and Asia Programs Director at the Paul H. Nitze School of Advanced International Studies at Johns Hopkins University, Washington, DC.

GAUTAM BHATIA is a Delhi-based lawyer and scholar of constitutional law. He is also a science-fiction writer.

HAFIZ AHMED is a social activist and poet considered to be the pioneer of the Miya poetry of Assam. He is also the founder president of the Char Chapori Sahitya Parishad, an organization that seeks to provide a platform to the literature from settlements along the river banks and riverine islands (*char chapori*) of Assam.

KHABIR AHMED is a poet based in Assam, and one of the early pioneers of Miya poetry.

LINA KRISHNAN is a poet and artist based in Bengaluru.

MIHIKA CHANCHANI is a Delhi-based researcher with a focus on communal violence in India and rights for excluded communities. She did her MSc in Violence, Conflict and Development from SOAS, University of London in 2018, where she was also a Chevening Scholar.

MIHIR DESAI is a human rights lawyer based in Mumbai. He is the co-founder of the human rights magazine *Combat Law*.

MOHSIN ALAM BHAT is an associate professor and the executive director of the Centre for Public Interest Law, Jindal Global Law School at the O.P. Jindal Global University, Sonipat.

NEELANJAN SIRCAR is a senior visiting fellow at the Centre for Policy Research, New Delhi and assistant professor of political science at Ashoka University.

NEERA CHANDHOKE is an honorary distinguished fellow at the Centre for Equity Studies and a former professor of political science in the University of Delhi.

NIRAJA GOPAL JAYAL is a professor at the Centre for the Study of Law and Governance, Jawaharlal Nehru University, New Delhi.

NIZAM PASHA is a lawyer practising in the Supreme Court and has fought cases related to the National Register of Citizens.

PAMELA PHILIPOSE is a journalist and researcher and a senior fellow at the Indian Council of Social Science Research. She is also the author of *Media's Shifting Terrain: Five Years that Transformed the Way India Communicates*.

PARISMITA SINGH is a writer, graphic novelist and educationist. Her publications include the graphic novels *The Hotel at the End of the*

World, *Mara and the Clay Cows*, *Crab Chronicles* and a collection of short stories Peace Has Come.

REHNA SULTANA is a poet, researcher and women's rights activist based in Guwahati.

SANJAY BARBORA teaches at the Centre for Sociology and Social Anthropology, Tata Institute of Social Sciences, Guwahati. He has written on the issues of human rights, agrarian change, migration and the media in South Asia.

SHAH ALAM KHAN is a professor in the Department of Orthopaedics at the All India Institute of Medical Sciences, New Delhi.

SHALIM M. HUSSAIN is a poet, translator and rights activist from Assam. His first book of poems *Betel Nut City* was published in 2018. *Post-Colonial Poems*, his translation of poetry by the Adivasi poet Kamal Kumar Tanti, came out in the following year. He was the 2020 Charles Wallace India Trust Literary Translation and Creative Writing Fellow hosted by Literature Across Frontiers at the University of Wales Trinity Saint David.

SHIVAM VIJ is a well-known journalist based in New Delhi. He has written on a range of issues for various national and international publications. He is a regular contributor at *The Print* and *Scroll.in* and is a New Delhi correspondent of *The Christian Science Monitor.*

VARNA BALAKRISHNAN is a researcher and human rights worker based in New Delhi, focusing on issues of citizenship, communal violence, and gender. She has been associated with Karwan-e-Mohabbat, the Centre for Equity Studies, and the Institute of Development Studies, UK.

ALSO FROM SPEAKING TIGER

SHAHEEN BAGH AND THE IDEA OF INDIA

Writings on a Movement for Justice, Liberty and Equality

Edited by Seema Mustafa

On 15 December 2019, police in riot gear stormed Delhi's Jamia Millia Islamia and attacked unarmed students protesting against the Citizenship (Amendment) Act (CAA), which makes religion a factor in the process of granting Indian citizenship. In neighbouring Shaheen Bagh, mothers and other relatives and friends of the students came out into the streets in outrage and anguish. They sat on a main road demanding repeal of the CAA, which, twinned with the National Register of Citizens (NRC), could make Indian Muslims aliens in their own homeland. Within days, similar protests broke out across the country.Free India had never seen anything like it.

Shaheen Bagh and the Idea of India examines how the sit-in by a small group of Muslim women—many of whom had stepped out of their homes alone for the first time—united millions of Indians of different faiths and ideologies in defence of the principles of liberty, equality and secularism enshrined in our Constitution. It also throws up many important questions: Can the Shaheen Bagh protests reverse the damage done to our democracy in recent years? How did the non-violent movement sustain itself despite vilification, threats and persecution by the establishment? Is this movement the beginning of new solidarities in our society? Will it survive the aftermath of the communal violence that devastated northeast Delhi in February 2020, and the witch-hunt that was launched under cover of the Covid-19 pandemic and lockdown?

This necessary collection comprises interviews with some of the brave women at the core of the protests; ground reports and photographs by journalists like Seema Mustafa, Seemi Pasha, Nazes Afroz and Mustafa Quraishi; and essays by thinkers, writers, lawyers and activists, including Nayantara Sahgal, Harsh Mander, Subhashini Ali, Nandita Haksar, Zoya Hasan, Apoorvanand, Enakshi Ganguly, Sharik Laliwala and Nizam Pasha. It is a book that must be read by everyone who cares about India's democracy and its future.